MSJC
P9-DSZ-126

Positive Strategies for Students with Behavior Problems

by

Daniel Crimmins, Ph.D.
Westchester Institute for Human Development
New York Medical College
Valhalla, New York

Anne F. Farrell, Ph.D.
University of Connecticut
Stamford, Connecticut

Philip W. Smith, Ph.D.
Westchester Institute for Human Development
Valhalla, New York

and

Alison Bailey, M.S.Ed.
Westchester Institute for Human Development
Valhalla, New York

Baltimore • London • Sydney

Paul H. Brookes Publishing Co.
Post Office Box 10624
Baltimore, Maryland 21285-0624

www.brookespublishing.com

Typeset by Maryland Composition Company, Glen Burnie, Maryland.
Manufactured in the United States of America by
Versa Press, Inc., East Peoria, Illinois.

This book was developed with support from the New York State Developmental Disabilities Planning Council; the Administration on Developmental Disabilities, Administration for Children and Families, U.S. Department of Health and Human Services; and the Maternal and Child Health Bureau, Health Resources and Services Administration, U.S. Department of Health and Human Services. The content and opinions herein do not, however, reflect the position or policy of these agencies and no official endorsement should be inferred.

The case studies appearing in this book are composites based on the authors' experiences; these case studies do not represent the lives or experiences of specific individuals, and no implications should be inferred.

Third printing, January 2015.

Library of Congress Cataloging-in-Publication Data

Positive strategies for students with behavior problems / by Daniel Crimmins ... [et al.].
p. cm.
Includes bibliographical references (p.) and index.
ISBN-13: 978-1-55766-878-3 (pbk)
ISBN-10: 1-55766-878-7 (pbk)
1. Classroom management. 2. Behavior modification. I. Crimmins, Daniel B. (Daniel Bernard), 1952– II. Title.

LB3013.P647 2007
370.15′28–dc22 2007004664

British Library Cataloguing in Publication data are available from the British Library.

Contents

About the Authors

Daniel Crimmins, Ph.D., Vice President for Community Programs, Westchester Institute for Human Development, Cedarwood Hall, Valhalla, New York 10595.

In addition to his position at the Westchester Institute for Human Development (a University Center for Excellence in Developmental Disabilities), Dr. Crimmins is a faculty member of the School of Public Health and the Department of Psychiatry, both at the New York Medical College. In 2002–2003, he was a Robert Wood Johnson Health Policy Fellow in Washington, D.C., where he worked in the office of Senator James M. Jeffords on health and education policy. Dr. Crimmins has a career interest in child development and disability with a particular interest in those issues that reflect the intersection of research, practice, and policy. He is coauthor of *The Motivation Assessment Scale* (Monaco & Associates, 1992) with V. Mark Durand and the *Autism Program Quality Indicators* (New York State Education Department, 2001) with V. Mark Durand, Karin Theurer-Kaufman, and Jessica Everett.

Anne F. Farrell, Ph.D., Assistant Professor, Human Development & Family Studies, University of Connecticut, One University Place, Stamford, Connecticut 06901-2315.

Dr. Farrell is a clinical and school psychologist in the Department of Human Development and Family Studies at the University of Connecticut. Her professional interests center on child development and disability, family partnerships and family-centered practice, and positive behavior supports. In addition to research and teaching, she provides program evaluation, consultation, and technical assistance on childhood disability policy, community integration, and interdisciplinary practice for children with special health care needs. Dr. Farrell serves on local, regional, and national advisory bodies concerned with quality care for vulnerable populations. She lives with her husband and son in Ridgefield, Connecticut.

Philip W. Smith, Ph.D., Project Coordinator, Westchester Institute for Human Development, Cedarwood Hall, Valhalla, New York 10595.

In addition to his work with the Westchester Institute for Human Development, Dr. Smith is a faculty member of the School of Public Health at New York Medical College. He has worked extensively in the area of positive behavior supports, developing and delivering training programs for schools, residential treatment programs, and families. He also provides technical assistance to schools conducting functional behavior assessment for students with the most challenging behaviors, and he maintains a caseload of individual therapy services for children and young adults with a combination of developmental disabilities, emotional disorders, and challenging behaviors.

Alison Bailey, M.S.Ed., Director of Administrative Operations, Westchester Institute for Human Development, Cedarwood Hall, Valhalla, New York 10595.

Ms. Bailey has a background in school counseling and instructs courses in classroom management, behavioral theory, and computer technology. Her professional interests focus on the development, delivery, and evaluation of quality training programs.

Foreword

I was a freshman member of the Congress in 1975, one of only 17 Republicans elected to the House of Representatives in the wake of the Watergate scandal. As such, I was named the ranking Republican on the Select Education Subcommittee and charged with helping to write what would later become the Individuals with Disabilities Education Act (IDEA).

IDEA was, and continues to be, a civil rights law. It guarantees the right of children with disabilities to a "free and appropriate" public education in the "least restrictive environment." It has given children the right to attend the same schools as their peers, to master the skills needed for success in life, and to participate in all aspects of school life. In virtually all respects, IDEA has been quite successful. It has improved the lives of millions of children and their families since its passage more than 30 years ago.

IDEA has meant that children with disabilities no longer face a life of institutional care. Rather, they are part of their families, their schools, and their communities. And, more and more of these children go on to get jobs, buy homes, and, yes, pay taxes. I consider the fact that so many students with disabilities are able to participate in the American dream to be one of the major accomplishments of my career in the United States Congress.

The path of IDEA has not always been smooth. We knew in 1975 that the cost of special education would be high. Because we saw this as a civil right guaranteed by the Constitution, we felt that the federal government should provide a significant portion of that funding. In the end, we arrived at the decision that 40% of the additional costs of special education should be paid by the federal government. But, we have failed to meet this commitment. Over these many years, the federal government has fallen short, even today, paying less than half of what it promised in 1975. Needless to say, this places an unfair burden on states and local school districts. The lack of funding played a major role in my decision to leave the Republican Party in 2001 and declare myself an Independent.

Since IDEA's original passage, it has been amended to ensure that the law continues to provide access to a special education for all students with disabilities. Examples of how the law has been amended include: extending the reach of IDEA to children from birth to age 3, providing assistive technology, and placing greater emphasis on the transition from school to adult life. We have also stressed the importance of teacher qualifications and clarified the role of parents as advocates for their children and as partners in the educational process.

In 1997, when I was the Chair of the Senate Committee on Health Education, Labor, and Pensions, the committee amended IDEA in regard to behavioral issues. Among our concerns at that time was the fact that the high school drop-out rate for young people with disabilities was twice that of their peers. Not only that, within the group of students with disabilities, there were also disparities in rates of students graduating from school. Students with visual impairments, for example, were almost twice as likely to complete school as those with emotional and behavioral disorders. We also found that students with behavior problems were far more likely to be educated separately from their peers, which precluded regular contact with peers and placed an additional financial burden on their school districts. When we took a closer look at this, it quickly became apparent that we had to clarify that IDEA protected the rights of all students to a special education—even those with behavioral issues.

We addressed this in the 1997 IDEA amendments by defining a process called *manifestation determination.* At the simplest level, this is an assessment to decide whether a problem behavior is caused by the child's disability. If it is, the school's response must take the disability into account, rather than just submitting the student to disciplinary procedures that may be inappropriate or ineffective.

We defined what we thought the school's response should be, not just for those students whose behaviors related to their disabilities, but for all students in special education whose behaviors interfere with learning. We proposed the use of positive behavioral intervention strategies, an approach that teaches students what to do, instead of just disciplining them for what they should not do.

We also introduced into IDEA the practice of functional behavioral assessment—understanding why the student is doing what he or she is doing. As *Positive Strategies for Students with Behavior Problems* demonstrates, this understanding can help teachers work with struggling students to find better ways to communicate, listen, participate, and behave. Indeed, addressing problem behavior needs to be an important aspect of a special education, because it opens new avenues for learning.

These were important additions to IDEA, and I feel they provided new opportunities for many students to achieve. They were new requirements for the schools, however, and we know that change sometimes comes slowly. In the Senate, we discussed whether these requirements should remain in IDEA in 2003 during the subsequent reauthorization. (In fact, Dr. Crimmins served as a fellow on my staff for part of this time while the reauthorization of IDEA was being considered.) Ultimately, we decided to retain the provisions for positive behavioral interventions and functional behavioral assessments that we first identified in 1997.

What we did add to IDEA when it was finally signed into law in 2004 was stronger language related to the training of school personnel in how to carry out positive behavioral interventions. This book outlines strategies that speak directly to this issue. All school personnel—teachers, related service providers, and administrators—need to understand why students persist in their behaviors, how to modify their classrooms to make students more likely to succeed, and, most importantly, which critical social skills should be taught to their students so that they might make it on their own. This book helps them to do just that.

This book is written in the best spirit of IDEA. It aims to help children whose behaviors prevent them from meeting their full potential. These children should also have their chance to participate in the American dream. We have come a long way since 1975, but we still have far to go.

Former Senator James M. Jeffords
Independent–Vermont

Preface

Today's educators face both exciting opportunities and daunting challenges in fulfilling their responsibilities to their students' academic and behavioral growth. The level of public awareness about student accomplishment is at an all-time high, paralleled by a recognition that optimal achievement results from quality instruction, healthy school environments, and adequate fiscal resources to support both. As educators seek to meet the needs of the many, they are also confronted with the mandate of ensuring that *all* students progress. As of 2007, schoolwide positive behavior supports (PBS), which focus on entire student bodies, are quickly becoming more common in United States schools. While both schoolwide and individualized approaches emerge from the rich traditions of applied behavior analysis and behavior therapy, *Positive Strategies for Students with Behavior Problems* addresses the needs of individual students. In this book, we translate current research in individualized PBS into practices that can be used every day in schools.

WHAT IS THE PURPOSE OF THIS BOOK?

Positive Strategies provides a starting point for educators supporting students with challenging behavior and provides a means to deliver effective supports that are grounded in research and anchored in a humanistic orientation. This book refers frequently to research on individualized PBS, classroom management, behavior therapy, and other related topics. We do not, however, intend this book as a comprehensive review of the literature on these topics. Rather, the chapters in this book summarize and convey only the most salient theory and research related to providing effective PBS. There is indeed a rich background and ample literature attesting to the effectiveness and acceptability of PBS and we provide numerous representative citations for readers who wish to pursue this topic further. Perhaps most importantly, we hope to provide concrete, effective strategies for ameliorating problem behavior and developing alternatives—helping students find a better way. We believe that PBS offers a means of improving quality of life in students with disabilities and are confident that educators, working in teams with other educators, professionals, and parents, can effect that change.

The term *Positive Strategies* derives from the use of humane approaches designed to capitalize on the best a student has to offer (positive) and the need to offer concrete, pragmatic approaches (strategies) to support them. The approach described in this book is multi-dimensional. Consider it a set of tools: becoming competent in *Positive Strategies* requires understanding the purpose of each tool, when its use is suitable, and how it can be applied to a given situation. With this knowledge and practice in the use of these tools in different situations, the user becomes an accomplished practitioner.

FOR WHOM IS IT INTENDED?

We expect our readers to include teachers, administrators, related services personnel, school counselors, school psychologists, family members, and student advocates. Ideally, our readers will first encounter the book in the company of working teams, as PBS are rarely initiated and delivered by single individuals. Recognizing the complex and demanding context of today's schools and the importance of collaboration in achieving positive outcomes, we emphasize a team approach in this book. Our definition of *team* necessarily includes students and their families, and we are committed to their full participation in this process. Nevertheless, we believe that this book will be helpful whether readers are learning PBS methods individually or as part of a team.

More experienced professionals may use *Positive Strategies* more as a reference for training, consultation, or intervention. We hope that readers view this book as just the beginning of learning about PBS. While it is written primarily for individuals working in schools, we have successfully adapted these methods for other providers and settings, such as nursery schools, child care providers, preschool staff, families, and direct support providers for adults in community settings. We are confident that our readers can do so as well.

HOW IS IT ORGANIZED?

Positive Strategies for Students with Behavior Problems comprises eight chapters and an appendix. In Chapter 1, we define challenging behavior, discuss the origins and values of PBS as a field, mention various applications of PBS in schools, and review the assumptions underlying *Positive Strategies* as one application of individualized supports. In Chapter 2, we outline the basics of applied behavioral analysis and behavior theory. Because these principles form the underpinnings of PBS as a technology, it is essential that the PBS practitioner be conversant with them. In Chapter 3, we discuss schools and classrooms as contexts for problem behavior and positive outcomes, as well as the importance of interlacing individualized PBS interventions and schoolwide efforts. Because engaging students is a powerful method of prevention, we also review some important features of successful classrooms and factors that place students at risk for problem behavior. In Chapter 4, we discuss the value and importance of teams in *Positive Strategies*: their composition, the skills and roles involved, and the characteristics of effective teams. In Chapter 5, we provide an overview of the entire *Positive Strategies* process, how it frames and previews the three elements—understand, prevent, and replace—involved in individualized supports. In Chapter 6, we address the process of implementing PBS beginning with understanding the function of behavior. In Chapter 7, we detail the steps involved in preventing problem behavior and replacing it with alternatives. In Chapter 8, we delineate issues and challenges in long-term maintenance of gains made through *Positive Strategies*. In the appendix, we provide photocopiable forms to be used to support teams through the *Positive Strategies* process.

Because learning PBS can be augmented through examples of practice, we include several case examples, each of which illustrates one or more features of the process of PBS. Within and across sections and chapters, we discuss several different students and address challenges each team would likely experience. We depict one student, Nathan, in great depth through several chapters, allowing readers to follow his team as the team members plan and conduct a functional behavioral assessment and behavior intervention plan.

WHERE DID THIS BOOK COME FROM?

In the early 1990s, we began working with teams to develop behavior support plans. We delivered training to individuals and teams in workshop and inservice formats. We provided on-site consultation and technical assistance to hundreds of schools and community agencies in urban, suburban, and rural settings. Over the years, as the research productivity, complexity and sophistication of methods, and recognition of PBS increased, so too did the *Positive Strategies* model evolve to incorporate these new findings and methods. We were struck by the labor intensity of training and supporting teams and individuals, and endeavored to streamline our training to respect the tremendous investment in time and effort that participants were making. Confronted by a burgeoning demand for training, we eventually adopted train-the-trainer models designed to ensure the consistency and fidelity of *Positive Strategies* dissemination efforts.

In an effort to support reliable adoption and application, we developed written manuals to accompany our training programs. The first manual we competed was *Positive Strategies: Training Teams in Positive Behavior Support* (Crimmins & Woolf, 1997); the second was *Positive Strategies: Case Studies from School-Based Teams* (Crimmins & Smith, 2001); and the third was *Positive Strategies: Developing Individualized Supports in Schools* (Crimmins, Farrell, Smith, & Bailey, 2004). Our choice to expand on those manuals and publish this book was rooted in our commitment to PBS and our goal to present *Positive Strategies* to a wider audience.

HOW DO WE SEE THIS BOOK BEING USED?

We believe this book is best utilized in conjunction with training and guided practice in providing PBS. This book and its activities can be assigned as part of courses relating to a range of disabilities and settings, such as education, special education, school psychology, and related fields. This book is designed to guide educators through the PBS process to support students requiring assessment and intervention. It is also is an informational resource on individualized PBS for those working within schoolwide applications. Whether it is used as a manual, reference, or source for examples, we trust that *Positive Strategies for Students with Behavior Problems* will assist readers to support students with challenging behavior.

REFERENCES

Crimmins, D., Farrell, A.F., Smith, P.W., & Bailey, A. (2004). *Positive Strategies: Developing individualized supports in schools.* Valhalla, NY: Westchester Institute for Human Development.

Crimmins, D.B., & Smith, P.W. (2001). *Positive Strategies: Case studies from school-based teams.* Valhalla, NY: Westchester Institute for Human Development.

Crimmins, D.B., & Woolf, S.B. (1997). *Positive Strategies: Training teams in positive behavior support.* Valhalla, NY: Westchester Institute for Human Development.

Acknowledgments

This book emerges from over 15 years of intensive *Positive Strategies* training and technical assistance. During that time, we collaborated with numerous school teams, administrators, colleagues, family members, and students. They guided us by ensuring that we addressed the practical realities of working in today's schools and communities, by their commitment to the inclusion of students with disabilities, and through their questions on how to resolve the sometimes competing priorities of teaching, learning, and growing. We thank them for the many improvements we took from them; any errors left behind are ours.

The input and support of many colleagues continues to enrich our work, and we wish to express our appreciation to some of those individuals. In particular, we owe a debt to Sara Woolf, whose role in the early development of these methods was invaluable. We wish to thank Carole Gothelf for her contributions to our early efforts at examining the effects of instructional settings on behavior. Louisa Kimball provided useful comments on an earlier version of the manuscript. We also thank Andy Bacon and our many Westchester Institute for Human Development colleagues who sustained us over the years with their commitment, support, collegiality, and friendship.

We acknowledge the school teams who participated in *Positive Strategies* training and provided crucial feedback about implementation. Special thanks to the team trainers, whose efforts both enriched their own school teams and assisted in the validation of these methods.

The New York State Developmental Disabilities Planning Council provided fiscal support for *Positive Strategies* initiatives between 1999 and 2006. Robin Worobey and Kerry Wiley, Director and Special Administrative Assistant for the Children's Issues Committee, encouraged our efforts and collaborated with us to disseminate this approach in New York State. The Administration on Developmental Disabilities funded some of our earlier training efforts between 1991 and 2001.

Our students at Hunter College, New York Medical College, and the University of Connecticut read and used earlier versions of this manuscript over the past several years. Their questions and comments helped us to improve our message while confirming the value of disseminating *Positive Strategies*. We are grateful for their enthusiasm and confident that they will improve the lives of the students they support.

We owe a debt of gratitude to the professional colleagues who created the vibrant field of positive behavior support and who guided us by their word and example along the way. While there are too many to recognize each individually, we would like to acknowledge the influence of Mark Durand, the late Arnold Goldstein, Ted Carr, Luanna Meyer, Rob Horner, Glen Dunlap, George Sugai, Bob Koegel, Lynn Koegel, Tim Knoster, Don Kincaid, David Allen, Albert Ellis, Dan Brenner, Michael Barnes, and Fredda Brown.

We are indebted to the staff of Paul H. Brookes Publishing Co., whose patience and care made possible the broad dissemination of *Positive Strategies*. Special thanks to Rebecca Lazo and Steve Peterson, as well as the entire production staff, who labored under a shortened timeframe to deliver this product. Three anonymous reviewers of an earlier *Positive Strategies* manuscript provided valuable comments and suggestions, and we appreciate their thoughtful input.

Our families' unflagging encouragement and support enrich our work—and this book—in ways both large and small.

Finally, to the students and families who have participated in these efforts, we acknowledge your patience as we struggled together to create a better future. More importantly, thank you for your gentle insistence that we address what matters most in your lives.

In the middle of difficulty lies opportunity.
—Albert Einstein

To our parents

Molly and Jack
Peg and Frank
Marilyn and James
Connie and Allan

Whose pride in the promise of their children
kindled our optimism and perseverance

Chapter 1

Introduction to Positive Strategies

CLARIFYING CHALLENGING BEHAVIOR

Let us start with the basics: most students misbehave at one time or another. How do teachers and other school personnel respond? Often, they simply tell the misbehaving child to stop. Sometimes, the directive "Stop that!" is paired with other consequences intended to discourage the behavior from happening again. Under these circumstances, many children will indeed stop engaging in the problem behavior, at least for a while.

Some children, however, do *not* stop. They continue to engage in behaviors that are distracting, annoying, counterproductive, and even dangerous, and, in turn, they typically encounter a sequence of increasingly serious sanctions. Compared with other students, they spend more time out of their classrooms, are the subject of more telephone calls to home, are discussed more often at staff meetings, and are considered more frequently for alternative educational placement. By definition, their challenging behaviors tend to resist interventions, frustrate the education process (and the educators), and defy understanding. Relatively inexperienced teachers may feel at a complete loss to manage these children, and seasoned teachers may feel they have tried everything to no avail. School personnel may feel thwarted, inadequate, resentful, victimized, or desperate. All the while, teachers must balance the demands of such students with the concerns of entire classes.

Challenging behavior evokes a range of responses. Fundamentally, educators just want such behavior to stop. This is an understandable and human reaction, but it is equally clear that stopping challenging behavior is not easy. A child may have a long history of problems with equally long efforts to get his or her behavior under control. Some children may cycle through relatively good years followed by one or more difficult ones. Among students with challenging behaviors, children with disabilities are overrepresented. Disabilities contribute to problem behavior directly through problems in self-regulation and indirectly through frustration that may be associated with instruction.

Teaching students who exhibit problem behaviors brings an additional complication. It is extremely difficult for any individual working with such children to develop and implement a workable plan. These students often require the combined efforts of a team of people who are committed to developing solutions for their behavioral (and often learning) difficulties. The team may be a formal instructional group or an ad hoc cadre assembled specifically in response to a student's problems. We have created *Positive Strategies for Students with Behavior Problems* for these teams. Although this book was initially developed to support a formal, yearlong training program, we have used these materials with educators in a variety of settings. As such, we are comfortable recommending that teams follow the steps outlined here on their own or with the assistance of a behavioral consultant.

The book is designed to help school teams develop appropriate and effective individualized solutions for the relatively small number of students (generally about 3%–5% of students in a school) with persistent behavior problems (Sugai & Horner, 2002). In this manual, we present a systematic method called *Positive Strategies,* which centers on two major activities: conducting functional behavioral assessments (FBAs) and developing behavior intervention plans (BIPs). *Positive Strategies* is grounded in a comprehensive, interdisciplinary literature on positive behavior support (PBS), central to which is the notion that understanding the function of problem behavior—how it meets a child's concerns in some way—is fundamental to successfully addressing the problem behavior.

This functional approach and other *Positive Strategies* components are mandated for some students with educational disabilities under the Individuals with Disabilities Education Improvement Act (IDEA) of 2004 (PL 108-446). We are confident that the steps in *Positive Strategies* will enable schools to meet their legal mandates, but our intent far exceeds compliance with regulatory requirements. Our primary goal is to improve quality of life for children with problem behaviors, for their classmates, and for the teams committed to their instruction and support.

OVERVIEW OF *POSITIVE STRATEGIES*

The term *Positive Strategies* refers to the specific approach we use to address problem behavior. *Positive Strategies* emerges from the fields of applied behavior analysis (ABA), psychology, and education and is shaped by professional literature, technology, trends, and influences in all three arenas. It is also consistent with and embedded within the larger field of PBS, which refers to the application of behavior therapy and behavior analytic principles to effect socially relevant change. Like all technologies, *Positive Strategies* is an applied science; it employs the laws of behavior to change behavior. *Positive Strategies* also involves careful application of contemporary instructional practices, as do all methods that fall under the umbrella of PBS. In this chapter, we outline the influences, assumptions, utility, and challenges involved in enacting *Positive Strategies.* The remainder of the book provides an overview of the behavioral principles that underlie intervention. The classroom and school are considered as contexts for students' behavior. Finally, the manual reviews our step-by-step approach to forming teams, conducting FBAs, and developing BIPs. These activities, singly and in combination, are intended for teaching students more effective ways of behaving.

Influences from the Field of Applied Behavior Analysis

The *Positive Strategies* approach evolved over more than 20 years and is shaped in part by two major trends in the field of ABA. The first of these, functional analysis, offers a technology for examining the context of problem behavior to determine its likely maintaining functions. Over the years, teachers and school psychologists have used ABA methods to manage a variety of difficult behaviors. Most educators are familiar, for example, with the classic antecedent–behavior–consequence (A-B-C) chain used to explain the relationship between behavior and environmental contingencies (more on this later). School personnel routinely apply the A-B-C chain and its underlying principles to improve student performance.

The second major influence on the development of *Positive Strategies* was the aversives debate. The term *aversives* refers to a range of interventions involving unpleasant consequences in-

tended to reduce the occurrence of problem behaviors. Aversives came into use when professionals encountered difficulty managing seemingly intractable patterns of dangerous or destructive behavior (e.g., self-injury, aggression), particularly among individuals with developmental disabilities. Aversive consequences included slapping, hitting, restraint, noxious odors, and mild electric shocks. Because aversives often involved pain, discomfort, or impingement on basic rights, their use became controversial in the 1980s, with debate regarding how difficult and dangerous behaviors should be managed. One side argued for freedom from harm, and the opposing side advocated for the right to effective treatment (Feldman, 1990).

The group advocating for the right to effective treatment argued that extreme and potentially dangerous behaviors warranted whatever treatments were necessary to bring them under control, including (in rare instances) high and intrusive levels of punishment. The viewpoint supporting freedom from harm was that consequences involving pain, humiliation, or deprivation of basic liberties had no place in education. The resulting debate, which continued from the early 1980s to the early 1990s, included animated discussion over whether any behaviors might be worthy exceptions (e.g., what should be done for forms of self-injurious behavior that pose a risk of permanent injury?) to a general disavowal of aversives. (The themes of the debate are chronicled in a volume edited by Repp and Singh and published in 1990.)

In the early to mid-1990s, the debate over aversive consequences to a large degree yielded to the development of the PBS framework, which emerged from the functional behavior analysis literature. PBS offered not only an understanding of why problem behaviors persist, but also a technology to address them. Importantly, the technology offered an alternative to a heavy reliance on punishment to reduce severe problem behavior. After several published studies demonstrated that extreme behaviors could be managed without aversives, the debate over aversives quieted, and the field witnessed an increased use of PBS. Today, the recommendation to use aversives would warrant careful ethical consideration, evidence that more positive approaches were ineffective, and indication that a failure to address the extreme behavior would itself constitute danger. Consistent with the entire PBS movement, the *Positive Strategies* approach opposes aversives on ethical and philosophical grounds. More detail on the *Positive Strategies* approach to the use of punishment as corrective feedback appears later in this chapter.

One distinctive feature of the PBS movement enabled it to supplant earlier ABA technologies that were based primarily on punishment: the emphasis on the prominent role of function in maintaining problem behavior. An emphasis on function and the corresponding need to develop alternatives to problem behavior was a shift away from the relatively simple A-B-C chain. Placing function at the center of understanding problem behavior led to the more contextualized approach that characterizes PBS today.

Empirical Support

Since 1990, a rich literature has demonstrated PBS outcomes that have included reduction in problem behaviors, enhanced functioning, and improved quality of life for thousands of individuals. We found more than 600 articles that included references to PBS in a review of the peer-reviewed social science and educational journals published between 1990 and 2005 (Farrell, Kimball, & Crimmins, 2005). This attests to the growth and effectiveness of PBS for both individualized and schoolwide efforts (Crimmins & Farrell, 2006). Broadly speaking, there is clear empirical support for three overlapping elements: careful assessment, data collection and emphasis on outcomes, and program evaluation.

Whether a team is working with an individual student or a school is revising its discipline procedures, success depends largely on careful initial assessment, without which there is little chance of accomplishing improvement or long-term change. A second aspect of effective PBS practice concerns ongoing data collection and focus on outcomes. Initial assessment involves the thoughtful identification of areas requiring intervention and benchmarks for improvement. These activities necessitate data-based decision making: schools engage in self-assessment and create effective infrastructures for monitoring implementation. This relates to the third component of effective PBS: program evaluation. To determine whether PBS efforts are successful, schools track several outcomes over time and alter their implementation plans accordingly.

Values Base

The PBS movement (and *Positive Strategies* in particular) derives from an empirically grounded science and emerges from a values base in person-centered planning. Jackson and Panyan (2001) discussed five central features of person-centered planning as an approach to organizing services and supports for individuals with disabilities. These include collaboration among all the individuals involved in the education and care of the child; focus on areas of strength and competency; creating a vision of broad outcomes that represent holistic, positive, and worthwhile ends for the student; translation of those outcomes into an action plan; and planned outcomes that benefit not only the learner but the entire learning community.

This approach goes hand in hand with another element of *Positive Strategies* values: full endorsement of the inclusion of children with disabilities in the mainstream of education. We believe that students with and without disabilities benefit when they learn together. Simultaneously, we acknowledge that the history of segregation in education presents continuing barriers to successful inclusion. Students with problem behavior are more likely to be placed in segregated settings, and students with disabilities are more likely than their peers to have problem behaviors. Even experienced teachers are apt to have little explicit training in managing behavioral diversity and behavior problems in the classroom. This is compounded by the fact that PBS represents a relatively new development in education. Further, school districts vary in their interpretation of IDEA'04's mandates, and some lack the resources to support full implementation of a PBS philosophy. Despite these challenges, we are optimistic that *Positive Strategies* and PBS have the potential to improve the education of students with and without disabilities.

Field Testing

In addition to scholarly and philosophical influences, field testing also plays a major role in the *Positive Strategies* framework. We developed, adapted, and field tested these methods with literally hundreds of school teams in their work with students. Our work continues; collaboration with families, educators, and related services personnel has informed and enriched *Positive Strategies* immeasurably. Field testing has also required us to consider the day-to-day challenges facing each team in its attempts to address problem behaviors.

Positive Strategies field testing occurs through the authors' direct consultation and team training delivered to many professionals working with children. We also teach undergraduate and graduate courses in PBS to students in education and related fields. Our consultation and training efforts reach a range of diverse settings for children, from early intervention programs to community residences. Training vehicles include school- and district-based in-services, single- and multiple-day training workshops, and train-the-trainer models. The *Positive Strategies* team training project, for example, involves a series of formal training sessions spread out over a period of months and interspersed with team activities and completion of case studies.

We work to ensure approaches that are effective, faithful to the tenets of ABA, ecologically valid, and, most importantly, responsive to the concerns of students, teachers, and families. Aware of the enormous time pressures and limited resources facing educators, we strive to make *Positive Strategies* methods accessible and pragmatic. Although *Positive Strategies* involves a technology, effective solutions to complex problems do not derive from a one-size-fits-all approach. In fact, it is difficult to imagine one BIP that would work equally well for two students. We anticipate that readers will adapt and individualize *Positive Strategies* materials based on the unique concerns of individual children and the educational contexts in which children learn.

THE POSITIVE BEHAVIOR SUPPORT FRAMEWORK

A recent definition of PBS described it as an integration of methods that is drawn from behavioral sciences, paired with practical interventions, and informed by social values, and that addresses issues at the systems level (Sugai & Horner, 1999). The context of PBS provides the interventionist with a frame for understanding its origins, goals, and effective implementation, with particular emphasis on applications in community and education settings.

Positive Behavior Support in the Community

PBS developed as a solution to the problem behaviors of individuals with disabilities participating in community education, living, and employment (Meyer & Evans, 1989). Concerns about problem behavior in community settings included potential for injury, lost productivity, disruption of programs, and social stigma. Historically, these concerns were used to justify the exclusion of individuals with disabilities from natural settings and the use of aversives to manage their behavior. The lack of adequate means to address challenging behavior resulted in lost opportunities for inclusion and stagnation in settings such as sheltered workshops and day programs. Over time, consumers and families successfully advocated for improved access to the educational and social mainstream. Along with this came the pressure on programs to develop better methods not only to meet the presumed concerns of individuals but to improve their quality of life.

Resulting shifts in services toward inclusion required an innovative application of behavior analysis that would be acceptable to the community. A number of developments in the 1980s made this feasible. Among these were an emphasis on participation in meaningful activities, an emerging methodology for conducting FBAs, and a recognition of the importance of developing alternative behaviors to replace problem ones (Durand, 1990; Helmstetter & Durand, 1990). Advances in behavior support combined with the changing cultural milieu to support the spread of FBA and its eventual incorporation into IDEA'04.

A major theme in the community development of PBS was its goal of measuring success in terms of improved quality of life, as opposed to just reducing the frequency or severity of problem behaviors. In PBS, meaningful progress is defined by positive changes in how a person lives, works, and learns. This notion of progress encourages adaptive behavior and participation, in contrast to the traditional goal of eliminating negative behavior, which pays little attention to what the student might do instead (Meyer & Evans, 1989). This transition in emphasis occurred in concert with a paradigm shift toward strength-oriented, family-centered, functional approaches to assessment and intervention in partnership with families of children with disabilities. Similarly, educators now advocate the use of proactive and preventive approaches to problem behavior over more traditional, reactive approaches. Because it awaits the occurrence of problem behavior, reactive discipline relies predominantly on punishment and often fails to consider the concerns of learners.

Beginning in the early 1990s, the literature on the effectiveness of PBS in improving quality of life for individuals with challenging behaviors expanded dramatically. This burgeoning literature included two edited volumes (Koegel, Koegel, & Dunlap, 1996; Lehr & Brown, 1996) detailing the successful application of PBS across different settings (e.g., community, supported living, vocational, school) and providers (e.g., families, direct caregivers, teachers, others). Before long, the emerging consensus in the published literature was that in addition to being acceptable to the community, PBS also helped individuals with disabilities achieve important life outcomes such as successful inclusion in the mainstream, reduction in pharmacological interventions, better vocational and residential options, and improved quality of life.

Positive Behavior Support in Schools

Before the 1997 reauthorization of IDEA (PL 105-17; hereafter referred to as IDEA'97), PBS was used in schools, although its use was scattered, unsystematic, and subject to the availability of local resources. Students in schools with commitment, fiscal resources, and access to expertise benefited from PBS methods, whereas those without such blessings were much less likely to do so. IDEA'97 acknowledged that students with disabilities were apt to lose valuable education services because of behavior problems stemming from their disabilities. The legislation provided a strong impetus for the use of PBS in schools because it contained specific language calling for the use of FBAs and BIPs when the behavior of classified students led to 10 or more days of suspension or consideration of an alternative educational setting. It also required FBAs and BIPs for students whose behavior was caused by their disability. IDEA'97 stipulated a process called manifestation determination for establishing the causal connection between disability and problem behavior. It also included the somewhat vague (but potentially quite inclusive) language, "In the case of a child whose behavior impedes his or her learning or that of others, consider, when appropriate, strategies including positive behavioral interventions, strategies, and supports to address that behavior" [Section 614(d)(3)(B)(i)].

The 2004 reauthorization (IDEA'04) maintained the essential requirements of IDEA'97 related to PBS. IDEA'04 continued the call for manifestation determination, consideration of PBS and interventions for impeding behavior, and FBAs and BIPs for suspended students. It required schools to examine the suitability and adherence to each student's individualized education program (IEP) as part of the manifestation determination. IDEA'04 also included several new references to PBS and interventions as a focus of training for current and future school personnel.

With the exception of the FBAs required by suspension or alternative placement, IDEA'04 lacks clarity regarding precisely what triggers an FBA. This has led to uncertainty, disagreement, and inconsistent application in schools across the country. Unfortunately, when teachers and administrators are uncertain as to whether an FBA is needed, they often elect not to complete one. We believe that this may be an error on a technical level—it cannot hurt to complete a quick FBA, and it might help. More importantly, it may also become an error on a legal level. Turnbull and colleagues (Turnbull, Wilcox, Stowe, & Turnbull, 2001) noted that PBS and interventions are the only approaches to dealing with behavior mentioned in IDEA'04; this essentially gives them a preferred status for consideration when a child has behavior problems. Because no other approaches are mentioned and IDEA'04 requires consideration of PBS for students whose behaviors impede learning, Turnbull and colleagues argued that this makes PBS the "intervention strategy of choice for the IEP team" (p. 14). We would anticipate that if an IEP for a child with behavior problems were going to be challenged, one of the first items to be examined would be how the team demonstrated their consideration of PBS strategies.

There are other clear advantages of broader rather than more restricted use of these procedures. One such advantage is that the technical aspects of conducting an FBA are best begun well before the events associated with a student's suspension or referral. Because FBAs rely on contextual assessment approaches, conducting them on children who are not in school is difficult (at best) and potentially invalid (at worst). A student being considered for alternative placement may have already burned bridges and have few remaining advocates in the school. Schools undoubtedly need to exercise caution before undertaking the time-consuming and potentially costly effort of conducting FBAs and developing BIPs; yet, as we will argue later, these costs are generally offset by savings in the time required to manage behaviors and the processes related to discipline and referral. In fact, we have generally found that as schools become familiar with PBS, they are increasingly willing to go beyond simple compliance with the law to make these approaches available for a broad range of students.

Current Trends

Two recent trends regarding the provision of individualized PBS in schools are worth noting. First, there is increased recognition of the relevance of PBS for students who have persistent problem behavior and do not have severe disabilities. Many school teams expend significant resources on students with mild disabilities who are in general education classes and who present discipline problems. FBAs may not be mandated in these circumstances, but they may be useful nonetheless. Second, PBS procedures are being used increasingly as an early intervention strategy for emerging problem behavior. An instructional team may undertake an FBA as part of prereferral efforts to prevent escalation of problems and the unnecessary (or inappropriate) classification of students with challenging behavior.

Although IDEA'04 lacks guidance on the optimal initiation of FBAs for students with disabilities, school districts are required to employ at least some elements of the PBS framework. These elements are likely to benefit students classified with disabilities and also students who are at risk. The strategies in this book provide a framework to guide school teams through the process of conducting FBAs and developing BIPs. Effectively implemented, the *Positive Strategies* approach is consistent with the law, is effective, meets high professional and ethical standards, and is practical for the entire school community.

Why Should Schools Invest Resources in Positive Behavior Support?

Three major benefits justify the investment of school resources in PBS efforts. First, the approach is useful in meeting the long-standing legal requirement of education in the least restrictive environment (LRE) for students with disabilities. This refers to the practice of placing students in the most natural (general education) setting in which they can learn with typically developing peers and also obtain individualized supports to meet disability-related concerns. Because behavior problems are a primary reason that students with disabilities are referred to more restrictive settings, a successful BIP may maintain a student in the LRE when this placement would otherwise fail.

A second reason for investing in PBS relates to a renewed emphasis on improving academic achievement. Problem behaviors are a significant challenge for schools inasmuch as they take up valuable instructional time. This has an impact on students with problem behaviors as well as classmates and teachers. As a result, overall productivity loss attributable to problem behaviors can be viewed as the net loss of instruction time multiplied by the number of students present in class. This calculation reflects more than the length of time the individual student misbehaves; it also reflects the time required for the teacher to restore order, reengage the class, and review material sufficiently to resume instruction. The loss of instructional time compounds existing pressure on teachers to complete an entire curriculum and support the achievement of all students. Effective behavior supports diminish such losses.

The third rationale for PBS in schools relates to the problems of school violence, bullying, harassment, and related ills that have received a great deal of attention since the early 1990s. Administrators are under tremendous pressure to demonstrate that their schools have zero tolerance for violence. In response to rare but appalling episodes of lethal violence (e.g., the mass shooting at Columbine High School) and chronic safety issues in many schools, the federal government has promulgated a number of initiatives to address school security and prevention of problem behaviors as central aspects of school safety. PBS is quite consistent with these approaches and has been shown to both reduce aggression and improve academic performance in schools (Sugai & Horner, 1999).

Broad Efforts Using a Positive Behavior Support Approach

Within the last decade, there has been considerable movement toward the use of schoolwide applications of PBS, generally referred to as positive behavioral interventions and supports (PBIS). Schoolwide PBIS are data-driven, population-based approaches to the prevention and reduction of problem behaviors in schools, employing long-term planning and commitment by the school to establish, encourage, and maintain positive behaviors among all students in the community (Sugai & Horner, 2002). The term PBIS is sometimes used synonymously with PBS; in other cases, it refers to broad school, district, or regionwide disciplinary practices and systems designed to foster positive learning and teaching environments for all members of the education community. Within the *Positive Strategies* framework, we employ the term PBIS in its latter sense to include universal discipline policies, safe school initiatives, social skills training programs, and antibullying efforts. Stated simply, PBIS endeavors, although potentially affecting many individual students, generally focus on the larger community, and *Positive Strategies* efforts tend to be targeted toward individual students.

School administrators sometimes ask whether they should use *Positive Strategies* or PBIS, but we do not see this as an either–or question. Our recommendation is to do a quick assessment of the proportion of students with persistent behavior problems. A school in which more than 10% of the students have behavior concerns is often best served by undertaking a schoolwide PBIS approach first and then moving on to *Positive Strategies* after that number has been reduced. If persistent behavior problems are restricted to 5% (or less) of the student population, we expect that the school has systemic interventions in place, and we recommend *Positive Strategies* training to address the concerns of the small proportion of students who require individualized supports. Optimally, a school will opt to interlace schoolwide and individualized approaches.

ASSUMPTIONS OF THE *POSITIVE STRATEGIES* APPROACH

Positive Strategies shares a values base and technology with the entire PBS movement. It has five underlying assumptions, which we review in this section and expand in the subsequent chapters of the book. Let us consider a brief vignette that illustrates a common classroom scenario as a starting point for a discussion of the major assumptions of *Positive Strategies.*

Consider a student, Sam, who gradually stops focusing on seatwork and starts talking loudly. Whether by design or by happenstance, these behaviors have consequences. The teacher is interrupted, other students are distracted and laugh, and Sam is reprimanded. Do these consequences influence the future likelihood of his disruptive behavior? What happens in school the next day? Does Sam repeat the behavior, or has he learned a lesson? Because this book is about developing individualized behavioral supports, we will assume that Sam repeats the behavior.

Problem Behaviors Are Functional

The *Positive Strategies* approach assumes that persistent problem behavior in some way makes sense to the student who is doing it; in other words, the problem behavior serves a function. This assumption derives from the recognition that the student who repeatedly engages in a behavior must be experiencing some benefit, even if the behavior is inconvenient or unpleasant to others. With regard to Sam, this means that if he repeats his loud talking, something that happened previously probably encouraged him to repeat the behavior; maybe he enjoyed the teacher's attention, or that of classmates, or the teacher was sidetracked and did not prompt students to finish their seatwork. We will not know which of these consequences was most important to Sam until we study the behavior more. We do know many students similar to Sam who are caught in a cycle of repeated misbehavior and increasing consequences for that behavior.

In a system that relies heavily on reactive procedures as consequences, a child with persistent problem behaviors is likely to experience these reactions repeatedly. When these reactive procedures are intended to decrease the behavior, we call it punishment, even if the form of the punishment is very common (e.g., scolding, redirection, reprimand). When these repeated attempts to control behavior are unsuccessful, increasingly intense and intrusive consequences often follow. In the case of Sam, he might first be reprimanded, then given a time out, and then sent to the principal's office. Each of these consequences may well have an immediate effect on Sam's behavior. But their effect is often short lived, requiring the next consequence to be even more intense to have an effect. The irony is that each of these intended punishments might actually be reinforcing to both Sam *and* the teacher. After all, the class runs much more smoothly after Sam's removal, and Sam receives a break from demands he may feel ill equipped to manage.

A reexamination of the A-B-C chain referred to earlier will introduce the reader to some fundamentals of *Positive Strategies.* These concepts are illustrated more fully in Chapter 6.

Within the *Positive Strategies* approach (and consistent with other PBS applications), we consider two types of precursors to problem behaviors: setting events and antecedents. *Setting events* (sometimes called slow triggers) are factors that increase the potential for a problem behavior to occur but that do not directly cause the behavior. Setting events contribute to behavior, but they are not sufficient to cause it; they set the stage. We consider setting events along four dimensions: *physical* (e.g., chronic medical conditions, disabilities, effects of medication, pain or discomfort, sleep disturbance); *learning and self-regulation* (e.g., learning disabilities, impairments in attention or behavior regulation); *social-emotional* (e.g., family crisis, argument with a friend); and *environment and routines* (e.g., a hurried morning routine, new caregiver, missed meal). *Antecedents* are immediate triggers for behavior—for example, being presented with schoolwork that taps a child's area of impairment, seatwork of a duration exceeding the child's workable attention span, or verbal instructions that surpass the student's comprehension level. Any such antecedent interacts with the setting event to result in the problem behavior. In addition, persistent problem behaviors necessarily have consequences that (often inadvertently) maintain the problem behaviors. This sequence is illustrated in Figure 1.

On reconsideration, it becomes clear that for each setting event–antecedent combination, there are actually two possible categories of outcome. The one pictured above is the focus of the FBA; the team seeks to understand how setting events, antecedents, and consequences influ-

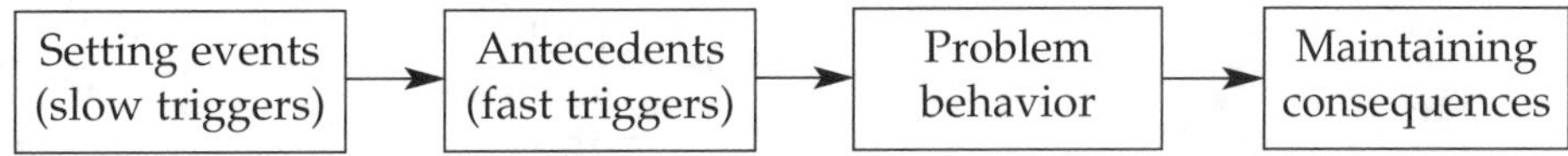

Figure 1. Precursors, problem behaviors, and maintaining consequences. (From *Functional assessment and program development for problem behavior: A practical handbook* [2nd ed.], by O'Neil, R.E., Horner, R.H., Albin, R.W., Sprague, J.R., Storey, K., & Newton, J. [1997]. Reprinted with permission of Wadsworth, a division of Thomson Learning. Web site: http://www.thomsonrights.com; fax: 800-730-2215.)

ence the problem behavior. The second type of outcome, shown in Figure 2, is the focus of the BIP. That is, we wish to support a student in such a way that the same sequence of setting events and antecedents triggers an alternative behavior. The alternative behavior then elicits natural consequences that encourage (reinforce) it, making it more likely to recur.

Although it seems fairly straightforward, anyone who has tried to wish away problem behaviors knows how hard it is to get from the state depicted in Figure 1 to that shown in Figure 2. The entire scenario is depicted in Figure 3. Here, persistent problem behaviors are a habitual, well-worn path. Although the problem behavior does not serve the student well in the long run, it persists because it meets an immediate need. On occasion, the student may even engage in the desired behavior in the same setting in which he or she is now misbehaving. In that case, the typical consequences for the desired behavior do not provide a level of reinforcement sufficient to maintain it. Instead, the student has learned that the problem behavior generates consequences that are more immediately satisfying in some way. For example, standing quietly in line involves boredom and listlessness. Joking and horseplay provide social stimulation, attention, and escape from the tedium of waiting. These consequences maintain the behavior in question. Note that the child does not necessarily realize that the problem behavior is reinforced; in fact, this is unlikely, and the child may even voice regret at not being better behaved.

As Figure 3 suggests, there are two major challenges to developing alternative behaviors. First, it is important for a team to develop a full understanding of how the problem behavior works for the student. Second, the team needs to identify an alternative that fulfills the same function as the problem behavior. Before we review alternative behaviors, an introduction to major functions of problem behavior is needed. (These functions, and the means by which teams assess them, are discussed much more fully in Chapter 4.)

Positive Strategies considers four major functions of behavior: *tangible,* meaning that the behavior results in acquisition of a desired object or activity; *sensory,* in which the behavior's primary purpose is to meet a sensory-driven need (e.g., for more or less input in a particular sensory domain); *attention,* in which the student's behavior reliably results in desired attention from others; and *escape,* in which the student is motivated to cease (escape from) undesirable activities or settings. Behaviors can serve more than one function. They sometimes develop to meet one need and evolve to meet other concerns over time. For example, disruptive behavior may develop from a student's desire to escape difficult tasks. The behavior might be maintained not only by that function but also by the attention that results from the disruptive behavior. Over time, the behavior and the environment's response may become so engrained as to qualify as habit. Positive supports require understanding the development of this habit and removing the need for it.

Reducing Problem Behavior Requires Increasing Alternatives

If a child's behavior is functional, it meets some need for the child. As such, understanding how the behavior meets that need is essential; the next step is to offer the child a better way to meet

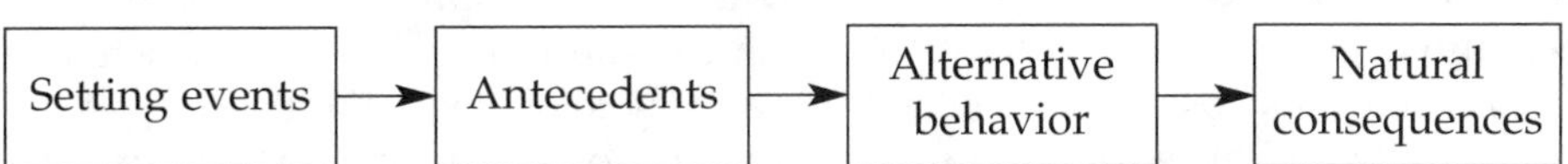

Figure 2. Precursors, alternative behaviors, and natural consequences. (From *Functional assessment and program development for problem behavior: A practical handbook* [2nd ed.], by O'Neil, R.E., Horner, R.H., Albin, R.W., Sprague, J.R., Storey, K., & Newton, J. [1997]. Reprinted with permission of Wadsworth, a division of Thomson Learning. Web site: http://www.thomsonrights.com; fax: 800-730-2215.)

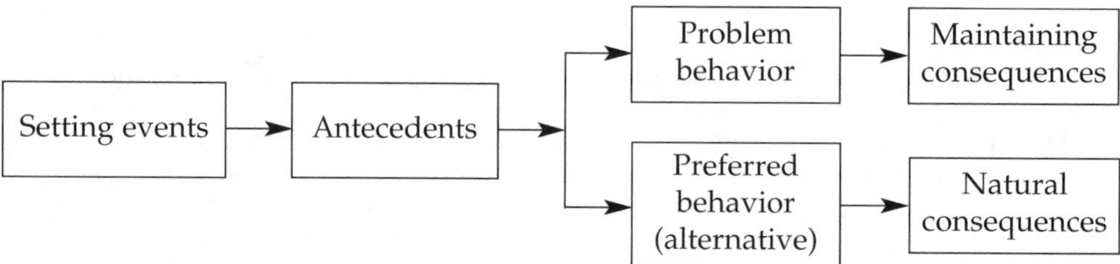

Figure 3. Positive supports entail understanding the function of problem behavior to develop appropriate alternatives. (From *Functional assessment and program development for problem behavior: A practical handbook* [2nd ed.], by O'Neil, R.E., Horner, R.H., Albin, R.W., Sprague, J.R., Storey, K., & Newton, J. [1997]. Reprinted with permission of Wadsworth, a division of Thomson Learning. Web site: http://www.thomsonrights.com; fax: 800-730-2215.)

the need. To illustrate, let us return to the example of Sam. His limited attention span and low tolerance for frustration may serve as setting events. Although Sam is able to succeed on many tasks throughout the day, being asked to do an assignment independently and quietly at his desk might serve as an antecedent for his verbal outburst. His behavior problem consistently gets him out of these assignments. The team's reliance on consequences that were intended to reduce his problem behaviors has been unsuccessful.

Ideally, the teacher and the team consider what the behavior is telling them: Sam cannot work independently for more than 5 minutes. An effective plan requires not only that Sam learn an acceptable way to communicate this message but that he also improve his ability to complete independent work. The alternative has to work as well as or better than the problem behavior, or its chances of success are slim. Thus, we would not recommend teaching Sam to say, "Sorry, I can only work for 5 minutes." Such a communication would probably be unwelcome and would not serve Sam in the long run. We might teach Sam to request attention after working for 3–4 minutes by saying, "Excuse me, but I'm not sure what to do next." This is far more likely to elicit support and direction from the teacher, which should serve to reinforce Sam's new behavior. A related plan to increase his frustration tolerance would aim to increase the amount of time he works independently before requiring support.

In Chapter 5, we more fully consider the types of skills that serve as alternative behaviors. In brief, we recommend consideration of the behavioral categories of self-regulation, communication, social, and academic skills. In the example above, we suggested teaching Sam a communication skill. Within our framework, we might also consider teaching him relaxation skills to use when confronted with challenging academic tasks (self-regulation), conversational skills with peers that would allow him to have pleasant sustained interactions (social), and analytic ability to determine which tasks are difficult and warrant requesting assistance from the teacher (academic). Any and all of these skills may benefit Sam; completing the FBA informs the teacher as to which specific skill is most likely to benefit Sam.

Problem Behaviors Emerge in Context

Positive Strategies activities require a departure from traditional conceptualizations of problem behavior. In psychology, traditional views of problem (maladaptive) behavior relate it to psychopathology, resulting from factors intrinsic to the individual (e.g., genetics), the early environment (e.g., family), and social and cultural influences. Problem behaviors are often described as if they emerged naturally from an underlying cause; that is, a child is self-injurious or has tantrums because he or she has autism. But not all children with autism have these specific problems. Rather, autism is associated with difficulties in communication, social interaction, and self-regulation that may make behavior problems more likely to develop. For the purpose of intervention, however, we would liken the diagnosis or classification of autism to a setting event.

Children with conditions such as autism may have many shared behavioral features, but the emergence of any specific behavioral pattern arises from interactions between underlying factors and a specific child's environment. As such, two children with very similar disabilities may demonstrate very different behavioral topographies or patterns of behavior, and one child may behave very differently in two different environments. Sound assessment practices determine not only when and where problems do occur but also when and where they do not. Although this may seem confusing, it can actually be helpful, because it can inform the team of strategies and contexts that promote positive behavior. *Positive Strategies* views the student in the context of classroom, school, and even home, with all of the associated instructional and social demands. Because problem behaviors arise in context, they must be addressed in context.

Hence, one difference between PBS and traditional approaches to behavior change is the focus of PBS on the relationship between behavior and environment. We view behavior as determined by a combination of factors, including personal factors, learning history and style, environmental triggers, and the consequences that follow. Because behavior emerges from multiple interacting factors, an FBA requires thorough evaluation of the student, the environment, and the relationship between the student and the context. This increases the likelihood of identifying how environment contributes to problem behavior, as well as the corresponding need to make changes.

Context, however, is often difficult to change. Our educational systems typically require students to adjust to schools, rather than having schools accommodate their students' concerns. Because of their difficulties, students with challenging behaviors often require changing, diverse, or intensive approaches, yet the suggestion that a school should change to fit a student invites significant resistance. Schools have historically emphasized control as a critical feature of classroom instruction, whereas more contemporary models stress more positive means of engaging students. As such, today's educators may be better prepared than their predecessors to increase efforts at creative instruction for children with challenging behavior. We observe wide variation in the amount and quality of preservice teacher preparation for managing behavior. Regardless of teacher experience or disposition, more discipline for a child with persistent behavior problems may only demean or disenfranchise the student, further reduce effective instructional time, and diminish more hopeful options. We discuss this further in Chapter 3.

Teams wrestle with another concern related to the tendency for schools to expect children to adapt (rather than the other way around). If elements of the environment contribute to or maintain behavior, does responsibility for the problem lie with an individual or within the setting? We do not assume that identifying contributory environmental factors is equivalent to assigning blame for problem behavior. Educators with the skills to manage learning and behavioral diversity may be in a better position to recognize the complex, multidetermined nature of problem behavior and be less concerned about blame. They may be more likely to circumvent some problem behaviors through proactive means, and they may feel more comfortable implementing positive supports. Yet, no one is immune to the experience of problem behaviors, and focusing on blame is usually a waste of resources. *Positive Strategies* assumes that behaviors emerge in context; it is concerned with answering how and why a problem developed only to the extent that the answer helps remedy the problem.

Punishment as Corrective Feedback Has a Place in Positive Interventions

When behavior problems occur, reproachful gazes or verbal reprimands typically follow. These are frequent, almost automatic reactions, intended as punishment in the technical use of that word. The teacher wishes to make it less likely that the child will repeat this particular behavior. Despite the pejorative connotations of the term *punishment,* the reprimand is intended as just that. If it works and serves to decrease the future likelihood of the problem behavior's occurrence, then the reprimand was, in fact, a punishment. Conversely, if the reprimand increases the future probability of the behavior, it has served as a reinforcer for the problem behavior. Note that we use the term *punishment* in a technical way rather than in its common connotation: it is punishment if it reduces behavior, but there is no requirement that punishment be harsh.

To avoid confusing these uses of the term *punishment,* some educators and interventionists adopt more neutral terms such as *consequences, discipline,* and *contingencies.* After the aversives controversy, many began to employ these terms to differentiate painful, humiliating, or uncomfortable consequences from more natural or benign ones. Teachers and parents necessarily rely on the use of contingencies to shape children's behavior, so punishment occurs even in the most nurturing relationships. Indeed, because all children misbehave sometimes, and caregivers wish to discourage misconduct, punishment is a basic strategy for shaping behavior. We would argue, however, that its effectiveness may well relate to its informational value to the child. Punishment informs a child that a given behavior was inappropriate to the situation. Its informational value is independent of its tone; harsh punishment introduces other factors likely to interfere with the purely informational component. For example, the demeaning, embarrassing or belittling aspects of punishment are likely to be more salient for a student than their intended informational content ("do less of that"). The student's response to those punitive elements is unlikely to resemble a positive alternative to the problem behavior.

Positive Strategies views punishment as a common response to problem behaviors in the world in which we live. Why? Punishments commonly employed by teachers and parents often lead to quick reduction or cessation of undesirable behavior. Punishment offers an immediate means of establishing control, which is reinforcing to the adult, particularly the teacher, for several reasons. An orderly environment is generally safer, tends to maximize the number of children engaged in tasks, and supports the adult in carrying out the responsibilities of instruction. It is the preferred context for children's learning, and it provides an environment in which children can further develop social skills. (Although we note that structured, organized environments have many advantages, we also discourage overemphasis on order and control in classrooms, and we encourage instructors to be tolerant of behavioral diversity.)

For these reasons, punishment (or discipline in the school context) is likely to remain with us. The *Positive Strategies* approach is not inherently antipunishment; rather, it assumes that punishment as corrective feedback has a place in shaping behavior. As stated earlier, however, we firmly oppose the use of aversive procedures. We also disagree with the use of punishment when it is a habitual, ineffective, demeaning, or unilateral means of responding to a student. When used too often for the same behavior, punishment is likely to be ineffective. Worse yet, the intended punishment may inadvertently maintain the problem behavior. Continuous reliance on punishment may signify erosion of the instructor's confidence or a lack of investment in addressing the problem. Overreliance on punishment for students with persistent behavior problems almost invariably leads to escalating cycles of behavior and increasingly punitive consequences.

Positive Strategies also recognizes that punishment alone is a poor instructional technique. It can only teach a child what *not* to do. Although few would espouse child-rearing philosophies that rely primarily on punishment, many environments offer few positive elements for a child with persistent behavior problems. In such cases, the neutral observer quickly sees the need for the child to experience more positive consequences. Because persistent behavior problems often develop over time and in response to escalating cycles, the individuals directly involved may not see how the environment has become discouraging for the child. Under these circumstances, the environment essentially offers the child few or no alternatives to the problem behavior, shaping a sense of hopelessness rather than a set of positive alternatives.

When a punishment is not working, the instructional team must acknowledge this and find a better way. The *Positive Strategies* approach offers a method for interrupting the vicious cycle of inappropriate punishment, inadequate reinforcement, and ineffective instruction. Indeed, the field of ABA has a rich literature attesting to the power of positive reinforcement and direct instruction in reducing (and sometimes eliminating) the need for punishment. *Positive Strategies* involves careful assessment of children's problem behaviors as well as their competencies, impairments, learning styles, and the consequences they find motivating. This permits the development of a BIP that considers both punishment and reinforcement as feedback on behavior to the student.

Positive Strategies Requires a Team Approach

Earlier in this chapter, we discussed how difficult it can be for any individual educator to address problem behaviors. At this point, the reader can certainly surmise the rationale for this assumption. Planning involves a review of past evaluations, assessments, and interventions; their characteristics; determining whether they failed or succeeded; and understanding why. Several individuals working together to achieve change have that many more creative solutions to consider and implement. Whether one is implementing an individual BIP or developing a schoolwide intervention, there are clear benefits to teamwork. As suggested earlier, multiple viewpoints (even those that at first seem contradictory) have the potential to enhance a plan because these viewpoints represent different contexts, perspectives, and analyses.

On the other hand, limited sampling of a student's behavior (e.g., excluding some instructors or settings from the assessment process) can restrict intervention success, because the planners might fail to foresee contextual demands or key skills necessary for student success. Teams that effectively implement BIPs tend to value the input of all members, tolerate and manage disagreement, communicate openly and assertively, and work toward consensus. Healthy teams share both the burdens of labor and the fruits of success. The multiple steps of conducting an FBA and then planning and implementing a BIP take time, effort, and perseverance. When a team achieves this, its members have enriched not only the individual student, but all their students and themselves. We further discuss characteristics of effective teams in Chapter 4.

POSITIVE STRATEGIES: UNDERSTAND, PREVENT, REPLACE

We summarize the *Positive Strategies* approach as consisting of three elements: understand, prevent, and replace. The management of persistent behavior problems begins with the FBA, a systematic approach to understanding why behaviors persist. This understanding is unique to the individual student and may vary across the settings in which behaviors occur. Once the team effectively identifies a behavior's function or purpose, the next step is to develop the BIP. The BIP outlines procedures and accommodations intended to prevent the problem behavior and provides a plan to teach replacement skills.

This formula may sound simplistic. And, on rare occasions, the process can even be simple. More often, success for students with persistent behavior problems requires complex, coordinated team efforts to carry out the activities of assessment, planning, intervention, and follow-up. This book, which outlines the steps involved in the FBA and BIP, is designed to support teams regardless of the complexity of the behaviors in question.

Field testing has made us highly sympathetic to the competing demands placed on teachers and other school personnel. Ensuring that the majority of students benefit from instruction sometimes conflicts with the time-consuming process of comprehensively addressing one student's concerns. To address this, we have routinely worked to streamline our procedures while ensuring that *Positive Strategies* remains faithful to the essential components of successful behavioral support. Maintaining a balance between efficiency and effectiveness is a primary consideration in our work. We have actively collaborated with many intervention teams who have successfully conducted *Positive Strategies* activities and provided input and feedback regarding our materials. During *Positive Strategies* team training programs, we ask teams to conduct case studies to provide a narrative synopsis of this approach in real-life settings.

COMMON CHALLENGES IN *POSITIVE STRATEGIES*

The *Positive Strategies* approach has enormous potential; however, there are six challenges to implementation, some of which arise when extensive efforts are focused on a single student.

Time and Effort

The first challenge concerns the reluctance of school personnel to devote the time and effort required to effect lasting change. This may be stated explicitly, or it may remain unspoken. Members of a child's instructional team may feel that it is unfair to devote disproportionate resources to an individual child in the midst of so many other concerns and demands. The reality, as discussed earlier, is that persistent behavior problems detract significantly from the amount of instructional time available to the entire class. This lost time compounds the stress of reacting to the problem behavior and concerns about such behavior's social impact on other students. In some cases, we work with reluctant team members to calculate the amount of time they spend each week unproductively managing problem behaviors. We encourage team members to reframe the FBA and BIP effort as a way to diminish their losses, essentially converting lost time to productive efforts. In combination with this pragmatic approach, we stress the values base presented earlier in this chapter. In Chapter 4, we discuss the crucial importance of administrative support of team efforts.

Reactive Culture

The second challenge involves moving away from reactive responses to problem behaviors. Team members often note that some *Positive Strategies* activities occur when their students are relatively well behaved. At these moments, it might be tempting to enjoy a respite from the student, focus instructional efforts on others, and wait for problem behaviors to recur. One common irony is that students with persistent problems receive a great deal of attention when in crisis and get little attention at other times. As organizations, schools tend to remain largely reactive to problems. Enacting positive supports requires a proactive stance.

Need for Accommodation

A third challenge concerns the reaction of teachers and caregivers to nontraditional approaches, particularly in the area of prevention. Based on the FBA, we sometimes recommend a period of reduced demands for a student, with the goal of preventing some occurrences of problem behavior. This approach is well grounded in the literature and derives from an assessment in which all team members participate. Despite this, school personnel and families may be uncomfortable with what seems like coddling or giving in to manipulation by the student ("He's getting just what he wants"). Many teams spend a great deal of time debating whether short-term prevention strategies are tantamount to giving in to problem behavior.

Once again, our response considers issues of pragmatism and ABA. First, from a practical perspective, intervention often means acknowledging a realistic starting point. Acknowledging the current state of affairs does not signify resignation about problem behaviors. Although no team member would be satisfied with an indefinite reduction in demands, a temporary reduction offers an opportunity for the child (and the team) to experience success, which, in turn, informs the work to follow. Indeed, an effective period of prevention informs all subsequent interventions and is just one of several strategies at work in the BIP. Further, the technology of ABA involves understanding the child's baseline and working from that to shape the acquisition and use of more effective skills.

We differentiate short-term strategies from long-term accommodations that might be identified during the planning process. Many students with challenging behavior benefit from instructional accommodations designed to make them more successful in the academic or social domains. These changes may be viewed as long-standing in nature and may be incorporated into the student's IEP and linked to the simultaneous development of replacement skills.

Establishing Teams

The final three challenges concern teamwork itself, which is clearly a crucial component of *Positive Strategies.* First, many schools do not have established teams, and personnel may be unfamiliar with the requisites of effective teamwork. Hence, establishing an effective team can be a challenge to successful implementation; it requires dedication, leadership, and practical mechanisms, such as planned meeting times. Even when teams are functioning, ensuring continuing resources to support their work may create additional complications.

Maintaining Team Momentum

Some *Positive Strategies* teams stop their work too soon. During the FBA and resulting accommodations, many students show dramatic reductions in problem behavior. Interestingly enough, this can create a problem. Because a student is doing better, there is a natural tendency to shift attention to other concerns. As a consequence, organizational support for continuing the intervention may wane at a crucial juncture. At the point that the student's behavior begins to improve, it seems unnecessary to invest the additional resources needed to teach replacement skills. Without ongoing support and instruction, however, there is a good chance that problem behaviors will reemerge or worsen. In the absence of good alternatives, students might develop new, equally problematic behaviors that serve the same function as the original behaviors. Maintaining the momentum achieved early in the process is key to not only addressing the problem but to preventing escalation and establishing enduring changes.

Teams Are Just One Piece of the Puzzle

Since approximately the year 2000, it has become increasingly clear that developing FBAs and implementing BIPs is just one aspect of an overall system of behavioral support. As discussed earlier, this book emphasizes individualized approaches, but we acknowledge the importance of the larger environment as the setting for behavior problems. Approaches to individual assessment and intervention outlined here work most effectively in classrooms and schools that meet the concerns of the vast majority of their students through sensible policies and sensitive curricula.

THERE IS NO BETTER PERSON TO DO THE JOB

In the spirit of encouraging you (the reader, teacher, school psychologist, principal, or whomever) to engage in this process of planning and action for your students, we say, "Go for it!" Dare to help the child whom no one else likes; dare to voice your belief that the system (or team) may be failing the child. Dare to care—and demonstrate it by going the extra mile.

In this book, we outline a process that works for a wide variety of students across a range of settings. Take your time as you read these materials; some aspects may be vaguely familiar, others quite so, and some will be entirely new territory. Talk to colleagues, meet frequently, and commit yourselves to working well together. In the end, you will be well served—and so will your students.

Chapter 2

Essentials of Behavior

How do problem behaviors develop? Why do they persist despite our best efforts to discourage them? What can be done to change behavior that is counterproductive or harmful? Better yet, how might problems be prevented? How can behavioral principles be applied to support the learning of social skills?

These are important questions to consider. Examining the history of education, one observes several different trends in understanding, influencing, predicting, and even controlling student behavior. Each trend reflects a unique set of social circumstances and an underlying set of beliefs about causes of behavior. For example, the adage "spare the rod and spoil the child" emerged from an era in which corporal punishment was commonplace at home and in school. This saying suggests that children need to be tamed, reflecting a belief that hitting is an acceptable (even necessary) approach to raising well-adjusted children. Today, very different views prevail, but our current perspective reflects underlying assumptions about the nature of children, how behavior is shaped, and effective ways to intervene when problems develop.

In this chapter, we discuss the central assumptions underlying behavior analysis and behavior therapy, presenting them within a *Positive Strategies* framework and placing them in an educational context. This material is intended for readers who consider themselves to be somewhat conversant with, but not necessarily expert in, behavior theory. In effect, this comprises an overview of the content covered in some college-level psychology courses.

WHY IS THIS IMPORTANT TO TEACHERS?

Teachers and other educators are necessarily concerned with changing student behavior for the better. We would argue that to predict and change behavior, we first have to understand how it works. Behaviorism offers useful explanations for behavior, and in this chapter we introduce some of behaviorism's most important principles. We consider behaviorism's explanations fairly straightforward, even if human behavior is complex and determined by many factors, and thus applying behaviorism's rules is not always easy. This is important for two reasons.

First, we look at student behaviors as having been influenced by multiple and complex factors that have contributed to a student's current repertoire of behaviors, both positive and negative. Second, to become competent in assessing and intervening with problem behaviors, teachers and others require a basic understanding of the behavioral concepts that underlie teaching and learning. This understanding frames our work with students, and it deepens with experience.

BEHAVIORISM'S EXPLANATIONS

Today, introductory psychology and related courses teach college students about Ivan Pavlov's salivating dogs and B.F. Skinner's ping pong–playing pigeons. Many readers may recall having learned about these scientists, and some may even recall how such research was applied to human behavior.

Classical Conditioning

Pavlov's work in classical conditioning demonstrates how environmental triggers come to elicit automatic behaviors or reflexes. From Pavlov, we learn why a war veteran might be startled when hearing a car backfire. We know that humans are hardwired to react to danger in predictable ways. On the battlefield, booming noise produces an automatic protective response, reflexively mobilizing the body for fight or flight. Repeated pairings of loud noise and danger produce a powerful continuing association for the soldier. Even without the presence of danger, a loud noise still results in a protective (startle) response, one that seems exaggerated or out of proportion in everyday circumstances. The body assumes a fight or flight stance even though the danger is no longer present.

Other aspects of the wartime circumstance can be conditioned: perhaps a type of building, an odor, or the unique color of military flares used to illuminate targets. Because these experiences and perceptions are associated so powerfully with danger, the soldier learns to expect danger when any of these cues are present, even though the danger may not be. The more closely a perception resembles the original (traumatic) situation, the more likely it is to evoke what Pavlov called the *conditioned response.* A conditioned response is a learned reaction: the body mobilizes reflexes in response to specific environmental cues. Pavlov's work examined associations between environmental cues and automatic behaviors—innate bodily reactions such as the eye blink, startle, and withdrawal from painful stimuli. The development of these associations is called classical conditioning. The emphasis is on the relationship between two external events (e.g., loud noise and danger) and the individual's automatic response.

In the realm of human behavior, classical conditioning plays a role not only in the development of negative emotions such as fear and anxiety but in the development of positive emotions. Behaviorists look at early development as a time in which the lifelong bonds of love between parents and their offspring are established. Similarly, a song associated with first love may evoke deep positive feelings when it unexpectedly comes on the radio.

Operant Conditioning

B.F. Skinner also conducted seminal work in behaviorism. Rather than study automatic behaviors, he examined how voluntary behaviors develop. Working mostly with animals, Skinner studied what he called *operant conditioning,* an approach that examined the relationship between voluntary behavior and the consequences that follow it. Skinner altered the consequences of behaviors that animals naturally engaged in. As a result, he changed the likelihood that those behaviors would occur in the future.

Skinner was influenced by the work of Edward Thorndike and his *Law of Effect,* which states that positive outcomes strengthen behaviors and that negative outcomes weaken them. The premise of Skinner's work was that when a positive consequence follows behavior, that behavior is more likely to recur. This principle (which readers might recognize as reinforcement) is one example of *contingency,* a functional relationship between behavior and the environment.

Some describe the contingencies as equivalent to switches that effectively turn behavior on and off. But there is more to operant conditioning than that; in the next section, we discuss how environment, individual differences, and consequences act in concert to influence behavior.

Applied Behavior Analysis

Whereas Skinner originated operant conditioning (sometimes also called *instrumental learning*), his work has been replicated and extended by many other researchers and clinicians. After Skinner's laboratory work in the 1950s and 1960s, others used the principles of operant conditioning to address human behavior. In the inaugural issue of the *Journal of Applied Behavior Analysis,* Baer, Wolf, and Risley (1968) wrote that

> an applied behavior analysis will make obvious the importance of the behavior changed, its quantitative characteristics, the experimental manipulations that analyze with clarity what was responsible for the change, the technologically exact description of all procedures contributing to that change, the effectiveness of those procedures in making sufficient change for value, and the generality of that change. (p. 97)

These authors asserted the legitimacy of applied behavior analysis (ABA) as a scientific endeavor and, in emphasizing its applied nature, also insisted that it focus on socially important behavior. For almost 40 years, behavior analysts have discussed the central relevance of function and emphasized the need to focus on meaningful outcomes. Although not all applications of ABA have realized this vision, positive behavior supports are a logical step in the evolution of this important technology.

We all apply behaviorism in our daily lives, whether it is tipping for good table service in a restaurant, offering privileges when children complete household chores, or placing a gold star on well-executed homework assignments. It is important to understand behavioral concepts because they can be used to enhance classroom instruction and learning. In truth, these principles operate whether we attend to them or not, so it makes good sense to put them to work on everyone's behalf. Our discussion of the essentials of behavior considers how environmental factors, individual differences, and contingencies act together to influence behavior. We discuss them in reverse order in the sections that follow and summarize them in the final section.

Behavioral Contingencies

Let us return to our discussion of operant conditioning. Skinner (1953) proposed that any behavior is followed by one of four possibilities: a) a positive experience begins, b) a positive experience ends, c) a negative experience begins, or d) a negative experience ends. These experiences refer to consequences delivered by the environment, whether deliberately or by accident. Imagine telling a joke to another person who is smiling, a consequence you experience as pleasant. As you reach the punch line, they might a) smile more broadly and laugh, b) stop smiling, or c) begin to scowl. Or, perhaps at first they were scowling (a negative experience for you), and when you finish your joke, the listener adopts a neutral expression (d).

In the first example (a), your behavior is met with something pleasurable. Your joke brings a smile, and that increases the chances that you will tell the joke again. Alternatively, if your joke removes a scowl (d), that might also increase its future likelihood of being told. Both of these experiences are examples of reinforcement. Example (a) is positive reinforcement, because something positive is added, whereas example (d) is negative reinforcement, because something negative is removed after you tell the joke. In both cases, you are pleased with the result. Reinforcement, whether positive or negative, increases the future likelihood of behavior. You are likely to repeat the behavior because it improved your experience.

Examples (b) and (c) are not pleasant consequences. In (b), the listener stops smiling as you deliver your punch line, and in (c) the listener actually scowls. Neither response increases the likelihood that you will tell the joke again. In fact, because they are somewhat undesirable consequences, they discourage you. In operant terms, the results are punishment because they decrease the future probability of behavior. You are less likely to repeat your behavior after this experience.

The term *contingency* refers to the conditional relationship between behavior and the environment. If your joke meets with pleasant consequences, you are more likely to tell it again; if it meets with unpleasant consequences, you are less likely to repeat it. Your experience of the consequences influences your future behavior, whether you realize it or not. Contingencies are key in shaping human behavior, but they are not the only influences.

Social Learning (Modeling)

The third major type of learning is *social learning*, or *modeling*. These terms are associated with researcher Albert Bandura (Bandura, 1977; Bandura, Ross, & Ross, 1961), who conducted classic experiments in psychology and is credited with integrating behavior theory and social psychology. Bandura and colleagues exposed children to adults who interacted with a toy doll named Bobo. The adults modeled either aggressive (hitting, kicking, punching) or nonaggressive behavior (ignoring Bobo). Children were later given the opportunity to interact with the Bobo doll. Bandura found that those who had seen an aggressive adult were much more likely to display aggressive behavior themselves, whereas children who had witnessed nonaggressive adults were rarely aggressive.

There are many implications to Bandura's concept of modeling, including recognition of the importance of appropriate role models for children, the risks of exposure to inappropriate models, and the potential of modeling to influence a range of behaviors from the classroom to the supermarket. Bandura and his colleagues also showed that modeled behavior is more likely to be adopted when the observer is similar to the model, when the model is admired or of higher status, and when the modeled behavior results in valued outcomes. Perhaps you are more likely to buy a certain laundry detergent if you identify with the actor in the television commercial, or your students might be apt to follow the lead of a popular student in class.

Bandura posited that four factors are required for *observational learning* to occur. First, the learner needs to be paying close attention to the model. Second, the observer must retain the modeled behavior in some way. These first two requirements refer not only to the complexity of the behavior modeled but also to the observer's ability to code, store, and recall (verbally or nonverbally) what he or she has seen. Third, to imitate, the observer must be capable of reproducing the modeled behavior. This implies the capability to process and reproduce the language and actions of the model, engage in some level of self-observation, and alter the imitated behavior as needed. Finally, Bandura suggested that motivation was critical for deferred imitation; the observer will reproduce behaviors that are enticing, functional, or likely to meet reward.

Given the prominence of imitation as a form of learning, it is important for educators to recognize factors that influence its occurrence. If modeling is planned as a component of an instructional intervention (the teacher first shows the student how to complete a task), success depends on careful assessment of the student's ability to attend to, retain, and reproduce the target behavior, as well as his or her motivation to engage in it to earn the reward. For complex tasks, the child may first need to learn its various components through modeling and, later, to imitate a model who incorporates the components into a whole.

Bandura's work exemplifies the interdisciplinary nature of applied behavior therapy in that it incorporates principles learned from related fields of social and cognitive psychology, behavioral genetics, and the study of individual differences. The four requirements for social learning tap underlying cognitive and memory skills, sensation and perception, self-observation, self-regulation and self-appraisal, concepts of reinforcement, and social referencing. Behavior theory began as the scientific study of animal behavior and is evolving into a multidisciplinary endeavor with roots and applications across education, health care, and sociology. Although social learning extends beyond behaviorism per se to include unobservable cognitive and social factors, it also is fundamentally behavioral in its assumptions regarding contingencies.

KEY BEHAVIORAL CONCEPTS

So far, we have introduced and distinguished three kinds of learning. *Classical conditioning* refers to automatic (reflexive) behavior, whereas *operant conditioning* concerns voluntary behavior, and *social learning* involves imitation of and learning from others using thought and memory as mediators. All three approaches share some terminology, but we focus most closely on operant conditioning in this chapter because it relates most centrally to positive behavior support (PBS) and classroom instruction.

Earlier, we suggested that there is inherent utility in understanding principles of operant conditioning and ABA because they are constantly at work whether we like it or not. Although we believe firmly that these principles can be used to the benefit of students and teachers alike, we also recognize that some readers are discouraged by the technical jargon and complicated graphs that sometimes accompany descriptions and case studies. As such, we attempt in this section to convey and define terms in straightforward language, using everyday examples.

Note that classical and operant conditioning are defined as forms of *learning*; although humans are hardwired to develop, grow, and change, our behavior is shaped by our interactions with our environment. Changes that emerge from those interactions are all forms of learning, even if they become somewhat automatic or habitual. We begin with a review of the basics of behavior, summaries of which appear in Table 1.

Reinforcement and Punishment

We mentioned earlier that *reinforcement* increases the future likelihood of behavior, whereas *punishment* decreases its likelihood. (As described in Chapter 1, our use of the term *punishment* is used here technically to include consequences that provide corrective feedback but that are not painful, humiliating, or infringing on basic rights.) In real-life interactions, reinforcement and punishment are frequently used in tandem. For example, a parent reprimands a child for failing to make his bed in the morning (or doing so sloppily) but praises him when he does it well and without reminder. The parental intention here is to maximize the likelihood that the bed will be made and to minimize the number of mornings that the bed is not made.

Most readers would note the absurdity of punishing a child who does not know how to make his bed for failing to do so. Yet, in some cases, students with problem behaviors do not possess viable alternatives to problem behavior. They are stuck in cycle of punishment until someone takes the time to explore the development of an alternative behavior that can be reinforced. A related problem concerning reliance on punishment relates to its consistency. Punishment is most effective when it immediately follows behavior, which requires the adult to be present and monitoring. When incidents occur outside of supervision, problem behavior is essentially reinforced, which strengthens it. Children can purposely or unwittingly discover the circumstances under which their behavior is likely to be noticed and then avoid such circumstances, thereby escaping punishment. Because of its inconsistent results and short-term effects, Skinner himself frowned on the use of punishment as a means of influencing human behavior.

Accepting that it seems unfair to punish a novice for poor execution of a complex task, let us return to the child who is learning to make his bed. How might you teach this skill to the child and encourage him to do so daily? In this case, parents would be likely to engage in *shaping,* which involves rewarding successive approximations of the desired (target) behavior. First, a parent might demonstrate bed making and ask the child to participate by pulling up some of the bedclothes, offering praise even when wrinkles remain. In the days to follow, the parents might offer praise for the child's efforts, even if the results are far from perfect—just pulling the covers up might be sufficient for reinforcement. Over time, the parents can naturally expect a little more from the child: fewer instructions, fewer wrinkles, and bedding tucked in more tightly.

In the first few days, the parent praises the child for simply engaging in the task. This eventually becomes an expectation, and soon, trying is not enough; instead, the child is praised only when all the covers reach over the pillow. Next, the child might be expected to smooth wrinkles and to tuck the pillow neatly beneath the top blanket. Rather than expecting him to master the entire task, the parents employ a gradual approach. Teaching often involves shifting criteria for reinforcement; in other words, successively smoother and neater bed making is necessary for the child to continue to receive rewards. This is a logical way to teach complex

Table 1. Key behavioral principles

Behavioral principle	What is it?	Example
Operant conditioning	Form of learning in which voluntary behavior is developed or inhibited in response to environmental cues and consequences	A person tells a joke; the listener's response determines whether the joke teller is likely to repeat it
Classical conditioning	Form of learning in which involuntary or automatic responses become associated with specific environmental cues; the individual demonstrates reflexive behaviors because these behaviors are associated with environmental cues	A veteran hears the bang of firecrackers, startles, and crouches defensively; a child who was bitten by a dog screams and flees when she sees one of a similar breed; a man is nauseated by the smell of an alcoholic beverage he has previously overindulged in
Reinforcement	A response from the environment increases the future likelihood of behavior	The teacher smiles, nods, and calls on a student who sits quietly with hand raised
Positive reinforcement	A positive experience follows a behavior, thereby increasing its future likelihood	A student who interrupts a teacher to ask a question finds the teacher's response receptive and helpful
Negative reinforcement	A negative experience ceases after a behavior, thereby increasing its future likelihood	The alarm clock's annoying buzz stops when a sleepy student touches the snooze button
Punishment	A response from the environment decreases the future likelihood of behavior	A student who interrupts a teacher to ask a question finds the teacher's response hostile and unhelpful
Primary reinforcer	Reinforcement that meets an innate need	Food when hungry, beverage when thirsty
Secondary reinforcer	Reinforcement whose value is acquired rather than innate	Money, points, or tokens that are exchanged for goods or privileges that are inherently rewarding to the individual
Antecedent	An event or cue that precedes behavior and relates to its occurrence	A student is asked to perform work or is told that he or she is not allowed to complete a preferred activity
Consequence	An event that follows a behavior and relates functionally to its future occurrence	Laughter of other students each time the individual engages in silly or disruptive behavior
Contingency	A specific temporal relationship between a response and a consequence	Student always begins calling out and disrupting class after the teacher starts reviewing the homework assignment
Baseline	The level at which target behavior occurs naturally, before intervention	When assessing a student's behavior, the team determines that the student has an average of 12 discrete episodes of aggression each hour
Shaping	Reinforcing successive approximations of target behavior	Reinforcing a child for picking up a pencil and trying to mark on the paper; once the child makes marks on the paper, prompting and reinforcing the child for tracing a line; once the child is successful at tracing the line, prompting and reinforcing the child for tracing a letter outline
Task analysis	Breaking down a complex skill or task into its component behaviors, subskills, or subtasks. Each component is stated in order of occurrence and sets the occasion for the occurrence of the next behavior.	For students with difficulty organizing themselves, packing a book bag could be broken down into steps: check planner; for each assignment, put book or worksheet in pack; check off subject in planner; put lunch box in pack; put gym clothes in pack; zip pack closed

Behavioral principle	What is it?	Example
Behavioral chain	A sequence of related behaviors, each of which provides the cue for the next, and the last of which produces a reinforcer	In bed making, a chain consists of steps such as pulling up the sheet, smoothing it out, pulling up the blanket, smoothing out the blanket, and so forth
Chaining	The reinforcement of successive elements of a behavior chain	Teaching and reinforcing a child for going immediately to his or her desk on entering the classroom, then reinforcing the child for going to his or her desk and taking out books, then reinforcing the child for going to the desk, taking out books, putting books in desk and backpack in locker, and so forth
Schedules of reinforcement	The response requirements that determine when reinforcement will be delivered; they may depend on the number or time of responses, and they may be fixed/consistent or variable	Receiving one's paycheck every other Thursday; slot machine that pays off at seemingly unpredictable patterns
Extinction	When a behavior is no longer reinforced, it ceases	Child stops asking for help with difficult work after repeated requests for help are ignored
Discrimination	Any difference in responding in the presence of different stimuli	Ignoring the teacher when first told to line up and come in for recess, but complying when the teacher repeats directions in a loud, angry tone of voice
Stimulus generalization	A behavior that has been reinforced in the presence of a specific discriminative stimulus also occurs in the presence of other stimuli	A student who has been rewarded for taking turns in physical education takes turns using the instruments in music class without being prompted
Response generalization	The spread of effects to other classes of behavior when one class of behavior is modified by reinforcement, extinction, or other means	A student being taught a new way to shape letters changes the way a number is shaped in a way that is similar to the new shape of the letters
Maintenance	Continuing to deliver the conditions that generated learning a new behavior	Having a student stop by the counselor's office (where he or she learned a new self-control skill) each day on the way to class, even though the student uses the skill consistently
Social learning	Learning of new behaviors through observing other people model or engage in that behavior	Taunting and humiliating younger students after watching a movie in which prominent college students haze incoming freshmen
Noncontingent	Reinforcement that occurs regardless of what a person is doing rather than being dependent on a specific behavior	Calling on a student who is motivated by social attention and using the student's work as an example, regardless of how many items the student completed or whether he or she is sitting and behaving appropriately in class
Fidelity	Extent to which a behavior plan or related procedure adheres to stated plans	Low fidelity: Teacher reports that a behavior plan did not increase student target behavior of raising his hand; investigation shows that teacher did not consistently call on student even when he did raise his hand

tasks; classroom teachers naturally employ these methods when teaching academic skills, from reading to algebra.

Rewarding consecutive efforts is called *shaping,* in which children are successively reinforced for more complete and proper execution of tasks. The process of breaking a larger task into discrete teachable components is called *task analysis.* If you have ever received telephone-based computer support, the technician likely walked you through several steps in the process of troubleshooting. For a personal computer user, this might begin with "from the main menu or desktop, click 'start.' Now, select 'control panel' by clicking on it." Each of these small steps is a component of the larger task. You might already know how to complete some of these steps, but you requested technical support because you did not know how to tie them together to solve your problem.

A related notion is the *behavioral chain.* A chain is a set of task components that form a more complex behavior. In bed making, the chain consists of steps such as pulling up the sheet, smoothing it out, pulling up the blanket, smoothing out the blanket, and so on. In chaining, you might choose to teach each of the component steps in order, providing reinforcement when the child demonstrates performance of previously acquired steps *and* performs the new one. Here, each link not only has its own purpose, it also serves to reinforce the prior step and to initiate the next one. In this way, the child reaches a level of independent performance in making the bed, expecting external reinforcement only for the last step in the chain.

Things do not always operate smoothly in child rearing. What happens when the child refuses to make the bed, or promises to do so, but watches television instead? Because there is little doubt that watching television is an inherently reinforcing activity, the parents insist that television watching be discontinued until the bed is made. This is an example of time-out, a frequently used consequence for problem behaviors. Time out is actually a shortening of the term *time out from reinforcement.* Although it is generally implemented as a punishment, time-out is based on the assumption that the problem behavior is reinforced by environmental consequences. Removal from the environment also removes the child from those reinforcing consequences. In this case, the child is receiving time out from reinforcement (i.e., television) until the bed is made, at which point television access is renewed.

Time-out has come to mean different things to different people. In families, it might take the form of a child being sent to his or her room or having to sit on the steps for several minutes. For teachers, it may involve ignoring disruptive behavior that is reinforced by attention, or temporarily removing valued materials if a student's behavior declines in their presence. It follows logically that the occurrence of behavior will diminish if reinforcing consequences are withheld. Unfortunately, time-out can be misused, especially when it involves excluding the child from the classroom. Exclusionary time-out entails removing an individual to a separate area or room as a consequence of undesirable behavior.

We tend to be cautious about the use of time-out in this way. Although it may be necessary in extreme cases to maintain safety, exclusionary time out may become a means of escape for the student with problem behavior. Removing a student who has just exhibited a problem behavior from the classroom may be perceived as a pleasant consequence by that student—demands are gone! Because the student experiences removal as negative reinforcement, exclusion inadvertently reinforces the problem behavior and has potential to aggravate it. For example, a student who disrupts math class and is sent to the office may learn that this is an effective way to avoid difficult math problems. Not only might exclusionary time-out fail to reduce problem behavior, it does not teach alternative responses and may even degrade the classroom environment.

There is another way to view the connection between bed making and television watching in the anecdote above. The child's parents could choose to link bed making, a behavior that occurs rarely, with one that occurs quite frequently: turning on the television ("You may turn on the television only after you've made your bed"). In this way, a contingency is established between a low-frequency behavior and a high-frequency behavior. This tends to increase the occurrence of the low-frequency behavior and is known as the *Premack principle,* or *Grandma's rule.* Grandma earns mention here because she presumably originated the contingency between eating your vegetables (low-frequency behavior) and having dessert (high-frequency behavior). The high-frequency behavior is often pleasurable (which is why it is so common), but it does not have to be. Grandma's rule is not foolproof: you might not be willing to endure Brussels sprouts to earn a measly ice cream cone! You might be too full to consider it, you might not like the flavor she has in the freezer, or you might just stubbornly refuse to consider the deal. An individual's likes and dislikes, current state, and motivation all combine to determine the effectiveness of this strategy.

Finally, what happens when the child has effectively mastered the skill of bed making? Many parents will simply expect their children to make their beds daily once they know how; they provide praise only while the skill is in development. Must parents provide continuing reinforcement for their children to continue to make their beds? Many behaviors, once achieved, certainly become enduring elements of children's routines. How is it that children do, in fact, continue to make their beds, even when they sleep away from home? The answers lie partly within operant conditioning and partly outside of it. Behavior theory and practice include a few additional concepts that help us understand how behavior is sustained over time. Among these are schedules of reinforcement, principles of maintenance and generalization, contextual or antecedent factors, and the transfer of control from extrinsic to intrinsic rewards. Perhaps outside the reach of behavior theory are explanations for behavior that rest more on our understanding of cognition, social influences, and motivation, to which we will return later.

Schedules of Reinforcement

Skinner's work includes careful analysis of how reinforcement affects the future likelihood of behavior. He examined different ways to deliver reinforcement and referred to them as schedules of reinforcement. A parent might deliver reinforcement every single time the target behavior appears (e.g., providing a reward every day the child makes his or her bed). This is called *continuous reinforcement.* Once the behavior has been mastered, reinforcing every single occurrence is burdensome, so the parent might choose to reinforce the behavior on a schedule of *partial reinforcement*, in which only some instances of the target behavior are reinforced.

Which is more effective in producing the target response: continuous or partial reinforcement? Continuous reinforcement produces the most rapid initial learning; with reinforcement, the child gets the message that the behavior has been executed correctly and that its regular appearance is valued. Partial reinforcement, however, produces higher and more consistent responses over time. Although this may seem counterintuitive, consider the slot machine, which pays on a variable ratio of reinforcement. *Variable ratio* refers to the fact that payoffs are unpredictable, seemingly random events. Management teams at casinos program slot machines to pay off at unpredictable intervals. The high level and consistency of gambling behavior relates directly to the fact that players do not know when the payoff is coming. If they did, casinos would no longer be in business. High rates of response are based on behavioral principles, whether the gambler realizes it or not. (People who operate the casinos certainly know this!)

In the long run, the most effective reinforcement is partial, not continuous, and it is delivered on an unpredictable schedule. A child will make his or her bed more often and more consistently if he or she does not know when the next reinforcement for doing so will come. This is convenient, given how challenging it can be to monitor behavior and deliver reinforcement with the perfect consistency that continuous reinforcement demands. Also, humans are prone to *habituation*; we easily become accustomed and somewhat immune to the effects of regularly encountered reinforcers and punishments. Because students habituate to contingencies, praise or scolding that initially increased or decreased behavior may lose effectiveness. Continuous reinforcement is less effective in the long run, is difficult to deliver, and leads more quickly to habituation or satiation. Use of partial reinforcement, capitalizing on natural reinforcement, and rallying other forms of motivation can enhance the effectiveness of planned change.

In the absence of reinforcement, will the behavior disappear? The answer is a qualified *yes.* In behavioral terms, *extinction* involves withholding reinforcement to decrease the likelihood that a behavior will occur. It is most often used to reduce undesirable behaviors, especially those that are inadvertently reinforced by environmental events. Recall the student Sam from Chapter 1; we can imagine that his classmates might laugh in response to off-task behaviors. Sam may well experience this attention as pleasant, even though he is being reprimanded by the teacher.

Although the best way to stop Sam's behavior might be to convince his peers to ignore his off-task behavior, we are skeptical that this can be achieved in many settings. If the classmates do ignore his behavior, we would expect it to stop. One caution with this approach is that because the student has learned to gain attention through off-task behavior, he may try several similar behaviors when he does not get the response he seeks. So, if Sam feels ignored when he usually gets attention, he may become louder, get out of his seat, bother another student, or otherwise escalate. This is called an *extinction burst,* in which the student tries a little harder to get the reaction that he received earlier. If the teacher and other students ignore the escalating behavior, we would expect the problem to diminish or stop. If they do not ignore Sam, he learns that increasing levels of behavior will be reinforced. This is a dangerous lesson for Sam, for the teacher, and for the rest of the class. Note that the process and effects of reinforcing an escalation of problem behavior may be outside the awareness of students and teachers alike. It is a mistake to assume that Sam is intentionally testing the limits, just as it is a mistake to assume that the teacher wants to reinforce problems of higher intensity.

Although permanent extinction is possible, the behavior in question may remain in the student's repertoire and spontaneously reappear. On returning from a week-long vacation, Sam's previously extinguished behavior may reappear, an example of *spontaneous recovery.* This is most likely to occur in circumstances that resemble the original learning situation. The behavior reappears because the individual has forgotten that the behavior was extinguished. In Sam's case, he returns from a hiatus to nearly identical circumstances and resorts to behavior that worked previously. Individual factors such as motivation, temperament, and cognition also influence the extent to which behaviors remain in an individual's repertoire (we discuss these later).

Maintenance and Generalization

Learning and positive behavior change are meaningful only to the extent that their benefits continue, spreading across areas of the student's life. *Maintenance* refers to the continuation of a desired response over time, within the original setting, and after completion of instruction or intervention. *Generalization* refers to continuing effects of behavior change across people and places without the necessity of intervention. The spread of change is purposefully obtained such that the learned behavior is evident even within circumstances in which no training occurred. Generalization includes the transfer of change (new skills, for example) into situations beyond the intervention setting and also refers to alterations in the replacement behavior itself. Generalization can occur spontaneously or as part of a planned intervention. Because a central concern of PBS is the ability to achieve lasting change with the aim of improving quality of life, maintenance and generalization are important considerations, even if they are not always easy to program or realize. These concepts are discussed again in this chapter and in further detail in Chapters 7 and 8.

Environmental Factors in Learning

Beyond the Antecedent–Behavior–Consequence Chain

Environmental or stimulus factors include various aspects of the environment that influence behavior. An *antecedent* is a specific environmental condition that precedes behavior. What occurs just before the target behavior to influence its appearance? A straightforward view of behavioral contingencies follows the A-B-C sequence. For a child who is learning to make his bed each morning, the sight of an unmade bed might be an antecedent. Related to this antecedent might be his parent's request (prompt) to make his bed. This is followed by bed making (behavior) and, in turn, by parental praise (consequence).

Stimulus Cues

Environmental events that set the stage for the appearance of the target behavior are *cues,* or *stimuli;* if the behavior only occurs when these cues are present, the behavior is said to be under *stimulus control.* In other words, the sight of the unmade bed becomes a *discriminative stimulus* for bed making. A common example of stimulus control is eating popcorn at the movie theater. You may rarely eat buttered popcorn while you watch movies at home, but the sights, smells, and sounds of popcorn at the movie theater may entice you into buying a bucket. Buying and eating popcorn are voluntary behaviors that can become habit. As a parent, you might hope that seeing the unmade bed will come to serve as a discriminative stimulus for your child's bed making, because you do not want to have to remind (*prompt*) your child every day ("remember to make your bed now"). In fact, you would probably prefer to gradually stop providing that prompt, a strategy known as *fading.*

Optimal instruction involves the smallest amount of prompting necessary and fades it as quickly as possible, to make sure that the student does not become *prompt dependent,* in which case the child does not demonstrate the behavior without a specific reminder or cue. Effective prompts can appear in a variety of forms, including verbal (reminders, requests, commands, hints), visual or gestural (point, nod, turn light on/off, sticky notes, Picture Exchange Communication symbols), tactile (light touch, vibrating), symbolic/pictoral (necklace signifying "your turn," photos of traffic signals for stop, go, and slow down), and auditory (music, sound of bell/tone).

Because environmental cues affect the extent, consistency, and execution of learned behavior, effective instruction considers their influence. In some cases, stimulus control might be quite desirable; for example, students learn that on entering their classroom, they should proceed to their cubbies, hang up their coats, take homework out of their backpacks, and head to their desks for quiet reading until the bell rings. The morning bell is a discriminative stimulus for standing and reciting the Pledge of Allegiance. The most effective learners have a knack for responding to similar cues in customary ways, so some students readily figure out which circumstances are appropriate for a particular routine or problem-solving approach. This is a form of *stimulus discrimination*: the learner differentiates the circumstances in which a particular response is indicated (and likely to meet with reward) from those in which it is not.

Stimulus Generalization

Discrimination is key to learning and happens quite spontaneously in children. The game Simon Says involves distinguishing when to imitate a behavior and when to refrain from imitation. Learning across academic subjects involves discrimination, whether it involves sight words, arithmetic symbols, or multiple-choice tests. Learning also involves *stimulus generalization*; for example, a new reader intuitively recognizes the word *dog* when it is printed in different fonts. The student might discriminate the two fonts but recognizes the fundamental components of the letters comprising the word, ignoring irrelevant differences.

As mentioned earlier, a student might also learn to discriminate circumstances in which punishment is likely to follow problem behavior and when it is not. An aggressive student figures out very quickly which peers will stand up to bullying and which will not. One might view the nonvictim as either simply refusing to reinforce bullying or actually punishing it, but the victim is in the unfortunate situation of unwittingly (and unwillingly) reinforcing the bully. Discrimination enables bullies to determine when they are unlikely to be caught and punished. They learn quickly to refrain from aggression when adults or socially powerful peers are present.

Effective teaching avoids overreliance on specific cues or stimuli; it is flexible and diversified. Teachers use routines to prepare the learning environment, but they rarely intend to present material in an absolutely rigid fashion, even when they adhere to a planned curriculum. Teachers commonly employ strategies such as multiple examples and different modes of presentation (e.g., oral, visual, tactile) to enhance the likelihood that students will learn and use skills in different settings and with new tasks. Such use, when appropriate, is likely to meet with natural reinforcement because it increases students' chances of being successful.

Because some students with disabilities may discriminate less effectively, varying instruction is crucial. A student with autism may respond to idiosyncratic features during a task, such as recognizing and addressing the teacher by name only when the teacher is wearing eyeglasses. In this case, instruction should include *multiple exemplars* of the concept "Ms. Jones":

with and without glasses, then in clothing of different styles and colors, standing and sitting, and involved in different activities. In this way, the child learns to extract the underlying constant "Ms. Jones, my teacher" from the multiple exemplars that represent her.

Stokes and Baer (1977) discuss the generalization of learning as fundamental; if learning is associated with a particular classroom and is not evident across people, places, behaviors, and times, its functional utility is quite limited. Fortunately, there are teaching approaches to promote generalization, such as *training loosely* (Stokes & Baer, 1977), a strategy in which multiple and diverse approaches are used. In this way, students can be taught to recognize and identify the most salient or relevant aspects of an academic problem or social situation and then apply a set of steps, rules, or procedures for handling it. Effective classrooms have just the right balance of routine (which encourages stimulus discrimination) and diversity (which encourages stimulus generalization).

Stimulus and Response Generalization

There are two different forms of generalization: stimulus generalization and response generalization. Stimulus generalization occurs when the desired response occurs outside the learning environment or in the absence of cues present during learning. Response generalization occurs when the target behavior arises outside the learning situation (e.g., the skill seems to spread). Less important than the distinctions between these two forms of generalization is the importance of diverse instruction and varied application of new skills. Stokes and Baer asserted in 1977 that a "train-and-hope" approach to generalization was commonplace. In such an approach, extensive efforts are invested in changing behavior; however, once change occurs, generalization is not actively pursued. Stokes and Baer further argued that train and hope was not sufficient to induce or sustain meaningful change. Unfortunately, train and hope is alive today. In PBS, the importance of generalization remains an area of emphasis; we discuss its benefits and challenges in the later chapters of this book.

Contextual Variables

In *Positive Strategies,* environmental stimuli or *contextual variables* represent the collective influence of the environment and, specifically, *setting events* and *triggers* that are associated with behavior. (Setting events and antecedents, also called slow and fast triggers, are also discussed in Chapters 1, 5, and 6, so we will refer to them only briefly here.) Contextual variables include a range of factors that may serve as precursors to problem behavior. As defined by Lohrmann-O'Rourke, Knoster, and Llewellyn (1999), "The term fast trigger refers to antecedents, or those events with a discrete onset and end point that are present immediately before occurrences of behavior" (p. 37). Lohrmann-O'Rourke and colleagues (1999) describe setting events or slow triggers as those occurring before or during the target response and causing an individual to behave atypically to a fairly typical set of circumstances. In *Positive Strategies,* we also consider setting events to include the transitory effects of perhaps more long-standing personal characteristics or situations. For example, students with disabilities are more likely than their peers to have health-related difficulties that influence sleep, mood, general well-being, or affect (emotion).

Setting events (slow triggers) are relatively enduring characteristics of the individual and the environment that exert an influence (sometimes indirect) on the appearance of behavior. Antecedents (fast triggers) are more immediate influences on behavior. One might liken the setting event to getting up on the wrong side of the bed. Imagine that another driver cuts you off during your morning commute to work. This might serve as the antecedent to an episode in which you unleash a torrent of ill wishes toward the other driver. On another day, you might be able to continue on your way unperturbed. But on this day, the setting event (bad mood) affects behavior by manipulating your threshold for tolerating frustration; antecedents are the immediate circumstances that set off your angry behavior. Slow and fast triggers interact with individual factors, other contextual influences, and behavioral contingencies to influence behavior.

From Extrinsic to Intrinsic Rewards

One criticism of operant conditioning in education is that students who are reinforced for their academic performance or behavior come to rely on reinforcement to sustain performance. Such use of reinforcement is referred to as an extrinsic reward, because the reinforcer is external to the individual. Extrinsic rewards are a legitimate concern if students remain dependent on them. This dependence might also suggest that behavioral objectives were only partially completed; a central goal of instruction should involve bringing behavior under the control of naturally occurring or intrinsic reinforcers. Stokes and Baer (1977) stressed the importance of teaching behaviors that *recruit natural reinforcement*; in other words, behaviors should be taught that are likely to be well received outside the intervention setting, thus being reinforced without being programmed.

Consider the example of teaching a child appropriate social skills for interacting with adults. The young child's parents are likely to provide very specific directions such as, "Say hello to Mr. Smith" and "Say thank you to Grandma." As the child gets older, the parent might use the general prompt, "Remember your manners" when the child is expected to draw on previous learning to formulate responses. Later, we would expect the child to interact with adults outside the parents' presence and to behave politely in these encounters. We would not expect that each adult would say "Oh, what a polite young person you are! Thank you." Although that might occur occasionally, it is probably not powerful enough to sustain the behavior. It is also preferable for the child to feel rewarded by the engagement, acceptance, and respect that increasingly mature interactions afford. The intrinsic rewards of social encounters assume the function that extrinsic rewards originally fulfilled.

In our lives, we engage in many activities that are reinforced both extrinsically and intrinsically. For example, we work to receive a paycheck, and we use that money to pay the rent or mortgage, purchase food and clothing, and put gas in the car. In this case, we use money, a *secondary reinforcer* because its value is learned, to purchase items that meet basic concerns (*primary reinforcers*). Many of us are also lucky enough to earn intrinsic rewards at our jobs, whether they involve helping others, watching children learn, bringing efficiency to an organization, or creating works of art. Earners also spend money on intrinsically valued items: we might use some of our money to buy books, go to museums, donate to charity, or save for the future. These are all examples of activities in which the reward relates to a sense of personal fulfillment or accomplishment. Note that many rewards seem influenced by personal experiences, beliefs, and values; contemporary behavior theory embraces the idea that experience and individual differences contribute to determine how much or what type of reinforcers an individual responds to.

Reciprocal Influences on Behavior

In the discussion of behavioral interventions, there is sometimes a sense that adults act and children respond. But children are not little automatons who respond to planned contingencies and fail to shape the behavior of others. As we examine problem behaviors in context, we see quickly that this is rarely, if ever, the case. Consider the example of a child in a grocery store with his mother; it is late afternoon and mother and child are both harried. Near the bakery, the child says, "I want a cookie." Mother responds, "No, it's too close to dinner time." The child moves to a louder and more insistent voice, and the mother repeats herself. The child escalates to a demanding tone, begins to cry loudly, and his mother says, "All right, just this once." She hands the child a cookie and he immediately calms down.

How do we understand this from the perspective of reinforcement? The child has obviously received positive reinforcement for the behavioral sequence of requesting, insisting, and crying. What about his mother? She is trying to get home with the makings of dinner, and she is a bit embarrassed by her son's loud voice and crying, feeling that people are looking at her and judging. The mother is also reinforced in this interaction when her son quiets down. Something negative ceases when she gives him a cookie, so she is negatively reinforced for her behavior. What will happen the next time she is in the store? The laws of behavior say that her son is likely to repeat his pattern of escalation in the future and that she is likely to give in. If she does not give in, she can expect her son to try harder: an extinction burst.

One can easily see the mutual influences in their behavior. We talk about the back-and-forth nature of behavioral influence as *reciprocity.* In the real world of human interactions, we regularly influence each other in long series of making requests, getting responses, receiving requests, and responding ourselves. Often, when these long chains of behavior are mutually pleasant (reinforcing), we think of these as good times, friendships, or loving relationships. Perhaps less often, we find ourselves in relationships that are mutually negative, in which both parties use unpleasant tactics to affect the other.

Gerald Patterson, a psychologist who studies the interactions of disaffected teenagers and their parents, describes a cycle of coercion in which each party escalates its negative behavior in an effort to control the other (Patterson, DeBaryshe, & Ramsey, 1989). Patterson and colleagues assert that problem behavior emerges from the interaction of a child's temperament and deficient parental management. Examples of poor parental management include insufficient monitoring, low involvement in key aspects of the child's life, and harsh or inconsistent punishment.

For a teen with inadequate supervision, limited perseverance, and few positive role models, adolescence brings great temptation. Strong social forces pull the teenager toward deviant behavior, and parents either respond inadequately (ignoring or failing to engage) or harshly (punitive yet short-lived responses that exacerbate the existing conflict). The teenager might affiliate with marginal or deviant peers and respond to those social models. Although more positive role models may be available, the teen no longer identifies with them (remember that social learning is most likely when the model is similar or valued). Despite this destructive cycle, Patterson and colleagues would not have us believe that all is lost. Their work involves a multifaceted approach that helps adults and teens, both separately and together. Parents learn to better monitor, communicate with, and discipline their teens. Teens are supported in learning new social behaviors that are likely to meet with natural reinforcement instead of the rejection they formerly elicited from well-adjusted peers.

We know that behavior is reciprocal, and when it is considered this way, its complexity is both apparent and daunting. Positive interventions such as Patterson's demonstrate that once change is mobilized, it can gather momentum that becomes self-reinforcing. When parents alter their communications with their teenagers, teens are likely to respond more positively, starting a more positive cycle. Maintaining that change can be quite challenging. Parents who face an extinction burst from their teenager have to resist falling into former, negative patterns of communication. The other people in the lives of students—teachers, peers, classroom aides—also comprise important contextual factors to consider in supporting them.

Individual Differences

As you read our examples of escalating students, gambling, the difficult teenager, and mother–child pairs at the grocery store, you might find yourself thinking, "Can all of this really be explained by reinforcement and punishment?" In the case of the mother in the grocery store, might some parents give in much more quickly, and some not at all? Does every child who reaches the teenage years in a household run by overly lax or harsh parents meet the same fate? A strict application of operant conditioning principles seems to imply that our actions are predicated solely on stimuli and responses, input and output. Further, if the laws of behaviorism were true, it would follow that our behavior would have infinite flexibility.

Of course, it does not. Siblings raised under the same roof can behave very differently. Without rehashing the decades-long nature versus nurture debate, we suggest that some variations in behavior emerge from innate sources—from within each individual. *Individual differences* is a term used to describe a range of variations in human behavior—how each of us might approach a situation uniquely, as opposed to characteristics we have in common. The laws of behaviorism apply to all of us; *that* we have in common. But each person has a unique response to them, which may be based on fundamentals such as temperament, personality, problem-solving skills, intelligence, threshold for pain, sensory processing, and a myriad of other characteristics.

The field of behavioral genetics tells us that some individuals are essentially hardwired toward certain proclivities or traits. You might consider yourself to be a risk taker or risk aversive; mellow or high-strung; an early bird or a night owl; an auditory or a visual learner; intolerant of frustration or highly perseverant; compulsively organized or enjoying chaos; quick on your feet or very slow; short-fused or slow to anger. There are many more examples of polarities in human behavior. Although you might not find yourself at all the extremes, there are certain traits you probably recognize in yourself. We are more or less born with some of these traits, yet they are shaped and molded during our lives. Exactly what human traits qualify as innate, and how much they are shaped by genetics or environment, is a continuing controversy, yet there is sufficient evidence to conclude that human tendencies are somewhat inherited. Besides clear medical and developmental factors, there are temperamental, intellectual, or personality traits that mediate learning and behavior.

For the purposes of this book, we suggest that individual differences emerge from relatively intrinsic and immutable factors such as genetics, medical and developmental factors, and temperament. Those differences are shaped by experience, but they present themselves to educators in such a way that their origins are invisible (and quite possibly irrelevant). Just as some students have a knack for math and others for science, children differ in the amount of modeling and repetition they require to learn, retain information, and apply new skills outside the classroom. They also differ in what motivates them, in their pace of learning, their perseverance, social skills, response to feedback, and so on.

Table 2 includes just a few of the organizing schemes developed by researchers to explain patterns of variation in human responses. Psychologist Howard Gardner (1993) proposes seven human intelligences. Thomas and Chess (1977) assert that temperament includes nine dimensions, and they further describe optimal parenting practices to meet the concerns of young children based on their profiles. Among adult personality theorists is Raymond Cattell (1965), who proposed 16 underlying personality factors that determine how individuals respond to the challenges of adulthood. Certainly, by adulthood, enormous environmental influences have shaped us, but our constitutional makeup remains constant. Numerous researchers have devoted careers to defining and categorizing individual differences. There is no best way to conceive of these; each method of conceptualizing them has advantages and disadvantages. We accept that some combination of genetics, medical and developmental influences, and experience shapes student behavior. Students arrive in a classroom as is. In *Positive Strategies,* we aim to describe the influences of individual differences on behavior, understand how well the classroom capitalizes on or thwarts those innate features (student–environment fit), and rally each student's unique strengths in support of positive change.

Contemporary behavior theory, then, does not ignore individual differences. Such differences are acknowledged as an essential component of understanding human behavior. In *Positive Strategies,* we discuss individual differences that influence behavior in terms of setting events and skill areas. We readily acknowledge that temperamental and sensory factors influence both the development of problem behaviors and the exercise of coping skills. Some setting events arise (at least in part) from innate factors. For example, an individual with Down syn-

Table 2. Examples of how individual differences are defined

Howard Gardner: Multiple intelligences (1993) Linguistic, logical-mathematical, spatial, bodily-kinesthetic, musical, interpersonal, intrapersonal
Thomas and Chess: Dimensions of temperament (1977) Sensitivity, activity, intensity, rhythmicity, adaptability, mood, approach/withdrawal, persistence, attention span
Raymond Cattell: Personality factors (1965) Warmth, reasoning, emotional stability, dominance, liveliness, rule-consciousness, social boldness, sensitivity, vigilance, capacity for abstract thought, need for privacy, apprehension, openness to change, self-reliance, perfectionism, tension

drome (a chromosomal anomaly) may have skin disorders that are responsive to stress, diet, and weather conditions. Symptom severity may be determined by a combination of those factors, and how the individual (and family) responds to those symptoms influences their outcome as well. The skin disorder, diet, and weather could all be considered setting events. The student arrives at school irritable after a poor night's sleep; the antecedent is the event that sets off an outburst, episode of tearfulness, or other atypical response to routines. In the chapters that follow, we discuss setting events more fully, placing them into four categories: physical; learning and self-regulation; social-emotional; and environment and routines.

Although setting events and antecedents are contextual or environmental elements of behavior, individual differences also play a role in determining student behavior. We frame the skill areas that are crucial to classroom success into four areas: functional communication, self-regulation, social skills, and academic skills. These are not exhaustive or mutually exclusive, but we believe that they are valid and pragmatic.

DESCRIBING AND MEASURING BEHAVIOR

Operational Definitions

The world of behavior theory is filled with terms to articulate learning and associational processes under study. It also has a vocabulary that helps describe behavior and behavior change efforts. Behavior plans, for example, involve pinpointing the amount, type, nature, frequency, severity, and duration of a behavior. Problems in school often arise from behavioral excesses ("too much") or behavioral impairments (not enough). Ameliorating problems often means addressing both. We suggest (colloquially) that these terms are necessary for determining a starting point and strategy toward positive outcomes. In planning a shared trip, you need to agree with your traveling companions (your colleagues) about starting place, route, and planned destination.

Similarly, there are two main reasons that we emphasize careful specification of behavior: it serves as a basis for shared communication and as a baseline for examining behavior. The first reason concerns communication and having a common vernacular. Elsewhere, we discuss the reality that several observers of the same situation may interpret and report it differently. One staff member may view a student's problem behavior as driving him or her crazy, another may describe it as unbearable, and a third might see it as not that bad compared with that of another student. We all behave differently within and across the various contexts of our lives, and students are no different. The differences in teacher reports of behavior may reflect differing perceptions or interpretations, but it may also reflect real differences in behavior across contexts. Whether they are focused on supporting mastery of academic skills or student self-appraisal of written work, teachers need to know a child's skill level. Student support teams need to come to consensus regarding skill mastery and the extent and impact of problem behavior. Once consensus is achieved, the team is in a position to formulate plans, goals, and objectives—the road map for the journey to come.

Rather than describing behavior in global terms ("He's never on task"; "She interrupts constantly"; "This is a huge problem because he disrupts the entire class"; "She has these incredible outbursts"), behavioral descriptions articulate the behavior in observable and measurable terms. These shared descriptions, called *operational definitions,* provide a basis for understanding the contextual influences and contingencies relating to a behavior and offer a starting point for instruction or intervention.

One would hardly begin to teach reading without knowing whether a student could recognize all the letters of the alphabet. Before beginning, it might be necessary to conduct an assessment to clarify students' current skill levels. Similarly, you would start planning your road trip only after identifying your current location on a map. You and your companions might alter your planned route or take detours along the way to your destination, but an agreed-on starting point is essential. When a target behavior is operationalized, it moves from being general, vague, and perhaps judgmental to a more objective, specific description. Although *off task* may describe a nearly exhaustive number of student behaviors, *on task* is easier to operationalize; the key in crafting operational definitions is focusing on the observable—the things students *do,* rather than what they think, want, or understand. In Chapter 6, we discuss how teams work together to operationalize target behaviors, and we provide several more examples. We also review several different methods for and approaches to measuring and quantifying behavior (collecting data).

This brings us to the second reason that behavioral descriptions are so important: they serve as benchmarks against which future change is measured. The term *baseline* refers to the level of behavior before intervention. It includes quantification of the frequency, intensity, and/or duration of a behavior that has been operationally defined. For example, "He is out of his seat for 10 minutes of every 35-minute lesson"; "During math class, she interrupted the teacher 12 times in 30 minutes"; or "Last week, her outbursts and interruptions resulted in a loss of 45 minutes of instructional time." The utility of the operational definition is its ability to specify exactly what constitutes an outburst and to count only those episodes that meet the definition. Instruction and intervention necessitate knowing how frequent the target behavior is and establishing a direction in which to head (increasing ability to request assistance, decreasing outbursts). This direction—which may be an informal plan, a behavior intervention plan, or an individualized education program—facilitates consistency, uniformity, and accountability. If things do not go as planned, the team returns to the starting point and reviews its definitions, baseline, and interventions. At this point, you may recognize the underlying theme of the communicative and measurement functions of the operational definition: precision.

Measuring and Assessing Change

It follows logically that ongoing assessment of behavior is necessary to understand how it changes. In fact, assessment and intervention are inextricably linked in our *Positive Strategies* approach. Once a baseline is established (for either desirable or undesirable behaviors), behavior interventionists track the occurrence of the target behavior to monitor it. There are many methods of doing this (which we will discuss in Chapter 6), but for now, it is important to understand that teachers may find themselves making hash marks to indicate occurrences of the behavior within specified time frames or filling out A-B-C forms to determine antecedents to behavior. Occurrence data are often graphed to display the frequency in a unit of time (e.g., three times per day, six times per hour). Graphs are an easy way to inspect and interpret data to assess change.

Single-Case Designs

Simple line graphs are commonly used in *single-case designs.* In a single-case (or single-subject) design, an interventionist measures the baseline rate of a target behavior for an individual student. This baseline phase, often denoted as Phase A, is followed by an intervention of some kind, denoted as Phase B. A student, Carina, is making careless errors on math assignments, and her teacher decides that Carina would benefit from a program to encourage self-correction of math problems. The teacher observes the percentage of correct answers on math worksheets for a week and finds that at baseline, Carina received scores of 83%, 88%, 85%, 88%, and 80% correct on math worksheets completed Monday through Friday, respectively. The teacher knows that Carina enjoys in-class free time, so she offers her extra free time for scoring above 90%, encouraging her to identify and correct any mistakes she discovers. During the week in which this plan is in place, accuracy goes up to 94%, 100%, 90%, 88%, and 96%. Is her improvement attributable to teacher intervention? Maybe something else changed—perhaps Carina's parents saw her grades and admonished her to be more careful if she was to maintain her privileges at home.

To determine whether the intervention (free time as reinforcer) is responsible for the change, the teacher returns to the baseline, Condition A (no reinforcement). Because the teacher has turned off the intervention and the student has not practiced self-correction long enough to make it a habit, accuracy is likely to return to baseline levels. This is now referred to as an

A-B-A design. The teacher could be more certain about the effects of her intervention if she adds one more phase, such that her intervention becomes an A-B-A-B; the graphic presentation of this design appears in Figure 4. This is called a *reversal design* because each step reverses the one preceding it. The teacher makes a series of baseline observations (A), introduces an intervention (B), removes the intervention to return to baseline conditions (A), and, finally, repeats the intervention (B). Figure 4 shows how these four phases of intervention might appear once the raw data have been transferred to a graph. Math scores are plotted for each day of the week. The lines with triangle markers connect the baseline phases, and the lines with square markers connect the intervention phases.

With the exception of one high score (93) during the second baseline condition, the graph suggests that the teacher's reinforcement has resulted in a higher percentage correct. On inspection of the graph, the teacher recalls the third Wednesday on the chart: forgetting it was not available to her, Carina came to her requesting extra free time. The teacher interpreted this as additional support for the intervention—the student was requesting reinforcement! The teacher was relieved to have an explanation for what otherwise seemed inconsistent and was happy to have informal confirmation that her plan might be working. Still, it is clear from inspection that the intervention phases produced better performance.

On the other hand, if the intervention (B) phases did not produce superior performance, the teacher might consider a few explanations. Did she, in fact, deliver the reinforcer on the days that the student self-corrected? This refers to the *fidelity of intervention* (was it delivered according to plan?); if reinforcement was not reliably delivered, we cannot reasonably assess its effects. Did the free time offer adequate motivation for the student to engage in extra effort? In other words, was it sufficiently reinforcing?

Suppose the teacher assumed that Carina could check her own work, discover mistakes, and self-correct, but Carina really did not have the self-monitoring skills to do this. In such a case, Phases A and B would probably resemble each other. The intervention could not be successful because the student would lack the skills needed to receive reinforcement. Analyzing data can be fairly straightforward in some cases; in other cases, the contrast between baseline and intervention might not be so clear. A great deal of variability may indicate that other un-

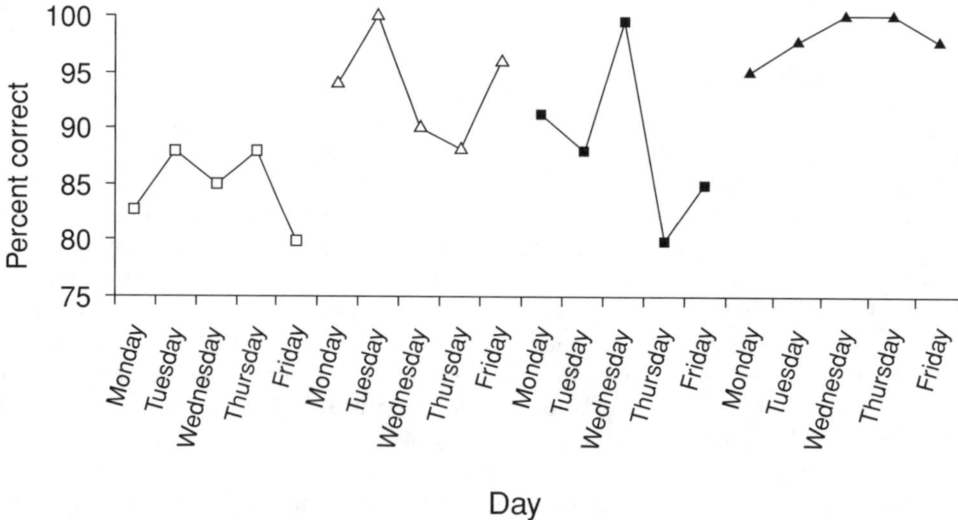

Figure 4. Reversal design (A-B-A-B). (*Key:* □ = baseline 1; △ = reinforcement 1; ■ = baseline 2; ▲ = reinforcement 2.)

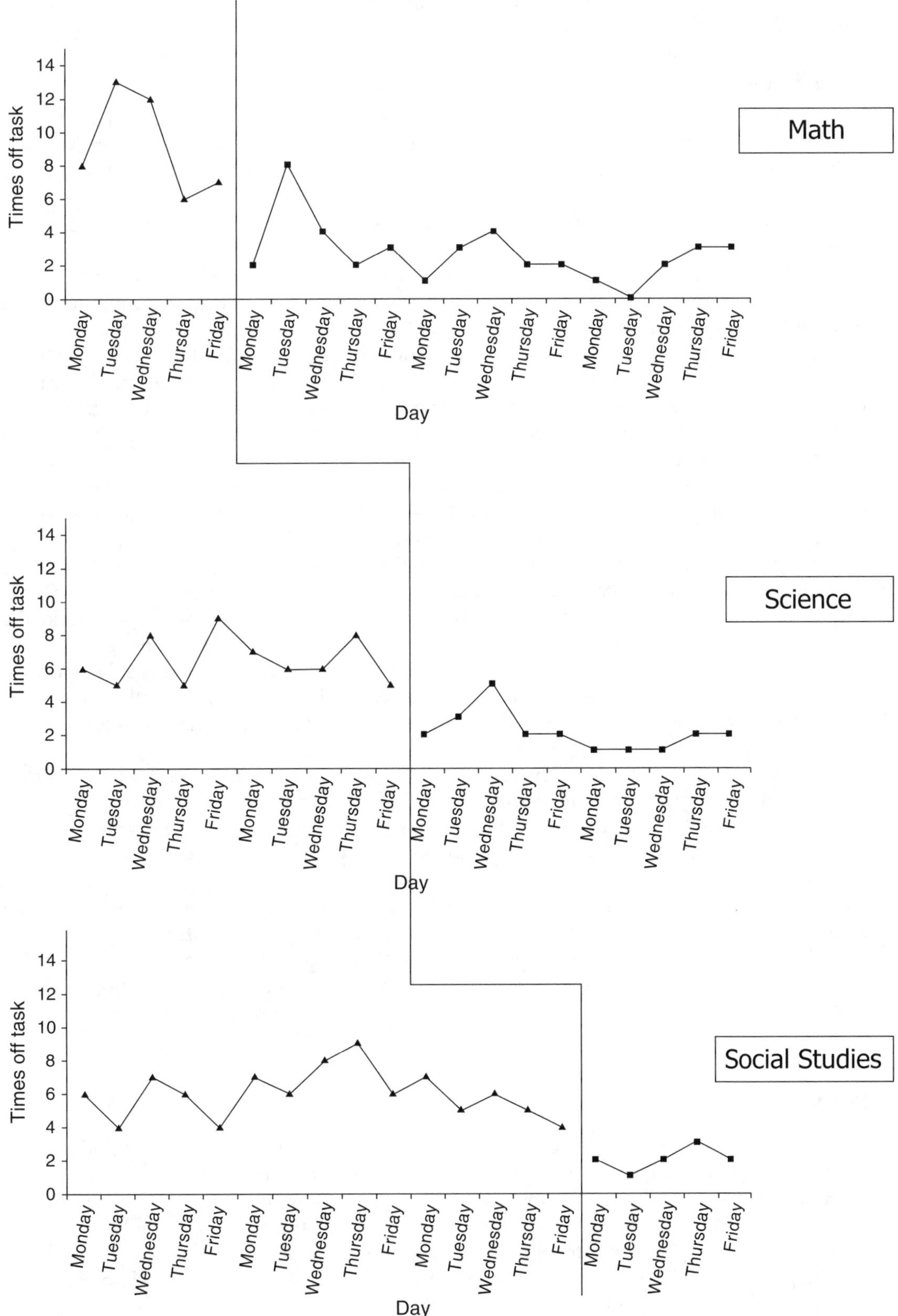

Figure 5. Multiple-baseline across-settings design. (*Key:* ▲ = baseline; ■ = reinforcement.)

monitored or uncontrolled factors are influencing a student's behavior. More assessment may be warranted.

Other Examples

Single-case designs allow for baseline and intervention to be compared within a single subject. The A-B-A-B design is one example. Other examples are multiple-baseline across-settings, multiple-baseline across-behaviors, and multiple-baseline across-subjects designs. We will illustrate the first of these designs.

The multiple-baseline across-settings design permits a team to assess the effects of a single intervention implemented in two or more settings. Perhaps a team wants to decrease a student's off-task behavior in more than one class. They might construct an intervention and then implement it sequentially across three different settings—introducing it first in math, then in science, and, finally, in social studies. Figure 5 displays the results of a multiple-baseline across-settings design for such an intervention. The instructional team has decided to offer this student (Anthony) programmed noncontingent breaks because they believe he does not have the perseverance to stay on task for an entire class period. They want to be certain that the intervention will work for Anthony, so they decide to test it first in math, the subject area in which he has the most frequent occurrence of off-task behavior.

The figure contains labels for each of the three classes. The team took baseline data for a week in all settings (math, science, social studies). The lines with triangle markers connect the baseline phases, and the lines with square markers connect the intervention phases. They begin the first phase of intervention in math class and implement it for a week, continuing to take baseline data in the other two classes. Intervention is added to science class in the third week and to social studies in the fourth week. The solid line that descends the graphs marks the time at which the baseline ends and intervention begins in each setting. One can see from the graph that Anthony was off task 8, 13, 12, 6, and 7 times in math class during the baseline period. With the exception of 1 day, the programmed breaks reduced his off-task behavior during the first week of intervention quite successfully. Similar findings are apparent for science and social studies classes.

Besides illustrating the effectiveness of a pilot intervention, this graph also displays other trends that might warrant the team's further examination. First, Anthony is off task on Wednesday more than any other day. Second, his improvement was perhaps most consistent in science. Why might that be? There might not be an easy explanation, but there may be some information about how Anthony interacts with specific instructional style or content. What if a multiple-baseline intervention reveals that the baseline rate of problem behavior is much greater in social studies than in other classes? Might aspects of the setting influence his behavior? The team could consider a range of contextual factors: how challenging he finds this subject, the time of day he takes it, the student seated next to him, the instructional style of the teacher, or where he is seated in the room. Any or all of these factors may interact to influence the student–environment fit and, therefore, the level of problem behavior.

CONCLUSIONS

In this chapter, we have reviewed a large number of behavioral concepts that underlie positive behavior supports in general and *Positive Strategies* in particular. We do not anticipate that readers new to behavior therapy will absorb, recall, and apply with ease all of the material. Rather, we hope you will return to this chapter and use references suggested in the bibliography as you begin your work in individualized behavioral supports. In fact, we expect you to turn back to this chapter to refresh your memory as you read later chapters. In the next chapter, we will apply these principles to classroom management.

Chapter 3

Setting the Stage: Classroom and School as Context

Teacher preparation involves a mastery of content areas, pedagogic and professional knowledge and skills, and an understanding of the norms of student development, learning, and motivation (National Council on the Accreditation of Teacher Education, 2006). Most teachers take on their first classroom assignment after comprehensive preparation that includes (among other topics) how to structure and arrange a classroom, analyze and implement state or district curricula, develop lesson plans, write and teach to goals and objectives, assess student readiness and performance, evaluate the concerns of students with disabilities, integrate technology, differentiate instruction, and engage in whole-class, group, and individual lessons. Many teachers arrive with theoretical and practical preparation in behavior management, whereas others do not. Some complete student–teacher practice with mentors whose teaching styles are effective and admirable enough to merit imitation; unfortunately, many others learn how *not* to behave as classroom managers.

Regardless of how prepared they actually are, many teachers *feel* unprepared to face the challenge of managing a classroom full of diverse learners of any age or grade. All other accomplishments rest on the teacher's ability to successfully manage the classroom environment. Many teachers are dissatisfied with their amount and quality of university training, district and school support, and professional development opportunities for general classroom management and student behavior (Nichols & Sosnowsky, 2002). With national rates of teacher turnover greater than 50%, and more than half of those leaving the profession citing student behavior problems as a source of dissatisfaction (National Center for Education Statistics, 2001), it seems clear that supporting a teacher's ability to manage student behavior should be a priority.

In Chapter 2, we discussed the elemental principles of behaviorism. In this chapter, we relate those principles, and aspects of universal PBS, to classroom management. We do not cover all aspects of classroom management, discipline, instruction, curriculum, or teaching style; there is a rich tradition and literature in education that most educators are familiar with, and there are dozens of books on those topics. Reviewing that literature is not only outside the scope of this book, it may not even be the primary topic of concern. Our experience—and national statistics—suggest that, despite their preservice preparation, teachers remain keenly interested in preventing and successfully managing problem behavior. Teachers of students with emotional and behavioral disabilities rank behavior management and social skills development as their most relevant competencies, ahead of administration, curriculum, and assessment (Fink & Janssen, 1993). Many teachers view classroom management as a developmental process influenced by personal and contextual factors and shaped by experience, some of which is trial and error.

Improving teachers' perceptions of their effectiveness as well as their actual competence in this area has the potential to diminish job stress, improve teacher performance, decrease attrition, and mitigate the erosion of team-based functioning. The benefits of teacher competence in classroom management extend directly and indirectly to students. Recent findings (Office of Special Education Programs, 2002) indicate that problem behavior contributes directly to noninclusive placements and disparities in graduation rates. In addition, problem behavior arising early in a student's educational career places the student at risk of long-standing attributional biases. For example, preschoolers with challenging behaviors are viewed by teachers as having lower academic potential, are at risk for continuing underestimation, and are less likely to establish warm, working relationships with teachers (Espinosa & Laffey, 2003). These pessimistic views may themselves contribute to observed disparities in achievement, graduation, and employment.

Research beginning decades ago (e.g., the Pygmalion Effect; Rosenthal & Jacobson, 1968) and continuing (McFadden & Marsh, 1992) indicates that educators operate with expectations based on student factors such as classification or ability grouping, gender, socioeconomic status, race, cultural–linguistic status, attractiveness, disability status, and so on. Educators are not unique in this regard; these same biases operate within all American institutions. Given the prominent role of education in the lives of children, it is crucial for the field as a whole and for educators as individuals to continually examine and address these perceptions. This self-examination is best begun at the preservice level and continued within schools, classrooms, districts, and across the field.

Perhaps the best way to affect attitudes toward challenging behavior is to prevent it when possible and to address it early when it occurs. With that in mind, we begin our discussion of classroom management with a brief overview of universal (schoolwide and classwide) PBS strategies. We then outline characteristics of healthy classroom environments, and we conclude with a discussion of how individualized supports can be initiated within existing universal supports.

Before we begin, clarification of a few terms is warranted. First, we use *classroom management* to refer to practices for preparing the learning environment, including the organization of the classroom, establishing rules and routines, and otherwise orchestrating student engagement. *Discipline,* on the other hand, refers to actions taken in response to behavior that violates rules, norms, or expectations. Most schools have formal discipline codes that stipulate global expectations for behavior and consequences for various infractions. *Instruction* includes all activities undertaken in support of learning.

POSITIVE BEHAVIORAL INTERVENTIONS AND SUPPORTS: SCHOOLWIDE POSITIVE BEHAVIOR SUPPORT

In Chapter 1, we introduced the term *positive behavioral interventions and supports* (PBIS) and stated that it is sometimes used synonymously with PBS. There is an emerging literature regarding classroom, school, district, and regionwide disciplinary practices and systems designed to foster positive learning environments for all members of the education community (Anderson, Munk, Young, & Cummings, 2006; Chapman & Hofweber, 2000; Colvin & Fernandez, 2000; Horner & Sugai, 2000; Lohrman-O'Rourke, Knoster, Sabatine, Smith, Horvath, & Llewellyn, 2000; Nakasato, 2000; Nersesian, Todd, Lehmann, & Watson, 2000; Scott, 2001; Taylor-Greene & Kartub, 2000; Utley, Kozleski, Smith, & Draper, 2002; Warren, Edmonson, Griggs, et al., 2003). We refer readers to these resources for a more complete discussion of universal supports. Examples of related systemwide or universal efforts include discipline policies, safe schools initiatives, social skills training programs, and antibullying and antiharassment efforts, some of which were inspired, developed, or revised in response to well-publicized episodes of school violence in the late 1990s.

We employ the terms *universal, schoolwide, systemwide,* and *districtwide* to refer to broad initiatives aimed at encouraging positive behavior in larger communities of learners. In some places, PBIS initiatives are state- or districtwide and involve extensive in-service training. In other places, school districts develop uniform principles and encourage personnel to individualize their implementation. Many such initiatives involve encouraging teachers to use universal supports both within their classrooms and in the common areas of schools. Of course, every fall, across the United States, teachers spend the first days of class orienting their new students to the rules and routines of their classrooms. Each of these examples demonstrates aspects of universal PBS. We briefly review the basics of PBIS as a backdrop for their application in classrooms.

POSITIVE STRATEGIES AND SCHOOLWIDE EFFORTS

Positive Strategies efforts are tailored to individual students, in contrast to systemwide endeavors that, despite their potential impact on individual students, focus on the entire student body. Although most schoolwide PBS curricula address individualized supports, their emphasis is global rather than individual. Like all PBS, schoolwide efforts aim not only to reduce problems (e.g., discipline referrals) but also to improve quality of life (e.g., creating safer school environments that allow for greater focus on student development).

Conceptually, universal behavior supports are not new; many schools and communities have engaged in communitywide, behaviorally oriented practices for decades. In the 1970s and 1980s, behavior analytic practices were perhaps most evident in programs serving children with disabilities, but they quickly penetrated a range of contexts, including inpatient, outpatient, and day treatment programs for children, adolescents, and adults with a range of problems and challenging behaviors. Indeed, the use of token economies was so widespread in these settings as to seem ubiquitous. Some researchers and practitioners blended the use of applied behavior analysis principles with those of milieu therapy, which stresses the importance of examining the implicit messages (versus the explicit rule structure or economy) in the environment and asking all members to take responsibility for their contributions to the culture. To the extent that they are both behavioral and interpersonal in focus, aspects of these historical efforts resemble contemporary applications of PBS to school systems.

SCHOOLWIDE SUPPORTS: AN INTRODUCTION

In addition to the broad philosophic dimensions discussed above, quality universal behavior-intervention systems adhere to several general principles. These are based on known dimensions of problem behavior and the level of effort required to address it, including a prevention perspective, long-term commitment and collaboration, continuum of supports, multisystem or integrated efforts, social values base, empirical orientation, and adherence to the law.

Prevention Perspective

In Chapter 1, we discussed the importance of early identification and intervention for individual students with challenging behavior. Walker and Horner (1996) proposed a three-tiered model of PBS based on public health models. Figure 6 depicts the relative prevalence of problem behavior and corresponding levels for prevention activities. A primary prevention approach intended to reduce the number of new problems is indicated for the majority of students. This is similar to the health-promotion efforts in medicine in which individuals are encouraged to exercise and eat properly for good health. Secondary prevention efforts are directed toward at-risk students, with the goal of reducing the number of new cases. A parallel in medicine would be dietary modifications and prescription medications for individuals with

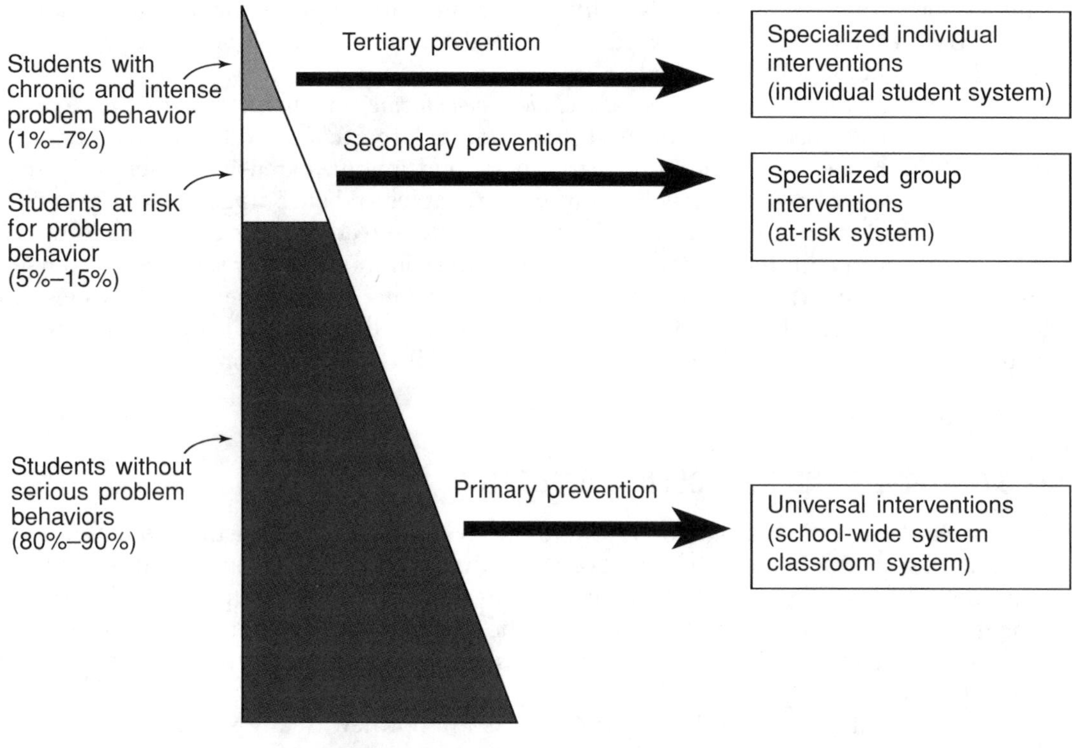

Figure 6. Prevalence and severity of problem behavior related to positive behavior interventions and supports. (Reprinted from Sugai, G., Horner, R.H., Dunlap, G., Hieneman, M., Lewis, T.J., Nelson, C.M., et al. [2000]. Applying positive behavior support and functional behavioral assessment in schools. *Journal of Positive Behavior Interventions, 2*, 131–143.)

high cholesterol but no history of illness (in other words, treatment for individuals who are clearly at risk). Finally, tertiary prevention is designed to reduce the amount, intensity, and complexity of existing problem behaviors. This includes individualized efforts such as *Positive Strategies* with functional behavioral assessments and behavior intervention plans targeted at specific students. This parallels the type of treatment one would receive from a physician after a heart attack or for ongoing management of diabetes.

According to Sugai, Horner, Dunlap, and colleagues (2000), more than 90% of students do not demonstrate behavior problems. Within this group, 5%–15% are considered at risk for problem behavior. Sugai and colleagues (2000) further estimate that 7%–10% of students do demonstrate problem behaviors; of this number, about half require individualized interventions because of the frequency and intensity of their problems. Schools that wish to create and sustain positive environments need to attend to all three levels of intervention, as illustrated in Figure 6 (Sugai et al., 2000).

Long-Term Commitment and Collaboration

Universal PBS, whether at the classroom or district level, require planning, resources, commitment, and support. Just as comprehensive individualized supports require development of an infrastructure including trained staff, internal and external expertise, and administrative support, universal supports cannot be achieved overnight. In fact, they require about 3 years of initial commitment. We believe that individual teachers and instructional teams can develop classroomwide supports with adequate teamwork, commitment, and support. This may be best pursued within a larger PBIS model, but important strides can also be made independently.

Effective systemwide interventions view and engage students, families, and other community members as partners in the process. This is realized in many ways, from including them in planning schoolwide interventions to eliciting their input in articulating a shared vision for school culture. For example, when developing expectations for student behavior, districtwide initiatives may include community members from both inside (students, faculty, staff) and outside the school (local officials, clergy, mental health personnel, child advocates, community youth organization leaders).

At the classroom level, the community includes teachers, students, aides, parents, and related services personnel. It also includes more transient members such as PBS coaches or consultants, family members, student teachers, librarians, and so forth. Ideally, all members of the community have a voice in and a shared understanding of classroom values, expectations, routines, and practices. In schools in which universal PBS is being implemented, teachers can reference schoolwide standards for behavior and key their classroom guidelines to them. Consistent with the multisystems perspective advocated by Sugai and Horner (2002), schoolwide PBS entails supporting teachers in their efforts to convey, encourage, and reward expected behaviors. When classroom guidelines relate clearly to those of the larger culture, they are more likely to become second nature.

Continuum of Supports

Related to prevention (and also illustrated in Figure 6) is the notion that effective schoolwide PBS efforts require a support continuum that is both broadly effective and that meets the unique concerns of individual students. A continuum implies that the type and level of support increase to match the concerns of the student(s) and the environment.

Effective supports for students at risk and with established problems may need to be comprehensive. The term *wraparound* refers to interventions that are arranged to fit the concerns of an individual child rather than requiring the individual (and family) to fit into existing support structures (e.g., crisis intervention, behavior supports, mental health, medical and public health services, transportation, recreation, financial supports, and social services). Because they draw from various parts of the community, effective systemwide PBS workgroups are also likely to produce comprehensive and integrated approaches to managing problem behaviors. Through universal PBS training, teachers and other team members learn early identification methods and school and community resources for children at risk. Freeman, Eber, Anderson, and colleagues (2006) provide a discussion of universal PBS in which they describe wraparound supports.

Multisystem or Integrated Efforts

The need for multisystem or integrated efforts relates closely to the first three features of PBIS. Sugai and Horner (2002) state that schoolwide PBS is characterized by emphasis on four elements: social competence and academic achievement, supported decision making, supporting student behavior, and supporting staff behavior. They assert that these four elements must be present across the school, in the classroom, in nonclassroom settings (common areas), and for individual students.

Values

Practitioners adopting PBS systems view aversive interventions as dehumanizing and unnecessary; behavior-intervention efforts should instead center on rewarding individual behavior and encouraging a culture of competence. This requires educational institutions to not only promote, but also *assume,* competence. The aim is to create a school environment in which interactions among students, faculty, and staff are predicated on mutual respect and a presumption of competence in all. Schoolwide PBS interventions welcome diversity and respect the fundamental worth and dignity of all members of the community. As such, effective schoolwide interventions are consistent with community values, implicitly embracing the inclusion of students with disabilities and aiming to improve quality of life, particularly for students facing disadvantages. Social values are constantly operating in the classroom, hopefully in support of explicitly stated priorities, but sometimes unwittingly working against them. Problem behavior is likely to be more common or more severe in the latter cases. A healthy classroom sets the stage for positive behavior; poor classroom management practices set the stage for problems.

An additional values element of PBS systems is their focus on strengths. A common first step in enacting a schoolwide PBS system is a needs assessment, the outcome of which is the identification of problems that need attention. This can inadvertently lead to a selective focus on problems. Like an individual functional behavioral assessment, if a school-based system ignores strengths, it fails to capitalize on existing skills, good habits, effective systems, and positive relationships. These can all be put to good use in a schoolwide plan. Focusing solely or predominantly on problems can be demoralizing to staff and can detract from positive efforts. A balanced assessment and intervention plan identifies both areas of strength and opportunities for improvement. This perspective is easily transferred to the classroom.

Empirically Validated Practices

Effective schoolwide PBS systems build on practices that have been demonstrated through program evaluation and external research to be effective. As discussed earlier, there is a rich and growing literature attesting to the effectiveness of PBS and systemwide efforts. Broadly speaking, these empirically supported practices have three overlapping elements: careful assessment, data collection and emphasis on outcomes, and program evaluation.

The research literature on schoolwide intervention includes applications in urban, suburban, and rural schools with both heterogeneous and homogeneous student bodies in terms of ethnicity and socioeconomic status. This literature reflects the increase in the number of districts offering safe schools programs during the 1990s, largely in response to several tragic incidents of school violence. This trend was given an added impetus in June 1998. After the fatal school shooting in Craigshead County, Arkansas, on March 24, 1998, President William J. Clinton directed the U.S. Justice Department and the Department of Education to develop a guide for school personnel, parents, and communities to use for early identification of and intervention for troubling and potentially dangerous student behavior. The resulting guide (Dwyer, Osher, & Warger, 1998) includes field-tested methods to assist school communities to identify early warning signs and develop prevention, intervention, and crisis-response plans. Several other approaches and intervention packages are available to assist schools in implementing schoolwide procedures; some are comprehensive guides to violence prevention, and others target specific areas of risk (access to firearms, harassment, students with discipline referrals, and so forth).

Schoolwide Positive Behavior Support and the Individuals with Disabilities Education Act

The successes of schoolwide PBS were recognized in several different ways with IDEA'04. The opening section on findings called for "incentives for whole-school approaches, scientifically based early reading programs, positive behavioral interventions and supports, and early intervening services to reduce the need to label children as disabled in order to address the learning and behavioral needs of such children" [Section 601(c)(5)(F)(i)]. Thus, PBS was clearly labeled as relevant to meeting the concerns of large numbers of children through proactive methods.

Later sections of the law state that IDEA'04 funds earmarked for professional development may be used to "provide training in methods of positive behavioral interventions and supports to improve student behavior in the classroom" [Section 654(a)(3)(B)(iii)(I)], that preservice and in-service personnel preparation programs "include training in positive behavior supports" [Section 662(a)(6)(D)], and that educational leadership programs focus on "behavioral supports in the school and classroom" [Section 662(a)(7)(B)].

In fact, IDEA'04 refers to schoolwide PBS in several other places, suggesting an endorsement of the approach by the U.S. Congress as important in making schools responsive to the concerns of students with disabilities. This is certainly laudable and offers the promise of increased use of schoolwide PBS in the future. Crimmins and Farrell (2006), however, offer one caution: schoolwide PBS is not enforceable as a civil right in the way that individualized supports can be. As noted in Chapter 1, individualized behavioral supports are a required consideration under IDEA'04 for students with impeding behaviors. This gives individualized behavioral supports the status of a civil right protected by due-process procedures and enforceable for the individual. IDEA'04 provides no mechanism compelling schools to provide schoolwide PBS in the way that individualized supports can be mandated.

How Does Positive Behavior Support Differ from Traditional Discipline?

Compared with traditional approaches, universal PBS approaches offer a proactive stance with respect to behavior. The traditional school culture views behavior management and socialization of students as outside its primary responsibility. Nonetheless, whether one examines the teaching process itself (interactions among adults and children) or the fact that students learn in a social context (in groups with other children), education is a largely social endeavor. The history of discipline in education is rife with examples of how students with disabilities, behavior differences, atypical learning styles, and behavior problems have experienced undesirable consequences ranging from time-out to placement in overly restrictive settings. From the beginning of formal education programs until fairly recently, removal of marginal students was the predominant means by which educators managed problem behavior. As such, it is hardly surprising that our methods to adequately address challenging behaviors are still evolving.

If the charge of schools is academics, however, it follows that all students should have equal access to learning opportunities. Behavior difficulties are a major barrier to learning and absorb a disproportionate amount of instructional time that could otherwise be devoted to the entire school community. Schoolwide and classwide supports, by addressing not only the small number of students with challenging behavior but also their peers, have the potential to enhance education. Such supports can effectively reduce the extent to which students with disabilities are excluded and enhance the learning environment for children and adults alike. To accomplish this, educators need to combine PBS with efforts to improve learning and academic achievement. The corollary benefits, including a healthy school milieu that socializes students to positive social customs, are consistent with educational objectives and are beneficial to all community members.

As discussed in earlier chapters, traditional approaches to problem behavior are largely reactive. Within a reactive school culture, there is a code of conduct that students, families, and faculty may be familiar with, policies for managing problem behavior, and few clearly stated positive expectations for behavior. In some cases, these strategies may work adequately for a significant proportion of students, but they do a disservice to those demonstrating persistent problem behaviors. When problems occur, time spent managing problem behaviors detracts from learning. In other schools, risk factors that are present in the community manifest as widespread problems because the learning environment lacks systematic or equitable attention to behavior.

In some reactive cultures, consequences for rule infractions might exist but are not widely known. In such cases, consequences cannot serve as effective deterrents or be reliably implemented by faculty and staff. Adherence may be short term or episodic. For example, a classroom may have an explicit rule system in which students behaving responsibly earn points to redeem for privileges or tangible items. If reinforcers are not reliably delivered, the system is doomed to be ineffective for the majority of students who are well behaved *and* for students demonstrating problem behavior.

Unfortunately, we have seen reward systems mismanaged and (in some cases) turned into punishment strategies. For example, a reinforcement program is neglected until one or more students misbehave. Staff respond by assigning reinforcement points quite volubly to all students *except* those who have misbehaved. This is problematic in two ways. First, although the strategy is intended to prevent the behavior from recurring, it is not likely to be effective. Second, this violates most school policies in that it demeans students for showing problem behavior. In our experience, this is most likely to occur in schools facing multiple stressors and diminished resources, without a true commitment to positive support.

In sum, reactive school cultures, inadequate systems of positive support, and failed adherence to existing codes for behavior detract from the likelihood that schools and classrooms can create and maintain positive environments. A schoolwide system of support must be sustained in effort and proactive in stance to enable better outcomes for all members of the learning community. We believe that the environment created within schoolwide PBS may prevent some, perhaps even most, problem behaviors. Because some problem behaviors will, nevertheless, occur—especially among students with disabilities—individualized supports will always be needed.

Example of Positive Behavior Support in the Classroom

You enter a seventh-grade classroom and see several different hubs of activity. Two groups of students huddle together at tables in quiet conversation. Another group sits at computers arranged in a circle (seats inside). These students are working quietly but conferring with each other and sharing resources. A fourth group is seated at a cluster of desks and is engaged in active discussion among themselves and with the instructor. From time to time, the instructor leaves the discussion and checks in with the other groups. The class is active and has a moderate noise level, but students can speak in low conversational tones and are easily heard. Occasionally, one group or student becomes loud, resulting in shushes from within the group and a nod from the teacher. Seven minutes before the end of the class period, the teacher strolls around the room, informs each group that they have about 5 minutes to wrap up, reminds them of the assignment due the next day, and asks them to finish their discussions. Two minutes before the bell rings, the students are preparing for the transition to their next subject.

A few doors down, in another seventh-grade classroom, an instructor stands at the front of the room, lecturing to the students and writing on the board. The room is arranged in long rows of desks. Student engagement covers the range of imaginable academic behavior—active interest and looking, notetaking, daydreaming, text messaging on a cell phone, and slumber. Two students are reminded by the teacher to raise their hands if they have comments to add, and when they shrink down in their seats, it becomes clear that they were not conferring about the course content. The teacher asks a question, which is answered by a very engaged student, and then the teacher moves on to other material. Three minutes before the end of the class period, students begin closing their books and preparing to leave. The instructor reminds them that the class is not over until the bell rings, but most students continue packing up. Over the noise of students shuffling out of the room, the instructor reminds them about the assignment due the next day.

In a third room, desks are arranged in groups and the teacher is seated at one of them. Some groups of students are working independently at desks, and others are talking loudly. Another group is working at the computer, with sounds from multimedia programs quite audible across the room. One student who is seated at a desk near the computers frequently leans back to speak to the students working at the computers. These students look over at another group and then laugh loudly. The other group glares in response and begins talking together. The teacher attempts to get the class's attention but, having trouble being heard over the noise, tells students to discontinue their group work and return to their assigned seats. The instructor then informs the students that their disruptive behavior will result in a loss of group project time the next class period. The students groan and then look to the teacher for further instruction. The teacher asks the students to read quietly until the bell rings. Some take out books, and others sit at their desks idly. A few minutes later, the bell rings.

POSITIVE BEHAVIOR SUPPORT IN THE CLASSROOM

These three classrooms depict diverse learning environments, student behaviors, and instructor management styles. As you read the descriptions, a number of questions might come to mind. You may wonder whether the classes are heterogeneous or homogeneous, whether teachers previously communicated expectations and implemented consequences for student behavior, or how the instructors typically respond to escalating or problem behavior. Does each teacher use the same fundamental strategies with every class? You may have an opinion of which classroom most effectively supports engagement, self-regulation, learning, and positive behavior. You might also have considered the extent to which the instructor effectively matches management strategies to student characteristics. Your analysis examines important classroom dimensions to be considered in understanding student behavior. These dimensions represent interacting factors that influence classroom environments; they determine the extent to which classrooms promote positive behavior or, conversely, trigger problem behavior.

CLASSROOM ESSENTIALS

Some essentials of healthy learning environments are already obvious: clear expectations for behavior, explicit consequences for behavior, and consistent application of both. It is also clear that effective pedagogy stimulates and engages students and may itself prevent problem behavior. But is not competent management a necessary prerequisite for effective pedagogy? Here, the interrelated nature of classroom management and pedagogy is evident. Chapter 2 contains several clues to structuring classrooms that encourage adherence to routine but also provide the flexibility to adapt to individual differences and circumstances. Table 3 lists a number of factors that influence the classroom environment, all of which might be considered contextual factors. They are discussed below.

Table 3 includes four main contextual factors that influence student behavior and performance: structure, instruction, expectations for behavior, and teacher and relationship factors. Although we list these factors separately, they are obviously interdependent and interact with student, school, and community factors.

Structure refers to the physical environment of the classroom, as well as the extent to which time is structured in service of engagement and order. The temporal organization of the classroom (how well and how explicitly time is allotted and managed) contributes to a sense of routine, and a variety of cues and prompts may help promote student adherence to structure and routine. Clearly visible schedules, cues for changing classes or exchanging materials, and previews and preparation for transition encourage task investment and discourage distractions. Routines are helpful because they become rather automatic, and with less attention paid to managing oneself and time, students can more readily engage in classroom activities. Effective classrooms provide ample stimulation but are managed in such a way that members are not chronically overstimulated or overwhelmed. They are developmentally appropriate and culturally inclusive.

Instruction encompasses all activities designed to promote learning. Here, the term *learning* refers not only to academic achievement but also to the development of self-regulation and metacognition. Metacognition is a higher-order learning skill that permits students to reflect on their own thoughts and behavior. It includes planning how to approach a task, monitor comprehension and progress, and evaluate success (e.g., edit or review one's own work).

Some authors (McCombs & Whisler, 1997) have used the term *learner-centered* to refer to classroom and school environments designed specifically to capitalize on the current knowledge about learning preparedness. Essentially, learner-centered environments optimally support individual student learning and achievement by considering cognitive, metacognitive, affective, personal and social, developmental, and individual factors. Learner-centeredness resembles both differentiated instruction and student–environment fit. Research indicates that effective instruction also requires careful planning and organization, access to quality curricula, high-quality instructor support, and diversified approaches to teaching and learning.

Other aspects of instruction that influence behavior include task demands, the amount of reinforcement and support available, and the extent to which instruction is targeted at a level that brings adequate success to the majority of students. We suggest that teachers target instruction to permit 80% accuracy in students. This level of success tends to motivate students and can contribute to a sense of learning efficacy that is helpful under more challenging circumstances.

Table 3. Factors influencing classroom environment

Factors	Examples of effective application
Structure	
Physical layout	The environment is comfortable, well lit, and decorated with student products. Space is arranged to encourage engagement and is appropriate to grade level, content, and instructional approaches. Multiple stations support diverse learning activities. Boundaries between personal (student desks and cubbies) and common spaces (reading area, computer center, bookshelf) are clear. Furniture is sized appropriately, and integrated seating is available for individuals with mobility impairments.
Temporal organization	Predictable routines capitalize on habit and environmental cues. Routines encourage self-regulation and development of autonomy rather than emphasizing control (Frede, 1995; Rosenberg & Jackman, 2003). Activities are planned so that students are dispersed to various learning centers, avoiding crowding and conflict (DeVries & Zan, 2003).
Stimulation	Level of sensory input (e.g., noise level, visual input, movement, number of simultaneous activities) is adequate to promote engagement and participation, but is not overwhelming.
Appropriateness and inclusiveness	The layout, materials, and level of structure available in the classroom are appropriate to the developmental level of the students (e.g., child care, preschool, primary grades, middle school and high school, and distinctions within each). Wall hangings such as photos and art prints represent the diversity of the community (Freeman et al., 2006).
Transitions	Schedules are posted; students are cued in advance of transitions. Transitions are smooth and orderly, maximizing time available for learning.
Instruction	
Learner centeredness	Routines, instruction, coaching, modeling, and reinforcement all support the development of self-regulation. Support for metacognition promotes student learning and autonomy (McCombs & Whisler, 1997; Porter & Brophy, 1988; Wenglinsky, 2003).
Planning, organization, curricula	Teachers allocate sufficient time for planning and instruction (Stronge & Hindman, 2003), have clear instructional goals (Porter & Brophy, 1988), communicate goals to students (Marzano, Marzano, & Pickering, 2003), and use curriculum-based assessment to tailor instruction (Tyler-Wood, Cereijo, & Pemberton, 2004). Published instructional materials enhance instruction when carefully selected and flexibly employed (Porter & Brophy, 1988).
Instructor support	The instructor supervises learning activities and is available to provide support, guidance, and direction without interfering with student creativity. Student engagement and rule compliance are promoted by teacher movement around the classroom (Kehle et al., 2000).
Instructional style	Opportunities for success and challenge are available. Diverse learning activities include direct instruction (individual and group instruction), hands-on learning, problem solving, questioning, and guided practice (Stronge & Hindman, 2003). Differentiated instruction provides students multiple options for information processing (Hall, 2002).
Expectations for behavior	
Origin	Expectations are developed and stated early and positively, with clear links to the schoolwide behavior code. Students of all ages are meaningfully involved in developing classroom behavior code; instructors facilitate links between student-generated rules and existing schoolwide standards (Cothran, Kulinna, & Garrahy, 2003; Sailor, Zuna, Choi, Thomas, McCart, & Blair, 2006; Sugai & Horner, 2002; Sugai et al., 2005).
Accessibility	Expectations for behavior should be stated positively, concise (e.g., limited to five), and readily accessible (posted in the room, signed by students, available as a handout; Taylor-Greene & Kartub, 2000; Sugai et al., 2005).
Teaching and responding	Procedures are in place for teaching expected behaviors; precorrection, praise, and feedback are offered in direct, predictable, nonjudgmental ways (Sugai et al., 2005; Sailor, Zuna, Choi, Thomas, McCart, & Blair, 2006).

Factors	Examples of effective application
Teacher and relationship factors	
Preparation, skill, expertise	Teacher's own test scores, certification, quality of teacher education, preparation (Whitebook, 2003; Rice, 2006), and expertise in content area (Porter & Brophy, 1988) are associated with good student outcomes. Teachers are knowledgeable regarding federal, state, and local benchmarks (Hall, 2002).
Personal attributes and behaviors	Students prefer teachers perceived as caring, respectful, empathetic, open, energetic, warm, accessible, flexible, and having a sense of humor (Bratton, 1998; Cothran, Kulinna, & Garrahy, 2003; Sanders & Rivers, 1996). Effective teachers are assertive, use a neutral tone, appear equitable, and take a personal interest. These teachers have fewer behavior problems in their classes (Marzano et al., 2003). Effective teachers are dominant, providing clear purpose and strong guidance regarding learning and behavior (Marzano et al., 2003); students prefer this type of dominance over permissiveness (Chiu & Tulley, 1997).

There is a growing base of empirical support demonstrating the effectiveness of developing behavioral expectations, teaching appropriate behavior, precorrecting foreseeable rule infractions, and applying praise and consequences fairly and uniformly in classroom management. Jones and Jones (2003) offer several teacher strategies for preventing and responding to disruptive behavior: 1) seating patterns should permit the teacher to move about and monitor students; 2) the teacher should regularly scan the classroom for potential problems; 3) the disruptive influence of teacher direction or intervention should not be greater than the disruptive behavior that triggers it; 4) the teacher should avoid angry responses, which create a negative ripple effect, increasing defiance; 5) the teacher should practice calm, direct, prompt, and nonjudgmental responses, which create positive ripple effects; and 6) the teacher should practice responses to disruptive behavior that will guide the student back to task rather than requesting explanation or drawing attention to it.

The last set of factors involves teacher characteristics and teacher–student relationships. When teachers are trained well in their content areas and in pedagogy, achievement is higher and behavior problems are less common and less severe. The U.S. Department of Education (NCES, 2001), although acknowledging that there is little consensus on how to define high-quality teaching, notes that research emphasizes two broad dimensions of effectiveness: *teacher knowledge and skills* (as measured by preparation and qualifications) and *classroom practices.* Elementary and high school students express a clear preference for teachers whom they perceive as caring, respectful, empathetic, open, energetic, warm, accessible, and flexible. Although this is not surprising, it is helpful when combined with other research indicating that students also prefer teachers who manage classrooms effectively by establishing rules and routines and by asserting positive control (dominance) rather than by more authoritarian approaches.

Thus, teaching is a complex role, and effective teaching requires a well-rounded, multifaceted, multitasked approach. First and foremost, the effective teacher establishes a supportive, appealing climate that engages students as individual learners. Porter and Brophy (1988) describe good teaching as

> . . . a tightly coupled rational process in which background and milieu factors influence teachers' development of professional pedagogical knowledge and routines. These, in turn, influence the planning of instruction, which influences the nature of instruction that actually occurs. And this instruction (along with student aptitude and motivation factors) influences students' immediate responses to instruction and, ultimately, its long-term outcomes. There is also a self-correcting mechanism: Good teachers reflect on the feedback they get. . . . This reflection in turn enhances their professional knowledge and affects their future instructional planning. (p. 75)

CONSEQUENCES OF EFFECTIVE CLASSROOM MANAGEMENT AND INSTRUCTION

Most adults can recall at least one favorite teacher whose influence extended well beyond the subject matter or course content. Teachers are important role models and mentors. The most effective ones can not only shape children's classroom behavior, study habits, and achievement test scores—they arm students with lifelong learning skills, influence career choices, inspire imitation, and improve self-efficacy. Although these relationship effects are mostly intangible, the field of education is beginning to examine the relationship between teacher effectiveness and specific student outcomes.

What are the measurable consequences of effective teaching? Recent research reviews and meta-analyses define effective teaching and elucidate its consequences. Sanders and Rivers (1996) and Wright, Horn, and Sanders (1997) evaluated the impact of effective and ineffective teachers on student achievement. The earlier study indicated that successive years with effective teachers resulted in substantial advantage—a gain of 52% in achievement scores. In contrast, students placed with ineffective teachers for successive years were at an extreme disadvantage. Subsequent placement with a highly effective teacher, although associated with significant gains, was not adequate to redress the loss. As teacher effectiveness increased, lower-achieving students were the first to benefit, and students of all abilities benefited from top-performing teachers. Minority students were more likely to be assigned to ineffective teachers. As such, Sanders and Rivers (1996) asserted that the effects of teaching are "both additive and cumulative." Mendro (1998) reported similar lags in remediation for students moving from ineffective to effective classrooms.

Wright, Horn, and Sanders (1997) examined the influence of classroom heterogeneity, class size, and student skill. None of these factors were significantly predictive of student achievement. Although their work has been criticized, these authors dismiss the claim that heterogeneous student ability (not teaching) is responsible for poor student outcomes. They assert that decades of research on ability grouping have demonstrated its failure and that this has come to be reflected in prevailing values in education. Wright, Horn, and Sanders (1997) state that "*effective teachers appear to be effective with students of all achievement levels, regardless of the level of heterogeneity in their classrooms*" (p. 63, emphasis original).

Stronge and Hindman (2003) found that students of low-performing teachers (bottom 25%) scored significantly lower than their peers. The impact of teacher effectiveness was apparent even when controlling for class size, student gender, ethnicity, socioeconomic status, English proficiency, and school attendance. In a recent meta-analysis, Marzano, Marzano, and Pickering (2003) found that teachers who had good relationships with students had 31% fewer discipline problems than teachers with low-quality relationships. Downer and Pianta (2006) controlled for home and child care factors affecting early reading and found that classrooms that spent more time on basic literacy, language, and math instruction produced higher scores in reading achievement, phoneme knowledge, and long-term retrieval. Apportioning instructional time seems to be an important teacher behavior as well.

Emerging research suggests what many parents know intuitively: a child's education may only be as good as the child's teacher. But because teachers have very little control over which students walk into their classrooms each fall, how can they possibly override the significant influences of student and school factors? (Some of these factors are listed in Table 4.) Effective teachers construct environments that fit both the shared and unique characteristics of their students. Despite the many challenges that teachers face, it is possible to override multiple risks and negative influences.

CLASSROOM AS CONTEXT FOR PROBLEM BEHAVIOR

Problem behaviors occur even in highly effective classrooms. If behavior problems are mostly transient, mild, or quickly mitigated by teacher intervention, it is likely that the classroom environment sets the stage for positive behavior. In effective classrooms, however, there may still be individual students who demonstrate problem behaviors. These students are more likely to have disabilities, histories of problem behavior, or both. In this case, individualized, team-based

Table 4. Student and school factors that influence behavior and achievement

Factors and aspects	Examples
Student factors	
Demographics	Demographics of student, school, and neighborhood affect individuals and classrooms; demographic factors include socioeconomic status, language, gender, race/ethnicity, neighborhood, school funding, and so forth (Guin, 2004; Losen & Orfield, 2002)
Family characteristics	Family structure, parental education, home environment, discipline practices, support for self-regulation, autonomy, prosocial behavior, expectations for academic achievement (Downer & Pianta, 2006; Duncan & National Institute of Child Health and Human Development Early Child Care Research Network, 2003; Fan & Chen, 2001)
Individual factors	Functional communication skills, self-regulation, social skills, cognitive/academic skills
School factors	
Availability of resources	Federal, state, and local funding affect the amount and availability of resources, classroom size, and staff compensation and retention (Buckley, Schneider, & Shang, 2004; Guin, 2004)
Schoolwide policies and expectations	Schools with clear expectations and uniform adherence have fewer discipline problems. Demographic factors (above) predict the prevalence of problem behaviors (Donovan & Cross, 2002; Losen & Orfield, 2002)

behavioral supports may be needed (we turn to teams in the next chapter and delve into individualized supports in the remaining chapters).

What if high rates of problem behavior occur in a classroom? We consider significant rates to include more than one significant disruption per class period, 10% or more students demonstrating persistent behavior problems, more than 10% of students being off task at a given time, or higher-than-average rates of disciplinary rates compared with those of other classes in the school. If many behavior incidents occur in a classroom, it may reflect some student characteristics (e.g., students with limited or immature self-regulation), but it also suggests that the instructor may not be doing everything necessary to manage these challenges.

Focusing on the classroom as a context is important when problem behavior is common or intense. In fact, it may be more efficient to address the concerns of several students (or the entire class) than to attempt to develop multiple individual plans. During the assessment phase of *Positive Strategies,* the student–environment fit is assessed. This process may identify classroom or teacher characteristics that serve as antecedents to problem behavior for more than one student. It may be prudent to examine the classroom structure, instructional style, behavioral expectations, and teacher factors that set the stage for problems.

Careful observation may reveal a classroom, location within the class, time, or activity that serves as a "hot spot" spurring problem behavior. Snell (2006) suggested that these problems may be circumvented by specialized group interventions, such as rearranging the environment, constructing monitoring systems (e.g., check-in/check-out cards), adult mentoring, or explicit instruction in social skills. When a classroom is identified as a hot spot, an individual teacher may feel defensive, sheepish, or helpless. Regardless of the teacher's reaction, identifying the hot spot can be framed as opportunity for positive change. For example, a brief, targeted intervention to improve the effectiveness of teacher commands and to increase the teacher's use of verbal praise can significantly increase student compliance, improve engagement, and reduce disruption (e.g., Matheson & Shriver, 2005).

CONCLUSIONS

Schoolwide and classroom PBS efforts combine naturally with individualized approaches to problem behavior and share many of the same philosophic and methodological origins. It is important to note that schoolwide systems cannot be successful without effective classroom implementation, and classrooms are unlikely to be managed well if instructors do not adopt PBS approaches or, at least, the underlying behavioral principles of such approaches. Schoolwide approaches lead to effectively reduced discipline referrals, suspensions, and expulsions; they have also proven valuable in improving school culture and addressing quality-of-life issues (Scott, 2001; Utley et al., 2002; Warren et al., 2003). Although they require dedicated resources, schoolwide interventions have the potential to streamline compliance with legal mandates and community-derived priorities.

Schoolwide efforts that reflect and respect the values and priorities of the community achieve much more than compliance; they improve the participation of individual students and enhance entire learning communities. Because a small percentage of students present a challenge for even the most effective schoolwide programs and classroom teachers, they are necessarily supplemented with individualized supports. We offer *Positive Strategies* to assist schools in meeting the concerns of these students, and we are confident that doing so benefits all students.

Chapter 4

*Positive Strategies Teams

Ensuring effective implementation of *Positive Strategies* requires a number of organizational tasks: assembling a team with skills to complete the work, developing procedures for responding to requests for student support, selecting individual students, reviewing and discussing relevant case materials, conducting FBAs, and developing BIPs. Teams undertake these activities in the midst of multiple, competing demands; managing all of this requires dedication, planning, resources, and close collaboration. In this chapter, we discuss why a team approach is so essential to success. We also detail how teams interface with other school entities; enumerate key staff competencies; discuss how teams select students with whom to work, roles of members, and attributes of effective teams; and underscore the impact of setting on using *Positive Strategies*.

WHY A TEAM?

Implementing *Positive Strategies* is a complex undertaking. And, although a single, well-trained individual may be capable of assessing a specific behavior and implementing a support plan, a number of predictable obstacles make that a very difficult individual endeavor. Within the classroom, the teacher's primary challenge is to implement a grade-level curriculum while managing a class of students with diverse abilities, behavioral styles, and learning concerns. Other challenges in the school environment involve managing related services, creating and delivering lessons, juggling personnel demands and schedules (e.g., lunch, physical education, arrival and dismissal coverage), and arranging time for faculty to confer. Outside school, families face community commitments, sports, religious activities, household demands, and the need for parental involvement in school. A range of perspectives is needed to address all of these arenas of potential concern in a child's life.

To ensure that teams obtain the most complete picture of the student possible, *Positive Strategies* teams generally include parents, teachers, teaching assistants and aides, related services personnel, and administrators. Later, we discuss the contributions made by each of these, but it is important to emphasize the value of having this mix of viewpoints in conducting the FBA and implementing the BIP. There are three major reasons for this.

Multiple Perspectives and Contexts

First, multiple perspectives enrich the team's understanding of a student's concerns, abilities, and possible motivations. Students interact with many people during the course of a day, and each person experiences the student differently. No single individual possesses all the information necessary to understand, appreciate, and support a student's behavior across contexts. The inclusion of staff with varied responsibilities and perspectives makes it more likely that the team will develop an informed, valid understanding of issues and priorities.

Within some schools, classroom staff and personnel who work in other capacities (e.g., school counselors) may view the same student in dramatically different ways. Teachers (or parents) may have more experience with the negative aspects of behavior and may emphasize its effects on academic performance, on other children, and on the classroom (or family) as a whole. In such cases, however, principals and school psychologists may view students with challenging behavior more dispassionately. Their perspective involves comparing the individual student with the total population of the school, in which case this student's problems may not seem particularly bad. The team structure is a vehicle for consolidating these views of a child and building consensus about what needs to be accomplished.

Collective Advocacy for Resources

Second, school personnel face a wide range of responsibilities for their students. Today's teachers are expected to meet higher academic standards without sacrificing sensitivity to students' individual learning, emotional, and behavioral concerns. Given these demands, it can be extremely difficult to determine the priority for FBA and BIP activities. A team can serve to encourage its members, validate problems, provide perspective, and furnish the support needed to obtain key resources. The team may also request time and human or other resources to address behavioral concerns. When advocating for resources, a diverse group of educators concerned about students has a distinct advantage over an individual teacher.

Shared Burdens and Rewards

Third, collaborating with fellow team members enhances the support process, making it more enjoyable and interesting. Students with persistent behavior problems consume large amounts of time and energy. At their most difficult, they can be tremendous sources of frustration. A team provides a forum for sharing both the burdens and rewards of developing effective interventions. In addition, teams provide opportunities for mentoring, role release, and shared responsibility among members.

In reality, school teams are a bit like families: you don't get to select their members. Teams vary in their size, structure, authority, autonomy, composition, division of labor, and in how well they get along. Like families, they change over time, have explicit and implicit rules, and can be healthy or dysfunctional. Because it is beyond the scope of this book to discuss all aspects of team functioning, we discuss the aspects that are most germane to operating in support of students with problem behaviors.

ORGANIZATIONAL STRUCTURE FOR POSITIVE SUPPORTS

Effective behavior supports require careful consideration and effort from the top down and from the bottom up. Administrative support and commitment make teamwork possible, and the dedicated and innovative efforts of teams contribute to discipline and educational accomplishment within the school. In this section, we discuss how schools constitute behavior support teams and how these teams relate to other educational functions, such as prereferral supports for students at risk, special education services, and building-level discipline efforts.

A Note about Terminology

Before we discuss team composition and functions in detail, a brief clarification of terms is warranted. In Chapter 1, we state that *Positive Strategies* is just one exemplar within the field of PBS. We also emphasize the importance of schoolwide policies and infrastructure for PBS, regardless of how this is implemented. Size, policy, and community characteristics dictate the specifics of how teams serving individual students relate to each other, building-level initiatives, and districtwide PBS practices. Although nomenclature varies greatly within and across regions and states, Figure 7 illustrates how these structures might be interconnected within a school district and represents only one way to configure various structures. There is no single ideal structure for PBS entities, because the optimal arrangement is determined by contextual factors in the community, school(s), staff, student body, and faculty.

For the purposes of this book, we refer to the buildingwide team as the *behavior support workgroup*. Because most ad hoc (temporary) teams form in response to the challenging behaviors of individual students, we refer to those as *student support teams*.

Note that during *Positive Strategies* team training initiatives, we sometimes refer to the school teams participating in training as *Positive Strategies* teams. These teams are made up of general and special education teachers, parents, teaching assistants, one or two related services providers, and an administrator. Ideally, those selected as team members include natural leaders who might eventually serve as mentors to others; we have also found it best to carefully consider the participation of first-year employees, teachers new to their grade level, and others who are already facing significant professional development demands. The *Positive Strategies* team serves as a student support team for its case study student, and we expect that many of these individuals will also serve on the school's behavior support workgroup.

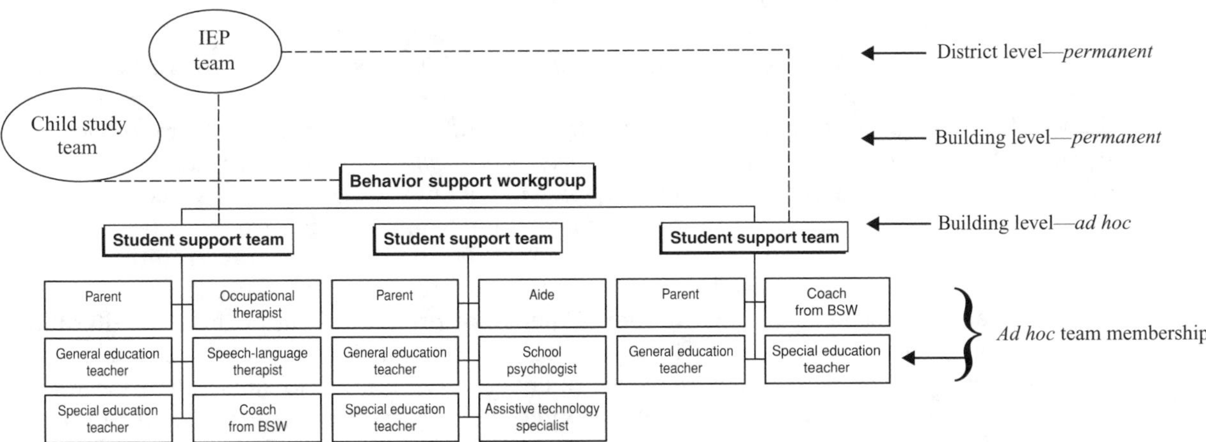

Figure 7. Illustration of the relationship among positive behavior support (PBS) elements in a school district. A permanent, buildingwide workgroup maintains overall responsibility for PBS. Ad hoc teams address the concerns of individual students. Dotted lines portray relationships, formal or informal, among existing special education entities, ad hoc student support teams, and building-level workgroups. The number and composition of support teams for individual students varies. Some teams have several members, including teachers, aides, and related service providers. Others are smaller and represent fewer disciplines. A behavior support workgroup consisting of individuals with diverse backgrounds, professions, and expertise enriches all PBS efforts because its members are available as coaches (liaisons and consultants) to individual teams. (*Key:* IEP = individualized education program; BSW = behavior support workgroup.)

Positive Behavior Support Entities in Schools

No matter how teams relate to their larger organizations, it is important that overall responsibility for individualized PBS (IPBS) rest with defined group(s) functioning within the school or district. The behavior support workgroup may be a subset of a larger entity, such as the IEP team or school support team, because the function of the behavior support workgroup relates so closely to the mandates of the IEP or school support team. Please note that for clarity, and consistent with the language of the IDEA'04, we employ the term *IEP team* to refer to those individuals collectively responsible for the development and implementation of individualized education programs. Schools, states, and regions may employ slightly different terms to refer to these groups (e.g., committee on special education [CSE], committee on preschool special education, pupil personnel team, and child study team). Our use of the term *IEP team* is not intended to preclude the involvement of any individual or role that is not stipulated in IDEA'04. In addition to the behavior support team, there may be several teams within a school that focus on different aspects of student behavior. As noted in Chapter 1, many schools have schoolwide initiatives that include school climate committees responsible for developing universal initiatives to support positive behavior for all students. In such cases, overlapping responsibilities and initiatives require coordination of effort. However constituted, the behavior support workgroup must have an explicit identity within the organization to be effective. Members should meet regularly, roles on the workgroup should be explicitly assigned (not assumed or added informally to staff workloads), and staff and parents should know how to refer students to the team.

To ensure that its activities are appropriately reflected within and coordinated with the student's IEP, the team should communicate with and be recognized by the IEP team. At any given point, a member of the behavior support workgroup may be participating in one or more student support teams and serving as the liaison between those teams and the IEP team. Perhaps this person is also a qualified member of the IEP team (e.g., the school psychologist or special education teacher). Alternatively, a teacher or related services provider (e.g., speech-language pathologist, occupational or physical therapist, school psychologist) may simultaneously serve on one or more student support teams without having PBS-related roles outside those responsibilities.

On a student-by-student basis, the behavior support workgroup recommends or assembles a student support team that includes people who work regularly with the referred student. Workgroups themselves are most effective when they have stable leadership but allow for revolving membership based on concerns and expertise. The workgroup may recruit new members on the basis of experience, interest, and expertise. A staff member who initially refers a student to the workgroup might become part of that child's student support team and later be recruited to join the buildingwide *behavior support workgroup*. This flexibility can be inviting to other members of the school, encouraging the sharing of knowledge about these techniques and the use of positive supports with more students, both formally and informally.

The relationship among various student support efforts is also portrayed in the interface between PBS and formal special education mechanisms, as depicted in Figure 7. Indeed, *Positive Strategies* can assist schools in meeting requirements for prereferral supports as an alternative to direct special education referral. These rules require schools to designate personnel responsible for identifying students who are at risk of being referred for, and subsequently classified into, special education. The goal of prereferral intervention is to develop a set of short-term, targeted supports to reverse a pattern of academic difficulty for identified students. In many schools, the prereferral endeavors are undertaken by an ad hoc team that also has formal ties to the IEP team. Prereferral efforts might take the form of a limited number of sessions with a resource room teacher, counseling, or other supports and services that might be available to all students (e.g., Title I, Section 504 services and accommodations). The team retains responsibility for the student and, if the prereferral effort is insufficient, ensures access to routine CSE referral and classification processes.

The behavior support workgroup might operate similarly. After receiving and reviewing a referral (generally from instructional or administrative staff handling discipline issues), core members of the group would invite the student's parents, teachers, and relevant support staff to an initial planning meeting. This new entity is considered the student support team. Collectively, these individuals are responsible for conducting the FBA and developing the BIP. Selected team members may collaborate to gather data, develop classroom accommodations, and set up in-class instruction. The team's efforts often clarify which nonclassified students need to be referred to the CSE and how modifications of the instructional program may be useful for students already receiving special education services. This implies ongoing coordination and communication among designated members of the student support team, the behavior support workgroup, and the CSE. Often, this coordination is achieved through the involvement of one or two key staff members.

COMPETENCIES IN POSITIVE BEHAVIOR SUPPORT

Individual and Shared Expertise

Table 5 lists a number of competencies that are necessary for effective delivery of *Positive Strategies.* Although we do not expect a single person to demonstrate all of these competencies, it is critical that all members possess some of these competencies and that the behavior support workgroup collectively possess all of them.

Areas of shared expertise improve a team's chances of weathering transitions, retirements, resignations, reassignments, and other commonplace personnel changes. Given the varied backgrounds of team members, some inevitably possess more advanced competencies than others. For example, the special educator, school psychologist, or administrator may have a commitment to professional development in PBS. It would be natural for these people to assume greater responsibility for the process. When we conduct *Positive Strategies* training, we expect at least one or two team members to develop advanced competencies. It is extremely helpful for one of them to assume the role of the champion for PBS within the school. It is also important for several members to become comfortable serving as coaches to student support teams.

Developing and Enhancing Competencies

Team members develop competencies in behavior supports through preservice and in-service training (workshops, professional meetings, and so forth), reading, and supported practice. The *Positive Strategies* team training project requires teams to participate in formal training, to complete reading assignments and PBS activities between sessions, and to present case studies and continuation plans for their school teams. Training sessions include a review of PBS philosophy,

Table 5. Collective competencies needed for providing *Positive Strategies*

Communicates the philosophical basis and empirical support for positive behavior support
Discusses potential functions of problem behaviors
Conducts functional behavioral assessments (FBAs) using a variety of methods and procedures, including observation, interview, survey, and questionnaire
Assesses the fit between the student and the instructional environment, including skills, preferred activities, and learning style
Conducts hypothesis test to examine the functional assessment hypothesis
Consistent with an FBA, develops a positive behavior intervention plan (BIP) with prevention strategies and a plan to teach functionally equivalent alternative behaviors
Designs behavior management strategies that protect interests of the student and others
Evaluates the effectiveness of the BIP and modifies it accordingly
Ensures that positive changes in behavior generalize across settings and are maintained over time
Possesses a broad range of skills in education, including instructional methods, classroom management, curriculum development, disabilities, cultural competence, and assessment/evaluation

technical and empirical support for PBS methods, and ample dialogue regarding case material. During and after training, *Positive Strategies* trainers provide technical assistance to school teams and buildingwide activities. This may sound exhausting, but each element is important to teams wishing to successfully adopt and continue the approach. Many schoolwide PBS curricula embed training in IPBS within universal models, providing an opportunity for involved staff and faculty to become conversant with principles of prevention and behavior change on several levels.

After completing formal training, many school personnel desire ongoing contact with external supports. Even with reasonable competence in *Positive Strategies,* it can be helpful to have technical assistance and strategic consultation from outside one's school or agency. This enables teams to maintain perspective and commitment to PBS and to obtain advice on challenging cases, observation by outside experts, and updates on methods of assessment and intervention. The *Positive Strategies* team training project, for example, provides ongoing consultation in person, by telephone, and over the Internet.

WHICH STUDENTS ARE RIGHT FOR *POSITIVE STRATEGIES*?

Minimum Standards in the Individuals with Disabilities Education Improvement Act

IDEA'04 lists some circumstances under which schools are compelled to conduct FBAs and BIPs. As Chapter 1 mentions, however, IDEA'04 and its amendments do not stipulate exactly when or how positive supports should be offered. The language regarding FBAs and BIPs refers to classified students whose behaviors impede their own learning or that of others, cause the CSE to consider alternative placement, or lead to disciplinary suspensions totaling more than 10 days. This covers a potentially enormous range of students and behaviors, and yet it is still open to interpretation regarding which students should be the focus of FBAs and BIPs.

In fact, one application of individualized supports mandated under IDEA'04 involves students who have been suspended for more than 10 days or for whom alternative placement is recommended. Elsewhere (Crimmins & Farrell, 2006), we have noted that conducting IPBS for these students is quite challenging; they may have engaged in low-frequency, high-intensity behavior, the kind most likely to result in serious consequences within the school discipline code. If a student is in crisis, out of school, or in a temporary placement, how can a team effectively work to assess and support him or her? After all, IPBS requires careful consideration of contextual issues, and the context may be altered significantly. These situations may require more experienced personnel because of the nature of the problem behavior and the need to adapt IPBS strategies. These unusual situations draw attention to the value of enacting PBS proactively rather than reacting to escalating or entrenched problems.

Broader Use of Positive Supports

Why, then, do we advocate even broader use of positive supports for individual students? We view IDEA'04's guidelines as minimum standards rather than best practices, and we envision using FBAs and BIPs earlier and more frequently than IDEA'04 requires. We also recommend broad use of *Positive Strategies* for students classified with disabilities under IDEA'04 and for those who are not. Although IPBS strategies originated in support of individuals with severe, typically low-incidence disabilities, there is a growing literature (Quinn et al., 2001; Scott et al., 2000) demonstrating their utility for students with mild, high-incidence disabilities, in some cases specifically for students who do not receive special education.

There are good reasons for this. The assessment and intervention technology offered by FBAs and BIPs is highly applicable to students regardless of disability status. Little is saved by restricting these procedures to classified students with the most significant behavior problems; these are the most time- and resource-intensive situations that we confront. Investing resources early is usually returned many times over in better safety, higher rates of learning, and improved morale.

Where to Begin?

New teams, whether or not they are participating in *Positive Strategies* training, often experience pressure to take on the most challenging student first. We advise against doing so for two reasons. First, this is quite frankly too much for any newly formed team. We propose that this student be handled with available procedures, or with an outside consultant, until the team has succeeded with one or two other students. Second, the student with the reputation of having the worst behavior is often in crisis; this often requires a series of short-term fixes that make it far more difficult to conduct the FBA. This student is also generally receiving a fairly high level of support and scrutiny, and others may have somewhat unforgiving attitudes toward him or her. These are obviously difficult systemic challenges for a new team to overcome.

In selecting the first and even the second student for initial efforts, a new team (and its administration) benefits from recognizing the importance of initial success. Because the buildingwide credibility of the team is important, we recommend selecting a student who is widely known but who is not in immediate crisis or jeopardy of losing placement. (This acknowledges the unfortunate reality that our students are usually preceded by their reputations.) These factors provide the team with the time to do its work but also with the knowledge that they have selected a student who warrants the investment of human resources required by the process. Success with a well-known student can convey valuable credibility for the effort, the team, and the methods.

Once the team has worked through the FBA process and successfully implemented an initial *Positive Strategies* BIP, they begin expanding their efforts to address a broader range of concerns. This entails diversifying the student behavior problems the team addresses. There are no rules about which students should receive positive supports, but it is important to establish a plan to extend access to other students and faculty. Expansion is best conducted in conjunction with an assessment of buildingwide concerns (discussed elsewhere in this book) so that systematic prevention, referral, and management procedures can be developed.

WHO SHOULD BE ON THE POSITIVE STRATEGIES TEAM?

The short answer to the question of who should be on the team is any who care and all who matter. Recall that we differentiate the membership of the relatively permanent behavior support workgroup from the student support team. Although we addressed aspects of team membership in the previous sections, in this section we examine the unique contributions brought by each member to either the behavior support workgroup or the student support team.

Parents

Because they experience the consequences for years to come, families are the most important stakeholders in education planning. This is particularly true with regard to behavior problems. Schools' abilities to engage parents in positive supports range from superb to extremely poor, and the reactive cultures of schools tend to complicate parent–school relationships. The responsibility for failure can rest with schools that fail to offer parents meaningful opportunities to participate, with families who resist a school's earnest attempts to involve them, and everything in between.

Although a full discussion of methods to promote meaningful family involvement in education is beyond the current scope of this book, the routine challenges schools face in this regard are amplified when students demonstrate persistent problem behaviors. We have seen circumstances in which communication between the school and family has grown increasingly hostile and contentious. More frequently, there is an established routine in which the school makes multiple contacts with parents about incidents of inappropriate behavior, but few productive collaborative change efforts emerge. The faculty contacting the family may feel that nothing will change, and the parents may experience the contacts as mere complaints about their child. The situation can be very tense if there is a need to discuss crisis intervention, alternative consequences, or change in placement. When there are difficulties in the parent–school relationship, the *Positive Strategies* process is not a panacea, but it can open new lines of communication. Including parents as full members of the student support team can lead to improved relationships between schools and families.

Challenges of Working with Families

For some teams, including parents in the PBS process is a real challenge, albeit an essential one to meet. We see two major reasons that collaboration with families can be challenging. First, family partnerships are most difficult for educators working in schools and classrooms that lack meaningful ongoing communication and collaboration with families. The stress of managing problems and resolving conflicts can be tempered by preexisting lines of communication, particularly if they involve information sharing that does not revolve solely around problems. In the absence of these routine conduits, educators and families are forced to quickly establish working relationships in times of actual or impending crisis. The implication is that healthy home–school communication routines are not only implicitly beneficial, they are a form of relationship building that enhances the work of student support teams.

Second, collaboration with families is difficult for teams inasmuch as members may lack explicit training on this topic. Although the field of disability has a rich literature on family partnerships, it is much less common in the training of educators and related services personnel. Hence, educators may lack the knowledge, skills, and confidence needed to foster effective collaboration. This may pose relatively minor barriers to working with engaged families, but it is likely to present substantial barriers to collaborating with families viewed as less approachable.

Elements of Effective Collaboration with Families

We have identified several team elements that contribute to successful collaboration with parents, including team preparation, family preparation, an atmosphere of shared commitment, cultural and linguistic competence, and a range of acceptable options for family participation.

First, effective collaboration requires adequate preparation by school personnel. Although this optimally entails previous training and experience, many teams lack professionals with such preparation. Nevertheless, most teams can identify one or two members who possess the interpersonal skills, communication style, and empathy to serve as primary liaison(s) with individual families. Effective school teams often make strategic, case-by-case decisions about which member(s) should work most closely and maintain contact with parents. Considerations include past encounters with the family, the nature of the behavior problem, consequences to date, and the match between family characteristics and the specific styles and expertise of team members.

Second, working effectively with families requires planning with them and helping them prepare. Although collaboration implies working toward shared objectives, a partnership involves the recognition that each member is of equal value. This does not require equivalence in the type of expertise but, rather, equivalence in each member's ability to share the expertise and resources he or she does possess.

Because they are not formal members of the school system, families sometimes come to the process with little explicit knowledge about policies, routines, and processes. Effective teams acknowledge this and provide parents with the information they need to participate as informed team members. This involves time and consideration. Teams who wish to engage meaningfully with families should prepare them in advance through individual contacts. For example, when calling parents to invite them to a meeting, the liaison should share the agenda, clarify the family's role, and explain how the family members might ready themselves. Possessing information helps many families feel in control and prepared to collaborate.

Third, a healthy team process provides a framework for shared responsibility and cooperation in addressing problem behavior. If the team is working well, the parent is joining a group with a visible shared commitment to developing solutions. This is a markedly different atmosphere than the one often present in meetings to inform parents about behavior problems. When parents understand that the team is not seeking to blame the child (and, by extension, the family), they are less likely to feel threatened or defensive. Recognizing that problem behavior is functional helps the entire team focus on positive alternatives. This is almost always consistent with family aspirations.

The fourth element of effective family collaboration concerns cultural and linguistic competence. Effective teams appreciate the challenges faced by racial, cultural, and linguistic minorities and make ongoing efforts to recognize, respect, and reflect the values and preferences of the family in their discussions and plans. This may involve minor accommodations such as adapting communication style to scheduling meetings in keeping with family schedules, or more substantial efforts may be required (such as obtaining a translator or working closely with the family to encourage empowerment).

Finally, successful team collaboration involves careful consideration of family roles. Effective teams offer a range of acceptable options for family participation. Just as each student presents uniquely, so does each family. Accordingly, there is no one right way for families to collaborate, and flexibility is key. In some cases, families are involved in the FBA process and are kept informed throughout, but they do not participate in meetings. In other cases, parents are present and actively participate each step of the way. We have collaborated with families who were working with mental health, medical, and education providers outside the school. In those cases, teams often found it helpful to offer the family the option of including those individuals or consulting with them. Consistent with basic tenets of PBS, we favor wide inclusion of stakeholders who may help realize or generalize the gains of the BIP. Less important than the amount of time parents spend with other team members is the team's ability to maintain ongoing consideration of the family's perspective.

When schools successfully engage parents as members of student support teams, benefits accrue to all stakeholders. These benefits extend beyond the immediate challenge of reducing problem behavior in school. By virtue of family participation, parents and educators may develop a shared vision for the child, effectively translate that vision into an action plan, and achieve gains across contexts (home, school, community). The collaboration itself has the potential to nurture trust between family and school and may decrease the likelihood of arbitration or litigation. In addition, all team members may feel better prepared to manage similar challenges in the future.

Teachers

Teachers have perhaps the most obvious motivation to reduce problem behavior in the classroom. The costs of problem behavior, discussed earlier, have the most direct impact on classroom staff. Whether they are members of the general education or special education staff, teachers are primarily responsible for instruction, a responsibility that is superseded by the need to ensure the safety of all students. Teachers are thus compelled to respond to problem behavior, both in the immediate sense and also via plans for managing future occurrences.

Teacher Roles

General and special education teachers have two essential roles within the *Positive Strategies* approach. These roles are not mutually exclusive and evolve over time.

The first role is as the teacher of a student who is the focus of an FBA. As a member of the student support team, this teacher is involved throughout the process, from the initial referral to the implementation and monitoring of the BIP. Within the school, teachers often have a great deal of ongoing contact with identified students and maintain responsibility for their instruction. By virtue of this, the teacher may have an established relationship with the student's family. In the best of circumstances, this consists of ongoing, healthy communication, on which other team members can build.

During the FBA, the teacher collects data, participates in interviews, completes questionnaires, and assists in designing and carrying out follow-up assessments. Without this input, it is virtually impossible to develop a legitimate understanding of why behavior problems persist.

When the BIP is developed, the teacher offers an essential perspective on which strategies are practical and likely to be effective for the student.

The second role for the teacher is as peer mentor, coach, and leader. Teachers who are trained and experienced in PBS possess important knowledge that can be leveraged to the advantage of colleagues. Valuable contributions include facilitating the planning process for less experienced teachers and providing input to multiple student support teams. The experienced teacher sometimes emerges as a schoolwide champion whose input regarding positive supports is sought through both formal (e.g., member of behavior support workgroup, or coach for a student support team) and informal means. As mentioned earlier, teachers sometimes begin this role as individual members of a student support team and assume leadership as they accumulate experience conducting FBAs and implementing BIPs. Such experienced teachers become highly valued coaches who can provide advice and consultation to student support teams.

Teaching Assistants and Aides

Other stakeholders to the IPBS process are teaching assistants and aides, sometimes referred to as paraprofessionals. We find that their input and team membership are sometimes overlooked, first because they often lack formal credentials, and second because of the outgoing need for these individuals to provide direct support to the student. Neglecting the input of the aide puts the team at a disadvantage not only in terms of collecting reliable information but also in ensuring that the team considers the practical advantages and constraints associated with intervention. Participation by paraprofessionals on the student support team has the additional advantage of establishing ownership in the findings of the FBA and the recommended course of action of the BIP.

Functions of the Paraprofessional

Paraprofessionals assigned to students with behavior problems often spend more time with the student than anyone else on the team. Their explicit role may be to minimize the number and impact of behavior problems. Ideally, the paraprofessional is amply supported in this role. We have, however, seen the misuse of one-to-one aides, whose de facto role is to serve as a buffer between the included student and typical peers. In this sense, the aide is expected to do what is necessary to minimize the student's disruptive effects on others, but that effort may not involve careful consideration of the student's social or instructional concerns. Whereas individualized supports ideally bridge the gap between students with disabilities and their peers, the aide as buffer effectively widens it. Because aides lack formal credentials and status within the system, they may not feel empowered to express concern about this.

A related function of the aide is as expert interpreter for the child. In this case, the aide who spends the bulk of the day with the student may recognize the child's cues and be adept at translating the child's attempts to communicate. The aide may also have a range of effective strategies to support coping efforts and de-escalation. Although the presence of such a resourceful and effective support is wonderful, there are occasions when it presents a disadvantage. Problems may emerge when this individual is absent, reassigned, or otherwise unavailable. In essence, this paraprofessional or teaching assistant has become a mini-support system on which the child and the rest of the team depend. A truly effective plan does not rely on a single individual. Under these circumstances, the aide's input is crucial to valid completion of the FBA. Knowing the conditions under which the student gets it right is just as important as identifying which factors increase the likelihood of problem behavior. The strategies the paraprofessional uses may eventually serve as components of the intervention, but this cannot be accomplished without the aide's participation. As such, it is critically important to include the paraprofessional as a member.

Roles of Paraprofessionals

Because they have to deal immediately with problem behavior, aides are often in the position of developing ad hoc behavior plans. In response to challenging behavior, they may separate the student from the group, require an apology, or present some other consequence. Although these reactions are sometimes effective, they may also inadvertently maintain persistent behavior problems. Participation in the student support team maximizes the likelihood that the paraprofessional will recognize this and seek to remedy it. Engaging the aide as a legitimate team member may motivate change more effectively than a directive from other, more involved personnel. Involving the aide in the FBA and BIP process often improves morale and can result in new skills and knowledge that can benefit future students and teams.

Including paraprofessional staff on the student support team assures that the process reflects this individual's wealth of observation, mobilizes change, and contributes meaningfully to an understanding of both effective and ineffective management approaches. Aides who spend hours observing children daily are perfectly situated to conduct several activities associated with the FBA. If paraprofessionals cannot regularly attend team meetings, their input is, nevertheless, critical. Team leaders can accomplish this by planning and preparing the aide's direct participation and by in-person follow-up and support. Direct input may lend the process a sense of personal ownership and responsibility, which may lead to better outcomes for all involved.

Related Services Providers

The behavior support workgroup is usually multidisciplinary, including two or three individuals from the related services staff: school psychologist, social worker, guidance counselor, educational evaluator, speech-language pathologist, occupational therapist, physical therapist, and so on. These individuals bring valued expertise to the team and may also serve buildingwide roles in PBS.

Recruiting Related Services Providers

It is helpful to recruit members of the buildingwide workgroup and the student support team based on several attributes, not solely on the basis of profession or discipline. For instance, although a school psychologist's training is more likely to include behavior assessment and management, this individual may have a limited amount of time to commit to the process. In this case, it may be more effective for a social worker or guidance counselor to serve on the team, calling on the psychologist as a consultant when needed. Alternatively, an assistive technology specialist may be a key member of a student support team for a child whose disabilities make it challenging to develop replacement behaviors involving communication. Although it is obviously important to involve staff who know the student well, it can also be useful to recruit other staff and faculty who can approach the problem from new perspectives.

Roles of Related Services Providers

Related services staff bring unique personal and professional perspectives to assessment and planning. First, they frequently have specific and unique expertise in assessment and intervention approaches. Second, they come from outside the classroom, which means that they are not generally part of the ongoing response to the behavior in question. They can visit the classroom without having to focus on lesson plans, preparation of materials, or group management. In many cases, this provides an opportunity for feedback on teacher–student interactions and on the clarity and objectivity of observations. Providers who typically work one on one with the student can observe the problem behavior in a different context, and those without prior acquaintance with the child contribute a fresh set of observations. Finally, because these related services providers are often called on to deal with problem behaviors throughout the school, they usually have a vested interest in achieving the goals of PBS interventions. As such, they may also be recruited as members of the behavior support workgroup and as coaches to student support teams.

Administrators

Other stakeholders who are often members of both buildingwide and student-directed efforts are school administrators. Although their efforts often focus on discipline and enforcement, key contributions to the team relate more to the administrator's responsibility for program supervision and coordination. Implementation of behavior management efforts may not fall squarely in the job duties of the administrator; however, persistent behavior problems, growing parent worry, and extended classroom disruptions quickly become administrative concerns. Because of this, there is a natural fit between team concerns and administrative interests, and both can be served by effective use of PBS.

Administrative Team Members

Schools often have little choice about which administrator becomes a member of the behavior support workgroup. This is often determined by the size of the school and the allocation of responsibility for discipline. If one has the luxury of choice among several administrators, we recommend considering factors besides job assignment or position title. Such factors include motivation, flexibility, experience, and ability to work toward consensus. Successful teams tend to have administrative members who can adapt their leadership style to collaborative teaming.

Another consideration in selecting an administrator is that person's role power: specifically, their position in the school's chain of command or table of organization. Although it is not necessary for this person to have autonomous decision-making authority, effective teams have administrators who are well respected, have the confidence of and access to higher administration, and possess a record of decisive action regarding resource allocation.

Administrative Roles

There are two major dimensions of team activity in which administrative support is essential: allocation of resources and supporting team efforts.

First, for *Positive Strategies* teams to be effective, assigned staff members need adequate time for assessment, planning, and implementation. Administrative support is crucial to ensure that time and meeting space are available and that PBS activities are assigned as a priority in the team members' job duties. This entails troubleshooting staff schedules and assigning alternative staff when student support team members require separate time for meetings and other PBS-related activities.

Second, because *Positive Strategies* emphasizes behavior in context, intervention plans may involve changes in the environment, the student's IEP, or even a policy exception or modification. The presence of an administrator on the team increases the likelihood of a clear and defensible rationale for these recommendations, which is critical if they come under scrutiny. In cases in which a modification is not approved, a skilled administrator may identify alternative ways to achieve the same goal.

SHARED CHARACTERISTICS OF EFFECTIVE TEAM MEMBERS

Besides the qualifications and perspectives of individual team members, there is another set of considerations that contributes equally to the likelihood of success. Particularly when *Positive Strategies* is newly introduced, it is helpful to recruit participants based on their personal characteristics and potential for good chemistry as a group. Table 6 lists member characteristics that are likely to contribute to team success.

This is clearly an idealized list—we wish all our colleagues had each of these attributes. We know, however, that teams go through different stages of development and that maximizing these characteristics is helpful as teams get together, begin working, struggle with the process, and need to communicate successes to their colleagues.

As suggested by our earlier comparison of teams with families, we understand that schools often lack control in the selection of team members. We offer this list as a starting point and recommend that teams use it as a self-study mechanism. Open discussion of these attributes can lead to individual self-evaluation and constructive feedback and can help establish a milieu in which forthright discussion is accepted and welcomed. In some cases, teams who are struggling because they lack some of these characteristics can benefit from training and consultation focused specifically on team functioning and group dynamics.

Table 6. Characteristics of effective team members

Flexible, adaptable, open to change
Effective communicators
Committed to quality educational outcomes for all students
Task oriented
Effective problem solvers
Resilient
Willing to evaluate their own and the team's performance
Accountable to each other, the student, and the larger school community
Supportive and respectful of each other
Respected by members of the school and community

COACHES

Coaches for student support teams need to demonstrate expertise in PBS and possess key personal characteristics that promote working partnerships. Hanft, Rush, and Sheldon (2004) describe five qualities of effective coaches that are easily recognized by colleagues and families: competency, objectivity, adaptability, caring, and honesty. We review them briefly here in relation to school teams. Of course, these traits are welcome in all team members, but coaches who exemplify these characteristics are especially valued.

Teams look to coaches for expertise and assistance in problem solving. As such, the coach's competency encourages teachers, related service providers, administrators, and families to approach them when they desire information, skill development, and support. Effective coaches help members recognize their own skills and knowledge and encourage ongoing development. To some extent, the coach is placed in the role of facilitator or mentor, always promoting reflection and self-discovery.

Second, effective coaches are objective. They understand and acknowledge that team members approach problems with unique perspectives, experiences, values, and biases. The effective coach clarifies these issues in fair, nonthreatening ways, always focusing the team's efforts toward effective supports for students with problems that can be very frustrating. The coach bases conclusions and actions on data, effectively resolving apparent discrepancies within and across contexts. An objective stance toward the student and the problem behavior makes for more accurate assessments and more effective interventions.

A third characteristic of effective coaching is adaptability. Although teams may invest time and energy in their plans and roles, the coach models flexibility, particularly when faced with the need to modify plans on the basis of new information. Coaches also model role release by volunteering to conduct activities outside their defined professional roles (e.g., cover the one-to-one aide's role for a period of time to provide a break and better understand that person's role) and demonstrating interest in learning *from* others. Enacting *Positive Strategies* requires adaptability from all members of the team. The coach can support this through modeling and by advocating for flexibility within school structures.

Fourth, effective coaches are caring, as demonstrated through a commitment to principles of student-centered planning (outlined earlier in this book). The effective coach demonstrates warmth, empathy, and encouragement to all members, exemplifying the ideals of collaborative partnerships. Caring implies a nondefensive stance, even under stress, and a sincere desire to support the achievements of students and fellow team members.

Finally, good coaching requires honest, forthright communication. Effective coaches provide constructive feedback and criticism in an accepting manner. Coaches set the tone for an effective process of reflection by modeling fair and direct appraisal of team efforts. Direct communication refrains from protective withholding (sometimes referred to as protective dishonesty); this refers to the tendency to avoid discussion of difficult matters based on the rationale that the individual(s) cannot handle or tolerate a more forthright approach.

In addition to these key qualities, effective coaches possess a number of the general characteristics outlined in Table 6, have a wide repertoire of skills in the areas of collaboration and mentoring, and are experienced and expert in *Positive Strategies.*

FINDING THE TIME

Team meetings, collecting and interpreting data, and developing plans each require a significant investment of staff time. With all the academic demands of the school setting, it can be difficult to appropriate the resources necessary to implement PBS, regardless of how effective research has shown it to be. Although we clearly support explicit time allocations, we also wish to remind the reader of a misconception about the total time investment required for PBS. A student whose behavior problems are significant enough to prompt the formation of a team is already consuming a considerable amount of staff time and energy. The challenge of PBS involves devoting resources proactively instead of reactively; there is really no question that staff will continue to spend time on the student's behavior. Engaging in PBS rarely takes more time over the long run.

To be proactive, it is necessary to protect the time team members need to devote to obtain accurate and valid results. Administrative support is usually crucial in making sure that time and meeting space are available and in assuring that PBS activities receive sufficient priority in the team members' job responsibilities.

How much time is needed? As a rule of thumb, we initially advise teams to commit at least as much time conducting an FBA as they are already spending on the problem behavior. If they are spending 2 hours each week in managing a behavior, they are likely to need that much time in assessing the behavior and carrying out an intervention plan. When the team begins the FBA, it may even require a temporary increase in the amount of time staff spend on the student. Even very competent teams will not achieve immediate, lasting results when addressing a problem behavior that may have been years in formation.

Reviewing the literature on FBAs, we examined the amount of time school teams working in partnership with expert researchers required, from approximately 3 days to about 20 days (Crimmins & Farrell, 2006). Most reports suggest that teams interspersed their FBA activities over time, such that observations conducted during a period of 15 days might involve a total of 22–25 hours. Kern and colleagues (2004) reviewed 20 published reports and concluded that the variability in problem behavior and team approaches makes it impossible to estimate with confidence how much time an FBA requires.

No matter how much time is required, an effective plan often means that the staff recoups much of the time they invested in the FBA and BIP. Teams often develop accelerated approaches for new or resurgent behaviors. In addition to devoting resources to assembling a behavior support workgroup and establishing procedures, schools just beginning formal PBS efforts also find that these activities require more time at the outset. In Chapter 5, we illustrate how context interacts with aspects of the behavior problem in considering FBAs of varying complexity and the resulting BIPs. Because there is not one right way to conduct an FBA or BIP, there is no standard method for getting it just right.

Most importantly, when the process is effective, there is a shift in how available time is used. Instead of engaging in interactions that might be confrontational, frustrating, and offering little hope of improvement, *Positive Strategies* fosters interactions that are more constructive. Success in this regard can lead to improved job satisfaction for the staff, better working relationships with families, and improved learning and quality of life for the student. Diminishing disruptive behaviors improves the learning environment for all stakeholders.

USING THE TIME

Finding the time for *Positive Strategies* teams is difficult, yet crucial. Equally important is using the time well. Team leaders and members face competing time pressures and duties, so efficient, effective time management determines how team activities are valued. Meandering meetings that accomplish little may detract substantially from motivation and effective action on behalf of students. Advance preparation by team members increases the likelihood that meetings will involve productive discussion, result in decision making, and aid the development of action plans.

Team meetings should be time limited (clear start and end time), adhere to a schedule or agenda, and involve a facilitator (often the leader or coach) who is implicitly responsible for maintaining the pace of the meeting. The leader needs to be skilled in effectively reconciling different perspectives. This does not assume that the leader's contribution is of superior value to those of other team members; rather, it recognizes the practical reality that teams can be sidetracked. Disagreements often emerge over details, and healthy teams learn how to reach consensus despite diverging views.

CONTEXTUAL FACTORS IN INDIVIDUALIZED POSITIVE BEHAVIOR SUPPORT

Because context is so crucial to the process of PBS, it necessarily influences many aspects of a team's composition, activities, and roles. Contextual factors include features of the student, the environment in which problem behaviors occur, the other settings in which the child functions, and the various physical and sensory characteristics, supports, pressures, challenges and advantages that these settings offer. The settings in which we've conducted *Positive Strategies* range from early intervention programs for toddlers to community residences for adults with developmental disabilities. Settings differ along several dimensions, including age, grade, and developmental level; community features (urban, suburban, rural); education model (from inclusion with push-in or pull-out related services to special education classes in which all students have disabilities); and the organization's history of behavior management and behavior support.

Each of these features influences the demands on school personnel, the resources available to teachers and students, and the ways in which student support teams assemble and function. Although we have alluded to several of these dimensions already, in this section, we briefly review some team considerations based on educational level. Because the underlying assumptions about behavior are fairly universal, unique aspects of the setting tend to be more influential in determining team activities than are the specific characteristics of the problem behavior. The best interventions consider multiple features and are informed by contemporary instructional (pedagogic) methods.

Early Childhood Programs

Like other education programs, toddler and preschool classrooms use curricula; however, learning frequently occurs in very small groups through structured activity and play, with teachers acting as both facilitators and nurturers. In contrast to emphasis on adult-led instruction and behavioral control in elementary school, current trends in early intervention (e.g., Bricker, Pretti-Frontczak, & McComas, 1998) stress child-initiated interactions and natural activities. Early childhood settings include special education programs, inclusive settings (designed to support children with and without disabilities learning together), and typical nursery schools (mainstream or natural settings in which some students with disabilities may be enrolled).

Regardless of educational model, the early childhood setting tends to focus primarily on the developmental concerns of children across developmental domains, with more explicit emphasis on adaptive function skills and self-regulation abilities than one finds in elementary and secondary education programs. Because effective early childhood programs embrace the centrality of family in the lives of young children, they tend to engage in ongoing contact with families. This is facilitated by the fact that parents, especially in inclusive settings, may have regular direct contact with the program (e.g., the opportunity for daily contact at drop-off and pick-up).

Children with disabilities in early childhood programs experience a range of education models quite similar to that seen in elementary schools. Frequently, the teacher and aides collaborate with one or more related services providers to form a small team. Special education and related services are either embedded in typical classroom activities or are delivered in one-to-one or small-group sessions. Although the actual involvement of parents in planning for the child's program may vary considerably, most programs recognize the central role of parents and structure their services to provide regular communication with the family. Because of this, existing lines of home–school communication can serve as a foundation for meaningful family participation in a student support team.

Optimally, early childhood programs demonstrate flexibility in approaching and accommodating the diverse range of developmental skills and temperamental features. This flexibility can be advantageous to the student support team, which will experience a corresponding array of approaches to the FBA and BIP. On the other hand, the everchanging demands of serving very young children can make it quite challenging to complete the activities associated with *Positive Strategies.* As such, careful planning and allocation of resources is essential. Early childhood teams need to be well acquainted with developmental expectations, possess an understanding of disability issues, and have a range of strategies for modeling, teaching, coaching, and reinforcing self-regulation and prosocial behavior.

Because of the potential to prevent the development of intractable behavior problems, we strongly advocate the use of positive supports in early childhood. Depending on the setting, early childhood teams may be constituted very similarly to those serving older children, although the involvement of the family is, perhaps, more crucial. Explicit and active family participation in planning increases the likelihood of success in clarifying developmental expectations and socializing children to accept nonpreferred activities. This requires fortifying the child's ability to follow the routines and rules of the early childhood setting and requires that the parents and child accept that congregate care necessitates occasions when choice of activity or timing is not an option. Although we almost always prefer finding and offering choice, we also acknowledge that becoming socialized to education also means tolerating the demands of schedules and transitions. Within these parameters, there are often small but meaningful opportunities for adults to offer choices that encourage self-regulation and adaptive behavior.

Elementary Schools

Within the elementary school, the organizational focus is the individual classroom, where teachers are responsible for the students within their classes. Providing supports through *Positive Strategies* involves connecting a primary teacher with members of the ongoing behavior support workgroup to evaluate and plan for the individual child.

Early in elementary school, classrooms tend to be more child- and developmentally focused than they are in the later grades. Relative to early childhood programs, kindergarten and first grade represent the shift from a developmental focus to an academic one, which is typically accompanied by a decreasing acceptance of temperamental and behavioral diversity. With each passing year, there is an ever greater focus on academic instruction and achievement, to the degree that many elementary educators are reluctant to invest significant efforts in the behavioral regulation and social functioning of their students. As a result, it becomes increasingly difficult to convince elementary school staff that coaching in skills related to social and emotional functioning should take place within the school. The earlier elementary years focus to some extent on the process of learning these skills, but by about second or third grade, the focus tends to shift to the content of instruction, as exemplified in the expression "from learning to read to reading to learn."

Education occurs in a social milieu, and all elementary school teachers spend time socializing children to changing demands. When problem behaviors emerge from children's skill impairments, educators have the option of maintaining a reactive stance or investing proactively in teaching alternatives. (This relates to our discussion in Chapter 1 about the reactive stance of schools as a challenge to implementing *Positive Strategies.*) Teachers who manage their classrooms effectively offer children explicit behavioral guidance and manage to provide individualized supports to selected children. Some strategies employed in classrooms exemplify the preventive approaches emphasized in schoolwide and universal supports, including the notion of engaging students as a means of prevention.

When elementary classrooms are more reactive in stance, it can be difficult to shift from short-term intervention to long-term planning and support. As discussed earlier, comprehensive district policies, effective school leadership, and teacher advocacy can be tremendously helpful in securing resources in support of positive behavior interventions. The dynamics and challenges of organizing teams and conducting *Positive Strategies* tend to be relatively straightforward at the elementary level.

Middle and Junior High Schools

At the middle school level, most students have multiple teachers, perhaps a homeroom or primary teacher, and several subject instructors. Children usually change classes throughout the day. As a result, there may not be a clear leader among the student's instructors, and in some cases there exists a diffusion of responsibility that can make managing behavior more difficult. In the latter cases, accessible buildingwide behavior support workgroups can be extremely helpful. Such a workgroup reviews the referral, then collaborates with and likely coaches the student support team as it conducts the FBA and plans and implements the BIP. Workgroup leadership can be important in securing resources for the team, negotiating and sharing duties among instructors, and managing attitudinal and stylistic differences among the instructional group.

We have worked with a number of middle school programs, both in developing formal case studies and in short-term consultation. Despite challenges presented by the setting, many middle school teams are quite successful in conducting FBAs and implementing BIPs that provide children with valuable alternatives to problem behavior. One important advantage that contributes to effective implementation of *Positive Strategies* is that many middle and junior high school staffs already work in multidisciplinary teams. Staff members may work together to address the concerns of the students on their team or house. This can provide a forum to assemble staff for meetings and allows a framework within which the teachers take responsibility for the student's support concerns. It also provides a structure within which ownership of the problem can lead to creative and divergent solutions.

High Schools

At the high school level, class assignments and teacher responsibilities are typically shifted to a departmental model. With the exception of programs designed primarily for students with significant disabilities, programs usually relate to individual disciplines (e.g., English, math, science, physical education) rather than to multidisciplinary teams. As a result, the teaching staff rarely works in ongoing teams. Barriers such as logistical difficulties and diffusion of responsibility may be substantial. At this level, teaching staff may have greater reluctance or even resentment when asked to address the self-regulation and social-skills concerns of students. Given the many demands facing them, they are focused predominantly on providing quality instruction for those students who are ready to participate; supporting students who are resistant to social or academic expectations is generally a far lower priority. In addition, challenges that are present in the middle school or junior high environment may be magnified by the sheer number of students attending high school.

Although all of this can present formidable challenges to the *Positive Strategies* process, there are still convincing reasons for using this approach. First, school personnel are responsible for dealing with behavior problems that impact the safety and effective operation of the school environment; some responses are mandated under IDEA'04. When behavior problems rise to this level, staff are often motivated to engage in crisis management efforts. In this instance, continuing engagement may be more challenging, especially if faculty question (either privately or publicly) the appropriateness of the student's placement. It is essential to address these questions explicitly, to use the team time efficiently, and to outline a prompt course of action. Once this has been done, ongoing coordination by the core behavior support workgroup is crucial.

Other complicating factors at this level are peer and out-of-school influences. Although students of all ages experience them, out-of-school influences can be more persuasive for high school students. Families of younger students often mediate some of these pressures. Assuming that a family or home setting is not directly contributing to the behavior, school personnel often work with the family to pursue community resources and supports. For many high school students, however, the student is in the process of making the transition to more independence within the community. Behavior problems can be exacerbated not only by family issues, but also by peer pressures such as experimentation with alcohol and substances, association with students engaging in antisocial behavior, and the many other social pressures associated with adolescence. An effective student support team considers these influences and assigns them appropriate prominence in the FBA and BIP.

HOME AS A CONTEXT FACTOR IN POSITIVE SUPPORTS

Discussions within school teams often turn to the dynamics of the relationship between home and school. Sometimes this is prompted by concerns about a problematic home environment in which the child encounters stress as a result of socioeconomic challenges or other family problems. At other times, the discussion reflects frustration over the perception that family efforts to address behavior problems are inconsistent with school-based plans or are thought to be totally lacking. In some cases, the school staff struggle with the parents' perceptions that the former are not doing their job to manage behavior. This may be hinted at through reports that the child is not presenting behavior problems at home, or it may be directly expressed via a parent's statements about the team's responses to date.

Ideally, effective working relationships with families exist when teams set out to evaluate behavior and develop BIPs. As discussed earlier, family involvement enriches the FBA by offering alternative contexts within which to examine behavior. Parents contribute to school-based assessment with data on factors that might influence the child's mood and readiness to participate in school on a given day. Families can support and implement skill development efforts. School–family collaboration permits the development of additional supports outside the school environment. If they are well coordinated, these efforts can only improve intervention.

There may be discrepant perspectives among school teams and the student's family, even when parents and teachers approach both education and behavior management with a collaborative attitude. After all, we recognize and accept that informed, reasoning adults are likely to bring a variety of different perspectives, values, and opinions to an issue. This is part of the rationale for establishing a student support team with diverse members to conduct the FBA in the first place. The challenge is to recognize and accept reasonable differences between school personnel and parents, communicate as clearly as possible about these issues, and use the benefits that derive from multiple perspectives.

Along with this difference in perspective, it is also important to recognize that the home and school are very different environments, each with diverse expectations and varying supports. Because *Positive Strategies* focuses heavily on environmental influences on behavior, acknowledging differences across context is especially important. It is tempting to conclude that discrepancies in the frequency and intensity of problem behaviors across contexts are attributable primarily to the *consequences* the settings offer. The *demands* of those settings, however, are equally likely to contribute to the occurrence of problem behaviors. Each school day demands several hours of a student's attention, compliance, autonomy (as appropriate for age) and focus; the home environment rarely comes close to taxing the child's self-regulation capacity that heavily. PBS stresses the importance of equal consideration of contextual factors (instructional demands or methods, task difficulties) and behavioral contingencies (environmental consequences for behavior). This reflects the assumption that disruptive or other problem behaviors may correspond more to the setting than to the consequences enacted by the adults who are present. Snell (2006) argues that a disproportionate effort tends to be placed on consequential approaches, when altering problem contexts may be more effective in reducing some problem behaviors.

Sometimes behavior problems are fairly consistent across settings. When teams begin conducting FBAs in these cases, parents may hope that difficulties that are being resolved at school will also improve at home. Similarly, school personnel express reservations about investing time and energy without reassurance that a plan will be implemented consistently at home. We often find these concerns unfounded because of the significant role that environment has on behavior and because of the amount of attention and supervision available to support students at home and school. When the concerns are founded, they are best addressed by direct collaboration and ongoing contact between the family and the team. Understanding the function of the problem behavior in various settings can lead to effective solutions that ease such concerns.

There also are a relatively small number of students with a high level of need that extends across all settings—home, school, and community. Teams working with these students may have to consider a more intensive model of wrap-around supports, whereby planning is coordinated among school personnel, family members, and community agencies.

The home context as a contributor to both problem behaviors and effective solutions underscores the need for active, working relationships with families. The value of working in teams derives from multiple perspectives, collective advocacy, pooled talents, and the shared burdens and rewards resulting from it. Collaborating with colleagues, families, and students to achieve a shared vision is an indispensable step toward improving student outcomes and, ultimately, quality of life.

Chapter 5

Introduction to Functional Behavioral Assessments and Behavior Intervention Plans

The core tasks of *Positive Strategies* are to *understand* problem behavior, *prevent* it when possible, and *replace* it with alternatives that serve the student now and in the future. These steps are implemented in two major phases: conducting the FBA and implementing the BIP. This chapter provides an overview of how teams prepare for and complete these activities, outlining the sequence of steps in which FBAs and BIPs are undertaken. Chapters 6 and 7 detail the steps involved in each. This chapter also reviews the common underlying elements of FBAs and BIPs and raises issues for teams to consider in planning. We remind readers of the assumptions of *Positive Strategies* and of how these assumptions drive the important work involved in supporting students, framing the philosophy of *Positive Strategies* in relation to its actual elements. We conclude this chapter with the stories of three students for whom teams developed FBAs and BIPs.

Because our methods derive fundamentally from applied behavioral analysis (ABA), many of its essential principles underlie *Positive Strategies* activities. This includes the inextricable link between assessment and intervention. Although we present and discuss the FBA and BIP in sequence, we also assume that assessment is ongoing and that teams are prepared to track the occurrence of problem behaviors and the use of alternative behaviors throughout the *Positive Strategies* process.

ADDRESSING PROBLEM BEHAVIOR REQUIRES A TEAM APPROACH

In Chapter 4, we stressed that the positive outcomes of *Positive Strategies* teamwork are most effectively accomplished with ample training, support, and preparation. We also reviewed characteristics of successful teams. Although it is certainly preferable for teams to embark on their first student support initiatives after extensive preparation, teams sometimes develop naturally out of efforts to support individual students. Under those circumstances, formal and informal team practices and standards may develop.

Both new and experienced teams that hope for success engage in thoughtful review of their prior activities. Teams do this to avoid repeating errors, such as communication problems, resource shortages, and inadequate follow-through, as well as considering how they can further develop and refine their skills. Errors and oversights in one student's support plan are important vehicles for performance improvement that can result in better planning for the next. Through each step of the process, successful teams pay attention to the allocation of resources and assignment of work. Without clear communication, responsibility, and accountability, *Positive Strategies* efforts have limited chance for success.

The effectiveness of behavioral interventions also depends on the fidelity with which they are implemented. This refers to the extent to which the intervention effort is faithful to the specifics of the BIP, and to the ABA principles in general. An intervention that is not enacted according to plan might produce results that are less than satisfactory. Successful teams do more than formulate good plans; they also monitor their efforts for reliability and fidelity to ensure consistency with those plans.

PROBLEM BEHAVIOR IS FUNCTIONAL

Because *Positive Strategies* assumes that challenging behaviors are functional, developing and testing a hypothesis about function are central team activities. Effective BIPs emerge when teams engage in thoughtful, valid, and complete assessment activities before designing interventions. A good BIP depends on valid assessment of the function of behavior.

Reliability and validity are also essential to good FBAs. Reliability refers to how consistent or replicable assessments are, or how accurately they represent what is actually happening in the student's life. For example, two simultaneous observations are perfectly reliable when they result in the exact same frequency counts and prompt identical conclusions about the antecedents and consequences. Obtaining reliability requires teams to observe and record behavior under fairly typical circumstances—for instance, during the same activities, with the same individuals present, and at same time of day that problems most often occur.

For assessments to be reliable, all observers must share a common definition of the problem in behavioral terms and engage in multiple observations of behavior. *Positive Strategies* does not require teams to complete perfect assessments, but an accurate determination of function requires sampling an adequate number of behavioral incidents. The team should feel that the number and quality of observations reflects the typical ways in which the behavior occurs. When this is done well, various team members draw similar independent conclusions about the relationship between the behavior and the environment.

A reliable FBA has a good chance of being valid. When it is consistent and accurate, the FBA does a good job of explaining the circumstances surrounding the problem behavior. Consistent, accurate, and diverse assessment methods each add to the likelihood that the FBA will lead to an effective plan for change. If any of these elements are subtracted, the potential effectiveness of the FBA diminishes. The best FBAs involve multiple observations but different observers across contexts, using various methods to collect information.

A reliable and valid FBA is essential to developing a successful intervention plan. Occasionally, when teams test hypotheses, they discover that the original hypothesis holds true only for some instances of behavior. They might then develop and test an alternative hypothesis regarding a second function the behavior serves. Although this adds to their work, the team completes the FBA phase with a reliable (consistent and accurate) and valid (explaining the behavior adequately and making sense to all involved) set of hypotheses. From there, the team decides which instances of the behavior to prioritize for intervention, whether the behavior can be prevented, and what replacement skills are relevant under each condition.

PROBLEM BEHAVIOR EMERGES IN CONTEXT

Because problem behavior emerges in context, FBAs and BIPs are best carried out in the same settings as the problem: the classroom, the playground, the gym, the cafeteria, and so forth. The team observes problem behavior in context to understand how it relates to the specific demands present in the environment and to determine the consequences that follow it. In vivo observation is unmatched in terms of the rich data it provides about the student and the context. The

FBA, done in the actual setting, can also clarify skill impairments that contribute to challenging behavior. The BIP includes specific methods for teaching and reinforcing new alternatives, again in the natural context. This requires team members to consider how others in the environment will respond when the student does something unpredictable.

There are two broad exceptions to the general rule that *Positive Strategies* activities are undertaken in the same context as the problem behavior. In the first case, an FBA cannot be performed in context for a student who is no longer in school. Some students with problem behaviors are suspended or assigned to alternate placements. Under these circumstances, the team relies on reviews of available records, interviews with knowledgeable informants, and direct interaction with the student in the alternate setting. Viewing the child out of context places the team at a disadvantage and illustrates the importance of initiating the FBA before a crisis emerges. In some cases, teams have to assess children out of context to plan for the child's return. This often requires assessing behavior in the alternative setting, doing an independent appraisal of the placement to which the child is supposed to return, and considering the information together.

Other *Positive Strategies* activities sometimes occur out of context. These include initial instruction and coaching in replacement skills (e.g., social, communication, and self-regulation skills) in a counseling office or other private area. Other than these preparatory activities and team meetings, FBA and BIP activities occur principally in the same settings as problem behaviors.

REDUCING PROBLEM BEHAVIOR REQUIRES INCREASING ALTERNATIVE BEHAVIORS

The first phase of *Positive Strategies,* the FBA, helps the team *understand* why behavior persists. With this information, the BIP identifies how to *prevent* the problem behavior and effectively *replace* it.

Developing replacement behaviors requires that teams possess a range of competencies surpassing those of any single discipline; indeed, as later examples demonstrate, this often requires close collaboration among several team members and, potentially, the need to consult with external sources. For example, a student's BIP may call for social skills, anger management, or another form of self-regulation training, but the student support team may lack expertise in these areas. In such cases, the team may need to consult the professional literature or recruit a coach to assist them in developing an instructional plan for these alternative skills.

CONTINGENCIES HAVE A PLACE IN POSITIVE BEHAVIOR SUPPORT

By developing replacement behaviors, teams hope to discourage problem behaviors. Effective plans, however, realistically examine how staff will respond to continuing incidents of problem behavior. Teams need to not only teach and reinforce replacement behaviors but also formulate plans for staff to respond differently to problem behaviors if and when they do occur. This involves rethinking how the typical consequences for the behavior may be reinforcing it and developing new routines for students and educators.

PHASES OF POSITIVE STRATEGIES

The two phases of *Positive Strategies* each have a series of steps that are illustrated in Figure 8. In this section, we provide an overview of the two phases in preparation for a more detailed discussion in succeeding chapters.

PHASE 1: CONDUCT THE FUNCTIONAL BEHAVIORAL ASSESSMENT

Develop Student Profile

Developing a student profile is a critical first step in the FBA. The process of creating the profile involves gathering and analyzing background information, assessing the fit between the

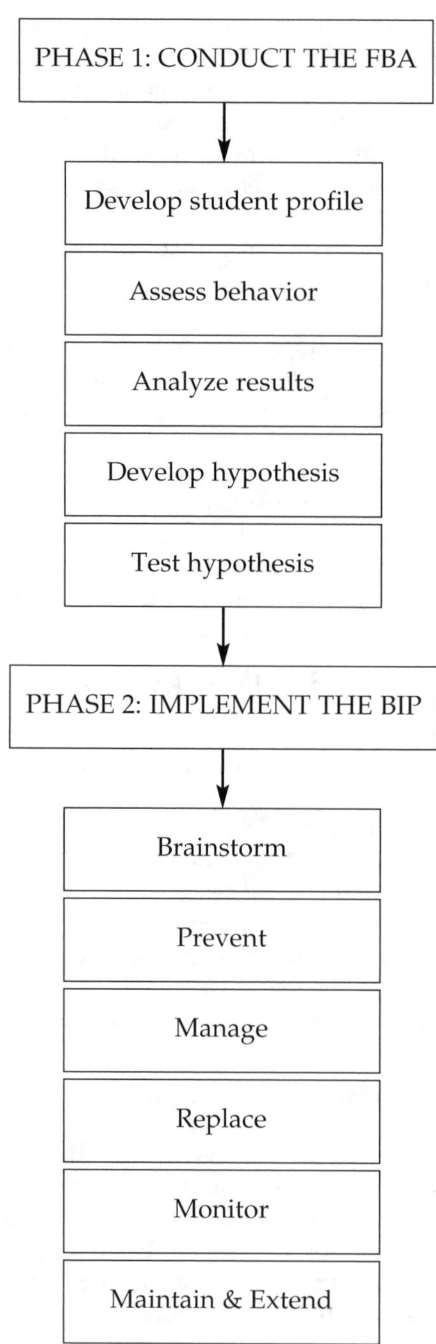

Figure 8. *Positive Strategies* has two phases, each with distinct steps. (*Key:* FBA = functional behavioral assessment; BIP = behavior intervention plan.)

student and the instructional environment, and defining and prioritizing problem behavior. A full profile includes the team's consensus regarding the definition and priority of target behavior and represents their understanding of student competencies, concerns, and history. It is helpful to synthesize existing information about the student in a written summary.

Assess Behavior

Once team members have defined and prioritized a student's challenging behavior, they are ready to begin the FBA. The term *FBA* is part of the basic technology of ABA and is a mandated activity under IDEA'04; it appears in several different systems or approaches to PBS (Jackson &

Panyan, 2001; Knoster, 2000; Scott & Nelson, 1999). Thus, the term *FBA* means different things to different people. Generically, it refers to an assessment process that identifies the function served by problem behavior; it answers the overarching question: Why does the student behave this way?

The specific activities associated with FBAs vary greatly within and across schools, communities, and even among model PBS programs. Most employ facets of ABA and other contemporary behavior intervention modalities with specific methods tailored to the concerns of different settings and student populations. We developed the *Positive Strategies* methods for conducting FBAs in our work with hundreds of teams during a period of more than a decade. The approach is designed to support constructive changes in student behavior in a manner consistent with federal law.

A good FBA leads the team to understand how student characteristics and environmental factors interact with consequences to influence behavior. Often, there is a link between the slow and fast triggers that switch on a problem behavior and the functions that maintain it. To illustrate, Table 7 relates triggers and consequences to the four functions of behavior introduced in Chapter 1.

For example, a student (Sam) with attention-deficit/hyperactivity disorder and limited perseverance (setting events) is required to sit quietly at his desk during whole-class instruction (antecedent). The language level of the instruction strains his processing abilities (antecedent). Sam begins to occupy himself by doodling and then crumpling papers and shooting them toward the wastebasket (problem behavior). Other students watch him, and one joins in (consequence: peer attention and peer engagement). The teacher stops her lesson, asking Sam to take a break in the hallway (consequences: teacher attention and escape). In this example, there is a logical link between triggers and the consequences that maintain the problem behavior. Sam's personal characteristics as a learner (setting event) interact with the classroom context (antecedents). The consequences clearly meet Sam's need for attention, and they also provide escape. These consequences maintain the behavior and will continue to do so until the team addresses the triggers and consequences that contribute to it—that is, until he is able to regulate his own attention (setting event), instruction is better matched to his learning style (antecedent), and he finds more suitable means of gaining attention (consequence) and getting breaks from classwork (consequence).

Analyze Results

An effective FBA obtains information using at least two methods or approaches to assessment (e.g., interviews, direct observations, checklists, questionnaires, multiple informants). It begins where the student profile leaves off, with a priority target behavior, and it is guided by ques-

Table 7. Relationship among functions of behavior, triggers, and consequences

Functional category	Triggers	Consequences
Attention	Difficult task; need for social interaction, recognition, assistance, or engagement	Social engagement, attention, assistance, sustained interaction
Escape	Learning difficulties; limited perseverance; undesirable circumstance, person, place, or work activity	Avoid nonpreferred activity, demand, place, or person; relief at cessation of demand
Sensory	Difficulty regulating states; disrupted internal state; overstimulation, boredom; atypical sensory needs	Generates desired input; produces sensory experience; drive reduced
Tangibles	Desire or need for object or activity	Obtains access to preferred object or activity

Note: Triggers are also known as setting events and antecedents. Consequences are also known as results and outcomes.

tions about function: When does the behavior occur? What setting events (slow triggers) increase its likelihood of appearing? What immediate environmental antecedents (fast triggers) are associated with its occurrence? What motivates and maintains the behavior?

Referring again to Table 7, it is clear that careful analysis of the FBA results is essential to understanding why the problem behavior persists. It requires examining how student characteristics and environmental factors interact. Because some problems meet a clear single function, whereas others meet multiple and complex concerns, teams need to reflect carefully on how these factors interact.

Develop a Hypothesis

Once team members conduct and analyze functional assessment data, they form a working hypothesis about the problem behavior. This specifies the team's educated guesses about the influences (slow and fast triggers) and consequences for problem behavior. A working hypothesis might appear in this format:

> [Student's name] engages in [problem behavior] when or after [antecedent], because when he or she does, [typical consequence]. This is more likely to happen when or because [setting events].

A team derives its hypothesis by careful analysis of a large amount of information; arriving at a working hypothesis is one of the most important steps in the entire behavior support process. An example appears in the next paragraph.

Test the Hypothesis

Once the team has a working hypothesis, it is often tempting to move right into intervention planning. We advise teams, however, to test hypotheses before embarking on involved plans. How do teams test their hypotheses? Because this hypothesis-testing process may be unfamiliar to readers, we examine it here and review it further in Chapter 6. To illustrate, let us return to our earlier example regarding Sam's disruptive classroom behavior. Sam's student support team has the following working hypothesis:

> Sam engages in disruptive behavior when asked to complete independent seatwork, because when he does, he avoids (escapes) having to complete the work. He lacks strategies for refocusing (self-regulation skills). This is more likely to happen during afternoon classes.

In this example, the team engaged in careful observation and assessment, concluding with a hypothesis that escape is the motivation for Sam's behavior. They observed that he has few strategies for refocusing on his work, causing disruptions that worsen as the afternoon wears on. There are a few aspects of the hypothesis that lend themselves to verification; the most obvious one is the escape motivation. If Sam's problem behavior is motivated by escape, and the team removes the need for escape, the problem behavior should diminish dramatically. To test the escape hypothesis, the team conducts a hypothesis test by altering some contextual factors and watching for a corresponding change in behavior.

A hypothesis test examines whether the presumed function of behavior is accurate and serves as an experimental simulation of the eventual intervention plan (or some of its components). It serves two purposes: one, to confirm the team's working hypothesis about what factors trigger and maintain behavior; and two, to establish the effectiveness of one or more accommodations or consequences that might be used in the eventual BIP. The hypothesis test usually begins with a baseline that represents typical current circumstances, followed by a sequence of one or more test conditions, alterations in the setting, antecedents, or consequences. Corresponding changes in behavior are tracked. Often, several hypotheses could be tested in a given situation.

For Sam, the hypothesis test might involve manipulating any of several factors: removing demands for independent seatwork, providing individual support to help him refocus, permitting (programmed) breaks every 5 minutes, or allowing him to request and receive breaks as needed. Each of these strategies makes his need for escape (function) unnecessary. If the team's hypothesis is correct, any of these conditions would reduce the problem behavior. The test may involve manipulating several factors, including setting events (for Sam, supports to increase his attention span), antecedents (remove demands for seatwork), or consequences (frequent breaks). These manipulations occur in sequence (not simultaneously) with a return to baseline (typical conditions) in between.

Figure 9 shows the results of a hypothesis test for Sam that compares a baseline set of observations with two test conditions. First, a baseline (Condition A, no change) is presented, followed by reduced demands (Condition B) and programmed 5-minute breaks (Condition C). To ensure that any change in behavior is attributable to the manipulation rather than extraneous environmental factors, each condition is presented twice, resulting in an A-B-C-A-B-C sequence. Please note that in formal applied behavior analysis, the sequence would more likely be A-B-A-C-A-C-A-B-A, with the baseline condition between the two test conditions and an alternating sequence to control for possible order effects. This level of experimental rigor is often impractical and unnecessary in schools. During Condition A (baseline), Sam has an average of two incidents in each instructional period. In contrast, he averages less than one incident in each of the two test conditions. Assuming that the conditions were reliably presented, the team may safely conclude that the reduced levels of Sam's disruptive behavior in Conditions B and C are direct effects of the manipulation. The hypothesis test supports the team's assertion that Sam's behavior may be motivated by escape. It also yields potentially valuable information about accommodations that may assist him.

PHASE 2: IMPLEMENT THE BEHAVIOR INTERVENTION PLAN

After the FBA, teams often experience considerable pressure to begin their interventions, especially after spending time on assessment activities whose goals may not have been clear to outside observers. It is crucial at this point for teams to allot specific time to meet and discuss past activities, plan next steps, and assign responsibility for tasks. We recommend that teams preparing to develop BIPs engage in a succinct review of activities and results to date, including all salient information gained from the FBA.

Brainstorm

The preferred strategy for preparing for the BIP is a brainstorming session—a tactic used by groups to generate creative solutions to problems. We ask teams to consider the FBA hypothe-

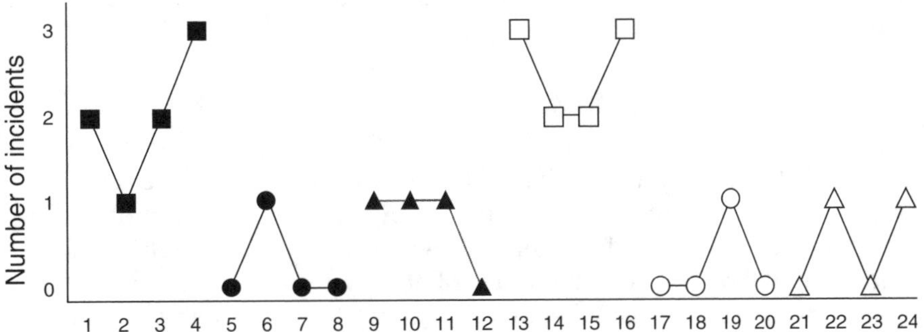

Figure 9. Results of Sam's hypothesis test. (*Key:* ■ = baseline 1; ● = reduced demands 1; ▲ = scheduled breaks 1; □ = baseline 2; ○ = reduced demands 2; △ = scheduled breaks 2.)

sis as a problem requiring a solution, which might take the form of prevention strategies or instruction in replacement behaviors. The group's task is to propose solutions that specifically address the function of behavior, as well as the setting events, antecedents, and consequences that influence it. During brainstorming, all ideas are welcome and criticism is not permitted. It is useful for one group member to serve as scribe and another as facilitator.

Prevent

An important element of the BIP is preventing the problem behavior by rendering it unnecessary. The team may have already used some such manipulations in a hypothesis test. In any case, preventing behavior often involves making changes to bring setting events and antecedents below the threshold at which they trigger problem behavior. Prevention approaches include short-term strategies that may buy time for the team to coach the student in alternative (replacement) behaviors, as well as long-term accommodations. The latter are environmental or instructional modifications that have the goal of making the student more successful academically or socially. (Recall the discussion in Chapter 1 on the need for accommodation as a challenge to implementation.) Good BIPs recognize that prevention strategies cannot be maintained indefinitely, so they consider long-term instructional accommodations and include teaching replacement behaviors.

Manage

Despite the best efforts of all involved, some problem behaviors persist. We recommend that teams expect problem behavior to continue at its baseline rate for a week or two after their efforts begin. This implies the need for a management plan to deal with continuing occurrences of problem behavior. Such a plan stipulates how the team will respond to problem behavior on an interim basis. It may be very straightforward, involving no more than following established school policies for behavior. Problem behaviors that are more serious, highly disruptive, or threatening may require a crisis intervention plan, necessitating specific staff training and monitoring.

In the general case, our caution for teams is that some components of a school's discipline policy may inadvertently reinforce problem behavior. For example, if school policy requires the student to leave the room and go to the office to speak to the principal, the student is both escaping and receiving attention. This is problematic for a student with escape- or attention-motivated problem behavior. This student's team faces several strategic questions. First, can the school policy be ignored without jeopardizing the safety of all involved? Second, can the potentially reinforcing aspects of the plan be mitigated by, for example, requiring the student to bring assigned work to the office and minimizing interaction with him or her? And, third, can access to the potentially reinforcing consequence(s) be provided noncontingently at other times during the day? That is, can the student leave the classroom to go to the office and speak to the principal about positive events or behavior?

Replace

Effective BIPs identify alternative behaviors that serve the same function as the problem behavior, indicate the extent to which they are in the student's current skill repertoire, and include plans to teach, coach, and reinforce these alternatives. In the BIP, the team states its plans for monitoring the development and use of alternative behaviors, especially in relation to continuing instances of challenging behavior. Without feasible alternatives, students are unlikely to relinquish problem behaviors that meet important—and legitimate—functions.

Just as the team plans to react to problem behavior, it considers the response that replacement behaviors are likely to receive. Although it is beneficial to have a good plan on paper, if the replacement behavior does not recruit natural reinforcement, the student may not be motivated to repeat it. Teaching and rewarding a student for prosocial behavior will not be effective in the long run if the behavior does not accrue natural payoffs in the environment. A team might teach a student to request a break (escape) for difficult seatwork. If the typical response the student receives is being told to wait, he or she is not likely to repeat the replacement behavior. The best replacement behaviors are those most likely to elicit a reinforcing response from others without specific training.

Monitor

With careful preparation, the BIP has a good chance for success. Sometimes, however, teams find that their plans do not result in the change they hoped for, or the change does not last. On other occasions, it is clear that the plan is not working. More commonly, the plan seems to work for a while and then fades over time. This does not necessarily mean the plan can no longer be effective, but recognizing a plan's waning effectiveness early is key to salvaging the team's efforts. This is only possible if the team monitors the implementation of the plan, incidents of the problem behavior, and the extent and circumstances under which the student demonstrates the replacement behavior.

A monitoring plan permits the team to evaluate the ongoing effectiveness of the BIP. Close monitoring might result in the recognition that although problem behaviors are diminishing, alternatives are not increasing. In such a case, the student is responding to accommodations and other team efforts but is not learning or using new, more adaptive behavior. Under these circumstances, the team needs to consider why this is the case and modify the BIP. As such, monitoring BIP implementation, evaluating outcomes, and modifying the plan are essential.

Maintain and Extend

Once the student has accomplished important change, team members may experience a sense of relief and satisfaction, but their work is not yet done. As we discussed in Chapter 1, students with significant problem behaviors often have a history of waxing and waning difficulties. The team that develops an effective BIP does so from an understanding of prior interventions, their successful and unsuccessful elements, and their short-lived or long-standing success. Because of that, the team is also in a good position to anticipate challenges that may lie ahead. On the basis of their experience with the student, teams can often forecast when a lapse or relapse may occur. A lapse is a time-limited recurrence of a behavior problem, whereas a relapse signifies a return to problematic levels impacting function.

By reviewing the student's history, the team can identify future high-risk circumstances that may trigger a resurgence of problem behavior. This includes recalling and forecasting setting events (stressful events or transitions such as new class or grade, illness, family problem, and so forth) and antecedents (academic demands, peer interactions, and so forth) that are characteristically difficult for the student. When the student faces new demands that tax his or her coping and self-regulation skills, lapses may occur. Teams need to foresee these circumstances and prepare students for them. If students manage new setting events and antecedents successfully, this promotes a sense of competence and encourages positive expectancies for all involved.

Consideration of evolving consequences (whether the behavior continues to receive sufficient reinforcement to maintain it) for new behavior is also important. By monitoring the student's use of replacement behavior, the team is prepared to assess how well it recruits natural reinforcement that is likely to maintain it.

ENHANCING CHANCES FOR SUCCESS

In Chapter 1, we discussed challenges to implementation of *Positive Strategies*. Our focus in this chapter is on key elements of *Positive Strategies* that are associated with success. Conversely,

Positive Strategies efforts lose potential for success when the work of any phase is not thoroughly conducted. In Table 8, we mention several potential pitfalls and constructive alternatives within the *Positive Strategies* process, as well as their consequences. Although it is not exhaustive, it does contain a number of common difficulties teams encounter, and constructive alternatives to these difficulties. These examples are drawn from the PBS literature and from our personal experiences as team members, consultants, and trainers. Table 8 depicts various potential pitfalls by phase, indicating their consequences and suggesting constructive alternatives and their outcomes. Although some of these pitfalls can be viewed as consequences of procedural mishaps (e.g., no assessment of student–environment fit), they may also reflect the amount of shared commitment among the team, the amount of expertise on PBS, or even the level of optimism team members have about the future. Based on the current state of practice in individualized supports, we now turn to an overview of elemental considerations for planning and implementation.

KEY CONSIDERATIONS

Throughout this book, we discuss the importance of team collaboration in the development and testing of hypotheses about the function of problem behavior. These efforts are conducted with hope and in good faith; because they signify investment in altering future outcomes for a student, PBS efforts are fundamentally optimistic. The existing evidence suggests that this optimism is well founded. When FBAs identify and confirm the function of problem behavior and are followed by intervention plans that consider the function of behavior and its context, beneficial change is likely to occur.

Published reports on the state of PBS practice in various contexts are growing in number and scope (see references in sections to follow). This literature has described some common challenges experienced by teams of diverse composition serving children with a range of concerns. A thorough discussion is beyond the scope of this book, but we include a brief description of key considerations that appear in the literature, organized chronologically along the FBA–BIP process, to serve as a backdrop for elucidating critical steps in student support.

Initiating Individualized Supports

All too often, individualized supports are initiated only when they are required by law or dictated by an emerging crisis. For example, Van Acker, Boreson, Gable, & Potterton (2005) examined the timing behind FBA referrals and found that 85% occurred when the student was in crisis; in their sample, only 1 of 13 FBAs were initiated for problems that had been occurring for less than a year. We strongly urge school staff to consider proactive classroom management strategies with the aim of preventing problem behaviors and to initiate individualized supports as promptly as possible after the appearance of problem behaviors. Early intervention works best.

Identifying Function and Testing Hypotheses

Reports of FBAs conducted in schools and other applied settings suggest that school teams identify one or more functions of problem behavior in the majority of cases (Ervin et al., 2001; Scott et al., 2005; Van Acker et al., 2005). Consistent with recommended practice, most teams seem to use several approaches (interviews, observations, rating scales) to collect FBA data (Snell, Voorhees & Chen, 2005; Van Acker et al., 2005; Ervin et al., 2001; Kern et al., 2004).

Some published reports (e.g., Van Acker et al., 2005; Snell et al., 2005) indicate that teams engage in hypothesis testing only about half the time, whereas another review (Ervin et al., 2001) conveyed more promising findings, such that hypotheses were validated close to 90% of the time. We believe that hypothesis testing is an important step that it is especially useful when problem behavior is entrenched, severe, long-standing, serving multiple functions, or inconsis-

Table 8. Potential pitfalls, constructive alternatives, and their consequences

Phase(s) and potential pitfalls	Consequences of pitfalls	Constructive alternatives	Consequences of alternatives
FBA: Inadequate consideration of previous evaluations and interventions underscoring elements of success and failure.	The team may replicate unsuccessful past efforts, fail to consider helpful aspects of previous plans, or not recognize areas of strength to build on.	Careful review and synthesis of prior evaluations and interventions produces a full picture of the child's functional competencies and history of problem behavior.	The team develops a holistic view of the student, ascertains successful and unsuccessful aspects of prior interventions, and builds on student strengths.
FBA: Failure to assess the fit between the student's functional skills and the instructional environment (contextual fit).	Plans developed may be thwarted by the student's ongoing frustration with instruction that is above the student's level or that does not permit adequate success.	The team pinpoints areas of mismatch that trigger problem behavior and that detract from the student's emerging sense of competency.	The team uses its expertise and knowledge of the student to better engage him or her in learning, thereby reducing the need for problem behavior.
FBA: Failure to adequately define or sample the target behavior, especially across context; incomplete FBAs or one that fails to uncover the function(s) of problem behavior.	Hypothesis and resulting BIP may not reflect context-specific influences on behavior; BIP may be partially or completely ineffective. Problem behaviors may resurge or new ones may develop.	Careful, detailed FBA results in accurate hypothesis; team understands multiple influences and consequences that reflect complexity of behavior. Team is poised to develop tailored BIP.	Team is able to bring setting events and antecedents below threshold at which they trigger problem behavior. BIP reflects influences of context and teaches skills likely to be reinforced.
FBA and BIP: No or limited consultation with family members; failure to include, welcome, or integrate input from team members, especially student and family.	Team view of student does not reflect home and community input, so key influences and competencies may be ignored. FBA and BIP will not receive family support or may be undermined.	Team welcomes family to process, seeks and values their input, and gains information about setting events, antecedents, and consequences at home and in community. The family works to generalize replacement skills to home and community.	Effectiveness of FBA and BIP increase because family input adds to their validity. BIP has greater likelihood to be enacted across multiple contexts, resulting in more gains and improved quality of life.
FBA and BIP: Maintaining a disintegrated or deficit-oriented view of the child that fails to capitalize on areas of skill and strength.	FBA not grounded in understanding of child's functional skills, so BIP does not leverage these. BIP may be unsuccessful, or success may be short-lived.	Team understands child's competencies, especially in the communication domain, and builds on them in BIP.	Students develop replacement behaviors that serve them well in the current context and into the future. Students learn to communicate needs directly, rather than through behavior.
BIP: Underelaborate BIPs, especially with regard to teaching and reinforcing replacement skills, monitoring efforts, and modifying intervention.	Initial BIP implementation, especially if largely consequence based, may prove successful, but success wanes as student becomes sated to reinforcers.	The BIP specifies and the team enacts a careful plan to teach, coach, and reinforce functional skills, replacing problem behaviors.	Students learn and use new skills, reduce problem behavior, increase instructional time, and experience improved quality of life.
BIP: Inadequate monitoring of outcomes over time and/or failure to forecast future challenges.	Student may demonstrate short-term gains and lapse or relapse as new setting events or antecedents emerge.	The team monitors ongoing incidence of problem and replacement behavior and modifies BIP as indicated. The team forecasts and supports student as new challenges emerge.	The student not only maintains gains but also generalizes them to new contexts, resulting in improved sense of competence and better educational achievement.

Key: FBA = functional behavioral assessment; BIP = behavior intervention plan.

tent. Underlying functions, whether operating singly or in combination, are not always clear until after hypothesis testing is complete, and hindsight is little comfort when valuable resources have been expended without benefiting the student. As such, we advocate even abbreviated hypothesis testing if the function of behavior seems straightforward.

Some authors (Quinn et al., 2001; Scott et al., 2005) indicate that published reports of hypothesis testing often reflect the contributions of expert researchers in addition to team members themselves, such that the feasibility of hypothesis testing in schools is difficult to assess. Our work with experienced school teams suggests that hypothesis tests are feasible and can be conducted effectively without ongoing expert support. Novice teams are advised to seek technical assistance from a PBS coach or consultant as a means of developing team competencies in this area. For this reason, our team training model includes ongoing access to and support from expert trainers, and teams are required to report on their FBA and BIP efforts as part of the training process.

Linking Functional Behavioral Assessment Findings to the Behavior Intervention Plan

We argue elsewhere in this book that the BIP is the culmination of prior team efforts, even those occurring before the initiation of the *Positive Strategies* process. Given that the purpose of the FBA is to identify and validate a working hypothesis, readers may be surprised to find that FBA findings are sometimes neglected in subsequent planning and intervention steps. Of course, this may be complicated if the hypothesis was not validated to begin with. Either way, the result of a failure to understand problem behavior may be an inability to prevent or replace it.

Ervin and colleagues' (2001) review reveals trends in the type and number of functions teams identify. The most common function for students with disabilities was escape, but this was rare in students without disabilities. Gaining the attention of an adult was a common function of problem behavior in students with and without disabilities. Multiple functions were more common in students without disabilities, suggesting that their FBAs might be more complicated.

Scott and colleagues (2005) found that teams did not consistently develop interventions that were logically linked to the function of problem behavior, and teams tended to rely on intervention strategies that were used previously (even if they were not effective). They related this trend to the tendency for schools to be somewhat reactive and punitive in their approach to problem behavior. Similarly, Van Acker and colleagues (2005) found an explicit link between the function of problem behavior and its replacement in less than half of BIPs they reviewed. When function is meaningfully considered in BIP development, its results are apparent—it improves the chances of good outcomes. For example, Ingram, Lewis-Palmer, and Sugai (2006) compared function-based and non–function-based BIPs and found that the former were associated with greater reductions in problem behavior.

If considering function is so critical, why would a team neglect it? In our experience, there are three main reasons. First, teams sometimes grow impatient or experience pressure to act quickly, especially when problem behavior is nearing or reaching crisis levels. They move into the BIP without having ensured that they understand the factors that trigger problem behavior or the functional relationship between behavior and its outcomes. Second, if initial attempts to clarify function are not entirely successful, it might seem more expedient to move toward intervention nevertheless. In the long run, this can consume resources needlessly and increase the student's chances for failure. Successful strategies require moving beyond a short-term perspective.

A third reason for failing to meaningfully incorporate function into the BIP relates to team functioning. Some teams lack perceived or actual knowledge and competence regarding effective strategies to teach communication, self-regulation, and social and academic skills. In their statewide study of BIPs, Scott, McIntyre, Liaupsin, and colleagues (2006) found no team that had selected interventions from outside their existing repertoire. Rather than turning to external resources such as training, education, textbooks, or consultants, teams tended to employ a limited set of interventions already in place in their schools. As Quinn and colleagues (2001, p. 266) state, the BIP may "more closely resemble a list of behavior change methods rather than a specific plan linked to the function of behavior." This statement reflects the tendency to rely on a set of familiar strategies rather than a fully integrated plan.

As we discuss later, the success of a BIP relies on whether it supports the development and use of replacement behaviors—more of the same rarely rallies significant change for students. Incorporating function into the BIP requires attention to team dynamics as well as the individual skills, knowledge, and attitudes of team members, specifically the ability and willingness of team members to engage in divergent thinking, seek external training and skills development, and use expert consultation. These themes are further elaborated in Chapters 4, 6, and 7.

Areas of Emphasis

Positive Strategies, like other PBS approaches, accentuates consideration of prevention and replacement of problem behavior in addition to (or instead of) consequence-based plans. This requires assessment of setting events and antecedents (contextual factors) that trigger behavior, as well as specific replacement skills. To what extent do school teams consider these factors? Ervin and colleagues (2001) found that both antecedent- and consequence-based interventions had been considered in most cases they examined. Others (Van Acker et al., Scott et al., 2005) found more limited attention to altering contextual variables (slow and fast triggers) and to developing and bolstering replacement skills.

Scott and colleagues (2006) found that school personnel relied predominantly on punitive and exclusionary approaches to problem behavior, regardless of its function. A clear theme of the literature (and this book) is that effective individualized supports cannot be achieved if intervention is viewed predominantly through the lens of reactive behavior-management approaches. The implication for teams is ensuring that plans contain elements of prevention and replacement, and willingness to reconsider plans that do not.

Acceptability of Interventions

Acceptability refers to the extent to which constituents view an intervention as appropriate to the problem, effective in reducing negative outcomes (and increasing positive ones), and fair and humane (Finn & Sladeczek, 2001). Although little has been written about acceptability in individualized supports, it is consistent with the values base of PBS and has potential to increase commitment and adherence to the BIP.

We believe that family involvement can influence the acceptability of interventions. This may occur partly because parents (in particular) may steer educators away from punitive approaches. Family partnerships result in more holistic student profiles—specifically, those that address student concerns, interests, and strengths. Further, research (Vaughn & Horner, 1997; Cole & Levinson, 2002) suggests that providing students with opportunities for choice making influences problem behavior. Moving away from the traditional conceptualization of the student support team as synonymous with the IEP team (on which parents and students may be marginally represented) or restricted to the core instructional team may have important consequences for students and educators alike.

Thus, incorporating the perspectives and contributions of students, families, teachers of nonacademic subjects (art, music, physical education), and other school personnel is likely to bring more creative and less reactive strategies. Plans that reflect contextual variables, capitalize on strengths, and support student choice increase the acceptability of interventions. This, in turn, may motivate adherence by all constituents and improve the fit between the student and environment.

Monitoring, Maintaining, and Extending Change

Later in this book, we discuss the crucial importance of follow-through in supporting students to maintain and extend positive change. This is an important challenge not only within a school year but across multiple grades and school placements—for example, as a student moves from elementary to middle school. Monitoring the effectiveness of a BIP is necessary to determine whether it is being reliably implemented (also referred to as fidelity of intervention) and whether it produces the intended effects. Effecting, maintaining, and extending change across time and place are necessary if individualized student supports are to influence quality of life.

The published literature (e.g., Carr et al., 1999, Van Acker et al., 2005; Quinn et al., 2001) suggests that teams rarely monitor the fidelity or effectiveness of their interventions for more than a few months, and the same can be said for long-term efforts to promote maintenance and generalization. In our experience, there is often a noticeable disconnect between IEP goals and the FBA–BIP process. This is unfortunate because the IEP is central to the education of students with disabilities throughout primary and secondary education. Although there are multiple reasons that the IEP and BIP remain distinct, there are also compelling reasons to ensure that both remain current and relevant.

Despite challenges to achieving long-term focus in school-based supports, some reports of longitudinal outcomes are emerging (e.g., Kern et al., 2004; Koegel, Koegel, Boettcher, & Brookman-Frazee, 2005). In many schools, taking a long-term perspective requires extraordinary commitment; we suggest that individual team members coordinate their efforts through schoolwide or districtwide initiatives. We have been involved in many cases in which this kind of concerted, long-standing focus is present, and it results in significant benefit not just to students but to the entire learning community.

What Does It Take to Provide Effective Supports?

We hope that this brief review of research regarding practice issues conveys three main points. The first is that teams struggle to rise above many of the challenges and barriers discussed in Chapter 1. Second, effective supports are possible with diligent effort, creative thinking, close collaboration, and equal attention given to all steps in the process. The final point, based on the literature and our experiences as trainers and implementers, is that effective supports really make a difference to students, their families, and the entire learning community. Perhaps delivering effective supports is not easy, but its rewards are meaningful.

HOW MUCH TIME?

Teams frequently ask how much time and effort is required by *Positive Strategies* activities. In Chapter 3, we discuss these issues generally, and in this section we place questions about time along a continuum. At one end are relatively straightforward behavior problems of low intensity and severity that have emerged relatively recently. At the other end are seemingly intractable problems of great intensity, severity, and duration. The latter clearly warrant more intensive team efforts because of the likely existence of an extensive problem history, corresponding records, multiple informants during the FBA, and the need to invest a great deal of effort in developing replacement behaviors for the BIP.

The process of conducting FBAs and BIPs is as varied as the problem behaviors that require them. Teams that function efficiently, base decisions on reliable data, and focus efforts on crucial behaviors conduct relatively brief FBAs and move rapidly into developing BIPs, particularly for less entrenched behaviors. In other cases, extensive efforts spent on the FBA will pay off in the form of ample and valid preparation for intervention. The challenge for teams, especially inexperienced ones, is determining when additional time is justified.

Teams bear in mind two main factors when determining the amount of time for FBAs and BIPs. The first is a consideration of how much time is already being invested in the behavior. The underlying issue driving the time investment is how substantially the behavior affects the student and the environment. In most cases, there is a positive correlation between these conditions: the more serious or disruptive the behavior, the more resources are devoted to it. In any case, the time being consumed by the behavior justifies an investment in strategies that will decrease its frequency. In contrast, it is probably not worth investing time conducting a protracted FBA on a behavior that has relatively little impact.

Earlier in this chapter, we recounted research indicating that the length of time required to complete an FBA is difficult to predict. One reason for this may be that there are so many contextual factors operating. A major factor influencing the amount of time to conduct *Positive Strategies* is the complexity of the relationship between the behavior and the environment. A behavior that can be triggered by numerous antecedents, that elicits different responses under different conditions, and that serves multiple functions in different settings requires additional assessment time and effort for the FBA, and it also requires a BIP of corresponding detail.

To illustrate the range of effort involved in conducting FBAs and BIPs, we summarize three assessment and intervention scenarios in the vignettes that follow. These cases, drawn from our files, represent a range of efforts commensurate with the complexity of the problem behaviors. They exemplify, in sequence, a relatively brief FBA and straightforward BIP (Jorge); a more involved FBA and BIP (Michael); and a detailed, time-consuming FBA and BIP for a student whose problem behaviors developed over several years (Denice).

JORGE

Jorge was a fourth grader referred to his school's team for repeatedly calling out in class. Jorge was classified as having a mild learning disability for which he received resource room support and testing modifications; he otherwise participated in the general education program.

On the basis of Jorge's profile, the school psychologist conducted a preliminary behavior assessment. When interviewed, the teacher indicated that she felt Jorge was disrupting class to get attention. She also completed a Motivation Assessment Scale (MAS), which suggested that the behavior was motivated by escape. The psychologist observed Jorge during math, the period in which the problem behavior occurred most frequently. Jorge did not call out while the teacher was explaining the lesson, but he did interrupt several times as she began assigning word problems to the class.

The teacher and the school psychologist tested the escape hypothesis by letting Jorge skip word problems for a week. After Jorge's calling out diminished substantially, they developed a plan for Jorge to leave the room briefly when difficult work was being assigned. When he returned, Jorge received help working on adapted versions of the problems.

Jorge responded well to this intervention; his disruptive behavior dropped to a frequency comparable with that of his peers. For the rest of the year, the teacher collaborated with the resource teacher to enhance instructional supports for math and reading. Jorge also learned some strategies for relaxation and for dealing with frustration in the resource room.

Jorge's FBA required about 3 hours of staff time during a 10-day period. His BIP was developed in less than an hour. Ongoing BIP supports required only a few minutes each day when Jorge left the room, plus the faculty time required to adapt his assignments (5 minutes each). * * *

MICHAEL

Michael was a third-grade student who was diagnosed with pervasive developmental disorder (not otherwise specified) and an educational classification of "multiply disabled." His parents and teacher referred to his disability as high-functioning autism. Michael was enrolled in a mainstream class with a one-to-one teacher's aide. He was generally attentive and well behaved. The team was concerned, however, because of increasing incidents of crying, yelling, and arguing with other children on the playground and in gym class. Several times a week, these lasted more than 5 minutes, disrupted other children, and nearly escalated into physical confrontations.

To determine likely setting influences, the student support team assigned a consultant teacher who observed Michael in the classroom and on the playground. They also interviewed his gym teacher and playground monitor to identify typical antecedents to and consequences of the behavior. The monitor completed an MAS, and the aide kept an A-B-C chart for five incidents.

Two weeks later, the team reviewed their findings. They determined that Michael's behavior typically occurred in less structured settings and was triggered by his belief that someone had violated a rule. The typical consequence for the behavior was adult intervention to help Michael calm down and redirect him. The team hypothesized that Michael engaged in this behavior to restore his sense of order. Its inadvertent effect was to create more distress, which served to escalate his behavior.

The team developed a BIP that included proactive adult supports, and they taught Michael a set of guidelines to follow when students violated rules, which involved a procedure for requesting adult intervention. For the next several months, Michael participated in a social skills group in which he learned conflict resolution and social skills. With support, he also learned to ignore some rule infractions. As a result, he was less isolated from peers.

Developing Michael's FBA, including observation and data collection, involved about 10 hours of staff time. Four team members then met for 1 hour to review FBA results and develop a BIP. Before the team initiated the BIP, two team members met for an hour to detail Michael's guidelines, and they spent an additional 3 hours coordinating aspects of implementation, monitoring, and evaluation—planning his participation in the social skills group, choosing outcomes to measure and means of assessing them, assigning tasks to team members, and coordinating with the committee on special education. Implementation was fairly straightforward and required little time outside of regular instruction and related services. Michael's social skills group participation was included in his IEP, as were time-limited individual coaching sessions designed to promote self-regulation (i.e., relaxation, ignoring rule infractions). * * *

DENICE

Denice was a 10th-grade student diagnosed with moderate mental retardation. She attended a school program sponsored by her regional board of cooperative educational services. For several years, she had demonstrated increased levels of physical aggression that had recently resulted in a staff injury. Her student support team consisted of her teacher, two classroom aides, a speech therapist, the school psychologist, and the crisis intervention aide. The head teacher for her program, who served as team leader, conducted a thorough review of Denice's records and summarized them for the team.

The team also reviewed 3 months of data on her behavior and maintained a frequency chart for the remainder of the assessment. They collected observation data using an A-B-C format for 3 weeks, and then they maintained scatter plot data for an additional 3 weeks. After the first 2 weeks, they developed a hypothesis that Denice's aggression was motivated by her desire to obtain tangibles in the form of preferred activities. Interventions based on this approach, however, did not result in any reduction of the behavior, so assessment was continued. After reviewing the new information, the team arrived at an alternate hypothesis: Denice's behavior was motivated by attention from staff. Based on this hypothesis, they developed several BIP strategies. When her behavior still did not improve, the team engaged an outside consultant.

The consultant met with the team and reviewed actions to date. The teacher completed an MAS, and the team conducted supplementary observations. The MAS results supported the attention hypothesis. Interview findings indicated that Denice's aggression was directed toward staff and less assertive students. She was never aggressive toward students who were themselves assertive or who retaliated. The team conducted hypothesis testing, during which Denice received scheduled noncontingent attention, with staff approaching Denice at scheduled intervals rather than awaiting a request. Denice exhibited lower rates of aggression and completed more work during the high-attention portion of the hypothesis test.

The team then reviewed the existing BIP and determined that although prior interventions had provided attention according to plan, Denice did not experience the level of attention as sufficient. In retrospect, the team realized that the attention they had provided was superficial and fleeting, and it was not enough to prevent Denice from escalating. They revised her BIP, providing Denice with high levels of noncontingent attention. To accomplish this, the team had to justify the amount of time spent attending to her; the ensuing discussion led to an acknowledgement that this time had been spent productively rather than in damage control. Under the revised BIP, the team engaged Denice in more group activities and paired her with assertive peers. She demonstrated rare outbursts, was more productive academically, and became more social with peers.

Denice's FBA and BIP were complex and time consuming. Before engaging the consultant, the team spent nearly 40 hours assessing her behavior, planning interventions, and implementing them. Once the consultant joined the team, the ancillary FBA activities required an additional 6 hours of consultant time and another 15 hours of staff time in a 3-week period. BIP development and implementation were completed approximately 3 months after the first FBA activities were initiated. * * *

Chapter 6

Functional Behavioral Assessments

Throughout this book, we discuss how important it is for teams to develop intervention plans based on careful assessment. Faced with disruptive, annoying, threatening, even dangerous behaviors, many educators want to spring into action. They want to *do something* to stop the problem. An assessment may seem like an unnecessary delay. After all, most students referred for FBAs have had plenty of assessments; what they really need is action. Nevertheless, when challenging behaviors persist despite the best efforts of many professionals, more action may not be the best next step. Effective interventions are built on knowledge of what motivates and maintains the behavior in the first place. The FBA is where teams find that understanding.

The FBA is the foundation on which an effective BIP is constructed. Without understanding the function of problem behavior, school teams can flounder, piecing together interventions that may work in the short term but then fall quickly into disuse. A plan that acknowledges the student's unique style, strengths, concerns, and preferences can only come from thoughtful consideration of those attributes. As Figure 10 depicts, conducting an FBA begins with developing a student profile and concludes with testing the hypothesis, taking the team into BIP development.

In this chapter, we detail the process of conducting FBAs, and we describe various approaches and resources that teams may use. We include some of those resources in this chapter, referring readers to others available elsewhere. Table 9 lists these resources and relates them to the various steps involved in completing the FBA. Note that we recommend the use of the *Positive Strategies* FBA worksheets as a resource for organizing FBA activities and analyses. The sections of the FBA worksheets correspond to the steps of the FBA as they appear in this chapter.

DEVELOP STUDENT PROFILE

Developing a student profile readies the team to conduct the FBA by painting a holistic picture of the student. A contextualized profile prepares the team for the BIP by illuminating areas of fit and

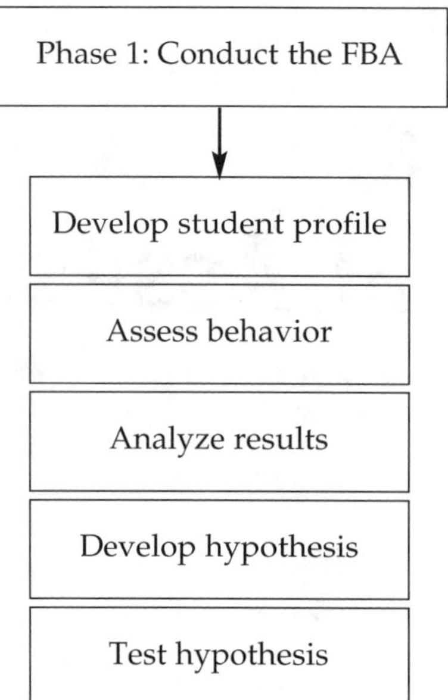

Figure 10. The steps in Functional Behavior Assessment (FBA), a compound of the *Positive Strategies* process.

mismatch between the student and the environment. Like so many aspects of *Positive Strategies* planning, the effort required relates to the depth and complexity of the behaviors addressed. To develop the student profile, teams engage in three somewhat overlapping tasks: gathering information, defining and prioritizing behavior, and assessing student–environment fit.

Table 9. Functional Behavior Assessment (FBA) steps, activities, and resources

Step	Activities	Resources
1	**Develop student profile** Gather background information Define and prioritize behavior Assess student–environment fit	Student Background Form Defining and Prioritizing Behavior Form Communication Style Assessment Learning Style Profile Preference and Interest Assessment Social Network Assessment
2	**Assess behavior** Interviews Observations Checklists and questionnaires	Incident Log Scatter Plot Antecedent–Behavior–Consequence (A-B-C) Chart Functional Assessment Observation Form* Motivation Assessment Scale (MAS)* Functional Assessment Checklist for Teachers and Staff (FACTS)* Setting Events Checklist
3	**Analyze results** Review data from observations, checklists, and interviews Identify areas of convergence Identify areas of discrepancy	FBA worksheets
4	**Develop a hypothesis** Team states working hypothesis as derived from FBA	FBA worksheets
5	**Test the hypothesis** Team tests working hypothesis about function of behavior Team meeting to review results and restate the hypothesis	FBA worksheets

*With the exception of the items noted, all FBA resources are included in the appendix.

GATHER BACKGROUND INFORMATION

There is often a great deal of information available on a student whose behavior requires an FBA. In the early phases of *Positive Strategies* planning, teams find themselves sifting through an accumulation of reports and concerns to arrive at a concise formulation of the problem. This activity can naturally form the focus of an initial team meeting regarding a student with challenging behavior; others might find it helpful for one or several team members to review this information ahead of time and provide a summary for the initial team meeting. The important point here is that this wealth of information not be overlooked, because many school-based teams are prone to missing or overlooking potentially significant relationships among such contextual factors and the student's behavior.

It is helpful for team members to examine and summarize the student's record, including:

- The IEP for students with disabilities
- 504 plans (i.e., accommodation plans for students with disabilities)
- Details about the current placement
- Medical conditions
- Progress notes and reviews of previous interventions
- Teacher notes
- Discipline reports
- Home–school communications
- Community provider reports (e.g., physician prescribing medication, therapist)
- Recent assessments and evaluations
- Other informative school data (e.g., state testing, prior behavior assessments).

We recommend that the team leader (or designee) prepare a brief synopsis of this information. If it is in written form, it should be distributed in ample time for review before a team meeting. Whether or not it is available before the initial meeting, oral presentation of the synopsis serves to organize information and positions the team for fruitful discussion.

This synthesis can be very informative. Starting from a synopsis of problem behavior, its development and history, and the student's areas of strength and weakness, the team is prepared to assess behavior. Because it entails a review of past interventions, the information-gathering process informs the team about effective and ineffective strategies for the identified student, yielding answers to guiding questions about intervention priorities. It also provides valuable clues to the student–environment fit and slow and fast triggers.

When a review results in unanswered questions or clear areas of need, it is beneficial to consider two sets of activities. The first involves an analysis of the *student–environment fit* to clarify areas of fit and mismatch between the child and the learning context. Second, the team is also advised to consider a range of additional supports that might be helpful. This may involve a referral for counseling supports, family assistance, or engagement in a schoolwide effort to promote positive behavior. If there is a clear need for such supports, the referral is best made early in the process; this increases the likelihood that services can co-occur and be coordinated with the FBA–BIP process.

The student background form allows teams to encapsulate the most salient information gathered in this early stage. Although some teams choose to develop a separate written summary, the background section provides a record of the team's synthesis in note format. In some cases, a review of a student's background may raise as many questions as it answers. For students with complex learning and behavioral difficulties (especially in combination with environmental or psychological stressors), the review and synthesis may illuminate student concerns that have not been previously identified, acknowledged, or addressed.

Nathan's Functional Behavioral Assessment: Student Background

Figure 11 has a sample student background showing information gathered on Nathan, a fifth-grade student. Nathan's problem behaviors include yelling at the teacher, muttering curse words, running out of the classroom, and hitting peers. A quick review of his background reveals that the student support team conducted a careful review of his history and prior assessments, examined his IEP, and consulted his family. The team's review yielded some unanswered questions about how Nathan's learning style interacted with context factors to influence his difficulties. Because of this, the team assessed the student–environment fit. We follow Nathan through this process and include his FBA results in the sections that follow.

Student: Nathan Jones Date: October/November

	Completed by	Date(s)
☑ **IEP and recent progress**	Teacher	10/21

(Note classification; summarize major goals and comment on their relevance to problem behavior)

10-year-old, fifth grade student, classified as learning disabled.
Major difficulty is in use of verbal and written language.
Average intelligence, achievement test scores are above grade level in math.
One of the top players on his basketball team.

☑ **Current placement**	Teacher	10/21

(Note location, type, staff-to-student ratio, inclusion opportunities, related services, and so forth)

General education class with 24 other students, mainstreamed for all subjects and activities.
Receives resource room twice a week as a supplemental support.

☑ **Medical and related conditions**	School nurse	10/23

(Note conditions affecting mood and behavior. List medications, especially for behavior, and effects)

Allergic to chocolate and peanuts.
History of febrile seizure prior to two years old—no indication that this has any impact on current behavior.

☑ **Family consultation**	Social worker	10/22

(List family concerns)

Family spends a great deal of time and energy focusing on Nathan's athletic ability as well as his lessons and performances with the local children's orchestra. Parents are advocating strongly to keep him included in the mainstream, both to stimulate cognitive function and encourage interaction with typical peer models. They are concerned that he may not be able to remain in his current mainstream class due to behavior, and note that this is a "school" problem and does not occur at home or in community.

☑ **Previous interventions**	Teacher	10/21

(Summarize results of individualized, classroom, or schoolwide interventions)

Implemented individualized classroom behavior plan consisting of "warning cards" and rewards at break time when no warning card received. Also, classroom-wide plan with beads placed in jar for periods of positive behavior and class party at end of week if enough beads. Neither reduced Nathan's problem behavior, though other students have responded well. Nathan does not respond to peer pressure regarding his behavior; although students sometimes laugh at his behavior, they also ostracize him at times.

☑ **Student–environment fit**	Teacher	10/21

(Overview of learning style, reinforcers, preferences, and needed accommodations related to behavior)

Good math skills: tests above grade level, but work is inconsistent. Solves problems intuitively, but frequently fails to complete assignments requiring explanation of responses and showing work.
Known weakness in expressive language is evident in poor writing skills and oral expression of ideas.
Need to look further at skill level and work presented in mainstream class.

Is formal consideration of student–environment fit indicated? ☑ Yes ☐ No

Figure 11. Nathan's student background form.

DEFINE AND PRIORITIZE BEHAVIOR

After gathering and organizing background information, the next step in developing the student profile involves defining and prioritizing behavior. This step is essential. Students whose behavior warrants the assembly of a student support team frequently demonstrate more than one problem behavior. Sometimes, the priority behavior is quite clear to team members and onlookers. In other cases, the student has multiple problem behaviors that need to be defined and delineated so that the team can decide which to focus on first. It is essential that the team achieve consensus about which behaviors should take priority and which can be addressed subsequently. This does not imply that some challenging behaviors are not worth addressing; rather, it focuses attention on the behaviors with the greatest functional impact. It also recognizes that behaviors long in development are not likely to disappear rapidly.

For each behavior of concern, the team develops a clear and specific definition in observable terms. As the team prioritizes behavior, its guiding questions consider safety, severity, frequency, and the relative impact of the problem behavior on the student's instruction and quality of life. This requires the team to elicit input from various sources (e.g., several teachers and staff members) and contexts (home, community, and school). Student support teams use the defining and prioritizing behavior form to document their definitions of behavior and to note the factors they have considered in establishing their priorities.

Defining Behavior

Formulating concrete, objective descriptions of behavior does not come easily to all teams. When initially asked to describe behavior, some team members may focus on presumed underlying motives, functions, and consequences. One team we worked with described a third grader's behavior as out of control and indicated that this occurred many times in a week; eventually, they refined their behavioral definition to state:

> Noncompliance—refusal to follow specific teacher instructions. This behavior occurs daily, often up to three or four times per day. Intensity is variable, ranging from ignoring directions to defiantly doing the opposite of what was asked. The more severe episodes (about once every other day) often escalate to agitated resistance, including kicking and flailing if efforts are made to remove him to a calm-down area.

This definition, which includes statements about estimated frequency and severity, suggests questions that remain unanswered—namely, the setting events and antecedents relating to the problem behavior, and its precise frequency. The FBA is the opportunity to answer those questions. Note the objectivity of the statement; such objectivity is key to setting a neutral tone and directing the team toward solutions rather than dramatizing the student's difficulties.

Many team members initially respond to this task with speculation about internal states, external influences, or personality traits. They might offer behavior descriptions such as "he's very angry," "she has poor self-esteem," "they let her get away with it at home," or "he's hyperactive." Although these statements may be accurate, they do not provide a clear starting point for assessment and intervention. At the definition stage, teams are advised to forego discussion of internal traits and external influences and instead focus on priority behaviors in which the student engages.

Teams may state their definitions formally (as above) or reach a consensus using an informal but clear set of terms or phrases. In another case, a student was described first as constantly off task, calling out, and making strange noises in class. The team also expressed a belief that these behaviors were related to a poor home environment, reflecting rumors about possible domestic violence. After discussion, the team described two target behaviors, and one member contacted the family. The behaviors were:

> Behavior 1: Off-task behavior: begins as fidgeting, escalates to calling out, making unusual noises, getting out of his seat, disrupting the entire class.
>
> Behavior 2: Calling out answers and comments during whole-class instruction.

The team recognized that the student's calling out did not consistently cluster with his more problematic off-task behavior. Although they were concerned that difficult family circumstances (setting events) might contribute to the behavior, the final definitions of the target behaviors were confined to descriptions that anyone might observe. Ascribing motive or causality at this step is premature; it also tends to oversimplify behavior and sidetrack the team from more productive efforts. Examples of effective behavioral descriptions include:

- Refuses to follow teacher directions; says "I don't want to," folds his arms, and refuses to speak
- Throws books into his locker, slams the door, and throws his backpack at or toward other students
- Bites herself on the forearm and hand, leaving a reddened area on the skin
- Makes bizarre or obscene sounds and gestures during class
- Sings loudly and talks to others while the teacher is giving an assignment
- Hums and sings (without apparent awareness) during lessons
- Calls out in class without raising his hand or being called on
- Physically aggressive; hits other students (punches and kicks)
- Taps a pencil repeatedly on the table

In sum, defining behavior requires three elements: delineating clusters of behavior that consistently occur together; developing a clear, objective definition for each; and providing an estimate of the frequency of the problem behavior. Effective descriptions do not reference presumed personality characteristics, motives, underlying causes, or effects of behavior.

Prioritizing Behavior

As stated earlier, an inherent challenge for many student support teams is that students requiring FBAs and BIPs often engage in several challenging behaviors. School personnel are under pressure to address all of them. Although this pressure is understandable, teams are much more likely to be successful when they prioritize behaviors in terms of functional impact and address them accordingly.

There are several reasons to address behaviors in sequence rather than attempting an all-encompassing assessment and intervention. First, multiple behaviors may serve a single underlying function. For example, a student may have two distinct sets of problem behaviors that are motivated by tangibles—attaining desired objects or activities. The team conducts an FBA on the first target behavior, uncovers its motivation, and develops a BIP that contains accommodations and teaches the student effective replacement behaviors. Although it aims to address only the cluster with the greater impact, a BIP may reduce both clusters of problem behavior.

A second reason to prioritize behaviors also concerns underlying functions of behavior and relates to the challenge of tailoring the intervention. When problems are appropriately prioritized, teams conduct FBAs and BIPs, incorporating short-term accommodations for prevention and a program to promote replacement skills. Sometimes, intervention effects wane; the accommodation ceases to bring the antecedent below the threshold at which it triggers problem behavior, or the student's appetite for the reward becomes sated. The team notices that the intervention is losing effectiveness and begins to discuss possible reasons for this. Under these circumstances, they are managing the impact of a single behavior and the plan to address it; even this is difficult. When teams deal with multiple, complex behaviors, it is extremely challenging to disentangle the many influences involved. Targeting assessment and intervention to a single cluster increases the team's ability to troubleshoot a support plan.

A third reason to prioritize behaviors is entirely pragmatic. Although it is theoretically possible to evaluate several behaviors simultaneously, this is not feasible or realistic in many schools. Addressing a single challenging behavior cluster often requires an ambitious plan and ample human resources. Undertaking more than one behavior diminishes the likelihood of successfully addressing any.

Defining and Prioritizing Behavior Form

Teams use the defining and prioritizing behavior form to organize discussion and reach consensus regarding which behavior or cluster of behaviors to address first. The defining and prioritizing behavior form allows for consideration of up to four problem behaviors. Although some students engage in more than four problem behaviors, teams necessarily limit themselves to discussing a manageable number. They begin by providing an operational definition of each behavior in observable and measurable terms. As mentioned earlier, this sometimes proves to be a stumbling block; an experienced coach can be very helpful in focusing the team's efforts toward behavioral descriptors.

We recommend that teams use this form, or employ a similarly structured process, to establish their priority behavior. The first step, if not already done, is estimation of frequency. Because this is a preliminary review, it is not necessary to provide formal baseline data, but teams should include it when it is available. Team members familiar with the student estimate frequency in terms of number of incidents per unit time (e.g., twice a day, three times per 35-minute class period).

Teams examine the impact by responding to 12 items on the defining and prioritizing behavior form. The team determines how that behavior affects the student's education, inclusion in the mainstream, and participation in the least restrictive environment. This appraisal is somewhat subjective, but teams often reach consensus regarding the functional impact of behaviors. We based the impact list on the defining and prioritizing behavior form on past research and professional discussion about selecting behaviors for intervention (Durand, 1990; Evans & Meyer, 1985) and adapted it during our work with teams in general and special education settings. Because it is not exhaustive, we encourage teams to consider other areas of impact that are relevant in their settings.

Establishing definition, frequency, and impact is extremely helpful in structuring team decision making. First, it encourages members to be objective and neutral; behaviors initially described as constant may actually occur only two or three times per week. Second, even behaviors of moderate concern are sometimes found to have relatively low impact. For example, behaviors that are annoying or counterproductive (e.g., tapping, noncompliance, thumb sucking, humming) do not warrant complete, formal FBAs and BIPs. Third, this activity relates closely to information gathering and assessment of student–environment fit. As teams complete this exercise, they sometimes decide to make short-term instructional or environmental accommodations to encourage and motivate the student, altering the need for further intervention.

Once they have considered frequency and impact, teams often find that their priorities are clear. The defining and prioritizing behavior section provides space for the team to denote which behaviors are first (and second) priority, with the option of stating a rationale. If a team has difficulty reaching consensus, it is wise to target behaviors that are part of an escalating behavioral sequence. For example, a student frequently yells loudly and sometimes escalates beyond that to hitting. In such a case, the team targets yelling as the first priority behavior and focus of the FBA, hoping to eventually replace both behaviors with more adaptive skills. If intervention successfully reduces the incidence of yelling, it will also reduce hitting.

Once priority is established, the team moves on to the FBA and BIP for that behavior, perhaps occasionally considering how lower-priority behaviors relate, but confining efforts to the first priority. Subsequent efforts then replicate the *Positive Strategies* process and use its resources in succession. An example of a completed defining and prioritizing behavior form for Nathan follows.

Nathan's Functional Behavioral Assessment: Defining and Prioritizing Behavior

Figure 12 contains the defining and prioritizing behavior form that Nathan's team completed. The reader recalls that Nathan's problem behaviors involved yelling at the teacher and cursing,

Student: Nathan Jones Date: October/November

Behavior: Using behavioral terms, describe the behaviors of concern. Provide actual or estimated frequency for a given unit of time (e.g., 15 times per day, 2–3 times per week).	**Frequency**
1 Yelling at teacher and cursing—raises his voice to teacher, makes rude comments, and then mutters "curse words"	4–6 times per day
2 Running out of the classroom	3 times per week
3 Hitting peers	2 times per month
4	

Impact: For each of the behaviors (as numbered above), check off the impact statements that apply.	**Behavior** 1	2	3	4
Poses a physical or health risk to the individual			X	
Places others at risk for injury			X	
Causes property damage				
Is a significant concern to student's parents	X		X	
Interferes with learning	X	X	X	
Interferes with participation in school	X	X	X	
Interferes with participation in community				
Disrupts classroom or other school routines	X	X	X	
Precludes participation in less restrictive environment	X		X	
Has recently escalated in frequency or intensity		X		
Is an antecedent to other behavior problems	X			
Other:				

Conclusions: Based on this review of frequency and impact for each behavior, indicate priority of target behaviors. As needed, provide a brief rationale.

First priority behavior: Yelling at teacher and cursing

This was identified as a top priority because of its high frequency, and the fact that it frequently serves as a precursor to the other behaviors, Nathan tends to run out of the class or begin hitting after an episode of cursing which has not resulted in his being sent out of the classroom.

Second priority behavior: Running and hitting

As noted above, these two behaviors tend to follow yelling and cursing, so team plans to conduct a functional behavior assessment and a behavior support plan regarding target behavior 1; will monitor leaving classroom and hitting.

Figure 12. Nathan's defining and prioritizing behavior form.

running out of the classroom, and hitting peers. Nathan's student support team discussed and defined all of these behaviors and concluded that yelling and cursing were the most prevalent problems. They also realized that yelling and cursing almost always occurred before hitting and running out of the room; in fact, the support team members were convinced that yelling and cursing were part of Nathan's escalation pattern. When he was losing control, Nathan first mumbled to himself, then raised his voice to the teacher, made rude comments, and muttered curse words. Sometimes his escalation continued, in which cases he struck other students, ran out of the classroom, or both. Because yelling and cursing were most frequent, and because they typically preceded the other problem behaviors, the team placed them at the top of intervention priorities. They hoped that targeting the first priority behavior might lead to a reduction in the other behaviors clustering with it. The team agreed to address yelling and cursing first and made a commitment to monitor hitting and leaving the room as part of the FBA and BIP.

ASSESS STUDENT–ENVIRONMENT FIT

Children often develop behavior problems because they lack skills to succeed in their school environments. Even when special supports are written into a formal plan, many students fail to benefit from the supports, for one reason or another. Examining the student–environment fit entails viewing the instructional environment from the student's perspective: given his or her skill set, can we reasonably expect the student to succeed in this classroom? To answer this question, the team examines the student's individual learning style, sensory preferences, valued activities and reinforcers, social interests, and communication style and skills. Viewing the student's profile of abilities, skills, interests, and preferences against what the environment offers can bring areas of mismatch into sharp relief.

The relationship between the instructional environment and the student's learning style is sometimes overlooked in behavioral assessment. Effective FBAs attend to environmental influences and student characteristics together. For many students with persistent behavior problems, there are functional gaps between potential and performance and between expectations and routine behavior. In some cases, instruction is regularly targeted to the student's frustration level rather than to promoting success a majority of the time. Discrepancies between underlying cognitive skills and academic performance may be obvious, but gaps also arise in other areas such as social capabilities, participation in group learning, ability to tolerate transition, and reactivity to environmental conditions (temperature, lighting, and noise levels). Often, as teams gather information and review prior intervention efforts, opportunities for improved fit arise early in the *Positive Strategies* process. Assessing student–environment fit is more than mere preparation for the FBA; it should be revisited and adjusted as the team comes to know and understand the student over time, because environmental changes and student growth can alter the dynamics of this relationship. The findings of this assessment can also take on renewed importance when it comes to long-term behavior planning, because this component of the assessment is often a vital component of planning for new skill development and for the establishment of alternative behaviors.

Teams sometimes forego formal assessment of student–environment fit when they have a clear sense of the student's interests, skills, and motivations (unrelated to problem behavior) and a forthright appraisal of the classroom context. Often, however, teams find it useful to assess student–environment fit during the FBA process. The more variable the student's profile of strengths and weaknesses, or the more complex the relationship between environmental factors and the student's behavior, the more important this assessment becomes. For students with a specific disability such as restricted or impaired speech and language skills, problematic behavior may serve functions that might otherwise be mediated by that skill area. Similarly, students who exhibit complex patterns of strength and weakness are also more likely to benefit from a formal analysis of their fit with the current educational environment. The more varied the pattern of strengths and weaknesses, the easier it becomes for educators to err in identifying areas of weakness and relative difficulty. All too often, we see students whose skill in one area contributes to the expectation that they will be able to perform at comparable levels in other areas.

To assess student–environment fit, one or more team members may conduct a direct classroom observation to consider physical arrangement, how the instructor engages students, how instruction is presented (e.g., use of oral, visual, kinesthetic, and written input), and how transitions occur. In whole-class and other forms of group instruction, the teacher strives to present material in ways that are effective for the majority of students. Assessment of student–environment fit considers whether the typical mode of presentation and level of difficulty are suited to the individual student and whether they permit enough success to sustain motivation. Teams often begin planning with knowledge of when problem behavior is frequent and choose those times for observation. Direct observation can readily reveal, for example, that the student with problem behavior loses motivation and becomes disengaged before other students do. Although this may reflect setting events for the student, it also indicates that the student requires instructional accommodations to be engaged and successful.

In the sections that follow, we describe four *Positive Strategies* tools that examine student–environment fit (Crimmins & Woolf, 1997). We designed these questionnaires to assist in organizing the observations and impressions of individuals who know the student well. They seek information about the student's likes and dislikes, functional communication skills, learning style, and social activities. The instruments are not organized around the student's disabilities or difficulties. They tap unique child characteristics and often illuminate fairly immediate steps that teams can implement to improve the student's school experience. For example, group instruction may be targeted well above a student's language processing abilities, causing frustration and apparent noncompliance. Immediate accommodations might involve using visual supports, incorporating the child's hobbies or interests into lessons, or providing supplementary language support for verbal instructions. Copies of the Communication Style Assessment, Learning Style Profile, Preference and Interest Assessment, and Social Network Assessment, along with instructions for using them, appear in the appendix.

Communication Style Assessment

This questionnaire supports assessment of communication skills. Teams often find it helpful to understand formal aspects of the student's communication style as assessed through traditional approaches: speech (articulation, fluency, speech sound production), language (vocabulary, syntax), and written expression (formulation, organization). In contrast to these abilities, the FBA requires understanding of *functional* communication skills: how the student expresses himself or herself, attends to communication, appreciates and applies nonverbal means (gesture, facial expression, tone), engages in dialogue (turn taking), and applies underlying language skills to communicate wants and concerns. These functional skills are integral to success in educational settings.

For students with problem behavior, examining functional communication is extremely important because challenging behavior often substitutes for other means of communication (Carr & Durand, 1985). Accordingly, effective intervention frequently involves teaching functional communication skills (Durand, 1990) that students can use in lieu of problem behaviors to communicate. Challenging behavior as communication originally gained attention when practitioners recognized its role in the problem behaviors of students with significant disabilities. Although those students often have limited functional communication repertoires, it is also clear that students with relatively strong verbal skills use problem behavior to communicate. This can develop when adults respond better or more consistently to behavior than to verbal requests. Recall our earlier example of Sam, who has difficulty concentrating for more than five minutes. In most school environments, even the most polite request to stop working on an assignment is likely to be met with a denial. So, rather than asking for a break, Sam just takes one by going off task.

A team that is informed about functional language skills is positioned to understand how the student's communication weaknesses contribute to behavior problems; this understanding may reveal functional skills the student needs to develop. Such considerations range from providing augmentative communication resources to instruction in a different language. In contrast to the IEP, the critical element distinguishing functional communication in the FBA and BIP is the goal of using communication to render problem behavior unnecessary.

Learning Style Profile

The concept of learning style is well established in the education literature; it holds that students demonstrate great diversity in how they learn most effectively and that there is no right or wrong style. Sometimes, however, when students receive group instruction, they are placed in environments that do not optimally match their learning styles. Instructional environments are usually conducive to the concerns of the average learner, to benefit the majority. In reality, several factors comprise the educational environment: the physical arrangement of the classroom, the teacher's style, and the availability of resources such as time, materials, and staff support. Although it is hard to accomplish, accommodation to individual learning styles greatly enhances learning.

A Learning Style Profile surveys student characteristics in terms of preferred modes for instruction, novelty, reinforcers, and other conditions associated with learning. A Learning Style Profile also surveys various dimensions of instructional and physical environments. Its goal is not to critique the program or the teacher; in our experience, most teachers work hard to adapt instruction to the concerns of learners. Rather, the goal of the Learning Style Profile is to identify areas of fit and mismatch that might contribute to a student's behavior.

Preference and Interest Assessment

This instrument is used to survey team members and families regarding the student's interests and preferred activities. As a result, teachers can adapt instructional material to reflect student interests and discuss appealing topics. Recalling that fewer than 10% of students have significant behavior problems, it is clear that the majority of students are relatively easy to engage, even when the material is not inherently interesting. If students are not motivated, or if they are distracted by other factors, challenging behavior is more likely. Although these practical reasons for incorporating student interests are sensible, routine incorporation of student (and class) preferences enhances motivation and learning for the entire class.

Social Network Assessment

Students with behavior problems, particularly those who also have significant disabilities, typically have a restricted number of social relationships. Challenging behaviors pose barriers to meaningful social relationships, which are in turn hampered by self-regulation impairments and inadequate social and communication skills. For some students, socialization in the community and school centers more on family, teachers, and other personnel than on peers. Examining and enhancing a student's social network can alter mood and self-esteem and provide peer models with whom the student can learn and socialize. In this way, improved social relations can diminish setting events by occupying the student's time more productively and by increasing self-esteem.

Social networks can also be overlooked in students without significant disabilities. Many students with recurring patterns of challenging behavior have social skills and self-regulation impairments, such that challenging and confronting others becomes their predominant means of relating to others. This is complicated by the reality that social skills are often considered to be outside the realm of education, making schools reluctant to invest effort in such instruction. Another consideration is the specific peer influences a student experiences at any point in time. If peers are involved in distracting, antisocial, or otherwise difficult behavior, the vulnerable student is exposed to situations that might trigger problem behavior.

A Social Network Assessment collects information about significant social influences in a student's life. Social network data can be collected via interview, observation of student interactions, and direct inquiry (asking students who their preferred peers are, or consulting a student's family). Although it is not critical to use this questionnaire, we recommend that teams give careful consideration to social influences on behavior. Before we discuss FBA methods in detail, let us examine how Nathan's team conducted an assessment of student–environment fit.

Nathan's Functional Behavioral Assessment, Step 1: Develop Student Profile

In Step 1 of Nathan's FBA, his team gathered background information, defined and prioritized behavior, and assessed student–environment fit. To assess fit, the team used a combination of approaches: analysis of learning skills and weaknesses as previously assessed (student background); observation by the consulting resource room teacher; and completion of the learning style profile. The team documented these activities in Nathan's FBA worksheets as shown in Figure 13.

STEP 1: DEVELOP STUDENT PROFILE

	Completed by	Date(s)
Gather background information		
☑ Consultation with family	Social worker	10/22
☑ Complete student background form	Teacher, social worker, nurse	10/21–10/23
Define and prioritize behavior		
☑ Complete defining and prioritizing behavior form	Student support team	10/29
Assess student–environment fit		
☐ Communication Style Assessment		
☑ Learning Style Profile	Teacher	10/30
☐ Preference and Interest Assessment		
☐ Social Network Assessment		
☑ Other: Observation and consult on accommodations	Resource room teacher	11/4

Figure 13. Step 1 from the Functional Behavior Assessment (FBA) worksheets, as completed by Nathan's team.

The team consulted Nathan's parents, and his mother joined the school staff for a team meeting. She was concerned that he might lose his current class placement because of his problem behavior, but the family felt somewhat at a loss to assist because he did not demonstrate these behaviors at home or in the community. Nathan occasionally got mad at home and sometimes argued with his siblings, but these were considered manageable and did not reach the same intensity. He had no behavior problems during athletic or musical activities. Team members concluded that Nathan's language-based learning difficulties probably had something to do with his behavior difficulties, perhaps acting as a slow trigger (setting event). They further assumed that because the behavior did not occur outside school, they needed to look carefully at the school context for fast triggers and maintaining consequences. Previously, Nathan had not responded to schoolwide and classwide preventive approaches; this surprised his family because he was very motivated for praise and recognition in other areas. As members of the team, the family agreed to keep in touch and said they would assist in any way possible, including enacting consequences at home if it would help.

To examine the school context, the team assessed the student–environment fit. The learning style profile completed by his classroom teacher indicated that Nathan worked best in small groups. He was most available for learning first thing in the morning and after lunch; the team conjectured that he was freshest at these points because they often followed times of little demand and some physical activity (walking to school, sports at recess). He responded best to instructions that were short in duration, that included visual and gestural cues, and that involved repetition. He also benefited from repeating instructions back, which was only possible in small-group activities. Nathan liked mathematics best and often did not even have to read the instructions for math problems; little to no support was required. For tasks involving reading (most subjects in his fifth-grade class), he worked best in short intervals. He often made excuses to get out of his seat and walk around. When reading or writing, Nathan was quite easily distracted, but he completed math problems as if in his own world.

Observation by the consulting resource room teacher confirmed and extended the classroom teacher's impressions. She noted that Nathan worked for very short durations on reading and writing tasks, becoming restless and fidgety after a few minutes. First, he sighed and then became more motorically active (shifted in seat, fiddled with pencil, looked around the room). At times, he returned to his work, and on other occasions, he raised his hand and asked to go to the bathroom, throw something away, or sharpen his pencil. On reading comprehension tasks, he showed less frustration on multiple-choice as opposed to open-ended questions. Math periods went well unless word problems were introduced, in which case Nathan usually showed less perseverance and more frustration. When the classroom teacher gave complex verbal instructions, Nathan seemed to tune out, averting his gaze; however, he often could repeat some of the directions and, with assistance, comprehend, repeat, and retain them. The consulting teacher was confident that she could suggest some accommodations that would reduce Nathan's frustration and support improved learning. We will return to Nathan's FBA at the end of Step 2: Assess Behavior.

ASSESS BEHAVIOR

In previous sections, we discussed the importance of using multiple approaches and informants to increase the likelihood of reliable and valid FBAs. We also detailed how effective FBAs prepare teams to develop BIPs tailored to a student's unique concerns and to reflect the realities of school contexts. In the section below, we present guidelines for FBAs and include several resources that teams use to conduct them. First, we enumerate a set of core questions (outlined in Table 10) to help teams match their FBA activities to the concerns of an individual student.

FUNCTIONAL BEHAVIORAL ASSESSMENT METHODS

With a specific behavior identified and a student profile in mind, a team embarks on the FBA. The first challenge they encounter is determining assessment procedures. Familiarity with the strengths and limitations of each method enables informed choices about the most useful tool for a particular behavior and setting. Because the preferred method depends on the nature of the behavior, teams base choices about assessment tools on information gathered for the defining and prioritizing behavior form. Logistical considerations combine with the frequency and impact of a behavior to influence which assessment methods are best for a given situation.

Given all the assessment strategies available, teams can be confused about which approach is best and how to combine information from a variety of sources to develop an effective BIP. Some teams resort to a routine set of procedures for every case—a cookbook approach. This is undesirable because overly standardized processes lead to unnecessary work in some cases and too little data in others.

As noted earlier, most FBA approaches fall into three broad methodological categories: interviews, observations, and checklists and questionnaires. In the next sections, we outline each, providing guidelines on when to use them. Figure 14 from the FBA worksheets illustrates the second step in conducting an FBA. Later in this chapter, we will examine Step 2 of Nathan's FBA.

STEP 2: ASSESS BEHAVIOR

	Completed by	Date(s)
Interviews		
❑ Student		
❑ Parent/family		
❑ Teacher (identify)		
❑ Other (identify)		
Observations		
❑ Incident Log		
❑ Scatter Plot		
❑ Antecedent–Behavior–Consequence Chart		
❑ Other		
Checklists and questionnaires		
❑ Motivation Assessment Scale		
❑ Functional Assessment Checklists		
❑ Setting Events Checklist		
❑ Other		

Figure 14. Step 2 from the Functional Behavior Assessment (FBA) worksheets.

INTERVIEWS

The first FBA method is interviews, conducted either formally (i.e., following a structure or protocol) or informally. Interviews involve discussing the student and the learning context with respondents who are familiar with both. In schools, key interviewees include students themselves, teachers, other classroom staff, related services providers, administrators, and anyone else with significant contact with the student. It can also be helpful to engage family members, not only to gather information but also to encourage their participation in the team. Team members may also interview the students themselves, assuming they are willing and able. Engaging students in their own assessment and intervention planning is consistent with person-centered planning; when teams allow students to participate meaningfully, it increases the likelihood that the eventual plan will reflect the student's interests, it capitalizes on momentum, and it encourages motivation. Preliminary research suggests that structured student interviews are comparable with staff interviews in revealing information about the context and consequences for problem behaviors (Wehmeyer, Baker, Blumberg, & Harrison, 2004).

The quality of interview data hinges on the interviewer's talent for eliciting information as well as his or her ability to avoid bias. Some proponents of functional assessment avoid interviewing, citing its subjectivity. For example, concerns include interviewer bias, when the interviewer's internal hypothesis about the function of problem behavior inadvertently influences the interviewee and skews the results. In the past, this and similar concerns led to a devaluation of the interview as a valid means of data collection. This is unfortunate because competent interview practices can yield valid contextualized data. Indeed, recent years have witnessed renewed interest in effective interviewing as a method of collecting information and developing hypotheses in school settings (Lohrmann-O'Rourke, Knoster, & Llewellyn, 1999).

To address legitimate concerns about subjectivity and bias, we recommend that teams use experienced members to conduct interviews organized around the central FBA questions presented in Table 10. It also is important to practice the generally recognized components of good interviewing:

- Ask clear, open-ended, nonleading questions.
- Engage in active listening and use follow-up probes.
- Allow the interviewee to elaborate when necessary, but guide the process.
- Avoid unnecessary interpretation of responses, and feed ambiguous information back for clarity.

To avoid some disadvantages that arise from personal interviewing style, some teams employ structured interview formats. A number of practitioners have developed guidelines for conducting this type of inquiry. Examples include the functional assessment interview (O'Neill, Horner, Albin, Sprague, Storey, & Newton, 1997) and *Screening for Understanding of Student Problem Behavior: An Initial Line of Inquiry* (Lohrmann-O'Rourke et al., 1999). The *Initial Line of Inquiry* format presents a series of leading questions with additional relevant information (i.e.,

Table 10. Questions associated with functional assessment

In clear, concrete, and observable terms, what is the behavior?
Where, when, and with whom does it occur most often?
Where, when, and with whom does it occur least often?
Is the behavior triggered by specific events or conditions?
Are expectations for this student realistic?
Does the environment provide opportunities for achievement, control, and mastery?
Does the environment support self-efficacy and self-esteem?
Does the student know a better way (sometimes behave and cope well)? Under what circumstances?
Does the student need to develop new skills (a better way)? What skills are needed?
How can we motivate this student? Can we adapt a successful class or schoolwide incentive program?

guiding questions for facilitators) noted. The questions in the *Initial Line of Inquiry* are designed to structure an interview process that identifies triggers for behavior.

OBSERVATIONS

The second major approach to assessment is observation. Like interviewing, observation has a long history and is probably the most common method that school support staff (psychologists, social workers, behavior specialists, and other consultants) use to assess behavior. Collecting data through direct observation is also one of the central methods of applied behavioral analysis. Although a great deal of insight can be derived from observation, it is important for teams to employ safeguards to promote reliability and validity.

There are two major types of observation, formal and informal; each of these is discussed briefly below. An FBA should include at least one observation conducted with the support of an assessment tool. In this section, we discuss the antecedent–behavior–consequence (A-B-C) chart, scatter plot, and the functional assessment observation form.

Formal (Structured) Observation

To protect against the biases inherent in informal observation, behavioral psychologists have developed several strategies for recording behavior in systematic and structured ways, which we discussed briefly in Chapter 4. *Positive Strategies* identifies several approaches that are well suited for use in school settings, and we outline several of these in this chapter. This is not an exhaustive list, and we encourage teams to use other empirically sound and efficient procedures. Before reviewing these observational methods, we raise four questions that teams should address as they embark on observations: 1) which staff member is going to be responsible for observation; 2) and 3) where and when are observations to be conducted; and 4) how long will the duration of observation be?

Informal Observation

Informal observation involves team members sharing incidental observations of the student's behavior. It may be planned as part of the FBA or it may rely on accounts from prior episodes of behavior (before the FBA). Because prior episodes were observed by staff, their descriptions can be valuable starting points in the FBA. They are, however, subject to errors in recall and other biases, so teams should supplement them with other data.

Informal observation occurs when an observer engages in casual observation of the child in the natural setting. In many schools, this happens when an outside observer (not a regular member of the classroom staff) visits the classroom to focus solely on the referred student. Frequently, this observer watches what is happening and makes notes; these observations are rarely systematic. Casual observation is useful because it provides an alternative perspective. An individual without distraction (e.g., organizing and conducting the lesson, attending to other students) watches for contingencies between student behavior and the environment. This may result in identification of subtle antecedents or other previously unrecognized patterns.

Limitations to casual observation include the fact that the observer is not an ordinary part of the classroom environment, and his or her presence may alter it. Casual observers are also subject to the same biases as interviewers; this includes attending predominantly to information that confirms one's own internal hypothesis and discounting observations that diverge from that impression. To minimize the effect of subjectivity, teams supplement casual observation with data collected and analyzed through more formal processes.

Who Should Conduct Observations?

At the outset, teams consider information from anyone who has made relevant observations and who is willing and able to share them. Accurate observations are best achieved, however, through structured interview formats, questionnaires, or survey forms (some are introduced in this chapter). Each method is characterized by strengths and weaknesses and demonstrates optimal fit only in selected circumstances. Systematic data collection requires that staff be adequately trained and have sufficient time to accurately record the relevant information. To minimize the impact of observer bias, collaborating team members work from a singular definition of the target behaviors and use consistent methods of notation.

Because the goal of collecting observational data is to obtain objective information, the question of which team member does the observing is significant. A number of factors enter into answering this question; they often include practical matters: Who has the requisite expertise? Which team members can be present when behavior problems typically occur? Is the problem of such complexity that substantial expertise is needed? This may require observation by staff who typically work outside the classroom. Personnel such as the school psychologist, social worker, or guidance counselor may be well qualified, although it is not always necessary for the observer to have a clinical background. In some teams, an administrator or consultant teacher conducts observations.

Good observers bear in mind that their presence has an impact on the setting. When visitors enter the classroom, students and staff may be conscious of the observer and alter their behavior. One way to address this is for observers to spend a significant block of time in the classroom, thus permitting students and teachers to habituate to their presence. Alternatively, trained classroom staff record observational data, after which the team compares those findings against others gathered by independent observers who have spent brief periods in the class. Consistency lends confidence to the team's assessment. Regardless of the details, effective teams consider reliability as they interpret findings. When individuals who know the child well indicate that findings coincide with their impressions, this is a positive (but not conclusive) indicator of reliability.

Where Should Observations Occur?

The second aspect of planning observations relates directly to the contextual basis of the FBA. Ideally, teams conduct their observations and collect data across as many settings as possible. This includes all relevant locations in the school (e.g., classrooms, hallways, lunchroom, common areas, and dismissal areas), home, work, day care, recreational activities, and other settings. Most critical, of course, is conducting observations in the setting(s) in which problem behavior occurs. Observing the student in other locations can provide useful information about the circumstances or conditions under which the student behaves appropriately.

There are a number of practical limitations that influence where school personnel can observe students and the type of data they can collect. Because the initiative for this process starts with the school, there is a clear mandate for observation and data collection in educational settings; collecting data from home and other settings can be difficult for school-based assessment teams. To accomplish this, teams need time, flexibility, and a good working relationship with the family. When a behavior occurs only in one setting, the temptation is to observe the student solely in that setting. Although observing other settings may be difficult, it can also be extremely valuable. Where direct observation is not feasible, many teams successfully employ interviews and other proxies.

When Should Behavior Be Observed and Documented?

Aside from the obvious need to document whenever behavior occurs, teams consider practical matters such as frequency. If the behavior occurs with low to moderate frequency, teams usually document most or all incidents. For high-frequency behaviors, constant recording may not be feasible, so teams use time sampling.

Time sampling involves designating a specific range of times during which observations are recorded. It is reliable when the sampling interval typifies what is happening the rest of the time. Periods selected for recording should be representative of a typical day (avoiding atypical days such as class trips, school assemblies, or state testing dates). Sampling decisions should consider settings, work conditions, and staff encounters that are typical during the course of the school day. This requires accounting for factors such as large- versus small-group instruction, morning versus afternoon classes, and beginning versus middle and end of instructional periods.

For How Long Should Observations Be Conducted?

This question is often asked before observation begins and is sometimes not answered until observation is in progress. It is not always possible to predict how long the observation period will be. To conclude the FBA with a useful working hypothesis, teams collect data until clear patterns emerge. Members begin to see the relationships among setting events, antecedents, consequences, and behavior. For high-frequency behaviors, this is sometimes accomplished in a relatively short period of time, whereas lower-frequency behaviors may require longer observation periods.

Frequency and context interact to determine the amount of time needed to confirm patterns among triggers, behavior, and consequences. It is usually necessary to observe up to 15 or 20 instances of low- to moderate-frequency behaviors (those that occur fewer than 10 times per day) to infer triggers and consequences. For higher-frequency behaviors (occurring 5–10 or more times per instructional period), it is usually necessary to observe two or more complete cycles of student activity (days, schedule rotations, instructional periods). For students whose behavior occurs once or less per instructional period, it may be necessary to record data for several weeks before a pattern emerges. Likewise, students whose schedules involve complex rotations (subjects presented at different times of day) may require longer periods of assessment.

When multiple functions are at work and the rate of problem behavior fluctuates without apparent reason, it can be difficult to glean patterns. Under these circumstances, teams are wise to supplement observational data with other functional assessment techniques that can be conducted simultaneously.

TOOLS FOR USE IN OBSERVATION

Antecedent–Behavior–Consequence Chart

An A-B-C chart is one of the most familiar methods of formally documenting observations. It requires logging all incidents of a behavior, along with the antecedents and consequences, for a specified time period. This approach has a long history of use in behavioral research and intervention. Like other instruments, an A-B-C chart has advantages and disadvantages.

An A-B-C chart provides richly detailed information, but the value of resulting data depends on how clearly it is recorded. First, entries have little use unless they document both antecedents and consequences in concrete, observable terms. A related concern is the reliability and completeness of data. Observers may miss some incidents or inaccurately describe an antecedent as pivotally influencing behavior when it does not, erroneously inferring causality between two events that occur in close proximity. A clear advantage of an A–B–C chart is its production of contextualized data; however, because it is prone to observer bias, teams generally supplement it with other forms of assessment.

Making entries is moderately time consuming; an average entry requires 2–3 minutes to record, and during this time, the observer can pay only limited attention to the environment. For high-frequency behaviors occurring more than several times per hour, detailed entries quickly become impractical or impossible. Several strategies might ameliorate these difficulties. First, teams may assign a person whose sole responsibility is to observe behavior and record data (an extra staff, paraprofessional or teacher's aide, or someone temporarily relieved of other duties). Alternatively, teams can use an A-B-C chart in a time sample. The observer makes entries in the chart during selected intervals (e.g., the first 10 minutes of each hour) or at times known to be problematic (e.g., waiting for the bus, a difficult subject, or transitions).

Scatter Plot

Another method for structuring observational data is a Scatter Plot. Although this approach does not provide the kind of contextualized detail an A-B-C chart affords, it is a quick and efficient way to record behavior. Completing a scatter plot involves checking off or tallying each time period during which the behavior does occur (secondary entries can also be made to record multiple incidents or high rates of behavior during a given time period). This is an efficient way to determine specific days or periods of time when the problem behavior occurs.

Data from a scatter plot are analyzed through visual inspection. The goal is to identify patterns of occurrence and nonoccurrence, as indicated by concentrations of data points in specific areas of the grid. Once a pattern of occurrence is identified, it is examined further in relation to setting events, antecedents, and consequences. This is done by interviewing key informants, reviewing the student's schedule, completing an A-B-C chart, and analyzing other factors (e.g., task demands) that might influence behavior.

If no clear pattern emerges on an initial scatter plot, teams can decrease the time interval for recording incidents. For example, it might be useful to observe in 10- rather than 30-minute intervals. Another strategy for recording high-frequency behaviors is reversal; teams record when the behavior is absent (or conspicuously infrequent), thus reversing the typical notation pattern.

Because a scatter plot involves relatively few recording demands (only a few seconds per incident), it requires few resources other than an observer. Recording can be done unobtrusively, having little impact on the behavior observed or on the environment.

Incident Log

Goldstein's (1999) Hassle Log inspired development of the Incident Log used specifically for *Positive Strategies*. The Hassle Log requires students to identify and record factors that affect their behavior; we used the Goldstein model to create an outline of important factors related to problem behavior, and we incorporated them into a checklist format. The log provides an organized method for analyzing incidents either singly or in aggregate.

We originally developed this Incident Log for use in a high school program through which many students participated in work-study preparation programs; although we subsequently broadened its focus, teams are nonetheless advised to customize it to their settings. Its intended use is logging incidents of problem behavior, noting which setting events, antecedents, and consequences were present. Observing multiple incidents is required to discern meaningful patterns of behavior. Depending on the consistency and complexity of the problem behavior and contexts, teams may need to log anywhere from half a dozen to 25 incidents.

A rapid visual scan of the Incident Log reveals that it requires the respondent to note the most salient features associated with the target behavior: context (time and location), setting events (more detail regarding these can be identified via the setting events checklist), antecedents, problem behaviors, consequences, and function. Because the log is usually completed during observation, it allows for fairly straightforward identification of antecedents. In addition to those listed in the log, Table 11 includes common antecedents for problem behavior in schools.

When identifying antecedents, teams determine which circumstances, conditions, or stimuli switch the behavior on. When completing an incident log (or otherwise ascertaining antecedents), it is useful to ask what might make the behavior stop happening.

Advantages of an incident log include its relative ease of use and contextualized approach. It comprises a range of triggers and consequences that might not otherwise be examined by teams. A related caution, however, is that it can be self-limiting because unique or idiosyncratic factors that are not part of this inventory may be ignored. The remedy is to combine the incident log with other forms of assessment to ensure that the team considers a range of triggers and consequences.

Functional Assessment Observation Form

A number of other methods for recording observations of behavior are documented in the literature. One example is the Functional Assessment Observation form (O'Neill et al., 1997). This chart allows an observer to record up to 25 incidents of several different behaviors for a period up to several days or weeks. The form allows respondents to indicate (by checking) typical pre-

Table 11. Examples of antecedents typically observed in schools

Given specific assignment or type of work to do
Being teased, called names, verbally abused, or berated
Victim of physical aggression, threat, or provocation
Told no after asking for something
Frustration or failure on a task
Task demands exceeded perceived or actual capacity or endurance
Interruptions, especially during preferred activity
Waiting
Performing tedious tasks
Transition between activities, classes, or contexts
Interaction with a specific person (teacher, principal, peer)
Crowded conditions, loud noise or other (over)stimulation
Reprimanded or redirected

dictors (antecedents), to notate perceived functions (apparent functions or motivators of behavior), and to record consequences for each behavior.

The Functional Assessment Observation form permits efficient recording of a considerable amount of information and organizes data for efficient analysis. The authors' description of their methodology for completing the form is rather extensive, and they caution that staff require 45 minutes of training to ensure accuracy.

CHECKLISTS AND QUESTIONNAIRES

Checklists and questionnaires are valuable, widely used tools for assessing behavior in contexts ranging from schools to clinical settings. Most involve a list of problems seen in children of particular ages, to which the respondent indicates whether a problem is present and sometimes rates its frequency, severity, or functional significance. Checklists and questionnaires are particularly useful for collecting, organizing, structuring, and analyzing information about a student or behavior. Norm-referenced checklists such as the Achenbach Child Behavior Checklist (Achenbach, 2006) and the Conners Teacher Rating Scale (1989), although of high utility in traditional assessment models, are less helpful in FBA applications.

Like the interview, many checklists and questionnaires are susceptible to respondent bias and other limitations (misinterpretation, limited insight, inadequate specificity, and so forth). Because of these limitations, and because few instruments had been developed at the level of specificity the FBA requires, researchers and clinicians initially spurned this approach and focused on more direct methods of assessment. Today, checklists and questionnaires are used in conjunction with other methods. In this section, we discuss the Motivation Assessment Scale (MAS), Functional Assessment Checklist for Teachers and Staff (FACTS), and Setting Events Checklist.

Motivation Assessment Scale

Of primary importance in the FBA process is identifying the function of problem behavior. The MAS is designed to do just that. Developed by Durand and Crimmins (1992), the MAS is a brief questionnaire completed by individuals familiar with the student and the behavior of concern. Because the MAS is relatively easy to complete and score (usually requiring 10 minutes or less) and provides information about the function of a behavior, it is often a useful first step in the FBA process. When completed and scored, the MAS provides a ranking of the contribution of attention, escape, tangibles, and sensory consequences.

Along with the benefits of the MAS, teams are cautioned about limitations and potential misuses. Most importantly, the MAS is not a substitute for an FBA. Although it demonstrates reliability and validity, results reflect respondent perceptions of behavior and are subject to bias. The MAS is designed to reflect the relationship between behavior and context, so several team members may need to complete it. As is the case with any single assessment tool, we advise teams to consider MAS results with other data; teams look for evidence that confirms or disconfirms MAS findings, pursuing avenues of convergence and divergence until a hypothesis is formed.

A second caution relates to the team approach. Some teams complete the MAS as a committee, entering responses after reaching consensus. The MAS was designed, and its psychometric properties examined, based on responses of single individuals. When it is completed by consensus, information can be lost or distorted, and the effects of context can be confused.

Whereas the committee MAS may suppress or distort information about function, assessments by separate respondents can result in different rankings. Inconsistent rankings underscore that the MAS relies on observer judgments. Discrepancies do not, however, indicate that one or more respondents is wrong about problem behavior. Instead, divergent rankings may indicate that the behavior is motivated and maintained by different factors in different settings. Understanding these discrepancies can lead to valuable insights that translate into change.

The Functional Assessment Checklist for Teachers and Staff

The FACTS (March, Horner, Lewis-Palmer, et al., 2000) is an interview format for school personnel to describe a student's problem behavior and to identify antecedents and consequences. Based on their experiences, respondents offer their impressions about possible functions of behavior. The team may use this information to develop a support plan or to guide more complete functional assessment efforts. The FACTS, which consists of two short forms (Parts A and B), can be particularly helpful for collecting information from individuals who encounter the student across different settings. At the elementary level, this might include music or art teachers, cafeteria staff, and playground monitors. At the secondary level, this might apply to instructors of various subjects.

The FACTS is designed to be a time-efficient method for the initial organization of FBA information. It permits fairly straightforward categorization of problem behaviors, routines during which they occur, related setting events, and consequences. It includes a summary section, in which teams can note their impressions, and a confidence rating regarding the accuracy of the summary.

The FACTS can be completed in 15 minutes or less, and respondent groups generally become more efficient with practice. A limitation of this tool is the degree to which documentation occurs in isolation from direct observation. The respondents reflect on their history of recent encounters with the student and draw conclusions about potential patterns among the typical antecedents and consequences. Because the form provides little structure or direction, personal judgments may shape findings to a large extent. As a result, key variables may be underestimated or overlooked, and incidental factors that made a strong impact on the observer may be stressed. Accordingly, it is important to combine results of the FACTS with direct observational data and other means of assessment.

Setting Events Checklist

Recall that setting events refer to distal factors (slow triggers) that exert an influence on problem behavior. The setting events checklist is designed to help teams ascertain several conditions that are not immediate antecedents of behavior and that may not be observed in the setting in which the behavior occurs. Originally developed by Gardner, Cole, Davidson, and Karan (1986), we provide an adapted version that presents additional factors relevant to educational settings. Because the setting events checklist taps slow triggers, family members and others not present during school are necessarily involved as respondents. Table 12 lists setting events commonly encountered in school settings.

The Setting Events Checklist includes these and other factors organized along four dimensions: *physical, learning and self-regulation, social-emotional,* and *environment and routines. Physical*

Table 12. Sample setting events affecting students

Physical
Neurodevelopmental disorder or physical disability
Physical conditions or illnesses (e.g., seizures, menses, allergies)
Missed medication, medication side effects
Disrupted sleep
Acute/chronic pain, illness, fatigue
Learning and self-regulation
Learning or developmental disability
Attention deficits
Hyperactivity
Organizational difficulties
Limited impulse, anger control
Atypical sensory needs
Slow to respond, needs high level of input
Social-emotional
Peer conflict rejection
Social isolation
Negative interaction (e.g., argument or confrontation on the bus)
Trauma, abuse, neglect
Significant family or social stressors (e.g., neighborhood violence, poverty, loss)
Environment and routines
Schedule change requiring adjustment
Substitute teacher or other caregiver
Family routine changed
Insufficient/excessive environmental input
Rushed or hurried routine
Time of day, day of the week, time of year
Change in school, class, routine

includes those that impact an individual's general sense of health and well-being, including such issues as chronic or transitory medical conditions, pain or discomfort, appetite or sleep disturbance, and so on. *Learning and self-regulation* triggers include both long-standing and time-limited effects of constitutional factors, such as neurodevelopmental disabilities (e.g., motor challenges, learning or cognitive disabilities, mental retardation, autism), related executive functions (e.g., attention, concentration, organizational skills), self-control (frustration tolerance, anger management), and affective and sensory regulation (e.g., atypical sensory issues). Setting events in the *social-emotional* realm include interpersonal stressors, both chronic (e.g., living in an unsafe neighborhood) and transitory (argument with a peer). *Environment and routines* includes any setting event that involves an alteration in routine, including scheduling modifications, changes or absences of a typical caregiver or instructor, and changes in the living environment.

Completing the Setting Events Checklist entails indicating which factors are present in a student's long-standing profile and recent experience. The form is often used for relatively infrequent behaviors (e.g., once a week or less) or when there is an unusual burst of higher-frequency behavior (e.g., a day with 10 aggressive incidents, relative to a baseline of an average of 2 per day). When problem behavior occurs, the setting events checklist helps teams examine slow triggers via consultation with instructional staff, family, and others involved in the daily life of the student. For example, a student may have particular difficulties on Mondays, after school holidays, or when required to awaken and ready for school in the dark (e.g., winter days when the sun rises late). These setting events may lower the child's coping threshold, making problem behaviors more likely under those conditions. As such, accommodations that ease the student's difficulties at these vulnerable points may diminish the occurrence of incidents.

Setting events influence behavior from some distance in time, which is why they are sometimes referred to as slow triggers. Within the category, however, their ability to influence behavior also ranges from relatively short-lived to long-standing effects. A disrupted morning routine, for example, is a somewhat transitory event that may set a tone of irritability for the rest of the day, but only that day. A long-standing factor, such as a learning disability or change in educational placement, may affect behavior for a long period of time.

For the purpose of the FBA, we are most interested in setting events that influence the specific behavior under consideration. Thus, we suggest that all potential recent events be noted in terms of gradually increasing timeframes (i.e., same day, the day before, or same week). For more long-standing influences, teams note which factors are likely to contribute to the behavior. For example, a short attention span may contribute to difficulties in peer relationships, but it is less likely to contribute to a behavior such as stealing. Note that many long-standing setting events may also be identified in assessing the student–environment fit, with plans developed to address them as needed.

Setting events have direct implications beyond the FBA to their efforts for teaching new skills (replacement behaviors). The student with attention impairments, for example, may need direct instruction and coaching in self-monitoring and self-control. If these self-regulation skills improve, the student may experience a diminishing of related setting event effects. This not only prepares the student for future learning opportunities but positively affects coping in other areas of the student's life.

Nathan's Functional Behavioral Assessment, Step 2: Assess Behavior

Step 2 of Nathan's FBA (outlined in Figure 15) employed all three methods of assessment: interview (consultation with Nathan and family), observations (scatter plot, A-B-C chart), and checklists and questionnaires (MAS, FACTS). On the basis of the student profile, the team assumed that Nathan's difficulties were linked to his learning skill impairments (setting events). Given that problem behaviors were confined to school, the team wished to further understand antecedents and consequences there. They used a scatter plot to determine the times and activities in which the behaviors occurred and the A-B-C chart to elucidate context elements and consequences in detail. The classroom teacher and resource room teachers completed the MAS and FACTS. When Step 2 was complete, the team met to review and analyze assessment results. Nathan's mother joined the rest of the team toward the end of the hour-long team meeting. In the next few sections, we interweave discussion of *Positive Strategies* steps with an overview of how Nathan's team analyzed behavior, formed a hypothesis, and tested it. Figure 15 depicts Nathan's Step 2.

STEP 2: ASSESS BEHAVIOR

	Completed by	Date(s)
Interviews		
☐ Student		
☑ Parent/family	Social worker	10/22 and 10/27
☐ Teacher (identify)		
☐ Other (identify)		
Observations		
☐ Incident Log		
☑ Scatter Plot	Teacher	11/3-11/7
☑ Antecedent–Behavior–Consequence Chart, during the 30-minute Language Arts class period each day	Teacher	11/10-11/12
☐ Other		
Checklists and questionnaires		
☑ Motivation Assessment Scale	Teacher	10/30
☑ Functional Assessment Checklists	Teacher and regular reading teacher	11/4
☐ Setting Events Checklist		
☐ Other		

Figure 15. Step 2 from the Functional Behavior Assessment (FBA) worksheets, as completed by Nathan's team.

STEP 3: ANALYZE RESULTS

What setting events were identified?	Physical	Learning and self-regulation	Social-emotional	Environment and routines
What antecedents are consistently associated with the target behavior?	Person(s)	Place(s)	Task or activity	Conditions
What consequences maintain the behavior?	Escape and avoidance	Attention	Tangible	Sensory
What function does it serve?	☐ Difficult task ☐ Prolonged work ☐ Social demands	☐ Peer ☐ Adult ☐ Group	☐ Food ☐ Object ☐ Activity	☐ Stimulation ☐ Sensory input ☐ Habit

What other consistent consequences were found?

What setting events or antecedents identified are associated with low rates of this behavior?

Figure 16. Step 3 from the Functional Behavior Assessment (FBA) worksheets.

ANALYZE RESULTS

How do team members analyze assessment results to arrive at conclusions about function? As suggested for many team activities, we recommend that Step 3 involve scheduling a meeting and establishing member preparation, timetables, and objectives in advance. One team member usually serves as leader and facilitator for analysis of FBA results. The team may organize their discussion around Steps 1, 2, and 3 of the FBA worksheets, also addressing the questions associated with functional assessment (as presented in Table 10).

Analysis involves review of each assessment method, using the FBA worksheets as a sequential index of activity. The worksheets follow the sequence of *Positive Strategies* activities and serve as a helpful organizer for the team. As suggested earlier, reviewing data involves analyzing areas of convergence and discrepancy within and across settings. By briefly discussing each FBA activity, the team summarizes the results of Steps 1 and 2 and then notes the results of its analysis on Step 3 of the FBA worksheets (shown in Figure 16).

Setting Events and Antecedents

Team discussion often results in a clear picture of the slow triggers that set the stage for problem behavior, the specific antecedents that serve as fast triggers, and the consequences that reinforce and maintain the behavior. In some cases, it may be difficult to distinguish setting events (slow triggers) from antecedents (fast triggers), and there are some factors that defy categorization. Precisely labeling a trigger as fast or slow, however, is less important than understanding its effect on behavior.

For example, the presence of a disliked substitute teacher may seem like an antecedent; during the course of one or more school days, however, the substitute's presence may exert a more slowly acting influence on behavior. Perhaps this teacher's presence alters the student's mood or changes the tenor of the classroom. What matters most is recognizing the relationship between the teacher's presence and fluctuations in the student's mood and behavior. Knowing whether this is a setting event versus antecedent is less important than considering accommodations that serve as effective prevention strategies. The team can also use this information to forecast future difficulties, which might predictably occur when this substitute teacher is assigned again or when the student experiences a similar disruption of routine. We recommend that teams forego extended debate on distinguishing setting events versus antecedents and instead focus on more salient aspects of analysis.

Step 3 of the FBA worksheets (analyze results) requires the team to note setting events (by category: physical, learning and self-regulation, social-emotional, and environment and routines) and antecedents (noting context factors such as person, place, task/activity, and conditions).

Specific context factors such as task characteristics, demands, interactions, and sensory conditions (noise, lighting, and so forth) may emerge as motifs in the team's analysis of the target behavior. The team gleans information about setting events and antecedents from all three FBA methods (interviews, observations, and checklists and questionnaires). Results listed in Step 3 reflect areas in which FBA data converge to indicate particular triggers influencing problem behavior.

Consequences and Functions

In addition to listing triggers, Step 3 requires the team to note results of assessment data relating to the function of problem behavior. The FBA worksheets permit the team to select from the four common functions of behavior (escape/avoidance, attention, tangible, and sensory), and the worksheets also provide room to indicate details about function. For example, recall Sam, who was discussed in earlier chapters. On the basis of the results of Sam's FBA, the student support team noted that Sam's disruptive behavior was motivated mostly by escape from independent seatwork, so his team would circle "escape/avoidance" and check "prolonged work." Another student whose hand biting is predominantly sensory in motivation may also engage in this problem behavior out of habit. If instruction ceases when the student begins biting, the behavior may serve as an escape function. As such, this student's team would note escape and sensory functions in Step 3.

Earlier, we cautioned against substituting the MAS for a more comprehensive examination of function, and we reiterate that caution here. Although the MAS is a logical source for this information, it is not the only one; teams also can obtain valid information about function from interviews, observation, and other checklists and questionnaires. Completing Step 3 involves understanding areas of relative consistency; the team will complete this section easily if their results point consistently to one or two functions.

It is critical that teams learn how consequences may inadvertently reinforce behavior. For example, consider a second-grade student whose father recently died (setting event). Rather than chatting quietly with peers while standing in line for the bus (expected behavior), he instead grabs lunch boxes from other children and teases them (problem behavior). Although lining up for the bus is routine for most students, it is a problem for this student.

Typical consequences for the expected behavior are mundane at best: the student is apt to be ignored and be bored, suggesting that a motivation for engaging in the problem behavior may be attention and an escape from tedium. This may emerge more clearly as a reinforcing consequence when the team finds that the student is receiving repeated redirection by numerous adults, dramatic reactions from peers, and escalating levels of negative attention. In this example (diagrammed in Figure 17), the student finds intense reactions and frequent adult attention more reinforcing than casual peer attention. Before the introduction of the setting event (loss of father), this child not only possessed preferred behaviors that gained attention, he also had sufficient behavior regulation to tolerate the antecedent (waiting). It is possible that the social-emotional stressor has affected his mood, affect, and self-regulation capacities. The resulting behavior change is reinforced by its consequences. As such, the target behavior is likely to continue until his prior coping skills resume or until the problem behavior is no longer reinforced, or both.

We mention elsewhere that effective FBAs note the contexts in which problem behavior is rare or nonexistent; Step 3 has space to denote this, along with consistent consequences that may not have been noted elsewhere. If a behavior meets a function other than one of the four listed on the forms, this can be noted just below the four functions, elucidated in Step 4. Once the team is satisfied with Step 3, they can move on to develop a hypothesis in Step 4.

When Analysis Is Challenging

Although some teams reach Step 3 with fairly consistent FBA results that point them toward a logical consensus, others may find that their results are not sufficiently consistent for the team to develop a hypothesis. For example, the team may have diverging FBA data about function, where it is unclear whether the behavior's primary function is attention or sensory. The team may face inconsistent MAS rankings by different respondents, and they might reach different conclusions about how consequences maintain the behavior. In such cases, team members engage in extended discussion about which conclusions are accurate.

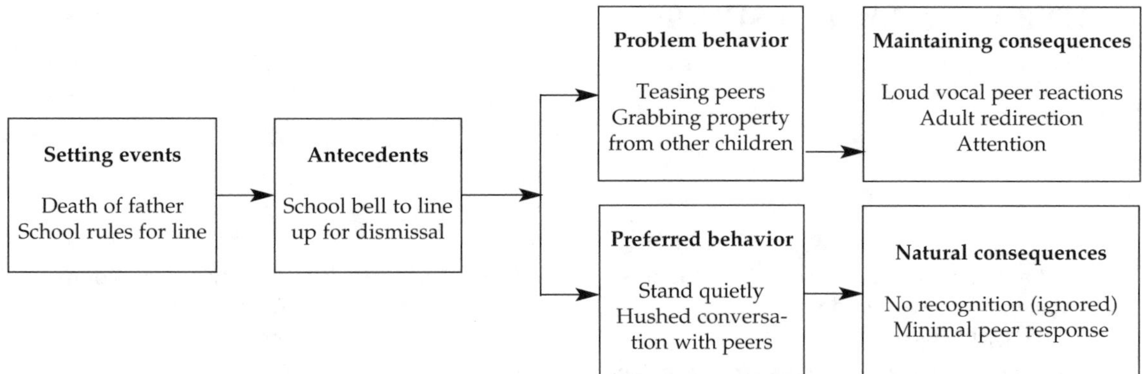

Figure 17. The relationship between setting events, antecedents, behaviors, and consequences. (From *Functional assessment and program development for problem behavior: A practical handbook* [2nd ed.], by O'Neil, R.E., Horner, R.H., Albin, R.W., Sprague, J.R., Storey, K., & Newton, J. [1997]. Reprinted with permission of Wadsworth, a division of Thomson Learning. Web site: http://www.thomsonrights.com; fax: 800-730-2215.)

If extended review and discussion do not produce a clear picture of the behavior, the team considers whether their FBA results have produced sufficient data and whether gathering more data is advisable. The most common reason for a team's inability to reach consensus in Step 3 is that they are analyzing complex, multidetermined behavior. Recall Denice, whose team's efforts were summarized at the end of Chapter 5. Initially, her student support team concluded that her behavior was motivated by tangibles, so they devised a BIP based on this hypothesis; when the interventions were unsuccessful, they resumed functional assessment. On the basis of the extended FBA, the team concluded that the primary motivator was actually attention.

In retrospect, Denice's initial FBA results did not converge to paint a clear picture of attention as the primary motivator. Did the team waste valuable time? Few teams may have been able to reach a more accurate conclusion with the same data. Denice's case illustrates the importance of examining areas of divergence. During analysis, the team might have asked questions such as:

- When is the behavior rare or nonexistent?
- Could behavior be motivated by different consequences in different settings?
- Why do various respondents rate function differently on the MAS?
- Why do MAS results not jibe with observational data?

Denice's case also underscores the value of formally testing the hypothesis in a way that also probes the effectiveness of proposed accommodations or interventions. In Denice's case, hypothesis testing would have produced equivocal results at best, suggesting that the team's hypothesis did not adequately explain the target behavior. This would have prompted reconsideration of the working hypothesis via extended FBA.

Another challenging aspect of analysis involves consequences. During the FBA, teams identify the circumstances that routinely follow the behavior and influence its future probability. They are usually examining immediate consequences delivered by the teacher or other adult. Although this information is a legitimate aspect of identifying consequences, it emerges from an adult perspective (recall our Chapter 1 discussion of punishment and reinforcement). To understand the function of a behavior, it is necessary to adopt the student's perspective. For example, a student engages in disruptive behavior, shooting rubber bands at classmates during a lecture; the teacher might describe the consequence as a disciplinary action—sending the student to the principal's office. Viewed from the student's perspectives, outcomes might include:

- Escape from a boring lecture or difficult work activities in class
- Being the center of peer attention; peer approval for disrupting the class lesson
- Status among peers for challenging authority
- Attention and engagement as the student goes to the office, chats with the secretary, and meets with the principal

STEP 3: ANALYZE RESULTS

What setting events were identified?	Physical	Learning and self-regulation Low frustration tolerance Language-based learning disability	Social-emotional	Environment and routines Classroom
What antecedents are consistently associated with the target behavior?	Person(s)	Place(s)	Task or activity Word problems Written tasks	Conditions
What consequences maintain the behavior?	Escape and avoidance	Attention	Tangible	Sensory
What function does it serve?	☑ Difficult task ☐ Prolonged work ☐ Social demands	☑ Peer ☐ Adult ☐ Group	☐ Food ☐ Object ☐ Activity	☐ Stimulation ☐ Sensory input ☐ Habit

What other consistent consequences were found?

What setting events or antecedents identified are associated with low rates of this behavior?
Group work, tasks Nathan is able to complete in collaboration with other students. Rare at home and in community.

Figure 18. Step 3 from the Functional Behavior Assessment (FBA) worksheets, as completed by Nathan's team.

- Intended discipline (being sent to the office) is no big deal (he has habituated to the consequence and does not find it upsetting)

For challenging analyses, it is especially helpful for teams to view the situation from the student's perspective. Although this scenario illustrates just one example, we encourage teams to consider the student perspective on setting events, antecedents, and consequences alike.

Many persistent problem behaviors are explained by the four categories of the MAS: escape, attention, tangible, and sensory; however, these categories do not account for all situations. Related and mixed examples of behavioral functions in school settings include provoking predictable reactions (e.g., the teacher responds predictably; the student gets a rise out of the adult), passing time, responding out of habit, and exerting control (e.g., power struggles, forcing adults to react).

Analysis is a challenging but crucial aspect of conducting FBAs. If teams confront complex behaviors that defy conclusions about function, we advise them to conduct a hypothesis test before initiating intervention and to consider support from PBS coaches or from external consultants.

Nathan's Functional Behavioral Assessment, Step 3: Analyze Results

Nathan's team met for an hour to analyze the results of his FBA. The team leader restated the target behavior and quickly reviewed the student profile. The team discussed results of interviews, observations, and checklists and questionnaires. Members agreed that Nathan's language-based learning disabilities and low frustration tolerance were *setting events*. Results of the scatter plot, A-B-C chart, classroom observation, and FACTS collectively suggested that word problems and written (verbal) tasks were *antecedents* to his yelling. Nathan demonstrated the problem behavior only in school and, more specifically, only when required to work independently on language-based tasks. On the MAS, escape was ranked as primary, and attention was ranked as secondary *consequences*. Scores for *tangible* and *sensory* functions were smaller and were considered inconsequential. The team noted its conclusions in Step 3, Figure 18.

STEP 4: DEVELOP HYPOTHESIS

____Nathan____ engages in ____yelling at the teacher and cursing____ when __he has__
[*Student's name*] [*problem behavior*]
____work with language demands____, because when he does, ____he doesn't have to do the work (gets
[*antecedent*] [*typical consequence*]
sent out of room) and peers laugh____. This is more likely to happen when __work requires complex
[*setting event*]
written or verbal expression____ and because ____he lacks frustration tolerance (self-regulation)____.
[*setting event*]

Figure 19. Step 4 from the Functional Behavior Assessment (FBA) worksheets, as completed by Nathan's team.

DEVELOP HYPOTHESIS

Once team members are comfortable that their analysis clarifies triggers and consequences, they synthesize this information into a hypothesis—Step 4 on the FBA worksheets. Step 4 requires the team to articulate

- An abbreviated term describing problem behavior (e.g., for Sam, becomes disruptive; for Nathan, yells and curses)
- Setting events (slow triggers—either long-standing, transitory, or both)
- Antecedents (fast triggers; context factors associated with problem behavior)
- Consequences (what typically occurs after the problem behavior) and function (what consequences motivate and maintain) the behavior

In Chapter 5, we provide a format in which teams can compose their hypotheses. Once the team feels that they can confidently fill in the blanks, they are ready to compose a working hypothesis.

> [Student's name] engages in [problem behavior] when or after [antecedent], because when he/she does, [typical consequence]. This is more likely to happen when or because [setting events].

With increasing experience in conducting FBAs, teams can confidently develop their own formats for writing hypotheses that contain these essential elements.

Nathan's Functional Behavior Assessment, Step 4: Develop Hypothesis

Toward the end of the meeting, Nathan's student support team composed the working hypothesis that appears in Figure 19. Note its succinct approach and clear stipulation of presumed relationships among triggers, behavior, and consequences. This flows logically from Step 3 earlier.

TEST THE HYPOTHESIS

In Chapter 5, we discussed testing the FBA hypothesis and provided the example of Sam. For purposes of context, we remind the reader that the test is an experimental manipulation of the working hypothesis and that it serves to evaluate the kind of intervention elements that might be included in the eventual BIP. As such, the test involves establishing a sequence of conditions that are predicted to influence the target behavior. Testing Sam's hypothesis involved the manipulation of two antecedents and resulted in impressive decreases in problem behavior compared with the baseline (no change; maintaining typical conditions).

Because of the seemingly technical nature of formally testing hypotheses, and the fact that some perceive such testing as postponing intervention, teams often forego this step. We urge teams not to take this shortcut, especially when problem behavior is complex or long in development. As illustrated earlier (Chapter 5) regarding Denice, formal hypothesis testing can result in improved efficiency when it demonstrates that a working hypothesis is invalid or that a proposed intervention component may be ineffective. If testing confirms the working hypothesis and validates proposed interventions, the team has proven strategies to replicate and extend within the BIP.

Testing hypotheses may involve manipulating setting events, antecedents, consequences, or a combination thereof. As discussed throughout this book, altering *setting events* and *antecedents* may be done as short-term prevention strategies or as long-term instructional accommodations. Sometimes, a prevention strategy is slowly withdrawn as the student learns replacement behaviors. For example, a student who bites her hand for self-stimulation and escape may be permitted scheduled breaks from instruction while she learns to tolerate longer intervals on task and better means of seeking sensory input. As she experiences success, required time on task is increased, and she is eventually required to request breaks using new communication strategies.

Manipulating *consequences* is advised when the team concludes that an individual motivational system may be the most powerful element in maintaining behavior and when the student possesses alternative (replacement) skills. For example, consider a student whose behavior is motivated by tangibles; she receives desired toys and activities when she acts aggressively toward peers. She knows how to ask assertively (replacement skill), and she waits for desired items (setting event: self-regulation) when requested by an adult (antecedent). Discrepancy analysis reveals that setting events are not highly contributory (she can wait in other circumstances), but particular antecedents (free play) and consequences (peers give in) reinforce the problem behavior. The team tests the hypothesis in a way that also involves assessing the motivational system (e.g., reward for refraining from aggression and using alternatives). A time-limited enactment of this system informs the team about the intervention's potential effectiveness compared with typical (baseline) circumstances.

Step 5 of the FBA worksheets permits teams to note which setting events (slow triggers), antecedents (fast triggers), and/or consequences will be examined during the hypothesis testing. Teams note baseline conditions (usually no change), conditions that were altered (accommodations or interventions), intended outcomes (what did the team expect?), and actual results (what happened?). Although more detailed documentation may exist elsewhere, teams use Step 5 to summarize the findings of their test and the conclusions they have reached regarding their hypothesis.

Nathan's Functional Behavioral Assessment, Step 5: Hypothesis Test

To test their working hypothesis, Nathan's student support team reviewed the qualitative details in his student profile and FBA analysis and chose to make two different instructional accommodations, multiple-choice questions and a peer buddy. The first accommodation, multiple-choice questions, involved reduced language demands. The resource room teacher converted all of the questions on Nathan's worksheets from open-ended to multiple-choice format. This accommodation primarily targeted the antecedent events: assignments with language demands. For the peer buddy strategy, a classmate named John read questions to Nathan and helped him compose his answers. This accommodation addressed Nathan's learning disability and low tolerance for frustration (setting events) by providing support. It had the added advantage of addressing peer attention, a likely maintaining consequence: Nathan received noncontingent attention from John, a popular student. A third intervention involved both accommodations together. The results of testing Nathan's hypothesis are depicted in Figure 20.

Data on testing Nathan's hypothesis demonstrated that both the peer buddy and multiple-choice accommodations were effective compared with typical classroom conditions (baseline). The average number of incidents per baseline interval was 2.3, in contrast to about 0.5 incidents per interval across all interventions. The most effective intervention was the combined multiple-choice plus peer buddy condition, during which Nathan had no incidents. Toward the end of the third baseline period, the team added the combination approach, which had not been planned previously. Aware that its effectiveness might be attributable to Nathan's success with the previ-

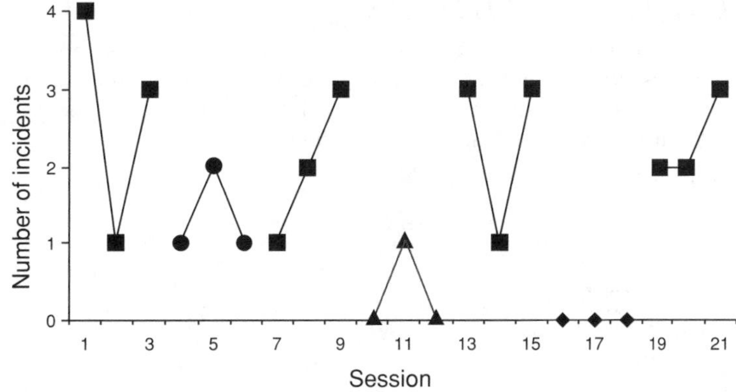

Figure 20. The results of testing Nathan's hypothesis. (*Key:* ■ = baseline; ● = multiple choice; ▲ = peer buddy; ◆ = multiple choice and peer buddy.)

ous accommodations, they were, nevertheless, pleased to see problem behavior eliminated during this condition. Thus, the team concluded that the modified instructional accommodation and peer buddy interventions were both effective. They noted their findings in Step 5 (test the hypothesis), as illustrated in Figure 21. Confident that their working hypothesis was valid, and aware that they had identified some interventions with proven (albeit short-term) success, they were ready to develop and implement Nathan's BIP.

At the completion of the FBA, Nathan's team conferred regarding the results. In preparation for the BIP, his classroom teacher and social worker met to write a brief summary of FBA activities and team impressions. The resulting document, an FBA summary, poised the team for a productive first BIP meeting. The summary became part of Nathan's record and is shown in Figure 22.

Chapter 7 (Behavior Intervention Plans) includes detailed discussion of the second phase of *Positive Strategies*: implementing the BIP. In Chapter 7, we discuss the methods teams use to prevent problem behavior, how students learn alternative skills to replace it, and strategies to maintain new skills in support of meaningful, lasting change. We also follow Nathan as his team formulates and implements his BIP.

STEP 5: TEST THE HYPOTHESIS

Conduct an experimental manipulation of setting events (slow triggers), antecedents (fast triggers), and/or consequences. Note baseline conditions (no change), conditions that were altered (interventions or accommodations), and results. While more detailed documentation may exist elsewhere, use this space to summarize the test findings and conclusions.

☐ Check here if formal testing was deferred.

	Results	Dates
☑ Setting events: Low frustration tolerance, learning disability		
Peer buddy, John—a preferred peer who is knowledgeable, friendly, and popular. For three-day period, John read the problems to Nathan and helped him compose responses.	Decreased rates of behavior compared to baseline—1 incident in 3 days compared to baseline average of 3 to 4 per day	11/9–11/11
☑ Antecedents: Work with language demands		
For a three-day period, work demands were reduced. Nathan was given adapted worksheets that required only multiple choice responses.	Problem behavior decreased to 0–1 incidents per day	11/15–11/18
Combination of peer buddy and multiple choice questions.	Completely eliminated behavior	11/21–11/24
☐ Consequences		
Not systematically addressed but peer buddy intervention provided noncontingent peer attention.		

Figure 21. Step 5 from the Functional Behavior Assessment (FBA) worksheets, as completed by Nathan's team.

Name: Nathan Jones Date of Report: November 30

Age: 10 years Grade: 5

Positive strategies team: Teacher, resource room teacher, school psychologist, social worker, school nurse, parents, and Nathan consulted on this assessment. Assessment activities were conducted between October 21 and November 24. Intervention planning is under way and several support strategies are already being implemented.

Reason for FBA: From the start of the school year, Nathan demonstrated an escalating pattern of disruptive behavior and disciplinary consequences. His teacher questioned whether placement in a mainstream class was appropriate and eventually requested consideration of alternative placement in a more intensive special instruction class, where Nathan might benefit from the reduced student–teacher ratio and increased support for learning and management of his challenging behaviors.

Challenging behaviors: Nathan's behavior problems include yelling at the teacher often combined with muttering curse words, running out of the classroom, and hitting peers. His FBA identified yelling and cursing as priority behaviors for two reasons—first, they occurred more frequently than the other behaviors (about 5 times per day), and second, yelling and cursing often serve as precursors to hitting and running out of the classroom.

Assessment approaches: (Results are recorded separately on *Positive Strategies* worksheets.)

Team consultation and discussion: Nathan's parents met with two team members and were also interviewed separately regarding their impressions of behavior both in and out of school. Two team members met with Nathan to discuss his view of triggers for his behavior.

Direct observation: Used by team members to conduct scatter plot and antecedent–behavior–consequence charts.

Checklists/Questionnaires: Team members completed the motivation assessment scale and functional assessment checklist for teachers and staff.

Student-environment: Fit was assessed through informal team discussion, the learning style profile, and observation by resource room teacher.

Background: Nathan is classified as learning disabled (language-based) and is enrolled in a general education class. He is mainstreamed for all subjects and attends resource room twice a week. Nathan's overall cognitive skills are in the average range. He has shown above–grade-level achievement in math, but has substantial difficulty with verbal and written language (significant aptitude/achievement gap). His parents prefer that Nathan maintain a regular education placement, but are concerned that his behaviors may make this difficult. They note that behavior problems occur mostly during school and are concerned a special education classroom may offer less intellectual stimulation and provide more negative role models.

Among Nathan's strengths is conceptual reasoning. He participates in the student orchestra and intramural athletics; he is a committed member of his basketball team. Nathan's primary teacher uses a classwide behavior intervention program to which Nathan responds intermittently. Before referring Nathan to the *Positive Strategies* team, his teachers employed warning cards and extra incentives; Nathan's behavior sometimes improved, but change was short-lived.

Findings: Based on the above-noted assessment, the team worked to clarify: 1) circumstances in which Nathan performed well, 2) slow and fast triggers (setting events and antecedents) relating to problem behavior, and 3) consequences of problem behavior. Nathan works best in small groups, especially early in the morning or just after lunch. He responds best to concise instructions accompanied by gestures or visual cues and repetition of key points. A pattern of escalation was identified: Nathan works intensely for a few minutes (even on reading and writing), then becomes restless and fidgety; from there, he may escalate to mumbling, yelling, screaming, cursing, and storming out of the classroom, depending on the circumstances. Thus, his language-based learning difficulties and limited frustration tolerance are slow triggers. Problems most often occur when Nathan works independently. Motivation assessment scale results indicate that escape is the primary motivation for Nathan's behavior, followed by attention as a secondary motivator. Following problem behavior, he was often sent to the office, with his work left incomplete; thus, the team surmised that leaving the classroom might unwittingly encourage the problem behavior. These findings are summarized in the hypothesis outlined below.

Nathan engages in problem behaviors when presented with difficult work. His behaviors typically result in avoidance of work, being sent out of the room, and laughter from his classmates. Incidents are more likely to occur when the work requires complex written or verbal expression, which may be a reflection of Nathan's limited frustration tolerance.

Hypothesis testing: The team tested the working hypothesis by implementing two different instructional conditions: 1) adapting Nathan's worksheets from open-ended questions to a multiple-choice format (reduce demands), and 2) providing a peer buddy (support). Peer buddy and multiple-choice format were both effective (the buddy a bit more so).

When these two approaches were combined, Nathan had no outbursts, compared to about 5 per day at baseline. Ms. Gonzalez conferred with all team members, including meeting with Mrs. Jones and Nathan together, to discuss these findings and seek input. All agree that the FBA conditions appeared to be helpful.

As this summary is written, the team is preparing to meet for initial behavior intervention plan development. Hence, results of this FBA and team feedback suggest that Nathan's plan should include elements of each component: adapted work and peer support.

This report was prepared by Eileen Coleman, Nathan's teacher, and Gina Gonzalez, social worker.

Figure 22. Nathan's functional behavior assessment (FBA) summary.

Chapter 7

Behavior Intervention Plans

Once the team understands the problem behavior, the FBA is complete. Implementing the BIP is the culmination of team efforts in *Positive Strategies.* Without it, neither teams nor students can engage in effective change efforts. Because it is so important, teams wishing for success embark on the BIP after careful planning and by rallying resources in service of their efforts. Their emphasis shifts from understanding to action, looking to replace the problem behavior with another that meets the student's concerns and strengthens his or her coping repertoire.

The effort invested in developing and implementing an effective BIP is generally in proportion to the severity and intransigence of problem behavior. A quality FBA (with a hypothesis that has been tested and confirmed) prepares the team to embark on some now logical student concerns. A clear hypothesis provides the greatest potential for an effective plan—one that addresses meaningful and valued goals that improve the student's quality of life and educational experience. The plan itself is part prevention and part management; this requires a team capable of anticipating difficulties, making accommodations, and figuring out how to manage challenges when they inevitably arise.

In this chapter, we provide an overview of the steps involved in planning and conducting BIPs and then take the reader step by step through implementation. Similar to the structure of the previous chapter on FBAs, the current one includes resources and references. As we guide the reader through each step of the process, we include a set of BIP forms that teams can use, adopt, and modify. The reader is reminded that although forms reflect the steps teams take, they should not be equated with the process itself. The best interventions revolve around students, not paperwork.

Figure 23 depicts the various steps involved in completing the BIP process. The reader will note that the BIP begins with a thorough review of the FBA (*understand*). The team then brainstorms a set of potential ways to *prevent* problem behaviors and to *replace* them with more acceptable alternatives. Because the problem behavior is likely to occur despite efforts to the contrary, the team considers how to respond to these incidents. Most importantly, the team considers elements essential to the student's evolving profile and team's efforts. Effective BIPs

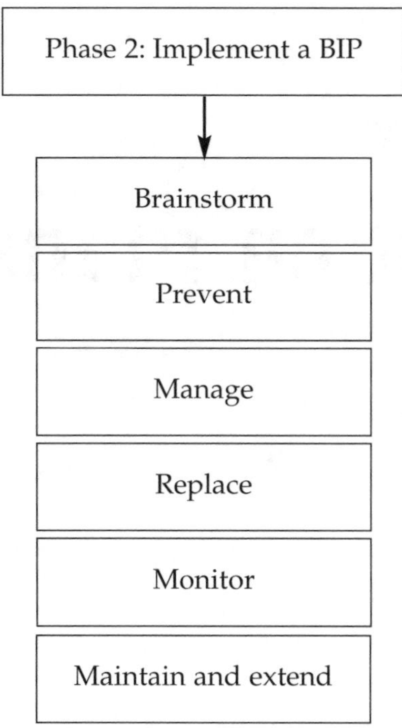

Figure 23. A steps in a Behavior Intervention Plan (BIP), a component of the *Positive Strategies* process.

stipulate means for evaluating intervention, assume that alterations and modifications will occur, and include plans for maintaining long-term change over time and place.

We developed the *Positive Strategies* BIP worksheets to support our own school consultation and team training efforts and modified them on the basis of experience and feedback; blank forms are included in the Appendix. We encourage teams to use the formats we provide here initially and to then customize the worksheets according to need and preference. Table 13 provides an overview of how the BIP worksheets relate to steps in the *Positive Strategies* BIP process.

Table 13. Overview of Behavior Intervention Plan (BIP) steps and corresponding activities

Step	Title	Corresponding BIP activities
1	Brainstorm	Review functional behavior assessment results Brainstorm how to manage, prevent, and replace behavior
2	Prevent	Develop short-term prevention strategies (temporary accommodations) Develop long-term accommodations to improve student–environment fit
3	Manage	Forecast and manage continuing incidents of behavior Develop a crisis management plan for serious problem behaviors Make necessary preparations for all aspects of BIP
4	Replace	Select one or more alternative behaviors to replace problem behaviors Teach, coach, and reinforce new alternatives Plan for generalization
5	Monitor	Track implementation Monitor incidents of problem behavior Monitor use of alternatives (replacement skills) Evaluate effectiveness; consider outcomes and related benefits
6	Maintain and extend	Forecast future challenges and prepare Assess maintenance of change and encourage skills across contexts

In the sections that follow, we detail the considerations and activities associated with each step of the BIP process. The succeeding sections follow the flow of activities outlined in the BIP worksheets. The reader may find it helpful to preview the worksheets and to have them accessible while reading the remainder of this chapter.

THE BEHAVIOR INTERVENTION PLAN

Teams base BIPs on what they learn about students in the FBA phase of *Positive Strategies.* A suitable means of preparing the BIP involves careful review of activities and findings to date. At the completion of the FBA phase, the team restates its working hypothesis. Let us return to Nathan, the student whose disruptive behavior and hypothesis testing were discussed in Chapters 5 and 6. At the completion of his FBA, the team's working hypothesis was

> Nathan yells at the teacher and curses when he has work with language demands, because when he does, he often doesn't have to complete the work as he gets sent out of room, and peers laugh. This is more likely to occur when work requires complex written or verbal expression and because he has difficulty tolerating frustration

Testing the hypothesis confirmed several aspects of the team's findings. Setting events (slow triggers) for Nathan include his language-processing difficulties and low tolerance for frustration. The most common antecedent for his aggression was independent seatwork with language demands. His aggressive behavior helped him escape frustrating situations and was maintained in part by attention from peers. Testing the hypothesis helped the team identify several feasible and effective intervention strategies. Knowing all of this, Nathan's team faces the tasks of building interventions that accommodate his learning style and teach him better ways to cope, get breaks from difficult tasks, gain attention, and tolerate frustration.

As any experienced educator can imagine, a BIP that achieves all of this requires flexibility, planning, and resources. It is likely that several talented and committed educators attempted to support Nathan before the assembly of the student support team. What can the team do now that will make a difference? One important feature of successful BIPs is creativity. After reviewing what they know, teams turn next to brainstorming BIP options.

BRAINSTORM

Brainstorming is a strategy used by groups and individuals to generate a diverse range of possible solutions to problems and questions. It is a time-limited activity during which novel solutions to problems are generated in an atmosphere unfettered by criticism and evaluation. Its application in *Positive Strategies* emerges from recognition that divergent thinking often produces innovative and effective solutions for behavior problems. Because teams begin brainstorming by restating the problem behavior, Step 1 of the *Positive Strategies* BIP forms involves a review of the target behavior and working hypothesis. The hypothesis becomes the springboard for lively, detailed discussion of the steps that follow. In this section, we discuss how *Positive Strategies* teams brainstorm elements of the BIP; in subsequent sections, we detail how teams consider and develop specific strategies for the steps that follow: prevent, replace, manage, monitor and evaluate, and maintain.

Brainstorming Guidelines

To be effective, *Positive Strategies* teams schedule time-limited brainstorming sessions followed by discussion. Because the session taps the expertise of team members and promotes an exchange of ideas, broad representation from different contexts and disciplines is beneficial. Many teams schedule a 30- to 45-minute meeting, devoting the first half to brainstorming and the second half to discussion and planning. The latter half of the meeting is used to hone ideas and to determine which solutions are most suitable to the BIP. Less important than the sheer amount of time the team schedules is how productively they use it. The pace of effective brainstorming and planning sessions should be quick, and their tone should be open, animated, and lively. Effective facilitation is key.

Brainstorming begins with a statement of the problem to be addressed—in this case, the target behavior and hypothesis. One member of the group assumes a facilitator role; this individual should be a member who is assertive enough to keep the team on topic and sufficiently tolerant of divergence to encourage creativity. Another member of the group serves as scribe, writing down ideas as they emerge from discussion (preferably on a flip chart or other plainly visible place). Inexperienced student support teams and those facing particularly challenging behaviors are advised to recruit a coach from the schoolwide behavior supports workgroup as facilitator. This person is unlikely to be distracted by minor details and has abundant experience from which to draw.

Effective sessions begin with a brief review of brainstorming guidelines and a restatement of the main questions under discussion. A more detailed list appears below. *Positive Strategies* teams may find it sufficient to consider three main questions as they begin discussion:

- Understand: What do we know about this student's problem behavior?
- Prevent: What can we do to make it unnecessary?
- Replace: What can this student do instead?

Brainstorming has several informal rules that assist teams in generating a menu of options for consideration. We discuss four guidelines that are important for *Positive Strategies* teams.

All Ideas Are Worthy of Consideration

The first rule of brainstorming is that all ideas are worthy of consideration. Unanimous participation is optimal. In group brainstorming sessions, there is an implicit risk that individual members will censor themselves. Further, socially powerful members may inadvertently quash creativity by directly or indirectly expressing disapproval of others' ideas. The scribe may choose not to legitimize some ideas by omitting them from the written record. When these or similar actions occur, the effective facilitator acknowledges them, redirects the group's effort, and continues the session.

Criticism Is Discouraged

Second, the brainstorming session generates ideas but does not entail evaluation of their feasibility. Because it cramps creativity, criticism is not permitted. For example, a member of Nathan's brainstorming team might suggest pairing him with a peer buddy for support. Another team member might express concern about Nathan's history of aggression, the team's liability of Nathan potentially striking a peer buddy, and the need to inform the buddy's parents. Another member might remind the team that a peer buddy intervention was unsuccessful 2 years ago. Although these may be legitimate issues for later discussion, for the purposes of brainstorming, they are nay-saying. If pursued in the brainstorming session, criticism sidetracks the team and diminishes the likelihood of generating effective solutions. Eventually, Nathan's team used a peer buddy successfully; an effective peer intervention might not have occurred if his team had been diverted by criticism.

When the authors conduct team training with multiple student support teams, we engage participants in an exercise that underscores the importance of an uncritical stance. Each team is asked to brainstorm BIP strategies based on hypotheses generated by another team. That is, teams swap student profiles and members develop potential BIP strategies for students they do not know. Members frequently develop the most innovative solutions for *other* teams. Although they are informed about the student profiles, they are not distracted by knowledge of student idiosyncrasies, bureaucratic obstacles, and other situational factors. The result is a refreshingly optimistic perspective that teams strive to replicate when they return to their own students.

Develop Team Members' Ideas

Third, effective brainstorming involves a balance between elaborating suggestions and limiting the amount of discussion any idea receives. Piggybacking occurs when one member suggests a strategy and another modifies or extends that idea. Consider a brainstorming session regarding a student, Nia, with very limited verbal skills and high rates of self-injurious behavior, mostly biting. The team's hypothesis is that Nia's self-injury is motivated primarily by escape and secondarily by sensory concerns. One member suggests that replacement behavior needs to effectively communicate the desire to take a break from instruction. Another team member suggests that Nia might learn to signal a need for a break by using a large jelly bean switch. A third group member responds by stating that Nia already knows the American Sign Language (ASL) sign for "stop," another possible functional communication strategy. Two or three other ideas follow. By piggybacking, the team generates several viable replacement behaviors in a short span.

The team then turns to discussion of other aspects of the BIP. Continued debate over the communication function and its replacement behavior might monopolize the session. Given time constraints, this may cause the team to inadvertently neglect prevention efforts and replacements for the secondary (sensory) function of Nia's self-injury. To prevent this, the facilitator asks whether there are any closing thoughts on communication (replacement) skills, then moves the team on to the question of identifying alternatives to meet the student's sensory concerns. As such, the facilitator and other team members exercise judgment and monitor time throughout the brainstorming session, permitting a sequential, time-limited discussion of each question.

Focus on Divergence and Novelty

As institutions, schools are often characterized by adherence to traditional practice, yet brainstorming requires focus on divergence and novelty. Of course, creativity does not preclude consideration of familiar practices, but it requires examining existing options in new ways. Teams that constrain themselves to habitual strategies stifle their options for supporting students. As such, each member might prepare for the brainstorming session by independently developing options they have never tried before. Sharing these strategies should not supplant spontaneous ideas generated during brainstorming, but preparation can be useful in promoting a rich range of proposed solutions.

In Chapter 1, we discuss the tendency for schools to require students to accommodate to them rather than the other way around. Because effective support considers environment from the student's perspective, teams engaged in brainstorming are advised to explicitly discuss options the *student* might generate. Indeed, we suggest that one or more team members discuss these issues directly with the student, offering choice whenever possible. Matching discussion and choice with the student's cognitive–linguistic capacities may be challenging in some cases; nevertheless, we advocate involving the student and supporting meaningful choices in support of person-centered planning whenever possible. Choice can be offered at many levels, from the content of assignments to preferred activities; staff who work with students with severe communication disabilities are expert in supporting the exercise of choice, and such expertise may be integral to including student input in the BIP. In some cases, it may be suitable to offer the student choices regarding activities, accommodations, and skills after the team has outlined draft BIP elements, and the input of family members can be enormously helpful whether the student engages directly in discussion or not.

Summing up the Brainstorming Session

Just as brainstorming begins with a statement of the questions to address, it also ends with them. Once the team has discussed the central questions before them, the facilitator concludes the discussion, again outlining three main areas of emphasis:

Understand

- What setting events, antecedents, and consequences contribute to this behavior?

Prevent

- What short-term strategies might prevent problem behavior?
- What long-term accommodations are needed to support this student?
- How do our brainstorming results relate to setting events, antecedents, and consequences?
- How might the team manage continuing incidents of problem behavior?

Replace

- What alternative behaviors or skills might effectively replace the problem behavior?

These questions are conceptual, not detailed. In summing up the brainstorming session, the facilitator encapsulates the discussion, brings it to conclusion, and prepares the team to transition into BIP development. Teams often choose to transfer several of their ideas and strategies into a written summary of the brainstorming session; this is best done immediately. In the next section, we follow Nathan's team as they brainstorm. Their summary, which appears as Figure 24, includes a restatement of the problem behavior and hypothesis as well as the results of Step 1, Brainstorm.

Nathan's Behavioral Intervention Plan—Step 1: Brainstorm

Nathan's student support team met for a 30-minute brainstorming meeting that preceded their BIP development session. The school psychologist, a member of the schoolwide behavior support workgroup, was the team's coach and served as facilitator for the brainstorming session. The coach began by restating the working hypothesis and then led the team in a discussion of various elements of the hypothesis, in sequence. (In the earlier section on critique, we discuss how parts of this brainstorming session might have gone.)

Behavior: *Yelling at teacher, cursing* FBA dates: *October/November*

Hypothesis (from FBA): *Nathan yells at the teacher and curses when he has work with language demands, because when he does, he often doesn't have to complete the work as he gets sent out of the room and peers laugh. This is more likely to occur when assignments require complex written or verbal expression and because he has difficulty tolerating frustration.*

STEP 1. BRAINSTORM POTENTIAL SOLUTIONS

A. Prevention: List setting event and/or antecedent modifications that might reduce target behavior. Check those validated by the FBA.

- ☐ *Do not assign written work*
- ☑ *Adapt written work (e.g., multiple-choice instead of open-ended questions)*
- ☑ *Provide social and affective support (peer buddy to help with work and provide attention)*
- ☐ *Allow frequent breaks*
- ☐ *Have resource room teacher available for one-on-one assistance*

B. Replacement behaviors: List replacement behaviors meeting the same function as problem behavior; consider coping skills that may reduce impact of setting events.

1. *Request breaks to provide escape*
2. *Gain peer attention through positive means, asking for help, collaborating on tasks that tap strengths*
3. *Improve frustration tolerance and time on task—assess task difficulty, rate frustration level, talk to self, take deep breath, ask for assistance, and wait for assistance to be provided*

Figure 24. Step 1 from the Behavior Intervention Plan, as completed by Nathan's team. (*Key: FBA* = Functional Behavior Assessment.)

First, the team discussed *setting events* affecting Nathan's behavior. Starting with his language-based learning disability and low tolerance for frustration, the team generated a range of responses to the question, "What could we do to prevent Nathan's problem behavior?" Among the ideas generated were assigning no reading or writing assignments, adapting his work to minimize his frustration, providing one-on-one teacher support, and providing a peer buddy to work with.

Because setting events and antecedents are often related, similar strategies emerged when the team considered *antecedents.* Prevention ideas included minimizing or eliminating language demands, providing frequent breaks, and giving easier assignments of shorter duration. Reflecting on Nathan's low tolerance for frustration as a setting event, the team realized that he was less likely to lose his temper when he received social support (attention) than when he worked alone. This support seemed to serve a regulatory function for Nathan; individuals working with him encouraged him with statements such as "hang in there, you can do it," and "just a few more to go." These supportive statements typically occurred just after Nathan first showed signs of frustration. As such, the team's brainstorming session involved a number of related setting events and antecedents; taken together, they had several prevention strategies to consider. The coach summarized these and suggested that the team move on to replacement behaviors.

The team quickly reached consensus about the broad types of *replacement skills* Nathan needed. Once again, these flowed logically from consideration of setting events, antecedents, and consequences (functions). First, they agreed that Nathan needed a better way to *escape* tasks that he found too hard to do. Second, Nathan needed to gain peer *attention* in better ways; he possessed many social competencies but was a bit isolated because of his problem behavior. The third cluster the team considered was related to *learning and self-regulation*—frustration tolerance and learning strategies. The team realized that Nathan could make better use of his learning potential; he needed to compensate for his specific weaknesses on language tasks and to handle frustration better when it occurred.

Once the team agreed on these areas, the coach solicited ideas on better strategies for Nathan. The multidisciplinary composition of the team was an advantage in this brainstorming session; partly by virtue of their diversity, they produced several ideas relating to each of their three criteria. A central role of the coach was to assist the team in categorizing their recommendations as either prevention or replacement. Related to Nathan's motivation to escape, the team suggested that he might learn to request breaks (replacement), to be offered a set number of breaks taken at times of his choosing (prevention), or to schedule breaks at predetermined intervals (prevention). For attention, the team suggested programming noncontingent (does not need to ask) attention from a peer buddy (prevention), teaching Nathan better strategies of gaining attention (replacement), having Nathan tutor his peers in math problems (replacement), or providing specific recognition for his mathematic abilities (enhancing consequences).

Finally, the team brainstormed several practices that might help Nathan improve his ability to regulate his own behavior. Teachers suggested instructional techniques that they could use (prevention) and eventually teach Nathan to use independently (replacement). The team also generated a set of self-control techniques to help him recognize frustration and calm himself down (replacement). The coach summarized their ideas, and the team began to discuss the BIP. Because they had tested the hypothesis, Nathan's team had the advantage of knowing that some of their accommodations worked.

We share how these ideas were shaped into a BIP as we discuss Steps 2 through 6 in the sections that follow. Figure 24 restates the team's working hypothesis and Step 1 of Nathan's BIP worksheets.

DEVELOPING THE BEHAVIORAL INTERVENTION PLAN

How Do Teams Prepare?

Once a team finishes brainstorming, they are ready to convert the fruits of their labor into a plan. When the FBA results in a clear picture of the student, and brainstorming produces potential solutions, the team has a wide array of choices about making a workable plan. Facing that array may be exciting, overwhelming, or both, depending on the circumstances. In some cases, desired outcomes are clear, but the team has difficulty envisioning strategies to achieve them. Like many elements of PBS, good BIPs are grounded in principles of applied behavior analysis and behavior therapy. Although BIPs require expertise, most teams find their efforts improve as they gain experience. Initially, teams may find the process of developing BIPs daunting. In Table 14, we provide a number of examples to illustrate how teams start with brainstorming ideas, including eventual corresponding BIP elements for each. We are confident that the majority of teams can brainstorm similar ideas.

Table 14. Problem behaviors, brainstorming ideas, and corresponding Behavior Intervention Plan (BIP) components

			Area of emphasis						
			Prevent		Replace				
Problem behavior	Initial brainstorming	Eventual BIP components	Setting events	Antecedents	Self-regulation	Communication	Social skills	Academic skills	Consequences
Preschooler cries and screams for 20 minutes when transition means end of preferred activity	Just give him whatever he wants until we can teach a better way	Postpone transitions for student		X			X		
		Picture schedule and cue transition	X	X					
		Offer choice of toys and activities		X	X	X			
		Teach coping with transitions			X				
		Reward successful transitions							X
Third grader becomes explosive during unstructured time	Keep her busy and do not make her wait too long	Occupy waiting time with activity		X					
		Teach self-monitoring, anger management, and assertion			X				
High school student loses focus and becomes overactive after seventh period	Do not ask him to do any new work after seventh period	Evaluate medication administration	X						
		Teach self-monitoring, self-control, and negotiation			X				
		Gradually increase demands and reinforce						X	X
Middle school student yells, curses, and storms out when demands are made	Do not make him to do any difficult work	Adapt materials to learning level	X	X					
		Allow frequent breaks	X	X					
		Teach learning skills and anger control			X			X	
Student flaps and claps when bored or under-stimulated	Provide frequent opportunities for movement	Minimize downtime		X					
		Offer alternative sensory input	X	X					
		Request peer buddy for social input			X	X	X		

Problem behavior	Initial brainstorming	Eventual BIP components	Area of emphasis						
			Prevent		Replace				
			Setting events	Antecedents	Self-regulation	Communication	Social skills	Academic skills	Consequences
Child has difficulty tolerating sensory input in cafeteria; paces and yells in line	Do not send him to the cafeteria anymore	Peer obtains beverage from line	X						
		Seat student on periphery of room	X						
		Student leaves for quiet place			X				
		Reinforce for staying and coping			X				X
		Develop lunchtime buddies					X		
Nonverbal student needs much staff attention; distressed if response is not immediate	Sit near her and pay attention all day long	Provide short-term one-on-one aide	X						
		Provide peer buddy	X	X					
		Provide periodic noncontingent attention	X	X		X			
		Teach to request attention				X			
		Gradually reduce attention given			X				
Junior high student sulks when his request to write about an alternate topic is denied	Let him choose any topic	With student, develop menu	X	X					
		Alternate student/teacher choice		X					
		Teach negotiation and anger control			X	X	X		
		Support writing skills and strategies			X	X		X	
Student perseverates and escalates with slightest change in schedule	Do not change the schedule	No schedule changes	X	X					
		Program manageable changes		X					
		Teach coping and relaxation			X				
		Ask to leave area to de-escalate			X	X			
Student irritable and withdrawn because he is hungry	Let him eat early	Allow midmorning snack	X	X					
		Snack after long bus ride	X	X					
		Snack on request; reinforce			X	X			X

Table 14 also delineates how these examples relate to sample BIP components. For example, during brainstorming, a team member suggests giving a preschooler whatever she wants to prevent crying—at least until the team can teach her to behave differently. The team notes this and moves on. Later, as they develop her BIP, the team considers how to meaningfully incorporate giving her what she wants into preventing and replacing problem behavior. Because they moved stepwise through the FBA, they are informed and confident about their working hypothesis. As long as they consider the elements of that hypothesis one at a time, they will produce viable support strategies. This team knows that the preschooler has a short fuse and that she takes a long time to calm down (setting events). When she is required to transition out of preferred activities (antecedent), she cries and screams (problem behavior), resulting in escape from demands (consequence and maintaining function).

Ultimately, her support team decides on two types of prevention: *short-term prevention* (postpone, prolong, or avoid transitions) and *long-term accommodations* (picture schedule; cueing transitions with verbal prompt and Ready Teddy, a stuffed bear who accompanies her to the next activity). They plan to use the short-term prevention strategy for a limited time until she is able to anticipate and manage transitions better. Long-term accommodations improve her tolerance for transition, and the plan also includes rewards for handling transition times well. At first, the team was not sure how they would use their brainstorming idea to accomplish these objectives; however, they did not let uncertainty derail them. (Please refer to Chapter 5 for a discussion of the key importance of linking BIP components to function, and how teams manage this.)

How, then, do teams prepare? Essentially, they come to the process with prior training, general knowledge about positive supports, and their own unique experiences and expertise. They develop BIPs by moving one step at a time. Once they adequately answer each question raised in the brainstorming session, the team's next task is to translate these ideas into a specific plan of action. Before discussing those details, some general guidelines for generating strategies are worth mentioning. We also remind readers of Table 8 (see Chapter 5), which details potential pitfalls and constructive alternatives for *Positive Strategies* teams.

Generating Intervention Strategies

Readers examining Table 14 may generate other (maybe better) ideas than those we list. This underscores two important points of BIP development. First, effective BIPs fit the ecology of the setting; each team is uniquely qualified to consider the resources, talents, and concerns of the school, team, students, family, and community. Second, creativity is crucial. We stress the importance of divergent thinking during the brainstorming process, but creativity is important in all phases. Novel solutions enhance potential for change, partly because they depart from past strategies. That is, more of the same is unlikely to promote change for a student with problem behavior. On the other hand, altering routines to accommodate one student may benefit several, enhancing the learning community.

Teams, especially inexperienced or homogeneous ones, are sometimes intimidated by the number and diversity of strategies that other teams produce. We offer reassurance and guidance. First, as stated earlier, team efforts become less overwhelming with experience. Second, team members know the student and the context well, and they almost invariably generate viable solutions. Access to knowledgeable coaches or consultants is an important means of both augmenting and validating team efforts (see Chapter 4 for a full discussion of teams and competencies). Effective practice in *Positive Strategies* requires teams to recognize their strengths and understand their limitations. For example, when Nathan's team completes its brainstorming activities and discusses his BIP, they confront their own concerns about whether the team has the expertise and experience to formulate and implement self-regulation training. Strong teams do not overstep the bounds of their proficiency; rather, they accept that their expertise is finite, and they seek external support as needed. Healthy teams often enjoy the opportunity to consult with external experts because the corresponding technical assistance is likely to enhance their own competencies. Nathan's team opted to use the school psychologist as a coach and resource when they recognized their own skills as limited.

ESSENTIAL ELEMENTS OF THE BEHAVIORAL INTERVENTION PLAN

Teams leave the brainstorming step with ideas about how to prevent and replace problem behavior. How do they translate this into a BIP? Developing a BIP requires both attention to detail and consideration of the big picture. We developed the *Positive Strategies* worksheets to prompt stepwise consideration of vital BIP elements. The worksheets provide a means to take the process step by step and to document team efforts. Blank copies of the BIP forms are located in the Appendix, and illustrations from Nathan's BIP are interspersed throughout this chapter. Essential elements of the BIP include

- Short-term prevention strategies and long-term accommodations (Step 2)
- Plans to manage (Step 3)
- Replace problem behavior (Step 4)
- Monitor and evaluate the BIP (Step 5)
- Maintain change (Step 6)

Implicit in each step is the need for an analysis of the resources needed for implementation. In the sections that follow, we provide an overview of each step, refer the reader to applicable sections of the FBA worksheets, and discuss how Nathan's team handled them. The reader is referred to Table 14 for examples of the multiple components of real BIPs.

PREVENT

One of the aims of the BIP is to eliminate the student's need for problem behavior. To illustrate, we return to Nia, whom we described briefly in the section above on brainstorming. Nia is a student with a very small functional communication repertoire and high rates of self-injury motivated primarily by escape. Her rate of self-injury is so high that she engages in virtually no instruction, and her team is concerned that she may lose her current placement. Attempts at instruction (antecedents) are regularly discontinued when she begins biting herself. Nia's long history of biting also meets a need for sensory input (setting event).

Nia's situation illustrates that behavior can be prevented in one of three ways, all of which relate to the function of the problem behavior. First, the team might alter setting events and antecedents that trigger the behavior. For Nia, that might mean removing or dramatically decreasing instructional demands (short-term prevention). Second, the team can formulate long-term accommodations so that Nia's instruction is less frustrating overall. The third way to obviate the need for escape is to teach and reinforce a more adaptive way to request breaks. (We talk more about this third option, replacement behaviors, in a later section.)

In earlier chapters, we discuss the resistance that prevention efforts sometimes meet. School personnel are often concerned about setting precedents by making an accommodation that other students or families might desire. Some team members (or observers) may equate accommodation with capitulating to the student's less attractive behaviors. Another concern is that prevention efforts will work briefly and then result in escalation. These were all factors in considering modifications to Nia's instructional schedule.

Effectively combined with other BIP elements, however, accommodations are a key component of intervention. For Nia, short-term accommodations permit the team to teach communicative alternatives. For a short time, suspending normal instructional demands provides Nia with the opportunity to practice using the ASL sign for "stop" and activating a jelly bean switch, two behaviors that are in her repertoire but are rarely used in school. When she executes them, the team offers her a choice of reinforcers; one provides deep pressure input (weighted vest), and the other provides pleasurable auditory input (listening to music on headphones). Earlier that year, various team members had tried unsuccessfully to get Nia to use ASL signs and assistive technology switches. The team now realizes that effort failed because Nia regularly discontinued teaching sessions by biting. They had offered her no meaningful reinforcement—when she signed, she received praise, followed by more instruction. Because Nia did not want instruction, she reinstated biting to discontinue it. Nia's plan demonstrates that effective prevention strategies reflect an understanding of the function of problem behavior.

In Nia's case, the team confronted external concerns about reduced instructional demands, as well as significant internal resistance from some team members who were wary of letting Nia off the hook during prevention. In the ensuing discussion, the team recalled FBA data indicating that Nia was off task almost 90% of her one-to-one instruction time. She spent about half of that time biting herself. Given that so little was really being accomplished, the team agreed to try prevention simultaneously with teaching alternatives.

There was an additional rationale for this approach. Nia's behavior was also motivated by sensory concerns; these would likely continue even when the team suspended instructional demands. The team recognized that Nia developed a habit of responding to frustration with biting (oral input). The team wanted to decouple frustration and biting. During the prevention period, Nia had free access to oral sensory stimulation in the form of a vibrating oral device. Toward the end of the accommodation, the team required Nia to sign a request for this device. She was highly motivated to do so, requesting it promptly, accurately, and frequently.

During prevention efforts, Nia's self-injury diminished to about 25% of its typical frequency. Without reduced instructional demands (short-term prevention in the form of antecedent modification), it is unlikely that Nia would have demonstrated such a dramatic reduction in biting. The team wisely chose to address her sensory concerns and helped Nia decouple frustration and biting. During this period, they prevented many incidents of self-injury and used the time to develop alternatives. It is worth noting that family input was crucial in determining which signs she might use and in understanding Nia's preferences for sensory input. In fact, her family provided the oral tool she used at school.

Short-Term Prevention Strategies

Short-term prevention strategies refer to temporary interventions to avoid incidents of problem behavior; they emerge directly from an understanding of setting events, antecedents, and consequences. Because teams use short-term prevention just long enough to permit developing alternatives, they must regularly evaluate their necessity.

To establish short-term prevention strategies, the team refers to the ideas they generated to answer the question, "How can we prevent this from happening?" The responses often entail removing or altering antecedents. For example, eliminating instructional demands (as with Nia) frequently reduces problem behavior. Because it is not always feasible or desirable to remove antecedents entirely, teams consider altering them so that their impact falls below the threshold at which problem behaviors are triggered. The team considers how setting events and antecedents work in tandem. For example, Nathan's setting events (learning disability, low tolerance for frustration) mean that language tasks are laborious for him and that he does not tolerate frustration well. Math problems (antecedent) with few language demands are manageable, even though he has limited frustration tolerance. Writing tasks (antecedent) tax both setting events, effectively triggering an outburst. The outburst results in escape (function) as well as providing attention (additional maintaining consequence). Short-term prevention strategies in his BIP need to address these setting events and antecedents.

Nia's BIP involved manipulation of antecedents (instruction). Less obvious is her team's gradual approach to her sensory concerns, which addressed setting events. In some cases, short-term prevention reduces the incidence of problem behavior, providing needed relief for the student, family, and team. Although it is easy for adults to recognize the stress involved in managing problem behavior, we sometimes neglect to acknowledge the stress of having it; from Nia's perspective, prevention meant a break from painful self-injury. In other circumstances, prevention is woven into a graduated plan to reduce problem behavior and to teach alternatives.

In Table 14, there are several prevention strategies that target either setting events or antecedents as their area of emphasis. In some cases, the initial prevention idea was enacted conceptually but not literally; in others, the need for prevention was so clear that setting events or antecedents were eliminated for a short time. For example, a student needing high levels of attention and support prompted the team's brainstorming idea: sit near her and pay attention to her all day long. That could be enacted literally by providing a one-to-one aide, or intermittently by providing frequent or noncontingent (no need to ask) peer and staff contact (every few minutes). In another case, a student sulked if denied a request for an alternative topic on an assignment. The team's brainstorming strategy was to let him choose any topic he liked. The eventual BIP included developing a menu of topics, alternating teacher and student choices, and teaching alternatives to sulking.

Teams list short-term prevention strategies in Step 2 of the BIP worksheets, along with the setting events and antecedents they target. They also indicate specific implementation plans and desired outcomes in this section. Finally, teams determine which members are responsible for implementing and evaluating short-term prevention strategies, specifying the first date the team will review them. These details ensure consistency and accountability for implementation.

Long-Term Accommodations

Long-term accommodations consider the student–environment fit. As such, they result in a better match between the student's learning and behavioral characteristics and the context in which learning occurs. In contrast to short-term prevention, these accommodations are considered indefinite in term, even though teams update and modify them on the basis of the student's progress and evolving functional skills. To generate them, teams refer to assessment of student–environment fit conducted previously in the FBA (Step 1). If formal assessment was deferred, the needed information is nonetheless available to the team (or is gathered before the BIP is finalized). To create accommodations, the team reviews its hypothesis, considering context elements such as task difficulty, classroom features, instructional style, and so on. The environment is ripe for long-term accommodations wherever there is a mismatch between the student's functional skills and the teaching environment.

Developing long-term accommodations involves the collective expertise of the team. It requires clear specification of strategies, desired outcomes, initial implementation plans, individuals responsible, and the monitoring period. Nathan's Step 2 appears in Figure 25 and is discussed below.

Nathan's Behavioral Intervention Plan—Step 2: Prevent

Immediately after their brainstorming session, Nathan's student support team initiated discussion of the BIP, starting with prevention. Considering prevention strategies, they already knew (from the hypothesis testing) that multiple-choice questions and a peer buddy reduced problem behaviors and that combining these two strategies eliminated yelling and cursing altogether. The team decided to extend both as *short-term prevention strategies.* In so doing, they determined a rotating schedule of peer buddies and a plan for coordinating instructional modifications. Step 2 in Figure 25 depicts short-term prevention strategies, lists the setting events and antecedents they target, and indicates the outcomes desired. Because her involvement would be required for these to be effective, the classroom teacher assumed responsibility to coordinate and monitor implementation of Step 2.

Next, the group considered student–environment fit. Their earlier efforts simplified this task, so it was clear that the typical language tasks assigned in Nathan's class were met with almost immediate frustration. Although the team hoped to teach Nathan to cope better with such antecedents, they also realized that both his low tolerance for frustration and his learning disabilities were setting events—in his case, constitutional factors that would exert continuing influence over his behavior and achievement. Accordingly, the team formulated two *long-term accommodations,* task adaptations and breaks. The task adaptation extended some of the elements of his short-term prevention strategies, with the aim of helping Nathan to eventually develop his own compensatory strategies.

Breaks involved short respites from challenging academic work. Nathan would initially be permitted to take three breaks per class period (this number was based on an observation of how long he generally worked on difficult tasks). Breaks could involve sharpening his pencil, walking around the room once, throwing something in the trash, and so on. The team decided to offer Nathan wide latitude as long as he was not disruptive. He was also permitted to leave the room if he signaled his coach or teacher by using a time-out or take-five sign.

STEP 2. PREVENT OR MINIMIZE OCCURRENCES OF PROBLEM BEHAVIOR

A. Short-term prevention strategies

Setting event or antecedent targeted	Strategy	Implementation plan	Outcomes
Low frustration tolerance; language-based learning disability; peer attention	Peer buddy	When math, language arts, and social studies require complex written or verbal expression, pair Nathan with valued peer who reads questions aloud and supports his responses Rotating peer buddies coordinated by classroom teacher with social worker support	Reduce number of incidents Learn from positive peer models Increase positive social attention
Language-based learning disabilities	Task accommodations	Resource room teacher to modify content for math word problems, language arts, social studies. Resource room and classroom teachers to coordinate Nathan's work and progress Daily, resource room teacher to meet privately with Nathan to explain and review accommodations	Reduce number of incidents Learn to simplify materials via daily meeting with resource room teacher Increase academic success

Staff responsible: Classroom teacher **Start date:** 12/11 **1st review date:** 12/20

B. Long-term accommodations

Setting event or antecedent targeted	Long-term accommodation	Implementation plan	Outcomes
Language-based learning disability	Make language tasks and verbal instruction easier for Nathan to process	Resource room teacher to provide continuing consultation to simplify instructions and adapt Nathan's work Resource room teacher to meet daily with Nathan to preview material and assignments, forecast trouble spots. Decrease frequency (fade) only with extended success	Better meet Nathan's learning needs Decrease frustration Increase success Decrease amount of labor Nathan expends on processing tasks and requirements
Low frustration tolerance	Breaks	Nathan permitted breaks from work to walk around room, sharpen pencil, and so forth without need for permission; must not be disruptive At outset, permitted 3 breaks per period. Number of breaks to be altered based upon progress	Reduce number of incidents Learn to simplify materials via daily meetings with resource room teacher Increase success

Staff responsible: Classroom teacher **Start date:** 12/15 **1st review date:** 12/20

Figure 25. Step 2 from the Behavior Intervention Plan, as compiled by Nathan's team.

Nathan's team also noted long-term accommodations within Step 2 of the *Positive Strategies* worksheets. Similar to short-term prevention strategies, the team indicated what the accommodations were, how they would be implemented, the setting events and antecedents targeted, and desired outcomes.

Relating Prevention to Function: Setting Events and Antecedents

Short-term prevention and long-term accommodation often entail modifying setting events and antecedents. It can be challenging to develop modifications to diminish the impact of these triggers. In this section, we relate prevention to setting events and antecedents.

Setting events are slow triggers, distal factors that influence behavior. They are sometimes neglected in BIPs because they are more distant from behavior. Some setting events are relatively immutable, such as a specific disability, learning style, attention impairment, or medical condition. Even though setting events may arise from relatively stable or uncontrollable factors, they often can be addressed or altered. For example, some students with attention impairments may respond well to a combination of instruction in self-regulation and medication. These interventions serve to reduce the overall impact of setting events (the child's attention impairment and its associated features). A good intervention plan would address setting events and antecedents in more than one way and also work to build better coping skills—this combined approach is consistent with current evidence that medication can result in increased focus but may not necessarily improve academic performance. The prevention plan is intended to reduce the impact of triggers, whereas other aspects of the BIP address replacement behaviors.

In Table 15, we include several setting events and corresponding accommodations that might be seen in schools. Note that this table includes only alterations designed to alter the impact of setting events; most BIPs attend to antecedents, consequences, and replacement behaviors as well.

Table 15. Sample setting events and corresponding accommodations

Setting events (by type) with implications	Corresponding accommodation (prevention)
Physical	
Student experiences pain, illness, allergies, other acute/chronic medical issues.	Provide treatment for physical conditions; ensure consistency (e.g., avoid missed doses, appointments).
Physical status makes sitting at desk painful.	Provide breaks, adapted exercise, physical activity; formal assessment of postural needs.
Student's sleep is disrupted/insufficient, impacting mood.	Work with family to address sleep difficuties; consultation with medical provider, other interventionist.
Student does not regulate states well, resulting in dramatic shifts in affect and behavior.	Monitor biobehavioral states: hunger, temperature, arousal; apply specific accommodations as indicated.
Medication side effects alter mood and behavior.	Consult medical providers (e.g., altered dose/dosing time)
Learning and self-regulation	
Student easily overwhelmed by noise, becomes agitated.	Present calming music, reduced lighting, or other environmental modifications.
Student is prone to distress over changes in routine or rule violations by peers.	Provide additional clarification of rules/expectations (picture schedule, cues, previewing, supplementary explanation).
Anxiety causes student to escalate or perseverate, disrupting own learning as well as that of peers.	Incorporate a relaxation routine into scheduled activities.
Enjoying the input, blind student plays only on swings at recess; monopolizes swing and annoys peers.	Provide alternate forms of sensory input; encourage peer interactions.
Attention difficulties make focusing very difficult.	Seat student near instructor; pair with good peer models; remove distractions; divide tasks into manageable segments.
Social-emotional	
Family in midst of divorce; student behavior declines.	Collaborate with family to address concerns.
Student is teased by peers after outbursts.	Coach peers to provide positive feedback for appropriate behavior; use socially valued peer as role model.
Student experiences traumatic event, with behavior problems worsening afterward.	Collaborate with family to address perceived safety concerns; consider therapist expert in trauma recovery.
Environment and routines	
Student occasionally arrives late to school and becomes very distressed and anxious.	Work with family to minimize lateness. Enact plan to help student cope with unavoidable changes.
Student is anxious about impending move to new school.	Visit new school and teacher; develop a pen pal or e-mail buddy in the new school; to encourage mastery, provide orientation, practice, reassurance, and coping supports.
Teacher going on leave; student tends to lapse into problem behavior with change.	Provide overlap with substitute teacher; develop interim plan in advance and share with student; allow student some choice in aspects of plan.

Teams sometimes find it difficult to formulate prevention strategies based on antecedents (fast triggers, circumstances that immediately precede problem behavior and serve to precipitate it). Often, it is useful in such cases to consider the links among antecedent and functions (which we first discussed in Chapter 5 and outlined in Table 7 [see Chapter 5]). In Table 16, we list several antecedents, indicate their functions, and suggest corresponding accommodations that may prevent behavior either in the short term, long term, or both. Because Tables 15 and 16 include several examples of setting event and antecedent manipulations, the reader may wish to refer to them when faced with the need to develop similar strategies.

MANAGE

Most of the time, problem behavior persists while teams complete the various activities associated with the FBA. Problem behavior usually persists even as the BIP is implemented—if eliminating it were that easy, the team would have accomplished it already. Because the prevent and replace steps take time, teams develop interim behavior management strategies. These fall under two main categories: crisis intervention and interim behavior management. Ideally, teams initiate individualized supports long before such supports are required by impending crisis or IDEA mandates; however, because this is not the reality in many cases, we outline some important considerations here.

Crisis Intervention

Crisis intervention occurs when problems are dangerous, threatening, or otherwise jeopardizing the rights, health, and safety of students, faculty, or staff. Optimally, teams avert the need for crisis intervention by engaging *Positive Strategies* interventions well before they face urgent situa-

Table 16. Sample antecedents and corresponding accommodations

Function	Antecedent and behavior	Corresponding accommodation (prevention)
Escape	Student escalates to threatening behavior when required to work on assignment.	Do not give assignments known to trigger behavior. Accommodate work to reduce antecedent impact.
Attention and tangible	Student becomes sullen and hostile when assigned to work with certain staff or peers.	Allow choice of peers in learning group; alter quality of reinforcement for task completion.
Escape	Faced with task of increasing difficulty, student divests effort and disengages.	Intersperse easy and difficult items. Adjust task difficulty to allow for 90% success.
Sensory	Student becomes overactive and agitated in certain parts of building.	Avoid those locations. Gradual exposure to tolerable level or length of time.
Tangible	Student has tantrums when required to relinquish desired item or activity.	Procure extras of desired toy. Cue transitions. Make preferred items/activities available for trade.
Attention and tangible	Student responds to direction defensively, quickly escalating until teacher capitulates.	Change tenor of interaction. Modify time and place where instructions are provided.
Sensory and escape	Tasks are difficult and boring for student who disrupts the class.	Target work to student's instructional level. Increase interest of material so work is stimulating.
Sensory	Student makes unusual noises during quiet classes.	Allow use of headphones to provide auditory input and decrease need to create it.

tions. When crises arise, teams are rarely in a position to engage in extended assessment and intervention efforts as required for FBAs and BIPs; in fact, teams may have to suspend those activities if a truly dangerous situation arises. Crisis intervention entails the provision of temporary measures designed to establish stability. Once stability is achieved, the team can plan for more effective and lasting change. Often, teams consider crisis management because behavior has the potential to become serious or has been serious in the past. As such, we discuss some general considerations for crisis intervention, referring the reader to more comprehensive resources elsewhere (refer to our bibliography for life space crisis intervention, strategies for crisis intervention and prevention, professional crisis intervention, and nonviolent crisis intervention). There are several generally accepted principles common to most approaches to crisis intervention: prevention, positive approaches, and the use of containment over restraint. (For more information on this topic, see, for example, Dawson, 2003; DeMagistris, & Imber, 1980; Grskovic & Goetze, 2005; and New York State Office of Mental Retardation and Developmental Disabilities, 1998.)

Prevention

As mentioned earlier, prevention is preferred over crisis management; supportive schoolwide efforts can diminish the risk of crises and provide guidelines to handle them. There is an emerging body of support for schoolwide approaches; some resources are included in the Appendices. This requires planning, implementation, and communication of policies; systems for responding to crisis; and debriefing and follow-up efforts.

Incident review and debriefing involve investigating the incident to determine any crucial lapses contributing to its occurrence. The ultimate aim of review is improving systems and responses to prevent and better manage future incidents. Because even healthy school environments with responsive schoolwide supports can experience crises, schools prepare through staff training and supervision. Faculty and staff need to be prepared in advance to handle a student whose behavior poses real or perceived danger to self or others.

Positive Approaches

Most crisis management guidelines stress the importance of defusing the crisis as positively as possible. Suggestions for doing so include offering choices (among acceptable alternatives) to students; avoiding use of ultimatums ("Do this or else"); a calm, honest, nonconfrontational stance (open hands, clear language, delivery on commitments, distance kept as indicated); and stating expectations and hopes in positive terms ("I know you can make the choice").

Consistent with the overall philosophy of *Positive Strategies*, effective crisis management assumes that, in the midst of a crisis, the student has no better way. Defusing the crisis means helping the student consider viable alternatives. When a crisis approaches more gradually, it may mean providing extensive temporary supports, such as one-to-one support or other highly supervised interventions. In these circumstances, we would advocate for prompt consideration of more thoughtful interventions; rarely does a crisis management aide result in good long-term outcomes for the student, the team, or the family. It is at best a holding pattern that is not designed to address the instructional goals of the student.

For problem behaviors with the potential to reach crisis, we sometimes recommend that teams forecast signs of impending threat and plan to respond accordingly. On the other hand, it is essential to maintain a neutral (if not positive) stance toward students. The risk of preparing for unlikely crises is that staff may become overly sensitized to escalation cues. When a crisis is highly likely, it is important for the team to have a plan to contain and manage it. The overarching goal of crisis management, however, is for staff to recognize these cues early and to provide the support needed to avert further incidents.

Containing Versus Restraining

Partly because of the historical use of physical aversives in education, many schools have policies forbidding physical restraint of students. Programs employing physical restraint have specially trained staff and tend to use it only as a means of last resort (e.g., harm prevention or reduction). Physical restraint is rarely used in schools, and most policies emphasize containing crises rather than using physical restraint. Staff are advised to contain aggressive and self-injurious behavior by removing others from the area to reduce risk and to intervene using the least intrusive means possible. Teams concerned about responding to aggression should seek specialized training, as noted earlier.

Step 3 of the BIP worksheets includes a place to note the need for crisis intervention plans. Because crisis management does not qualify as true intervention, and because teams often divert from *Positive Strategies* activities in the midst of crises, these plans are developed separately from the BIP. When teams assess that a crisis is likely, their plans need to be consistent with school policy, federal and state law, and tenets of PBS. In some cases (e.g., Nathan), teams incorporate prevention and replacement strategies from Steps 2 and 3 of the BIP. Collapsing strategies across various strands of the intervention plan is sensible because it provides a consistent approach, which benefits both staff and students.

Interim Behavior Management

Because problem behaviors continue even as BIPs are implemented, teams develop interim plans for managing them. The interim plan specifies early signs of the problem behavior (precursors), how the team will respond to precursors, and steps for reviewing incidents once they occur. Because BIPs are intended to reduce problem behavior, its occurrence necessarily triggers review. The review provides opportunity to reconsider whether the BIP effectively incorporates the student's concerns.

As mentioned in Chapter 5, interim management may require teams to reconcile conflicting approaches. For example, a school discipline policy may require that disrespectful or highly disruptive behavior leads to sending the student to the principal's office. If the behavior is motivated by escape, however, sending the student out of the classroom may inadvertently provide reinforcement. The team might have to negotiate an exception to this policy with administrators concerned about precedent.

Initially, Nia's team was concerned that the only way to manage continued episodes of biting was physical restraint. Instead, they decided to carefully monitor the frequency and severity of biting as her BIP was implemented and to attempt an initial management strategy. If she engaged in biting, her instructor would immediately establish eye contact, model the sign for requesting her oral sensory tool, and provide it. As long as her biting diminished in frequency and intensity, the team would continue this management approach. Given how frequently she bit herself before intervention, they agreed to tolerate a small amount of biting as long as she made progress. Nia's parents supported this management plan, which ultimately proved beneficial.

Even when hypothesis testing demonstrates that problem behavior can be dramatically reduced (e.g., Nathan), teams cannot expect problem behavior to cease completely. In fact, teams are often advised to expect behavior to continue at its average frequency, or possibly increase, just after the BIP is initiated. Although increases in frequency are rare, they sometimes occur, especially when teams make noticeable changes in the environment. For example, if a team decides to ignore problem behavior and respond quickly to alternatives, the student may show an *extinction burst*: a temporary increase in the behavior that wanes once the student uses the alternative and is rewarded. We recommend that teams diminish the likelihood of this burst by ensuring that alternatives are ready to use and are naturally reinforced. Because this does not always occur, good BIPs anticipate accordingly. When an extinction burst is expected, the team establishes a way to track frequency and establishes a ceiling, above which the BIP is reviewed.

Effective management anticipates and forecasts behavior problems and is consistent with the team's prevention and replacement efforts. Management strategies consider the typical reception the behavior will receive. They also reconcile differences between aspects of the BIP and typical consequences required by school policy. The team negotiates any such exceptions in advance so that the plan receives credible support from school leadership.

Step 3 of Nathan's BIP, which appears in Figure 26, outlines precursors to problem behavior, steps to take in response, and incident review procedures. Although his management plan was distinct from other aspects of his BIP, it used features of his prevention and replacement steps.

STEP 3. MANAGE CONTINUING INCIDENTS OF PROBLEM BEHAVIOR

Early signs of problem behavior: Escalation.

Nathan sighs, becomes restless, increases motor activity, makes excuse to take break (bathroom, pencil, trash can).

Steps to take in response to early signs of behavior: (Refer to replacement skills.)

Provide verbal prompt for Nathan to rate frustration. Based on rating, Nathan will choose type of break. At end of break, Nathan will be coached to use coping statements and relaxation strategies. When he has de-escalated, resume work.

Response to incidents of behavior: Include plan to resume activity or return to context.

1. If Nathan yells at teacher or curses, he will be coached to regain control and resume work as soon as possible by resource room teacher, social worker, or school psychologist depending on scheduled availability. If behavior continues, coach will escort Nathan from room and monitor until he is able to cooperate with coaching (Step 5 of the behavior intervention plan).
2. If Nathan leaves classroom, he will be required to make up work missed (with support if needed).
3. If Nathan hits another student, his parents will be called immediately. He will be required to discuss episode with social worker, assistant principal, and parents. In-school suspension will apply per school policy.

Steps to take following an incident: Describe procedures for incident review and strategies to minimize inadvertent reinforcement for problem behavior.

Classroom teacher, resource room teacher, and social worker will meet to review. Social worker will then review incident one-on-one with Nathan, discuss "better ways," ask him to share with parents, and confirm and consult with parents. Incident review will be opportunity to consider modifying plan.

☑ **Preparation required**: Consider staff training, student supports, other efforts needed.

In consultation with school psychologist, social worker will develop thermometer for Nathan to rate frustration and anger (see next page) and relaxation strategies. This will be finalized with Nathan and shared with parents in meeting. This will be developed, explained and practiced prior to implementation.

☐ **Crisis intervention plan is needed.**

Staff responsible: Social worker **Start date:** 12/15 **1st review date:** 12/20

Figure 26. Step 3 from the Behavior Intervention Plan, as compiled by Nathan's team.

Nathan's Behavioral Intervention Plan—Step 3: Manage

Given the successful testing of the hypothesis, Nathan's team was fairly confident that he would demonstrate a positive response once his BIP was initiated. Nonetheless, they predicted that a fairly frequent behavior (between two and three times per day) would not go away completely. The team had also committed to monitoring two related behaviors, storming out of the room and hitting peers. These were less frequent but were more serious than yelling and cursing; they also occurred later in Nathan's escalation pattern. Nathan's team decided to consider his three priority behaviors in succession and to develop management plans for each.

They began with the behaviors targeted for change in the BIP, yelling and cursing. Nathan's escalation pattern was predictable: when he was losing control, he would first sigh and become increasingly restless. Then, he would mumble to himself, raise his voice to the teacher, make rude comments, and mutter curse words. Sometimes, his escalation would continue, in which cases he might strike other students, run out of the classroom, or both. Because the restlessness and mumbling were identified as *early signs* indicating the potential for escalation, the team agreed that interrupting the sequence at the restless or mumbling stage was necessary to avoid yelling and cursing. This was also viewed as a good investment of staff time, because Nathan at this point could often be redirected with relatively little effort. The team linked this intervention to the replacement component of his BIP. They agreed that Nathan would be coached by the social worker to monitor his moods using a 10-point scale (1 = calm; 5 = getting antsy; 8 = very mad) and an image of a thermometer (levels of red to accompany each number). If he was becoming upset (restless or mumbling), he would be prompted to rate his level of frustration on a scale of 1 to 10. Once Nathan rated his mood, he would be prompted to engage in self-calming strategies (discussed in the Replace section, Step 5) until he was ready to return to work (e.g., self-rating of 4 or below).

Nathan's team also identified plans to *respond to incidents of target behavior*. In the event that his behavior did escalate to yelling, one of the team members would come to the room to coach him. The resource room teacher, social worker, and school psychologist agreed to coordinate their schedules so that one of them would always be available to provide individualized support. Whenever possible, they would work with Nathan in the classroom to assist him in calming himself. If he was judged to be out of control or not working to regain it, they would discontinue their interactions, escort him from the instructional area (or remove other students), and monitor him until he was able to cooperate. They would then coach him in the use of the rating scale and assist him in identifying alternatives that he might have used.

Nathan's management plan appears in Figure 26. It stipulates early signs of problem behavior, the team's response to these, and the steps they need to take *after an incident*. The BIP form also has a place for the team to denote any *preparation required* and whether a *crisis intervention* is called for (if so, a separate document might be required). In Nathan's case, implementation could not feasibly begin until mood monitoring and de-escalation coaching had been initiated and he and his family were fully aware of the plan. Before completion of the BIP, the social worker discussed ideas for the plan with Nathan's mother by telephone; she agreed with the plan and said she would support it. Nathan's mother also joined him toward the end of his first coaching session with the social worker, and she left with a copy of his BIP. They agreed that the social worker would call Nathan's parents once a week to discuss his progress, or immediately if there were concerns.

REPLACE

Replacing problem behaviors with more adaptive, effective alternatives is one of the most important activities of the student support team. In earlier sections, we discussed how teams brainstorm replacement skills, including the link between problem behavior, function, and alternatives. In this section, we outline several key considerations for formulating, teaching, and reinforcing replacement behaviors, and we complete this step by sharing how Nathan's team accomplished its objectives.

Characteristics of Effective Replacement Skills

Successful replacement skills have several shared elements, eight of which are listed in Table 17 and discussed in the sections that follow.

First, successful replacement behaviors are possible and plausible in the life of the student. That is, the student already demonstrates the skill, possesses prerequisites, or is *capable of learning and executing* it. The team carefully assesses the student's functioning, determining both the current skill level and the extent of support required for mastery. Successive levels of support are indicated for skills the student is not currently using or does not possess. Behaviors outside the student's repertoire require intensive instruction, support, and reinforcement to become effective alternatives. If the student has (and uses) prerequisites, the team first works to develop skills more fully and then to encourage their use. When neither a replacement behavior nor its prerequisites are present, the team faces a lengthy, complex instructional plan; we advise considering a less complex skill in the short term and training the complex one under a long-term plan.

Some replacement behaviors seem rather simple or straightforward; consider Nia's sign or Nathan's request for a break. Despite this, replacement skills have as yet eluded the student, at least in the contexts in which problem behaviors occur. As such, the team's assessment considers not only whether the student demonstrated the skill elsewhere but also how context might influence its likelihood.

Table 17. Criteria for replacement skills

Student can learn and successfully execute.
Serves the same function as the problem behavior.
Works as well as or better than problem behavior in meeting the student's needs.
Meets with natural reinforcement (positive consequences).
Provides socially acceptable alternatives to problem behavior to student and others.
Potential to enhance functional skills (self-regulation, communication, and social and academic skills).
Can enhance quality of life.

As such, effective replacement behaviors reflect the team's hypothesis about function; that is, they consider several factors together: the student's ability; setting events and antecedents (the potential interference of slow and fast triggers); and the function and typical consequences for the replacement behavior in the setting. Recall the example (in Chapter 5) of a second grader who engages in problem behavior while waiting for the bus. The most obvious replacement behavior, waiting quietly in line, is in the student's repertoire; however, expecting that he will change his behavior without some alteration in context—a prompt or cue—is not likely to succeed, leading to a sense of failure for both the student and the team.

To the extent that the replacement behavior reflects an accurate working hypothesis, it also *serves the same function as problem behavior.* If the BIP is to succeed, the team must consider the likelihood that the replacement behavior can be elicited in the problem context. The team also forecasts the reception that a replacement behavior is apt to receive. If the problem behavior results in attention, tangibles, escape, or sensory input, so must its replacement. If not, the problem behavior is likely to continue or be replaced by a functionally equivalent problem, sometimes of greater severity. For example, a reward system may motivate a student to stay on task for longer periods of time. The student wishes to do well and to please instructors, and he or she expends a great deal of effort, persevering well past his or her usual attention span. Despite a sincere desire to behave and earn rewards, the student lacks the self-regulation skills to persevere further, and frustration mounts, but the student has no viable means of escape. Unfortunately, the student ends up having an outburst of greater severity than usual, and in the midst of it the student curses the intervention plan and everyone involved in developing it. The team now faces a lapse in behavior as well as setbacks in confidence and motivation. To avoid this, teams should attend carefully to function and ensure that replacements are equivalent.

Because effective replacement behaviors meet equivalent functions, problems with multiple functions may require multiple alternatives. Teams may be able to develop a single replacement behavior that meets two or more functions, but this can be challenging. Further, more than one behavior is preferred unless the necessary instruction overly taxes the student. Recall Nia, whose behavior was motivated by sensory concerns and maintained by escape; she learned a replacement behavior (sign) to meet her escape concerns and had access to desired input to meet her sensory concerns. Her team first addressed these functions separately and then combined them (using a sign to request sensory items); this permitted them to evaluate how effectively she responded to each replacement skill. They progressed after initial success with each. When it comes to replacement, two behaviors are better than one; more alternatives mean that a student will be better prepared to cope.

The next consideration is that effective replacement behaviors work *as well as or better than* problem behaviors. If not, problem behavior will continue. If the second grader described above waits quietly in line, he will be met with (at best) minimal peer response and no adult attention. The problem behavior, however, results in cessation of boredom and the attention of staff and peers, consequences that are much more reinforcing than tedium. Because his disruptive behavior is maintained by adult and peer attention, an effective replacement behavior must procure this for him as well. To illustrate further, let us return to Nia, who bites herself; this works nearly 100% of the time in helping her escape from instruction. The replacement behavior (e.g.,

ASL sign for "stop") must work just as well, or it will fall into disuse. So, if Nia signs "stop" and her instructor continues the lesson, Nia will predictably bite herself, effectively ending instruction. Replacement behaviors that work are especially important for escape-motivated behaviors. The tantrum (outburst in older children) is 100% effective at interrupting, so any team hoping to replace it needs to find, teach, and reinforce alternatives that work.

Effective Reinforcers Are Natural

When teams wish to diminish one behavior, they teach a new one with its own rewards. Although artificial reinforcement (praise, tokens, privileges) is part of many BIPs, behaviors that recruit natural reinforcement are more likely to be used, reinforced, maintained, and generalized. Teams are wise to choose behaviors that are pivotal in nature. Pivotal skills (Koegel, Koegel, Harrower, & Carter, 1999) are likely to be recognized and encouraged by others, prompting natural growth of the behavior across time and context. Effective replacement skills result in some reinforcement that is programmed and some that occurs naturally—a beneficial side effect. Although replacements for serious or long-standing behavior problems may require artificial reinforcement at the outset, good plans will use this for initial instruction and then decrease its use over time.

Effective replacement behaviors provide *socially acceptable alternatives* to problem behavior. Sam, discussed in previous chapters, engages in disruptive behavior as a break from independent seatwork. One message behind his behavior is that he cannot work independently for more than 5 minutes. Although this message may be truthful, a team would be ill advised to instruct Sam to deliver it in this form, because doing so would be socially awkward and would not be welcomed by teachers. Instead, Sam's team might teach him to raise his hand for assistance, take seated breaks (close his eyes, take a deep breath), request occassional trips to the water fountain or pencil sharpener, and so on. Children with aggressive behavior are often motivated by legitimate concerns and desires, although they express them in socially unacceptable ways. Replacing aggression involves cognitive and behavioral components; the student learns to accurately appraise the situation, select an appropriate (assertive) response, and regulate feelings and behavior adequately to enact it. In this case, the replacement behavior is actually a cluster with some invisible components, cognitive and regulatory processes that nevertheless require instruction and practice.

Similarly, the replacement behavior must be acceptable to the student. It must be seen as nonstigmatizing if used with or in the presence of peers. For example, we worked with one student whose team had developed a highly effective BIP in a specialized program using a picture book communication system. This student transferred to an inclusion class in his neighborhood school and noted that none of the other students carried communication notebooks. He began to refuse to carry his book, and his behaviors reemerged. His new team had to develop a system that would be acceptable to the student in the new setting.

Effective replacement behaviors have the potential to *enhance functional skills.* We frame replacement skills into four major categories: self-regulation, communication, social, and academic skills. Although these categories are not all inclusive, they do encompass a range of functional competencies critical to success in school. Table 18 lists these categories and provides examples.

Functional communication skills refer to how an individual uses his or her language skills to make wants and concerns known. It includes any means a child may use to make requests, regulate others' behavior, play, and engage socially. In addition to formal language, functional communication includes pragmatic language and alternative or augmentive communication systems (ASL, voice output device, Picture Exchange Communication System). In Chapters 5 and 6, we discuss the central importance of understanding the communicative intent of problem behavior. That is, problem behavior often serves the function of communicating a student's concerns or wishes (see Durand, 1990, for further discussion of this topic). For example, Sam effectively communicates his limited attention span by taking a break (becoming disruptive). An effective replacement skill may require teaching better functional communication strategies; be-

Table 18. Replacement behaviors by type

Functional communication
Use language and nonverbals to request (attention, objects, assistance)
Regulate the behavior of others (initiate, ask for response, extend or cease interaction, and so forth)
Play (represent ideas, interact with others, coordinate activities)
Social functions (obtain attention, information or assistance, share information or feelings, engage in dialogue)
Alternative and augmentative communication systems (alternate means of communicating)
Self-regulation
Self-monitoring (observe own mood, affect, behavior)
Self-control; impulse regulation; delay of gratification; frustration tolerance; anger control
Organization and task approaches; attention and concentration
Relaxation; self-soothing and self-calming
Social skills
Managing relationships: assertiveness, negotiating conflict, response to authority
Cooperation with peers; compliance and respect for adults
Participation in activities; pursuit of interests, especially with others
Handle developmental demands of socialization
Academic skills
Specific learning strategies, skills, and approaches needed for various subjects
Processing and following directions (oral and written)
Responding to whole-class instruction
Reading, writing, and mathematics as appropriate for age and grade

fore his team establishes new communication goals, they need to understand his current communication repertoire.

Self-regulation refers to several aspects of monitoring and controlling behavior; during the course of childhood, it entails increasingly proactive, conscious (metacognitive) processing (Bronson, 2000). Self-regulation skills reflect setting events (slow triggers such as constitutional factors) and overlap with communication, social, and academic skills. Self-regulation is the cornerstone on which many learning, social, and communicative functions rest. Students with impairments in self-regulation often face difficulties in several areas.

Because education is a social endeavor, *social skills* are key. Students with problematic social relatedness (e.g., autism spectrum disorders, attachment disorders, social anxiety or phobia, conduct disorders, antisocial features) are at increased risk for a number of negative outcomes: school failure, dropout, and overly restrictive placements. Problems in social skills are also associated with socioeconomic status, lack of access to positive social role models, acute or chronic stress, and emotional trauma. Students with problem behavior *and* limited social skills require attention in this area for two reasons: first, to provide new alternatives, and second, to improve overall chances for success now and in the future.

Academic skills are obviously important in the lives of students; success in school is hardly possible without them. Although we do not intend to minimize the importance of academics, we also acknowledge that impairments in the three other categories tend to subtract from student achievement. Difficulties in communication, self-regulation, and social skills can become the lowest common denominator for students with problem behaviors; they have the potential to reduce the student's functional academics. Although we recognize that academics is the mainstay of education, *Positive Strategies* places relative emphasis on the other replacement skills. Our experience has taught us that the vast majority of educators struggle *not* with what or how to teach, but with how to prepare students to learn. Successfully addressing social, communication, and self-regulation skills prepares the student with problem behavior for instruction.

This brings us to our final criterion for effective replacement skills: they should *enhance quality of life* by promoting relevant skills and ensuring that they accrue meaningful benefits in the lives of children. Effective replacement skills do more than reduce problem behavior; by teaching a child new ways to cope, adapt, and communicate, they have the potential to result in meaningful outcomes. A child who is less aggressive and more assertive may do better in school, be accepted by peers, and show related gains attributable to confidence and self-efficacy.

Teaching Replacement Behavior

Several general considerations apply to teaching and encouraging the use of replacement behaviors. These guidelines and strategies are relevant regardless of the type of skill (communication, self-regulation, social, or academic skills) and include understanding functional competence, assessing the student's ability to observe himself or herself and learn rules, enactment, and practice with feedback.

As stated earlier, clear understanding of the student's *current functional competence* is necessary before the BIP is initiated. We encourage teams to first determine whether the student uses the target behavior in *any* context. If so, the team has probably come to understand the triggers that prompt its use (during the FBA, the team determines when problem behavior is absent and notes contextual features). If the student does not use the skill, the team's task is to determine whether prerequisites exist. Teams accomplish this by involving individuals familiar with the student in various contexts and by conceptualizing the behavior in terms of its discrete components (similar to task analysis).

Next, teams consider whether the student can *observe him- or herself.* This refers to the child's ability to monitor his or her own thoughts, feelings (affect), and behavior. The typically developing child is capable of minimal self-monitoring by preschool age ("I took that toy," "I was mad"). This ability matures and becomes more nuanced during the course of childhood. At first, children are capable of monitoring only visible behavior; over time, they develop the ability to think about their actions, contemplate choice, verbalize their own traits, identify and regulate feelings, and observe and resist impulses—abilities that are collectively referred to as metacognitive skills. Because the ability to observe oneself is helpful as students learn new behaviors, teams assess this ability. It is often helpful to build self-monitoring and self-evaluation into BIPs for students with effective self-monitoring capacities. For students with problem behavior, self-monitoring may be quite challenging, and for some students with significant disabilities, expecting this may be unrealistic in the short term.

Related to self-observation is *rule acquisition.* Here, the term *rules* refers not only to guidelines or policies for behavior (codes of conduct) but also to the rules of thumb that pertain to social and communication skills (interpersonal distance, turn taking in conversation, initiating and maintaining social discourse, social relevance and appropriateness). Students who readily learn and generalize rules are well prepared to acquire and use new ones. Alternatively, students who generally require high levels of structure, prompting, and repetition need rules in their BIPs.

For replacement skills to have utility, students must be able to *enact behavior.* Simply stated, the student must be capable of engaging in the behavior independently, or at least with support and prompting. This is an obvious point; we articulate it here because enactment is a fairly common oversight, leading to failed BIPs. Problem behavior arises because students do not have a better way or cannot find a better way when they need it. It is essential to observe the desired replacement behavior before expecting it in context. This may be feasible only in artificial circumstances (e.g., deep breathing and relaxation in the counselor's office, test-taking strategies practiced in the resource room), but the team needs to be confident that the student can do it when necessary.

A closely related point is the need for *practice with feedback.* Effective BIPs require only what students are capable of. Even replacement skills that are in the student's repertoire require full mastery to be enacted under stress. Because of this, overlearning is sometimes indicated. This refers to practicing a skill until it can be repeated without difficulty or error. Overlearning self-regulation, communication, and social and academic skills enhances the likelihood that the student will be able to access them in problem contexts.

STRATEGIES FOR TEACHING REPLACEMENT SKILLS

Table 19 encapsulates several general strategies for teaching replacement skills. These follow directly from the team's assessment of the student's functional status. Teaching can be conducted in a sequential fashion regardless of skill category. These strategies apply equally to teaching self-regulation, communication, and social and academic skills.

As this table suggests, teams should consider embedding instruction and enactment within a larger incentive or *motivational system* (system of rewards) for the student. Notwithstanding our earlier comment regarding natural reinforcement, programmed reinforcement may be necessary, especially when a student already possesses a skill but does not use it consistently. Effective motivational systems consider the interests, concerns, and preferences of the students and deliver reinforcement in meaningful, nondemeaning ways. As such, an incentive system cannot be an afterthought or hastily added BIP component. Formulating an incentive system requires the involvement of the student and family and includes information derived in the student profile and assessment of the student–environment fit as part of Step 1 of the FBA (Chapter 6).

Earlier, we mentioned that teams sometimes struggle to pinpoint replacement skills and develop instructional plans for their components. To assist them, Table 20 presents common skill impairments by type, provides examples of explicit skills to target, and suggests instructional methods. It is also worth reiterating that teams lacking expertise in teaching specific skill areas should consider consulting relevant literature, procuring external consultation, or both. The bibliography lists several helpful resources to assist teams in matching replacement skills to specific difficulties and effectively teaching alternatives.

Although we provide a few examples of common skill impairments in Table 20, a full discussion of teaching skills across these areas would require several volumes. We encourage teams to be creative and innovative in developing strategies for students. For example, a student with academic and self-regulation difficulties may be taught to rate task difficulty using a traffic light; difficult problems (red) require a *stop, calm, and think* response; moderate problems (yellow) mean *proceed with caution*; and easy problems (green) mean *move right along.* Another student may use an imaginary remote control to turn on feelings of calm or to turn down anger. There is a plethora of material available to support students with specific difficulties (learning disabilities, conduct problems, attention impairments, autism spectrum disorders, and so forth); many manuals, workbooks, and tracking forms are available to assist teams. We suggest that teams use and customize them to suit the concerns of their students.

Step 4 of the Behavior Intervention Plan Worksheets

Step 4 prompts teams to define alternative behaviors and list the skill areas to which they pertain; sometimes, more than one skill area is tapped by a replacement behavior. Teams denote the student's current skill level (uses skill, has prerequisites, lacks skill) and the amount of support the new skill will require (formal instruction, motivational system, assistive or adaptive technology). To clarify the relevance of the replacement skill, the team also indicates the in-

Table 19. Strategies for teaching replacement skills

Teach student to observe own behavior; if the student is not capable, develop clear means of providing feedback and tracking behavior.
Teach rules and pivotal (keystone) skills first.
Teach elements of behavior in stepwise (task analysis) fashion.
Ensure that the student has skills to perform the behavior; instruct any lacking elements.
Require practice; provide supportive feedback and coaching; consider overlearning.
Teach the student to evaluate own performance and compare it against standards.
Combine teaching with context accommodations and motivation systems.
Fade prompts and programmed reinforcement with mastery.

Source: Barnett, Bell, & Carey (1999).

Table 20. Skills deficits (by area) and suggested instructional strategies

Functional communication: Student does not communicate needs or desires.

- Determine most frequent communication skills needed (e.g., request).
- Assess whether needed skills are in repertoire (can student ask?).
- Expose students to models (observe actions of peers, staff, fictional characters).
- Teach, coach, and practice communication skill before requiring it.

Self-regulation: Student does not handle emotion adaptively (e.g., poor impulse control, low frustration tolerance).

- Assess self-monitoring ability and social skills repertoire.
- Teach emotion identification and self-soothing (role play, relaxation).
- Teach selection of optimal response (games, Stop and Think Program[a]).
- Teach problem-solving steps, self-talk.
- Construct motivational system that incorporates monitoring by self and others.

Social skills: Student engages in aggressive, nonassertive, disruptive, or socially inappropriate behavior.

- Assess self-monitoring ability and social skills repertoire.
- Educate regarding aggressive, assertive, and nonassertive behavior; teach social rules (games, curricula such as Skillstreaming[b], PREPARE Curriculum[c]).
- Use Social Stories[d].
- Teach, coach, and practice social skills before requiring them.

Academic skills: Student lacks learning skills needed to approach material or compensate for weaknesses.

- Assess underlying self-monitoring (metacognitive skills).
- As appropriate, assess organization, reading, writing, and related prerequisite skills.
- Link academic strategies to self-regulation ability.
- Teach rating of task difficulty, task analysis (step-by-step approach).
- Require self-evaluation, provide supportive feedback.

[a]Kendall (1992).
[b]Goldstein (1999).
[c]Goldstein & McGinnis (1997).
[d]Gray (2000).

tended long-term goal and its benefits. Finally, Step 4 involves a detailed instructional plan and anticipates ongoing instruction.

Logically, the instructional plan is based on the student's current skill level and the level of support the student needs. The plan stipulates procedures, staff responsible for instruction, the frequency and setting of instruction, materials needed, and reinforcement provided. This level of specificity is key to ensuring accountability and fidelity of implementation. Although the student's ongoing instructional concerns rely on initial progress, good planning anticipates next steps so that teams can prepare accordingly. Step 4 forms permit space for teams to outline two replacement behaviors. In some cases, teams will develop three or more and can reproduce this form in those cases.

To illustrate how a team might go about developing a detailed BIP, we return to Nathan and include Step 4 of his BIP.

Nathan's Behavioral Intervention Plan—Step 4: Replace

Generating a plan. From early in the FBA, Nathan's student support team had an emerging sense that his learning disabilities and low tolerance for frustration contributed to problem behavior. They surmised that his behavior initially served the function of escape and was being maintained by attention. It seemed clear that Nathan needed a better way, but how could they help him find one?

Initially, team members expressed uncertainty as to whether they could get Nathan to change. They had manipulated various contingencies before, and Nathan had not responded. They had tried reprimands, parent conferences, time-out, a motivational system, and informal counseling, yet the behavior had persisted. Although they were confident that their short-term prevention efforts would probably have some effect, they were not assured about teaching him to *replace* his problem behaviors. During the BIP meeting, the classroom teacher suggested that they simply talk to him again about how to behave, pointing out that he did not have outbursts elsewhere. Other team members responded with silence.

The coach asked team members to share their reactions and concerns. The coach then reflected the team's sentiments: most lacked confidence, leading to a sense of resignation. Essentially, they knew what Nathan needed to do: learn different ways to compensate for his learning difficulties and handle his frustration better. They felt at a loss, however, to make those things happen. The coach asked the team, "If you knew a student who lacked mastery of a set of academic skills, but you had no experience instructing them, what would you do?" Team members responded that they would consult authoritative sources on teaching, talk to colleagues, attend in-service or training, or secure a consultant. The coach said that these alternatives were exactly the kind they needed to pursue for Nathan. The team decided to take each of the two skill areas (learning skills and frustration tolerance), discuss them in turn, and note specific areas with which they might need assistance.

First, the team considered learning skills. Despite their initial lack of confidence, they generated several means to help Nathan master language-based materials. Many suggestions came from the resource room teacher—a learning disability specialist—who took the time to explain support strategies. Ideas also came from the classroom teacher, the social worker, and coach. The classroom teacher, who seemed to be encouraged by this discussion, commented, "But all the learning strategies in the world won't help him if he can't handle the frustration that comes with the territory." Now the team was prepared to discuss the question of how to promote frustration tolerance to give Nathan the perseverance he needed.

The coach sensed that the team felt unprepared to address self-regulation, and he asked about their skills and experience in coaching children. The social worker stated that this was part of her ongoing work with several children, but other team members said they had no experience at all. The coach made two observations. First, the social worker clearly had competencies that would be essential for supporting Nathan. Second, being an instructor involved teaching self-regulation skills every day; word attack skills, tackling math problems, and narrative composition all required helping children process instructions, assess tasks, formulate responses mentally (including breaking the task into several steps), write down answers, check work, stop and think, raise their hands, and wait to be called on. The coach reassured the team that although their experiences did not include teaching frustration tolerance, they nonetheless had many relevant skills and talents to draw from. The coach, who (as a psychologist) had expertise in teaching self-regulation skills, volunteered to serve as consultant to the team.

Next, the team considered a range of support strategies for Nathan. Recognizing the wisdom of the teacher's statement about frustration tolerance, they decided to front-end coaching in frustration and anger management and gradually require greater use of support strategies while introducing new learning skills. Thus, they developed plans for two clusters of replacement skills, both involving self-regulation.

Plan for replacement skill 1 (frustration tolerance). The first replacement skill was related to frustration tolerance and contained three major elements: mood monitoring, self-calming, and breaks, all supported by individual coaching with the team's social worker. For *mood monitoring,* the social worker (after conferring separately with the school psychologist) collaborated with Nathan to develop a thermometer. In coaching sessions, the social worker role played situations with Nathan, and he rated what his mood would be in those circumstances. Together, they created the thermometer that had numbers from 1 to 10, corresponding to frustration level. It was anchored with descriptions of feelings, thoughts, and actions that Nathan usually demonstrated at each level. For each number, they also listed specific self-control strategies and other coping means that Nathan could use. For example, by 5, Nathan could take a *break*: he could get out of his seat, walk over to the wastebasket, sharpen his pencil, and so forth. He would be permitted up to three of these breaks per instructional period; if he took more than three breaks in a session, he would be asked to attend a booster session in anger management with the social worker. Because Nathan's problem behavior was maintained by escape, breaks were considered an important feature of both prevention and replacement efforts; they qualified as self-calming strategies (interrupt escalation) as well as escape.

Self-calming skills would also be instructed and coached by the team social worker. These would include deep breathing, counting to 10, taking breaks, coping statements ("This is hard but I can do it—one step at a time"), and using an imaginary switch by which Nathan could turn on the calm, initiating use of calming skills.

Given her prominent role in this replacement skill, the social worker volunteered to coordinate this part of the plan and agreed to provide an initial progress report just a few days after initiation. From there, the plan would be regularly updated and modified to reflect progress and continuing concerns. During the initial coaching sessions, the social worker would supply a binder in which Nathan's mood monitoring forms would be placed. At each mood-rating interval, there was a place to note outcomes; the form required notation of what Nathan did after his mood rating and how long it took him to de-escalate. The form also had a "How am I doing?" section in which Nathan would judge the effectiveness of his self-calming. The binder served as a self-regulation support and a monitoring tool.

Nathan's team outlined an initial instruction plan and projected ongoing instructional concerns, which would depend on his progress. Although change was difficult to predict, the team nevertheless considered its next steps, including how to generalize Nathan's skill use. Initially, this included extending strategies to the home environment and providing reinforcement for unused breaks.

Plan for replacement skill 2 (learning skills). After noting the fundamentals for teaching Nathan's first replacement skill, the team briefly returned to learning skills. They reiterated some of the earlier strategies they had discussed, but they felt more confident that these might come to fruition if Nathan could first manage frustration. They also acknowledged that there had been times in the past when staff had been reluctant to approach Nathan because of discomfort over his potential escalation. The team expressed regret that his behavior had deteriorated, and they renewed their commitment to supporting him. They realized that their prior avoidance had only served to reinforce the escape component of Nathan's behavior.

As seen in Figure 27, supporting Nathan's learning skills involved careful planning and ongoing coordination. Because the team wished to support Nathan and prepare him for future challenges, they constructed a graduated approach. First, all language tasks would be adapted (per the short-term prevention plan); however, the resource teacher would review these adapta-

STEP 4. REPLACE PROBLEM BEHAVIOR WITH ALTERNATIVE BEHAVIORS OR SKILLS

Alternative #1: Predict "trouble spots"; use thermometer to monitor mood; use breaks, deep breathing, coping statements; effectively de-escalate before losing control.

Skill area: ☑ Self-regulation ☐ Communication ☐ Social skills ☐ Academic skills ☐ Other

Current skill level: ☑ Uses skill inconsistently ☑ Has prerequisites or aspects of skill ☐ Lacks this skill

Support needed: ☑ Formal instruction ☐ Improved motivation system ☐ Assistive or adaptive technology

Long-term goal and benefits: Improve frustration tolerance/anger management resulting in better performance, improved peer relations.

Initial instructional plan: Include procedures, instructor(s), frequency, setting(s), materials, and reinforcement.

Coaching: Social worker will prep materials and meet with Nathan and family before implementation. Social worker will instruct and coach self-regulation skills: mood monitoring, relaxation (deep breathing, imaginary "switch" that turns on calm), and coping statements ("This is hard, but I can do it—one step at a time").

1. **Mood monitoring:** Nathan will rate frustration level using numbers 1–10 with corresponding amounts of "mercury" (red) and descriptive terms (1=relaxed, 5=getting antsy, 8=steaming mad).
2. **Self-calming:** Nathan and social worker will develop strategies for calming and coping associated with each level on thermometer (e.g., 5=take break): relaxation, deep breathing, count to 10, coping statements.
3. **Breaks:** Based on mood rating, Nathan will take breaks (at desk, walk around room, enter hall, depending on frustration level). Higher mood ratings should prompt breaks and self-calming until de-escalated (rating of 4).

Ongoing instruction: Include plan to fade prompts and reinforcement as skill is generalized to other settings.

Nathan will be allowed a limited number of breaks each period—put one chip in jar for each break; initial daily amount established by number or breaks needed during behavior intervention plan to date. To generalize, family will help him practice self-regulation skills. After demonstrated success in school, homework assignments at home so frustration tolerance and self-calming skills are practiced there. Since progress should bring natural and programmed reinforcement, team expects more self-regulation over time and corresponding fading of supports.

Staff responsible: Social worker **Start date:** 12/15 **1st review date:** 12/20

Alternative #2: Rate task difficulty, predict "trouble spots," develop and use "attack" strategies first with support and then independently.

Skill area: ☑ Self-regulation ☐ Communication ☐ Social skills ☐ Academic skills ☐ Other

Current skill level: ☐ Uses skill inconsistently ☐ Has prerequisites or aspects of skill ☑ Lacks this skill

Support needed: ☑ Formal instruction ☐ Improved motivation system ☐ Assistive or adaptive technology

Long-term goal and benefits: Develop learning strategies for verbal material to improve success on language tasks and overall achievement.

Initial instructional plan: Include procedures, instructor(s), frequency, setting(s), materials, and reinforcement.

1. **Adapt materials:** After consulting with classroom teacher, resource room teacher will adapt learning materials and assignments in advance. Resource room teacher will meet with Nathan daily; will explain how materials were adapted.
2. **One-on-one support:** Resource room teacher will instruct and support Nathan on writing skills (e.g., main ideas, outlines, narrative writing diamond) and set aside one-on-one time to review and support written assignments.
3. **Diary:** Resource room teacher and Nathan will keep diary listing of accommodations and summarize them weekly.
4. **Supported self-monitoring:** After consulting with classroom teacher, social worker and resource room teacher will meet briefly (10 minutes) with Nathan each Friday to review progress. Social worker and Nathan will review with family (call).

Ongoing instruction: Include plan to fade prompts and reinforcement as skill is generalized to other settings.

As Nathan demonstrates success with behavioral control (see alternative #1), resource room teacher will begin to request his collaboration in adapting materials. This will prepare and tutor Nathan in identifying his need for accommodations. To generalize, after stable period of success, resource room teacher and Nathan will meet with parents to review self-accommodation strategies in preparation for homework. Continuing resource room assistance per individualized educational plan.

Staff responsible: Social worker **Start date:** 12/15 **1st review date:** 12/20

Figure 27. Step 4 of the Behavior Intervention Plan, as compiled by Nathan's team.

tions with Nathan each day. She would explain how the materials were adapted (e.g., convert questions to multiple-choice format, break word problems into steps, and so forth) and track their effectiveness for future review, summary, and reports to the team. Over time, Nathan would join the resource teacher in forecasting trouble spots by reviewing upcoming assignments, rating their difficulty, and developing adaptations. The resource room teacher would remain available to Nathan when narrative writing was required and would set aside individual time to support this activity. She would incorporate accommodations (e.g., increased computer use) as indicated. One of the long-term goals was for Nathan to learn self-accommodations that would serve him well into the future.

To encourage self-monitoring, Nathan was integrally involved in reporting progress. He would meet with core members of the team at the end of each week, and with the support of the social worker, he would discuss his progress with his parents (initially, on the telephone from the social worker's office; his parents would arrange a break from work for 10-minute conversations). Nathan's parents were pleased to be closely involved in the plan, but they expressed reservations about Nathan's comfort in discussing progress initially. As such, the team agreed to work closely with Nathan and to not place those demands on him until he was ready.

Nathan's team developed a plan that involved detailed specifications for initial instruction and projected ongoing concerns but that was flexible enough to accommodate varying levels of progress. It empowered Nathan not only by promoting positive change but also by involving him in monitoring and communicating his own progress. The eventual objective was for Nathan to internalize elements of his BIP: assess task difficulty, adjust his approach to work accordingly, recognize his own frustration, and take small, socially acceptable (i.e., nondisruptive) breaks, all in service of better academic achievement, enhanced social relationships, a personal sense of efficacy, and improved quality of life.

MONITOR AND EVALUATE

Effective BIPs specify behaviors to reduce, behaviors to increase, and plans for effecting these changes. Interventions can have positive, negative, mixed, or unremarkable outcomes. Once the plan is initiated, how do teams know whether their efforts are making a difference? Teams may consider their efforts successful when the student demonstrates noticeable change—change with functional impact. But what comprises such change is subject to judgment. Because evaluation of effectiveness should not be subjective, teams should establish clear criteria against which to benchmark progress.

The process of monitoring the BIP actually begins with the FBA. The team reviews previous assessments and interventions; conducts interviews, observations, and checklists; and completes questionnaires. All of these steps are intended to help the team understand when, where, and how often problem behaviors occur. Once baseline frequency has been established, monitoring actually becomes less complicated. The team has established its means and systems for observing and documenting behavior during the FBA. To evaluate intervention effectiveness, the team monitors change relative to the baseline levels in relation to explicit criteria.

Comparing change against established criteria also informs modifications to the intervention plan. Even the most effective BIPs require ongoing modifications. In fact, BIPs that are not evaluated and modified are unlikely to meet the student's continuing concerns. This requires a close link between assessment and intervention; monitoring and evaluation activities link these two phases.

What Do Teams Monitor and Evaluate?

Teams *monitor* two major areas, incidents of problem behavior and use of replacement behaviors (alternatives). They *evaluate* general outcomes and the impact of behavior change on academic and social performance.

Monitoring Problem Behavior

Monitoring problem behavior involves observing the student, tracking incidents, and noting triggers and consequences as needed. It requires the development of simple, accessible tracking methods that do not pose substantial documentation burdens for team members. The BIP monitoring plan lists each problem behavior and indicates its baseline rate (average rate before intervention). To establish benchmarks, the team projects optimal outcomes (goal achieved) and decides the rate of problem behavior that constitutes insufficient progress. If either benchmark is met, the team contemplates modifications to the intervention.

The monitoring plan, then, targets a level of problem reduction that signifies goal achievement. To determine this, teams ask what rate of problem behavior would be tolerable. Risky or dangerous behaviors may need to be completely extinguished, in which cases the rate at which a plan is considered successful may be zero. Behavior intervention research indicates that few behaviors disappear entirely from an individual's repertoire. Quite frequently, it is acceptable and realistic for teams to target a low (but manageable) level for a problem behavior. The team also establishes a rate at which review of the BIP is required if it seems to be ineffective or minimally effective.

Monitoring Replacement Behavior

Because effective interventions attend to problem reduction and corresponding improvements, teams track how much and how well students use replacement behaviors. The processes for doing so are quite similar to those for tracking problem behavior: the behavior is clearly defined (operationalized), there is a system to noting its occurrence (including relevant context information), and there are established benchmarks for acceptable levels of change and those that will trigger reevaluation of the intervention.

To illustrate these benchmarks, we return to Nia. If her baseline rate of biting herself were 25 times per day, her team might establish a goal of 5–7 times per day as representing a successful intervention. They would reevaluate their plan if biting remained at an average frequency of 15 or more times per day, at least at the outset. In data-driven decision making, outcomes are tracked daily and analyzed for days or even weeks. It is generally most helpful to consider average rates rather than examining daily fluctuations; this ensures that the team does not modify the plan in response to unusual circumstances (outliers). When there is concern about intervention effectiveness, fluctuations in behavior should be carefully monitored because frequency may covary with setting events, antecedents, and other contextual factors.

Evaluating Problem and Replacement Behavior

Because significant outcomes reflect more than mere problem reduction, evaluation focuses on improving overall function. In selecting replacement behaviors to coach and reinforce, the team chooses skills that relate meaningfully to education and quality of life. Before a BIP begins, the team assesses the relevance of each replacement skill, the benefits it will accrue, and the settings in which those benefits will be evident. They prepare to evaluate outcomes and benefits in multiple ways. When significant outcomes and benefits are realized, they are observable to various members of the team (the student's teachers, family members, counselors, related services providers) and to others (athletic coach, tutor, friends, peers). Some benefits are publicly observable (better behaved, more social, less angry or disruptive), whereas others remain relatively private (better grades, improved discipline record). A useful evaluation plan samples various contexts and individuals to understand the benefits (and limitations) of intervention.

Each BIP specifies benchmarks for progress, indicates levels of performance that trigger reevaluation, and stipulates procedures for modifying the BIP. The best initial BIPs are living documents that teams refer to, revisit, and revise frequently. Modifications can be minor (involving brief notes or addenda) or substantial (prompting the development of an entirely new BIP).

Nathan's Behavioral Intervention Plan—Step 5: Monitor and Evaluate

Aware that evaluation was not possible without tracking behavior, Nathan's team made plans for immediate monitoring. They established benchmarks for progress and developed markers that would indicate if the plan was not meeting with success. The team decided to track problem and replacement behaviors and outlined a very simple tracking form.

Incidents of *problem behavior* were subdivided into yelling and cursing, storming out of class, and hitting peers; all incidents of each were to be recorded. As they considered how to define success, the team examined Nathan's baseline for yelling and cursing. At the time of the FBA, he had about 2.3 incidents per day. Although the best possible outcome would be a complete cessation of incidents, the team realistically considered what they could live with and how much they could expect from Nathan. The team concluded that they would continue the BIP unaltered unless there were more than about 1.5 incidents per week. They agreed not to throw out the plan if Nathan had a few bad days. They concluded that more than 1.5 incidents per day for several days would trigger careful review and that the benchmark would likely be gradually reduced over time.

The team took a similar stance regarding storming out of the classroom; this behavior was unproductive but not dangerous. They felt that they could tolerate this behavior about once per week and that expecting more from the outset might not be fair to Nathan. Because hitting signified a substantial loss of control and violated the rights of other students, the team concluded that any future incidents would automatically trigger a review of the plan (as well as other measures stipulated in Step 2, Prevent).

Nathan's BIP included two main clusters of *replacement behaviors,* both of which entailed self-regulation and offered the chance to improve related academic and social outcomes. They chose three behaviors to track: taking breaks from work, mood monitoring and self-calming, and learning-accommodation strategies. Breaks could easily be tracked by a simple daily frequency count; the challenge was to determine what would signify progress. What if the learning accommodations worked so well that Nathan did not need all his breaks? In that case, breaks would not be a valid index of improvement. The team decided to track breaks and outbursts together. If Nathan did not take breaks and did have incidents, he had missed opportunities for self-calming. This might imply limited success and would trigger reevaluation of the plan.

Finally, the team wished to *monitor and evaluate* whether Nathan benefited initially from accommodation strategies and eventually engaged in self-accommodations. At first, team members felt this outcome was rather amorphous, and they struggled to operationalize it. Then, the resource teacher offered a strategy: because she and Nathan would be keeping a diary of his accommodations, they could also track whether they worked (and, later, whether he generated his own). She volunteered to incorporate this into the diary so that it could be used for evaluation. Figure 28 depicts Step 5 of Nathan's BIP, including problem and replacement behaviors to monitor, baseline rates, benchmarks for progress (goal achieved), and indicators that the plan needed review (e.g., he was not demonstrating sufficient reduction in problem behaviors or use of alternatives).

Immediately below the monitoring section in Nathan's BIP lies the evaluation section. Here, the team formulated expected outcomes for problem and replacement behaviors. They also emphasized the larger benefits resulting from those outcomes. In other words, it would certainly be a positive change if Nathan showed fewer outbursts and better self-regulation in school; it would be even better if those improvements benefited his academic and social functioning. Because these generalized outcomes were so meaningful, the team (including the family) viewed them as crucial. Figure 28 illustrates four outcomes his team chose to focus on and how they were evaluated; like many good evaluation plans, they sample various skill dimensions and settings.

Maintain and Extend

Positive behavior change is the goal of intervention. If change is achieved but is not durable or evident across contexts, how meaningful is it? Change is *generalized* when it is maintained (lasting) in a wide variety of settings and spreads to a variety of related behaviors. Spontaneous generalization occurs when students transfer skills without explicit programming; this occurs rarely. Thus, it is not enough to train and hope, implementing a plan and simply wishing for change to have a global impact. Effective plans foresee the diverse contexts in which new skills may be used as problem behaviors diminish. They develop specific plans to achieve those objectives, establish targets, and monitor change. In this section, we review several guidelines for supporting maintenance of change over time and across settings. We also discuss the importance of fortifying change by anticipating and planning for circumstances in which problem behavior may reemerge.

Promoting Maintenance and Generalization

Techniques for supporting maintenance and generalization take one of two approaches. First, by teaching, coaching, and reinforcement, they help the individual transfer skills to new settings. Second, they alter the environment to support maintenance of change (Rutherford & Nelson, 1988). By teaching replacement skills and making long-term accommodations, effective BIPs encompass both approaches.

STEP 5. MONITOR AND EVALUATE CHANGES IN BEHAVIOR, USE OF REPLACEMENTS, AND OUTCOMES

A. Monitor rates of problem behavior and use of replacement behaviors or skills

Problem behaviors (tracking methods)	Baseline (number per unit of time or opportunity)	Goal achieved (rate at which plan is considered successful)	Review required (rate at which plan modification is needed)
Yelling at teacher, cursing (tracking form)	2.3 per day	1 in 3 days .3 per day	More than 1.5 per week
Storming out of class, out of control (form)	3 per week	1 per month	1 per week
Hitting peers (tracking form)	2 per month	None for rest of year	1 incident
Replacement behaviors (tracking methods)			
Independently initiates breaks (frequency count)	None	3 or fewer per class	None
Mood ratings and self-calming (binder)		Uses as needed	Less than 1.5 outbursts per week
Accommodation strategies (recorded in diary)	Varied	75% of opportunities	50%

B. Evaluate generalized outcomes and impact of changes on academic and social performance

Skill area	Setting	Expected outcomes and benefits	Evaluation method
☑ Self-regulation ☐ Communication ☐ Social skills ☐ Academic skills	☑ School ☑ Home ☐ Community	Improved self-regulation: handle frustration without losing control	Monitoring incidents of problem behavior Daily with weekly review; then at longer intervals with progress
☑ Self-regulation ☐ Communication ☐ Social skills ☑ Academic skills	☑ School ☑ Home ☐ Community	Better "attack" strategies for language and writing tasks More confidence and access to strengths	Student, parent, teacher report, resource room teacher diary Weekly at first, longer intervals with progress
☐ Self-regulation ☐ Communication ☐ Social skills ☑ Academic skills	☑ School ☐ Home ☐ Community	Better performance-average grades in math, language arts, and social studies will increase	Team review of grades in math, language arts, and social studies in 3 months Meeting at report card time
☐ Self-regulation ☐ Communication ☑ Social skills ☐ Academic skills	☑ School ☐ Home ☑ Community	Better peer relationships, more friends, not ostracized, con tacts outside school	Parent and teacher observation and report, self-report Evaluate in 3 months at time of report card

Procedure for modifying behavior intervention plan: (Indicate how changes will be made to plan.)

Team will monitor progress daily and weekly; should behavior incidents increase or worsen, immediate team meeting to discuss and plan. If no or limited progress (see A above), team will reconvene to reconsider plan.

Staff responsible: Social worker **Start date:** 12/15

Figure 28. Step 5 of the Behavior Intervention Plan, as compiled by Nathan's team.

Several ways to promote durable behavior change are listed in Table 21. These strategies are best considered at the time of initial BIP development and revisited as the team observes the student's evolving progress. Without knowing how a student will respond to the BIP, it is impossible to program generalization into the initial BIP. Quick perusal of this table reveals several strategies that closely resemble strategies to promote *acquisition* of replacement skills; they appear again here because they also promote the *maintenance* of skills.

Several of the items listed reflect the need for skill instruction to be flexible and diversified. This includes the need to teach in natural contexts, with varied context cues, and with changing schedules and intervals of reinforcement. A pivotal skill such as self-regulation can enhance intervention effects across settings and classes of behavior (e.g., the student may show better impulse control in academic subjects, in art, at home, and at basketball practice). To maintain positive change, teams consider consequences that inadvertently reinforce challenging behavior. Elsewhere, we discuss equivalence of function in detail; here, we remind teams to evaluate and mitigate the impact of maladaptive consequences for problem behavior. Although peer attention is a common example of a maintaining consequence, more subtle and problematic ones exist. For example, students who gain a great deal of peer attention have to sacrifice a developing identity among peers. A student's aggressive behavior may be rewarded when peers acquiesce to demands, and a student's self-stimulatory behavior may actually occur in avoidance of uncomfortable interactions with peers. If these consequences are not managed, the intervention plan may show only limited success. Alternative consequences exert a strong pull toward problem behavior. As such, teams need to forecast high-risk situations, provide supports, and, ultimately, teach the student a better way to respond. In the next chapter, we discuss issues related to maintenance and generalization of behavior over the long term.

The effective BIP maintains change by anticipating high-risk circumstances and planning for them. Understanding that lapses are common, considering the student's past behavior, and building on success to date, the team formulates specific support strategies and develops a plan to enact them. In so doing, they hope to assure that lapses into problem behavior are not extended into relapse.

Nathan's Behavioral Intervention Plan—Step 6: Maintain

Nathan's team planned to support new skills and to evaluate whether they resulted in changes in his quality of life. Another question they began to consider was how they could support positive change across time and context. This would require a concerted team effort as outlined in Nathan's BIP, as well as considering bumps in the road ahead, as one team member put it. For Nathan, maintaining change would require forecasting high-risk situations and planning to enhance supports.

The team *forecast* two sets of risk, one in the relatively near term and one more distant. The first involved *unforeseen changes* in the classroom or support plan. What if an integral team member was out for training one day, or fell ill? The team agreed that they could minimize such disruptions by planning Nathan's assignments at least 3 days in advance. They would also en-

Table 21. Strategies for promoting maintenance

Employ natural reinforcement.
Eradicate/modify maintaining consequences for undesirable behavior (e.g., modify social attention for disruptive behavior; teach assertion to peers who were subjects of aggression).
Train loosely; do not adhere to rigid or scripted protocols for teaching behavior or evaluating response to training.
Train in diverse settings and conditions and with varied reinforcement.
Reinforce incidents of spontaneous and programmed generalization.
Incorporate self-regulation training: self-monitoring, self-instruction, and self-evaluation.
Vary context cues; use familiar ones (verbal prompts, play and learning materials) in initial teaching and generalization; fade these with mastery and replace with unfamiliar cues.
Conduct initial and follow-up (booster) teaching in natural settings.
Foresee and practice high-risk circumstances.
Teach the student to respond to lapses.

Sources: Stokes & Baer (1977) and Rutherford & Nelson (1988).

sure that at least two members of the team were intimately familiar with each aspect of his plan. In this way, if any one person were out, others could fill in without significant disruption.

This would allow time to adjust plans and shift resources. If reduced supports were available to Nathan when he needed them, the team would consider reducing his work as a means of prevention. Over time, Nathan's parents would implement BIP strategies at home, ensuring that Nathan's skills transferred across context and that continuing support would be available long after Nathan finished fifth grade.

The second forecast involved Nathan's *transition to middle school* the next fall. Although it seemed far away on the day they contemplated his BIP, the team knew that this would be a significant stressor for Nathan. To provide extra supports for the transition, the current team would contact the middle school instructional team in 3 months to begin planning. The hope was to develop an individualized transition plan for Nathan in addition to that afforded to the entire fifth grade.

The team also wanted Nathan's middle school team to respond to any upsurge in behavior in a way that would promote adaptive alternatives rather than reinforcing escape. To ensure the existence of a coping plan on the first day of sixth grade, the new team would receive a copy of Nathan's BIP and meet with his parents and student support team before the end of the current school year. The initial aim would be to continue prevention elements of Nathan's BIP (learning adaptations, self-accommodations) that effectively reduced problem behavior. It would be important for Nathan to have resource teacher support immediately on entering sixth grade. Should Nathan have resurgent self-regulation difficulties after achieving success in the fifth grade, similar mood monitoring and de-escalation strategies would likely be effective in sixth. Acquainting his new middle school team with these successes might eliminate future challenges for Nathan and his instructional team. His parents volunteered to continue coaching his self-regulation skills through the summer months.

Nathan's student support team noted their forecasts and corresponding support plans in Step 6 of his BIP, depicted in Figure 29. They agreed to review and update this step in 3 months, at which point they would initiate their contact with the middle school.

Effective BIPs emerge from extensive planning, assessment (FBA), and implementation (BIPs). They require the sustained creative energies of the entire student support team. In Chapters 5, 6, and 7, we outline the steps teams take to understand, prevent, and replace problem behavior and the tools they use to do so. *Positive Strategies* entails more than discrete activities and steps, however. Effective student supports involve careful allocation of resources, collaboration among stakeholders, and sincere commitment to meeting the concerns of individual students. In Chapter 8, we examine how meaningful changes can be maintained and extended to new contexts.

STEP 6. MAINTAIN POSITIVE CHANGES OVER TIME AND ACROSS SETTINGS

Periodic review: Outline plan to maintain change into future and enhance quality of life.

High-risk circumstances: Develop support plan that anticipates predictable future challenges.

Unforeseen changes: Teacher or coach absent, not available for support. Classroom teacher and resourse room teacher consult to adapt work several days in advance. In resource room teacher's absence, classroom teacher provides support; Nathan may obtain extra breaks, reduced work. With success, consider peer buddy support for mood monitoring.

Transition to middle school at end of year; departmentalized curriculum, more teachers, greater demands. Before year's end, social studies teacher to meet with middle school staff about Nathan. In addition to group orientation, provide Nathan a one-on-one orientation. Have coping plan and recourse room teacher support in place prior to 1st day of sixth grade.

Plan for relapse: Assuming initial success, outline plan for managing recurrence of problem behavior. If Nathan's target behavior changes or problem behavior reduces but positive outcomes not achieved, team will meet within one week to reconsider plan.

Staff responsible: Social worker **1st review date:** 3 months

Figure 29. Step 6 of the Behavior Intervention Plan, as compiled by Nathan's team.

Before we discuss Nathan's plan over the long term, we return to Nathan's team to examine how his BIP evolved over the course of the school year. As illustrated previously in this chapter, Nathan's team developed and initiated a BIP with elements of prevention and replacement skills. They monitored problem behavior, but they also kept track of how often Nathan took breaks, the extent to which he used newly taught coping skills, and his grades. The team met regularly during the first few weeks of implementation (beginning in December), and a bit less frequently as Nathan demonstrated fairly consistent progress. The whole BIP, as developed, is presented in Figure 30 on pages 156–160.

Student: Nathan Jones **Date:** December 18

Behavior: Yelling at teacher, cursing **FBA dates:** October–November

Hypothesis (from FBA): Nathan yells at the teacher and curses when he has work with language demands, because when he does, he often doesn't have to complete the work as he gets sent out of the room and peers laugh. This is more likely to occur when assignments require complex written or verbal expression and because he has difficulty tolerating frustration.

STEP 1. BRAINSTORM POTENTIAL SOLUTIONS

A. Prevention: List setting event and/or antecedent modifications that might reduce target behavior. Check those validated by the FBA.

- ☐ Do not assign written work
- ☑ Adapt written work (e.g., multiple-choice instead of open-ended questions)
- ☑ Provide social and affective support (peer buddy to help with work and provide attention)
- ☐ Allow frequent breaks
- ☐ Have resource room teacher available for one-on-one assistance

B. Replacement behaviors: List replacement behaviors meeting the same function as problem behavior; consider coping skills that may reduce impact of setting events

1. Request breaks to provide escape
2. Gain peer attention through positive means, asking for help, collaborating on tasks that tap strengths
3. Improve frustration tolerance and time on task—assess task difficulty, rate frustration level, talk to self, take deep breath, ask for assistance, and wait for assistance to be provided.

STEP 2. PREVENT OR MINIMIZE OCCURRENCES OF PROBLEM BEHAVIOR

A. Short-term prevention strategies

Setting event or antecedent targeted	Strategy	Implementation plan	Outcomes
Low frustration tolerance; language-based learning disability; peer attention	Peer buddy	When math, language arts, and social studies require complex written or verbal expression, pair Nathan with valued peer who reads questions aloud and supports his responses Rotating peer buddies coordinated by classroom teacher with social worker support	Reduce number of incidents Learn from positive peer models Increase positive social attention
Language-based learning disability	Task accommodations	Resource room teacher to modify content for math word problems, language arts, social studies; resource room and classroom teachers to coordinate Nathan's work and progress; daily, resource room teacher to meet privately with Nathan to explain and review accommodations	Reduce number of incidents Learn to simplify materials via daily meeting with resource room teacher Increase academic success

Staff responsible: Classroom teacher **Start date:** 12/11 **1st review date:** 12/20

B. Long-term accommodations

Setting event or antecedent targeted	Long-term accommodation	Implementation plan	Desired outcomes
Language-based learning disability	Make language tasks and verbal instruction easier for Nathan to process.	Resource room teacher to provide continuing consultation to simplify instructions and adapt Nathan's work; resource room teacher to meet daily with Nathan to preview material and assignments, forecast trouble spots. Decrease frequency (fade) only with extended success.	Better meet Nathan's learning needs Decrease frustration Increase success Decrease amount of labor Nathan expends on processing tasks and requirements
Low frustration tolerance	Breaks	Nathan permitted breaks from work to walk around room, sharpen pencil, etc. without need for permission; must not be disruptive; at outset, permitted 3 breaks per period. Number of breaks to be altered based upon progress.	Reduce number of incidents Learn to simplify materials via daily meetings with resource room teacher Increase success

Staff responsible: Classroom teacher **Start date:** 12/15 **1st review date:** 12/20

STEP 3. MANAGE CONTINUING INCIDENTS OF PROBLEM BEHAVIOR

Early signs of problem behavior: Escalation.

Nathan sighs, becomes restless, increases motor activity, makes excuse to take break (bathroom, pencil, trash can).

Steps to take in response to early signs of behavior: (Refer to replacement skills.)

Provide verbal prompt for Nathan to rate frustration. Based on rating, Nathan will choose type of break. At end of break, Nathan will be coached to use coping statements and relaxation strategies. When he has deescalated, resume work.

Response to incidents of behavior: Include plan to resume activity or return to context.

1. If Nathan yells at teacher or curses, he will be coached to regain control and resume work as soon as possible by resource room teacher, social worker, or school psychologist depending on scheduled availability. If behavior continues, coach will escort Nathan from room and monitor until he is able to cooperate with coaching (Step 5 of the BIP).
2. If Nathan leaves classroom, he will be required to make up work missed (with support if needed).
3. If Nathan hits another student, his parents will be called immediately. He will be required to discuss episode with social worker, assistant principal, and parents. In-school suspension will apply per school policy.

Steps to take following an incident: Describe procedures for incident review and strategies to minimize inadvertent reinforcement for problem behavior.

Classroom teacher, resource room teacher, and social worker will meet to review. Social worker will then review incident one-on-one with Nathan, discuss "better way," ask him to share with parents, and confirm/consult with them. Incident review will be opportunity to consider modifying plan.

☑ **Preparation required.** Consider staff training, student supports, other efforts needed.

In consultation with school psychologist, social worker will develop thermometer for Nathan to rate frustration and anger (see next page) and relaxation strategies. This will be finalized with Nathan and shared with parents in meeting. This will be developed, explained, and practiced prior to implementation.

☐ **Crisis intervention plan is needed.**

Staff responsible: Social worker **Start date:** 12/15 **1st review date:** 12/20

(continued)

STEP 4. REPLACE PROBLEM BEHAVIOR WITH ALTERNATIVE BEHAVIORS OR SKILLS

Alternative #1: Predict trouble spots; use thermometer to monitor mood; use breaks, deep breathing, coping statements; effectively deescalate before losing control.

Skill area: ☑ Self-regulation ☐ Communication ☐ Social skills ☐ Academic skills ☐ Other

Current skill level: ☑ Uses skill inconsistently ☑ Has prerequisites or aspects of skill ☐ Lacks this skill

Support needed: ☑ Formal instruction ☐ Improved motivation system ☐ Assistive or adaptive technology

Long-term goal and benefits: Improve frustration tolerance/anger management resulting in better performance, improved peer relations.

Initial instructional plan: Include procedures, instructor(s), frequency, setting(s), materials, and reinforcement.

Coaching: Social worker will prep materials and meet with Nathan and family before implementation. Social worker will instruct and coach self-regulation skills: mood monitoring, relaxation (deep breathing, imaginary "switch" that turns on calm), and coping statements ("This is hard, but I can do it—one step at a time").

1. **Mood monitoring:** Nathan will rate frustration level using numbers 1–10 with corresponding amounts of "mercury" (red) and descriptive terms (1=relaxed, 5=getting antsy, 8=steaming mad).
2. **Self-calming:** Nathan and social worker will develop strategies for calming and coping associated with each level on thermometer (e.g., 5=take break): relaxation, deep breathing, count to 10, coping statements.
3. **Breaks:** Based on mood rating, Nathan will take breaks (at desk, walk around room, enter hall, depending on frustration level). Higher mood ratings should prompt breaks and self-calming until deescalated (rating of 4).

Ongoing instruction: Include plan to fade prompts and reinforcement as skill is generalized to other settings.

Nathan will be allowed a limited number of breaks each period—put one chip in jar for each break; initial daily amount established by number or breaks needed during behavior intervention plan to date. To generalize, family will help him practice self-regulation skills. After demonstrated success in school, use on homework assignments at home so frustration tolerance and self-calming skills are practiced there. Since progress should bring natural and programmed reinforcement, team expects more self-regulation over time and corresponding fading of supports.

Staff responsible: Social worker **Start date:** 12/15 **1st review date:** 12/20

Alternative #2: Rate task difficulty, predict "trouble spots," develop and use "attack" strategies first with support and then independently.

Skill area: ☑ Self-regulation ☐ Communication ☐ Social skills ☐ Academic skills ☐ Other

Current skill level: ☐ Uses skill inconsistently ☐ Has prerequisites or aspects of skill ☑ Lacks this skill

Support needed: ☑ Formal instruction ☐ Improved motivation system ☐ Assistive or adaptive technology

Long-term goal and benefits: Develop learning strategies for verbal material to improve success on language tasks and overall achievement.

Initial instructional plan: Include procedures, instructor(s), frequency, setting(s), materials, and reinforcement.

1. **Adapt materials:** After consulting with classroom teacher, resource room teacher will adapt learning materials and assignments in advance. Resource room teacher will meet with Nathan daily; will explain how materials were adapted.
2. **One-on-one support:** Resource room teacher will instruct and support Nathan on writing skills (e.g., main ideas, outlines, narrative writing diamond) and set aside one-on-one time to review and support written assignments.
3. **Diary:** Resource room teacher and Nathan will keep diary listing of accommodations and summarize them weekly.
4. **Supported self-monitoring:** After consulting with classroom teacher, social worker and resource room teacher will meet briefly (10 minutes) with Nathan each Friday to review progress. Social worker and Nathan will review with family (call).

Ongoing instruction: Include plan to fade prompts and reinforcement as skill is generalized to other settings.

As Nathan demonstrates success with behavioral control (see alternative #1), resource room teacher will begin to request his collaboration in adapting materials. This will prepare and tutor Nathan in identifying his need for accommodations. To generalize, after stable period of success, resource room teacher and Nathan will meet with parents to review self-accommodation strategies in preparation for homework. Continuing resource room assistance per individualized educational plan.

Staff responsible: Social worker **Start date:** 12/15 **1st review date:** 12/20

STEP 5. MONITOR AND EVALUATE CHANGES IN BEHAVIOR, USE OF REPLACEMENTS, AND OUTCOMES

A. Monitor rates of problem behavior and use of replacement behaviors or skills

	Baseline (number per unit of time or opportunity)	Goal achieved (rate at which plan is considered successful)	Review required (rate at which plan modification is needed)
Problem behaviors (tracking methods)			
Yelling at teacher, cursing (tracking form)	2.3 per day	1 in 3 days: .3 per day	More than 1.5 per week
Storming out of class, out of control (form)	3 per week	1 per month	1 per week
Hitting peers (tracking form)	2 per month	None for rest of year	1 incident
Replacement behaviors (tracking methods)			
Independently initiates breaks (frequency count)	None	3 or fewer per class	None
Mood ratings and self-calming (binder)		Uses as needed	Less than 1.5 outbursts per week
Accommodation strategies (recorded in diary)	Varied	75% of opportunities	50%

B. Evaluate generalized outcomes and impact of changes on academic and social performance

Skill area	Setting	Expected outcomes and benefits	Evaluation method
☑ Self-regulation ☐ Communication ☐ Social skills ☐ Academic skills	☑ School ☑ Home ☐ Community	Improved self-regulation: handle frustration without losing control	Monitoring incidents of problem behavior Daily with weekly review; then at longer intervals with progress
☑ Self-regulation ☐ Communication ☐ Social skills ☑ Academic skills	☑ School ☑ Home ☐ Community	Better "attack" strategies for language and writing tasks More confidence and access to strengths	Student, parent, teacher report, resource room teacher diary Weekly at first, longer intervals with progress
☐ Self-regulation ☐ Communication ☑ Social skills ☐ Academic skills	☑ School ☐ Home ☐ Community	Better performance-average grades in math, language arts, and social studies will increase	Team review of grades in math, language arts, and social studies in 3 months Meeting at report card time

(continued)

Skill area	Setting	Expected outcomes and benefits	Evaluation method
☐ Self-regulation ☐ Communication ☑ Social skills ☐ Academic skills	☑ School ☐ Home ☑ Community	Better peer relationships, more friends, not ostracized, contacts outside school	Parent and teacher observation and report, self-report Evaluate in 3 months at time of report card

Procedure for modifying behavior intervention plan: (Indicate how changes will be made to plan.)

Team will monitor progress daily and weekly; should behavior incidents increase or worsen, immediate team meeting to discuss and plan. If no or limited progress (see A above), team will reconvene to reconsider plan.

Staff responsible: Social worker **Start date:** 12/15

STEP 6. MAINTAIN POSITIVE CHANGES OVER TIME AND ACROSS SETTINGS

Periodic review: Outline plan to maintain change into future and enhance quality of life.

High-risk circumstances: Develop support plan that anticipates predictable future challenges.

Unforeseen changes: Teacher or coach absent, not available for support. Classroom teacher and resource room teacher consult to adapt work several days in advance. In resource room teacher's absence, classroom teacher provides support; Nathan may obtain extra breaks, reduced work. With success, consider peer buddy support for mood monitoring.

Transition to middle school at end of year; departmentalized curriculum, more teachers, greater demands. Before year's end, social studies teacher to meet with middle school staff about Nathan. In addition to group orientation, provide Nathan a one-on-one orientation. Have coping plan and resource room teacher support in place prior to 1st day of sixth grade.

Plan for relapse: Assuming initial success, outline plan for managing recurrence of problem behavior.

If change below targets, or problem behavior reduces but positive outcomes not achieved, team will meet within one week to reconsider plan.

Staff responsible: Social worker **1st review date:** 3 months

Figure 30. Nathan's full Behavior Intervention Plan (*Key:* FBA = Functional Behavior Assessment; BIP = Behavior Invervention Plan.)

In February, the team convened to review Nathan's progress and prepared an interim summary of that meeting. The interim summary appears in Figure 31 and a graph illustrating incidents of problem behavior appears in Figure 32. The solid line in that figure depicts the day-to-day variation in Nathan's behavior. The broken line shows the overall trend in the number of weekly incidents.

During initial BIP development, team members mused about the eventual need to plan for Nathan's transition to middle school, regardless of how well the remainder of his school year went. As the end of the year approached, the team prepared for the annual review meeting that was required for all classified students in the school district. The team again convened. They discussed—and praised—Nathan's continuing progress. While he was not outburst free, he maintained a very low level of problem behavior, attaining better grades, doing better socially, and utilizing learning and coping skills more autonomously. Figure 33 depicts the summary developed in preparation for Nathan's annual review. It contains progress reports and also details current planning for the transition to middle school, a crucial consideration for his continuing adaptation and improvement. Figure 34 illustrates Nathan's outbursts and use of his replacement skills; Figure 35 depicts Nathan's academic performance in English Language Arts over the time period of his BIP.

Name: Nathan Jones **Date of Report:** February 10

Age: 10 **Grade:** 5

Background information: *Nathan is a 10-year-old student who is currently completing the fifth grade. At the beginning of the year, he was engaging in a variety of behavior problems including yelling at the teacher, cursing, storming out of the class, and hitting his peers. A functional behavior assessment was conducted in late October of the current school year, and a BIP was implemented in mid-December. The team has reconvened in order to review Nathan's progress, make any needed changes in his BIP, and begin to plan for his transition into middle school in September.*

Team: *Teacher, resource room teacher, social worker, school psychologist and Nathan's parents. The strategies and accommodations that follow were identified as part of Nathan's original BIP in December, and are being re-evaluated at this time to determine how well they are working, whether they should be continued, decreased, or modified, and to make recommendations for Nathan's transition to middle school.*

Short-term prevention strategies:

- *Rotating peer buddy for tasks requiring complex written or verbal expression*
- *Resource room teacher modifies content for math word problems, language arts, and social studies*
- *Resource room and classroom teachers to coordinate Nathan's work and progress*
- *Daily, resource room teacher meets one-on-one with Nathan to explain and review accommodations and preview work*

Long-term accommodations:

- *Resource room teacher simplifies instructions and adapts Nathan's work*
- *Resource room teacher meets daily with Nathan to preview material and assignments, forecast trouble spots*
- *Nathan permitted breaks from work to get up from his seat without need for permission*
- *Three breaks per period; altered based upon progress*

At this time, the prevention strategies and accommodations appear to be successful. At the time of the first team meeting in December, Nathan had an average of 2–3 episodes per day of yelling at his teacher; over the last six weeks he has averaged 3 per week, or less than 1 per day. The peer buddy system supporting Nathan for complex written and verbal tasks also appears to be strengthening his social skills. He is having more spontaneous interactions with his classmates, who are beginning to seek him out for other activities.

The resource room teacher is continuing to simplify some of Nathan's assignments and meeting with him every day to preview assignments and forecast potential problems. Nathan has indicated that he's looking forward to the time when he does not need to have his assignments modified, as he would like to be doing the same things as his friends are, but for now Nathan will continue to meet daily with his resource room teacher.

Nathan's use of "breaks" appears to be stabilizing a bit. Initially, it was difficult for him to limit his breaks to three per class, but this occurred most often at the end of the day when Nathan was tired and more likely to become frustrated with specific tasks. With support and encouragement from his classroom teacher, he has reduced his "break" times to an average of just fewer than two per class period during the past four weeks.

Replacement skills: *Nathan has been working on skills related to self-regulation. The school social worker reports that he has made tremendous progress in his ability to self-monitor his mood, and in using imagery strategies and coping statements to manage difficult situations before he loses control. Nathan's parents report that he engages them in practice sessions at home; this "homework" has become more important since Nathan has begun to bring an increasing number of school assignments home for completion.*

Nathan's resource room teacher and social worker continue to adapt materials and assignments for Nathan, and are coaching him so that he will be able to look at assigned tasks, rate them, and predict areas that may be challenging to him. Nathan feels that the one-on-one support he has been getting from the resource room teacher in writing skills has been a help to him in all his classes.

Recommendations: *The team agrees that the accommodations and adaptations identified and implemented in Nathan's BIP are indicative of a successful plan. Nathan's team is making these recommendations based on a review and evaluation of Nathan's progress during the past two months.*

The team and Nathan have agreed that he will no longer maintain a diary of accommodations; however, he will continue to meet with the school social worker and his resource room teacher at the end of each week to review his progress.

Classroom staff will monitor rates of problem behavior, continuing to use the adapted tracking form. If there are increases in Nathan's disruptive behavior (less than 3 episodes per week), the team will meet to discuss other options.

(continued)

As Nathan becomes more proficient at gauging the difficulty of assigned tasks and monitoring his mood, he will be encouraged to take fewer breaks during class time. The expectation is that breaks will be reduced to less than two or three per week by the end of the school year.

Nathan's parents have expressed some concerns about Nathan's move to middle school in the fall. The team will continue weekly telephone calls to his parents to keep them involved and informed.

Nathan's grades will be reviewed at the end of the third quarter; if no improvement, team will meet at that time.

The team will meet with the middle school staff in May to begin planning for Nathan's transition to middle school in the fall. It is expected that his team will familiarize middle school staff with the accommodations currently in place for Nathan, and discuss how these accommodations may be modified for middle school work.

Nathan will continue to work with his parents during the summer on coping strategies. His parents have also engaged a high school peer mentor for the summer who will continue coaching Nathan on his self-regulation skills.

Prepared by: *Eileen Coleman, classroom teacher, and Mary Dwyer, resource room teacher*

Figure 31. Nathan's interim Behavior Intervention Plan (BIP) review.

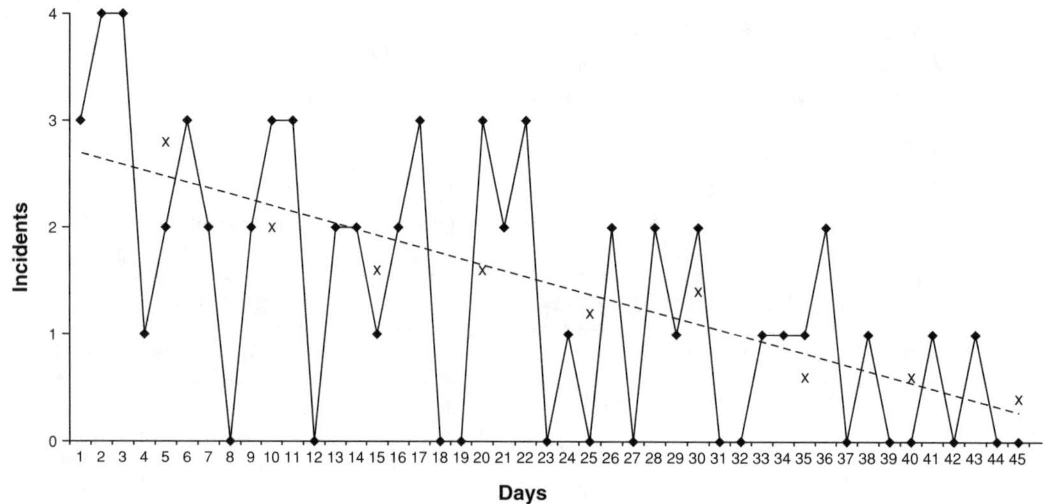

Figure 32. Graph of Nathan's outbursts. (*Key:* ♦ = incidents per day; x = mean number of weekly incidents; – = weekly trend.)

Name: Nathan Jones **Date of report:** May 15

Age: 10 **Grade:** 5

Team members present at review meeting: Teacher, resource room teacher, social worker, school psychologist, Nathan, and Nathan's parents, Mr. and Mrs. Jones.

Background information: Nathan is currently completing the fifth grade. At the beginning of the year he demonstrated a variety of behavior problems involving escalation, outbursts, storming out of class, and hitting peers. FBA and BIP were conducted and developed in October and December, respectively.

Since then, the team has conferred informally in order to review Nathan's progress, alter his BIP, and begin the process of transition planning. This summary is prepared in anticipation of Nathan's annual individualized education plan review and in preparation of his transition to middle school, and reflects the consensus of team members present at a meeting held last week.

Summary of assessment and intervention to date: Results of the FBA conducted in the fall indicated that Nathan possessed a number of strengths that serve him well and weaknesses, in particular in learning skills and self-regulation that served as slow triggers (setting events) for problem behavior. The behavior was maintained in part by the consequence of avoidance, which provided short-term relief for Nathan but brought negative attention from staff and peers and hindered his overall social and academic progress. The team developed a behavior intervention plan with short-term prevention strategies and long-term accommodations, including use of a peer buddy, one-on-one support from the resource room teacher (in the form of adapting tasks, previewing material, and teaching learning skills and compensatory strategies for Nathan's language-based difficulties), and teaching of self-regulation skills (sessions with staff).

An interim review and report produced in February of this year indicated that the frequency of behavior problems had diminished from 2–3 per day to less than 1 per day. All team members, including Nathan, view this as significant progress and credit him for hard work and perseverance. Nathan, his parents, and his teachers also report better interactions with classmates. In February, Nathan indicated that he would prefer to work toward less accommodation of his assignments.

In coordination with Mr. and Mrs. Jones, the resource room staff and teacher engaged in a learning skills intensive—a period of three weeks in which the team supported the development of more self-regulated problem-solving skills. Nathan left this intensive with a short list of strategies he could use to approach learning tasks identified as most difficult. Nathan now has regular resource room sessions, but his work is not regularly adapted in advance. This has met with varying success; a few problematic episodes were triggered by new academic material. When lapses occurred, Nathan met with a team member of his choosing to review the episode, as well as discussing it at home. Despite brief lapses, Nathan continues to be more independent in approaching his work. He has been quite successful in employing a number of cognitive–behavioral strategies (imagery, relaxation, coping statements, self-monitoring) for managing his frustration, and voiced a desire to discontinue his sessions with the social worker. Accordingly, Nathan now has a daily check in with his teacher, a monthly check-in with the social worker, and a daily check in at home. His grades have improved but are still considered to be somewhat below his potential, particularly in English Language Arts.

In sum, then, Nathan demonstrates a significant reduction in problem behavior and a corresponding increase in the use of replacement skills (coping, learning skills). The result is a youngster who has occasional lapses in the form of outbursts but who much more readily calms and returns to work. He continues to struggle with writing tasks, and this is an area that will likely cause continuing challenge for him as he enters middle school. Much greater autonomy will be expected of him in that setting.

Recommendations: The team agrees that the accommodations and adaptations identified and implemented in Nathan's BIP are indicative of a largely successful plan. The team makes the following recommendations:

- Staff will continue to monitor Nathan's use of replacement skills and the occurrence of any problem behavior, using the above-noted strategies and responses.
- The school psychologist will continue contact with middle school staff and will initiate the transition meeting between the two instructional teams (elementary and middle school). This is tentatively scheduled for later in the month.
- Nathan will attend the middle school visit along with the rest of his peers, and his parents will arrange a separate visit to meet his guidance counselor and school psychologist. Periodic email and phone contact between the family and staff will continue with meetings scheduled as needed or requested.

The elementary school staff will recommend that Nathan have at least an introductory session with either his guidance counselor or social worker early in the school year. Nathan has expressed concern about being stigmatized by these meetings, so the team will request specific consideration regarding meeting time(s).

The use of a peer buddy was discussed and will be further explored. Nathan would prefer not to have a buddy system and would like instead to rely on the system already in place in middle school (each student has two others with whom they collaborate to coordinate homework, assignments, and so forth). A decision was deferred for now, with concerns expressed about the increased stress of middle school without formal peer support. The team decided to await the meeting with the middle school staff and to monitor Nathan's progress through the end of June.

(continued)

Nathan will continue to work with his parents during the summer on coping strategies. His parents have also engaged a high school peer mentor for the summer who will continue coaching Nathan on his self-regulation skills. Nathan met with this student recently; his parents described their interaction as a bit awkward at first, and they will keep the team apprised of progress in this area.

It has been a pleasure working with Nathan and his family, and we look forward to planning a successful transition to middle school.

Prepared by: Eileen Coleman, classroom teacher, and Mary Dwyer, resource room teacher

Figure 33. Nathan's end-of-year summary. (*Key:* FBA = Functional Behavior Assessment; BIP = Behavior Intervention Plan.)

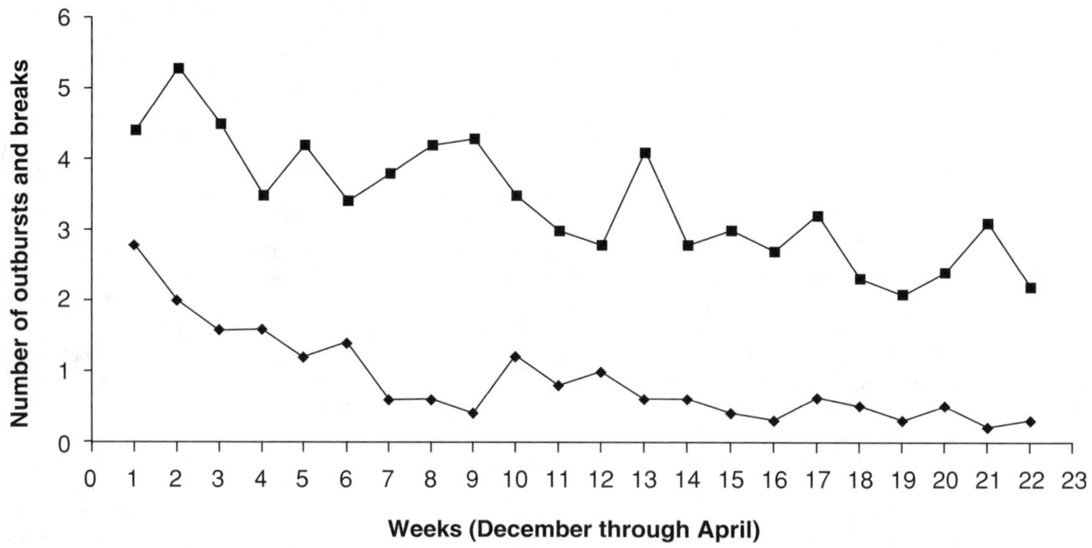

Figure 34. Graph of Nathan's outbursts and breaks taken. (*Key:* ♦ = average daily outbursts; ■ = average daily breaks.)

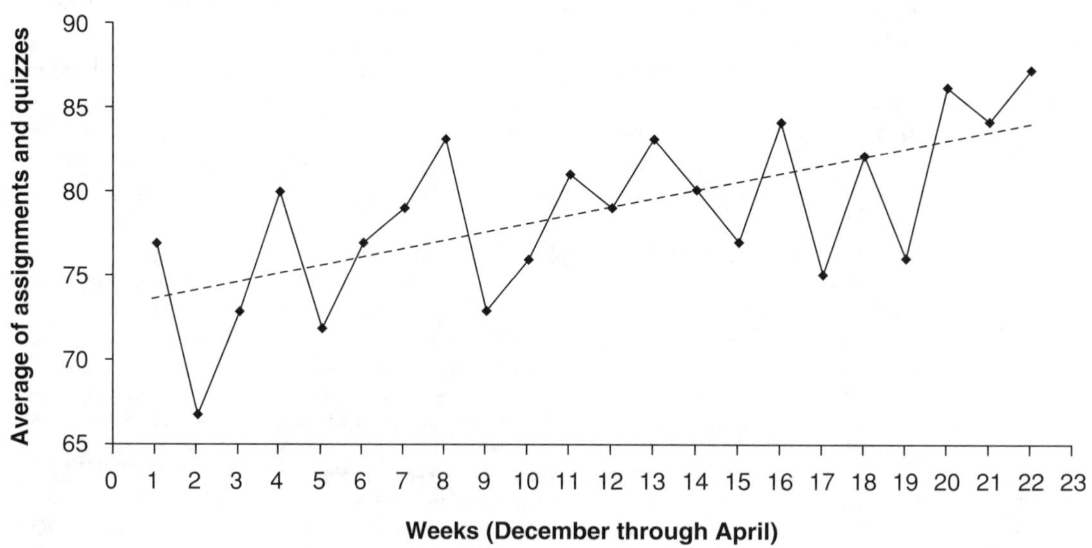

Figure 35. Graph of Nathan's English Language Arts class average. (*Key:* ♦ = Nathan's class average; – = Nathan's linear class average.)

Chapter 8

What Is Next? Promoting Long-Term Success

What does it mean to solve a behavior problem? Is it enough that the problem no longer occurs? With our emphasis on replacement skills, we clearly expect the reader to give a resounding *no* to the latter question at this point. But beyond the development of specific replacement skills, what more are we looking for? We are hoping that those skills are instrumental in opening new doors for the student: making friends, accessing different settings, and gaining opportunities for growth and development. Within this chapter, we point out some of the many changes that may occur for students after the BIP process, and we discuss some of the long-term goals for our interventions.

FOCUS ON ACCOMPLISHMENT

A concern in planning interventions is that the challenging behavior is often more problematic for others than it is for the individual student: classroom routines are disrupted for the teacher; peers experience a higher level of inconvenience than the student; all are frustrated. Clearly, the student is endangering his or her own success in the long run, but in the near term, he or she may not seem bothered by it. Behavior interventions nearly always start with an emphasis on making the problem stop. But, as we discuss in this chapter, quality of life means much more than that.

Some early behavioral theorists cautioned against classroom behavior interventions whose primary goals were for students to "be still, be quiet, be docile" (Winett & Winkler, 1972). The concern expressed by these authors derived from two observations. First, behaviors that had typically been defined as inappropriate shared a single characteristic: violating one or more of these directives. Second, interventions relying on this criterion were specifically designed to accomplish this outcome: still, quiet, docile students. Is that what we really want? Assuming it is achievable (which is unlikely), is it even desirable?

We would argue that stillness, silence, and docility are never legitimate targets for interventions, for one main reason. These qualities illustrate the absence of behavior, rather than specific alternatives or improvements. They might even be described, in the tongue-in-cheek words of Ogden Lindsley, as failing the dead man's test for behavior, which can be best summarized as "it is not a behavior if a corpse can do it." The dead man's test is attributed to Lindsley, one of the founders of the science and methods that have become applied behavior analysis (ABA) and behavior therapy; the phrase dates at least as far back as a 1968 paper cited in Eshleman (2000). We would expect a corpse to succeed spectacularly at the goals of being still, quiet, and docile. And, we accept that stillness, quiet, and obedience in children are positive states *for the teacher*; indeed, they may include some of the most pleasant moments of the instructor's day. Our contention is that they are not innately desirable or achievable *for the student.* We need to remain vigilant that the goals of instruction go far beyond a "rigid preoccupation with order and control" (Winett & Winkler, 1972).

So, what do we want for our students? Lindsley (1991) provides an anecdote that speaks directly to this question:

> In workshops on behavioral engineering, Tom Gilbert was plagued with practitioners not knowing the crucial difference between behavior and accomplishment. It was accomplishment that had value to the employing corporation, not behavior, so he developed what I have called the leave-it test for an accomplishment. Tom often showed a transparency of an archer with bow and arrow and said, "that's behavior." Then as he showed a target with an arrow in its bull's eye he said, "now, that's an accomplishment." I recently asked Tom when he first did this, and he said in workshops in 1962. He quoted a phrase he used then: "Behavior you take with you, accomplishment you leave behind!" (p. 458)

What we want for our students is accomplishment. Making friends is a significant accomplishment for a socially isolated student, going far beyond single behavioral dimensions, problem reduction, or replacement skills. Given its complexity and, perhaps, only loose relationship to a specific problem behavior, is accomplishment an appropriate goal for behavioral intervention? One might argue that accomplishment defies operationalizing. Nevertheless, we would expect the student's parents to consider this accomplishment the equivalent of the bull's eye in Lindsley's anecdote.

Meyer and Evans (1989) were among the first to categorize the outcomes of behavioral interventions into what we might consider accomplishments, including improvement in quality of life along such dimensions as happiness, satisfaction, and opportunities for choice and self-determination; inclusion in home, school, and community; expanded social relationships; and increased regard by others. These authors also noted a number of desired collateral decreases that might follow intervention. In the spirit of the dead man's test, we may not be able to call these decreases behaviors, but we can argue that they are highly meaningful to the individual, the support team, and the family. Wolf (1978) put this approach on the path to legitimacy in the field of ABA when he introduced the construct of social validity, referring to the assessment of the feasibility, acceptability, and importance of outcomes for behavioral intervention. Because its measurement is necessarily subjective—a significant point of departure from the methods of ABA at the time—social validity was controversial when first proposed. It has since become incorporated into practice as an important component of outcome evaluation.

In Chapters 2 and 7, we define maintenance and generalization and discuss specific strategies to promote them. We also stress the importance of thoughtful perseverance applied to ongoing modifications in the BIP. Our discussion of long-term change is not intended to supplant the suggestions for generalization and maintenance we offered in Chapter 7 (particularly in Table 21 of Chapter 7). It assumes that teams not only embed these strategies but that they alter them over time and also consider long-term change. Later in this chapter, we envision how Nathan's adaptation might have evolved over the long term.

POSITIVE BEHAVIOR SUPPORT OUTCOMES

Behavior support plans are typically designed to address the problems inherent to challenging behavior by reducing problem behaviors and increasing suitable alternatives. There is clear consensus in the field that long-term change is the ultimate goal of PBS and that train-and-hope strategies are insufficient. Thus, it is logical to wonder how long-term success is measured and which strategies are used to get there, especially when dealing with school-age children.

As mentioned previously, several reviews provide ample evidence that individualized PBS produces positive change when applied faithfully (Blakeslee, Sugai, & Gruba, 1994; Ervin, Radford, Bertsch, Piper, Ehrhardt, & Poling, 2001; Fox & Davis, 2005; Gresham, 2004; Horner, Carr, Strain, Todd, & Reed, 2002; Snell, Voorhees, & Chen, 2005). Although hundreds of published studies attest to its fairly immediate successes, relatively few address issues of social validity (Ervin et al., 2001; Kincaid, Knoster, Harrower, Shannon, & Bustamante, 2002). We believe that social validity includes accomplishments that families and students, not their professional providers, are in the best position to identify in the long term. Indeed, a volume edited by Lucyshyn, Dunlap, and Albin (2002) includes several case examples of family–professional partnerships in PBS as well as a discussion of research partnerships along the same vein.

Quality of Life

The concept of quality of life has been examined by disciplines from economics to medicine. It is generally understood to comprise a positive standard of living or state of wellness that goes beyond the absence of a problem or disease. In the field of disability, two early edited volumes (Goode, 1994; Schalock, 1990) outlined some of the major challenges facing the field. Subsequently, several authors have discussed dimensions on which to assess quality of life. Table 22 lists three such categorizations appearing in a comprehensive review of the concept (all categorizations listed below appear in Galloway [2006]).

Each definition references multiple areas of life, includes positive notions, and clearly invokes a notion of wellness rather than just freedom from problems. Two of the three definitions also reference productivity. At first glance, this may seem inapplicable to school-age children (including adolescents); however, within these frameworks, it is understood that school is the job of students and that substantive changes in that context might affect quality of life.

Our literature is replete with examples showing that positive outcomes can be achieved and maintained. Elsewhere, Crimmins and Farrell (2006) discuss the reality that few field-based research studies of PBS in schools replicate the day-to-day functioning of school teams; rather than evaluating the efforts of school personnel, most studies involve acknowledged PBS experts as primary investigators. Does this mean that these are typical results for all students?

Table 22. Current conceptualizations of quality of life in the field of disability

Authors	Definition	Proposed quality of life dimensions
Felce & Perry (1995)	"Quality of life is defined as an overall general well-being that comprises objective descriptors and subjective evaluations of physical, material, social and emotional well-being together with the extent of personal development and purposeful activity, all weighted by a personal set of values."	Physical well-being, material well-being, social well-being, productive well-being, emotional well-being, and rights (civic well-being)
Schalock (2000)	"Quality of life is a concept that reflects a person's desired conditions of living related to eight core dimensions of one's life..."	Emotional well-being, interpersonal relationships, material well-being, personal development, physical well-being, self-determination, social inclusion, and rights
Cummins (1997)	"Personal values as well as life conditions and life satisfaction interact to determine quality of life. The significance of either the objective or subjective assessment of a particular life domain is interpretable."	Health, material well-being, community well-being, work/productive activity, emotional well-being, social/family connections, and safety

Unfortunately, we do not know. The research literature is largely a product of academic educators and psychologists. Although many of their efforts are directed to real-world settings, these efforts are often under the direct supervision of a true expert, whose technical knowledge and skills may far surpass the average person working at the school. Does this suggest that individualized supports are not a worthwhile endeavor? Hardly, but continuing evaluation of the factors influencing its success is needed.

Does Positive Behavior Support Affect Quality of Life?

There is good reason to believe that it does; however, the PBS literature has not assessed long-term outcomes of PBS extensively enough to assert this with great confidence. Evidence from across the field of behavior therapy demonstrates maintenance, generalization, and improvements in quality of life for a variety of specific disorders, including depression, anxiety, impulse control, disruptive behavior, and more. Many of the same underlying principles and technologies, even the same strategies, are implicit in PBS, so it seems quite likely that positive effects and durable change can be attained.

Although few published studies have examined long-term outcomes, there are some exceptions. Kincaid et al. (2002) measured the impact of PBS on several outcomes, including quality of life among children supported by 78 different teams, mostly in schools. These authors found significant improvements in quality of life as rated by parents, direct care staff, and administrators. Of note was the tendency for ratings to be discrepant by source. Although all sources rated changes in the same direction (positive), the magnitude of change was seen as higher by parents and team members than by administrators. Although this may reflect differing access to and perceptions of certain students, it may also indicate that those with greater distance from a child may be less inclined to experience the full impact of change.

There are unmet challenges in PBS in measuring the long-term impact of individualized supports, particularly with respect to quality of life. This does not suggest that we should abandon our efforts; rather, we should sustain them, record them, and articulate which types and aspects of behavior intervention are likely to result in changes that are meaningful enough to impact overall quality of life. If change can be effectively initiated, maintained, and generalized, it is hard to imagine how it could fail to influence well-being in key areas.

On the other hand, we feel obligated to share some wisdom we have learned the hard way. In Table 8 (Chapter 5), we discussed several examples of how individualized PBS can go awry, linking these examples to various stages of the process. Holburn and Vietze (2002), in a discussion of person-centered planning, relates several sources of failure that can easily apply to PBS in schools. Among them are misunderstanding of the process and its time requirements; institutional cultures that do not adequately plan, support, and sustain new paradigms; unwillingness on the part of professionals to relinquish power and control; and absence of appropriate services to match student needs. Each of these factors could easily limit a team's ability to plan for an immediate intervention and would inevitably impede medium- to long-term planning. We have witnessed these pitfalls in action (and, no doubt, bear responsibility for some of them), and we share them here in the hope that knowing what *not* to do can be as helpful as knowing what to do in some cases. Because we are confident and hopeful about the power of quality intervention, we move to a discussion of some dimensions of sustained change.

COLLATERAL EFFECTS OF SUSTAINED CHANGE

Table 23 shows some of the potential long-term, life-enhancing effects of behavioral intervention. The initial BIP focuses on decelerative and accelerative goals—that is, reducing one or more specific problem behaviors and increasing appropriate alternatives as replacement skills. If an intervention is successful and changes are sustained, we hope to see collateral changes along a number of dimensions. This may include improvements in quality of life for the student and for the other people in his or her life. We may also know that things are improving on the basis of what is no longer being done—for example, discontinuation of one-to-one supports during transition times, or extra staff deployed in crisis management.

Table 23. Potential outcomes after successful behavioral interventions

Impact of problem behavior	Reductions in...	Improvements in...
Poses a physical or health risk to the individual	Emergency medical appointments Use of psychoactive medications for behavior control Medication side effects (e.g., sedation, sleep disturbance)	Health Engagement Independence and quality of life Life satisfaction
Places others at risk for injury	Emergency medical appointments Peer injury or incidents Staff time lost to work-related injury	Life satisfaction for peers and staff Acceptance by others
Causes property damage	Incident reports Replacement costs for damaged items	Freedom of movement Acceptance by teachers, other staff, administrators, and peers
Is a significant concern to student's parents	Time, stress, lost work productivity associated with problem behavior (e.g., calls from school, meetings) Ongoing worry about future	Family quality of life and satisfaction Interactions with relatives and neighbors Optimism
Interferes with learning	Need for intensive supervision Need for one-on-one instruction	Academic achievement Individualized education program content emphasizes academics Participates in state testing
Interferes with participation in school	Need for intensive supervision Level of accommodations Use of prevention strategies	Friendships and social relationships After-school activities
Interferes with participation in community	Level of accommodations Need for prevention strategies Time required for planning and intervention	Friendships and social relationships Increased community participation Greater range of options available for activities, outings, and jobs
Disrupts classroom or other school routines	Level of accommodations Need for prevention strategies Time required for planning and intervention	Friendships and social relationships Participation in group instruction Available choices More instructional time for all
Precludes participation in less restrictive environment	Referrals for more restrictive placements Specialized support services Supervision costs Out-of-district placements Transportation costs	Moves to least restrictive environment Increased time in inclusive activities Reduced stigma
Has recently escalated in frequency or intensity	Crisis interventions Office referrals Discipline reports Requests for evaluations	Diminished distress for individual and family Better outlook
Is an antecedent to other behavior problems	Global reduction in problem behavior	Self-monitoring and self-awareness of effects of triggers Increased self-efficacy, autonomy and self-direction

Table 23 illustrates these outcomes in contrast to the concerns that led to the initial selection of the behavior for intervention. This table presents examples of long-term outcomes of our interventions concerning the behavior identified during Step 1 of the FBA as part of the process and as they appear on the defining and prioritizing behavior form.

Table 23 shows that some of the desirable outcomes for intervention may involve reduction in negative events. (The principle of negative reinforcement is at work here; BIP efforts that reduce problem behavior are inherently reinforcing to staff.) These can include some obvious reductions—medical visits for emergencies, need for medications to control behavior, or injuries to others. We may also look for changes in the emotional or affective domain in terms of reductions in stress, worry, and anxiety, not just among family members, but also in peers and staff. The table also identifies reductions along those dimensions likely to bring unfortunate attention to the student in the school, such as office referrals, high levels of accommodations, and crisis interventions. Finally, we look for evidence that a successful plan may have resulted in significant cost savings to a school district because of a reduced need for one-to-one support or supervision, out-of-district placements with required transportation, and evaluations.

On the positive side, we are looking for evidence of accomplishment—a positive impression that the student leaves behind. Often, our greatest hope is that the child will have an expanded range of social relationships. Because personal identity is socially grounded, most students, and probably most adults as well, define themselves in reference to their friends, teachers, and other peers (and colleagues, mentors, and supervisors, for adolescents and adults). Indeed, shifting friendship patterns are a source of some of the major emotional upheavals of childhood and adolescence. But for many students with BIPs, the social realm is one of isolation from peers and even extended family, such that they experience only a restricted range of contacts. They may never have experienced the upset of a broken relationship, but they may be acutely aware of chronic rejection. Perhaps we should call this the *Tinman effect*—the Wizard of Oz can give you a heart, but there is a risk of it being broken.

The vulnerability inherent in relationships is a recognized and normative phenomenon, and parents of children with long-standing problem behavior would, no doubt, exchange their child's social isolation for openness to vulnerability. One collateral effect of sustained improvement in behavior may be the appearance of typical childhood social challenges. We would also hope to see greater calm and self-control reported by the student, peers, staff, and family. These changes, if persistent, may be recognized as improved quality of life.

Students with disabilities and problem behaviors ranging from mild to severe may experience corresponding shifts in identity that promote sustained change. Interestingly, shifts in identity both cause and result from behavior change. The student whose behavior is motivated in part by an emerging identity as a clown or troublemaker may instead find an outlet as a performer or musician. This may happen spontaneously, but it may also be very difficult for an adolescent to relinquish the power associated with his or her expected social role. The school team that helps students find constructive outlets for their unique qualities moves well beyond the mechanics of the BIP.

Consider the comedian Richard Pryor, whose grade school teacher permitted him to try stand-up comedy routines (no profane content) when he came to class on time and prepared. She clearly recognized the brilliance in this social outsider. Pryor was a reluctant, isolated student, partly because he lived in a brothel. Although Pryor remained a controversial figure because of his outspokenness and sometimes outrageous behavior, he is widely acknowledged as an important social commentator; he might not have achieved the same level of success if he had not possessed confidence in his ability to communicate. Pryor recalled his teacher with fondness, and one can only wonder about the power of her very simple encouragement. The message to teams is that not all aspects of change are conventional educational interventions; spontaneous, creative encounters can do much to nurture students, whether part of a BIP or not.

Table 23 identifies aspects of the instructional environment that may change, such as engagement in tasks, time in inclusive settings, participation in group instruction, going to after-school activities, and having increased freedom to move about the school. In the long run, we would look for improved academic performance, working on higher-level tasks, or even full participation in standardized testing.

How do we know a student is really doing better? When things work well, the reports will often come in on their own through spontaneous comments from peers, family, or colleagues. Sometimes, a note is received from home that the student is doing something the parents have never seen before. The student may seem to exercise more choice, and perhaps changes in behavior permit more opportunity for it. Family or school staff suddenly realize that they are spending less time on problems; or, better yet, they might note a highly pleasant interaction with the student. The important consideration for the team is ensuring that these positive changes are communicated and that a team member bears primary responsibility for monitoring and documentation of these and other outcomes.

ARE WE EVER DONE?

Do students who develop behavior problems serious enough to warrant an FBA and BIP get to a point at which they no longer require extra supports? Because the law does not require systemic monitoring, and there is scant research on the subject, we know very little about what happens in the long run for students with BIPs. First, it is unclear how most schools handle the BIP itself: it may or may not become part of the IEP. Second, it is difficult to ascertain whether BIPs are implemented as written. Third, there is tremendous variability in the amount of supervision and leadership provided in different schools and settings. We have encountered (more times than we would like to admit) that after about 6 months of implementing a BIP, a number of staff no longer know what it says or what they are supposed to do.

This is not always a bad thing. If the student were still engaging in problem behavior, the staff would likely be aware of the plan, but, in all likelihood, the problem behavior has subsided. Abandonment may indicate, however, that staff have given up or that nuances of generalization have fallen by the wayside. The extra support offered by the BIP is being faded without a specific plan and without sufficient attention to the establishment of replacement skills. Train and hope, indeed.

It is sometimes difficult to maintain a high level of effort with a student, particularly one whose behavior no longer seems difficult. There is a tendency for teams to want to move on to the next student. It is key to see the process through to some mutually approved time of discontinuation. Should cessation of team supports be warranted, effective teams assign one person to serve as liaison for individual school staff and family—just in case problems arise or continue. Although behaviors often come under control using various prevention strategies, it does not necessarily follow that replacement behaviors are well established. Resurgence of problem behavior can occur after periods of relative improvement, so ongoing monitoring and explicit attention to the long term are important. The following example seeks to illustrate the possible paths a student's school career might take depending on the decisions and actions of his or her behavior support teams.

NATHAN: 4 YEARS LATER

Imagine Nathan in 4 years. What course might his life take? We can pose two different scenarios—one clearly a better outcome for Nathan, but the other intended to be entirely plausible (based on experiences we have encountered all too commonly). He is 14 years old and in the first semester of his freshman year in high school. He continues to have an IEP identifying needed supports and accommodations.

Nathan: 4 Years Later—Scenario A

In our better scenario, Nathan has entered and left the middle school, surviving it with his share of ups and downs. This is quite significant because for Nathan, social, academic, and behavioral problems had the potential to be exacerbated during this transition. This success may be attributed to the hard work of the middle school team who helped him in making a smooth transition and who then provided continued support. They built on the plan developed in the elementary school, further developing the skills he had learned there. He received resource room services throughout all 3 years, with attention given to reviewing homework assignments so that he could complete them without modification. This was important to Nathan because he wanted to know he was doing the same work as his peers. The team felt that this would be an important skill for high school. At Nathan's middle school, each week's assignments were posted on the school web site on Mondays, with specific due dates for each assignment so that parents could help their children organize their time.

The family met with the team a few times a year, and they also came regularly to school events and open houses, where they made a point of speaking to each of Nathan's teachers. The resource room teacher was the designated point of contact for general parental concerns.

The team (including Nathan) agreed to forego a peer buddy system. Because several major assignments required students to work in groups of different sizes and members, peer support was built in, and all students learned to work cooperatively. This worked well for Nathan. He became more comfortable asking for assistance and explaining to peers which tasks he was well suited for and which tasks were more difficult for him. Nathan's individual assignments were structured to encourage a range of modes for responding, including assignments composed on the computer rather than in longhand, three-dimensional projects using different materials, and a videotape.

The middle school social worker continued some of the work that had been begun in elementary school on self-monitoring of mood, calming, and learning more about Nathan's triggers. Nathan particularly liked that the social worker offered to meet with him during an optional school breakfast time slot so that he would not have to leave class—and no one knew he was meeting with her. The beginning of each year and examination time proved stressful for Nathan. The social worker found it helpful to schedule 5-minute meetings each day of the first week of school and on examination days, providing specific cues to help him use his self-calming strategies.

Nathan enjoyed playing on school sports teams and received recognition for this. All coaches at the school had made a commitment to sports supporting the goal of schoolwide academic excellence. They monitored the academic status of each of their players and encouraged them to complete at least some of their homework before coming to practice.

At the beginning of his first season, Nathan demonstrated poor sportsmanship after an official's call—he swore, kicked the ground, and complained loudly about the call. The coach took him out of the game, discussed alternative ways to handle the situation, and required him to apologize to the official at the end of the game. The coach made it clear to all team members that disrespect for officials and players would not be tolerated. He spoke with Nathan's parents briefly, informing them that although Nathan had made a mistake, he had taken responsibility for it and now knew better. Nathan played the remaining games of the season without any similar incidents.

With Nathan making a relatively smooth transition into middle school, the behavior support team began planning his transition to high school when he was still in seventh grade. Nathan continued to struggle at most language-related tasks. His team was concerned about Nathan's ability to cope with higher demands for academic performance and autonomy. His social worker devised a strategy with him to go slowly in reviewing the exact requirements for each of his assignments, because he tended to get angry and upset when confronted with assignments that he did not understand, often thinking they were more difficult than he could manage. His middle school team arranged previews of high school work with individual instructors there.

He has made the transition to high school, where he is trying to find a niche among the many students and options available. Before the start of the school year, his middle school resource room teacher conferred with the guidance department on his schedule. A more important reason for the meeting was that this teacher, who had previously worked at the high school, was able to ensure that he would have several teachers who were likely to work well with him. This was considered to be critically important because Nathan is taking a general academic course load. He continues to receive resource room services 5 days a week, where he reviews his assignments with the teacher and outlines how he plans to approach each of them. He also has the services of a consultant teacher for his English class for one period per week, because the team anticipated that this would be a difficult subject for him and that he might require some instructional modifications or accommodations. Beyond this, the guidance counselor has agreed to meet with him weekly at first, then monthly, and then at least once each quarter and to be the contact person for any parental concerns or questions. Nathan has decided to try out for the freshman basketball team.

Nathan: 4 Years Later—Scenario B

In our less desirable scenario, Nathan has also entered and left the middle school, where he had some difficulties, but nothing that has been judged as out of the ordinary for a student with a history of learning disabilities and explosive behavior.

A representative from the middle school team met with the elementary team before the transition. This person was impressed with all that the elementary school team had done and thought that Nathan was in better shape than many other students. They agreed that it was important that he receive resource room support throughout all 3 years. As it developed, his resource room teacher went out on leave during Nathan's seventh-grade year, and he had a replacement teacher for the rest of the year, followed by a new teacher for eighth grade. Resource room sessions focused on immediate academic demands that he was confronting. Nathan managed to keep up with the bulk of his academic work, although a number of assignments were handed in late after his parents were informed that he had missed deadlines. Nathan was a C student.

The family met with the team a few times per year and came regularly to school events and open houses, where they sought out each of Nathan's teachers. Some of the team members viewed Nathan's family as a bit overinvolved and interfering. No single person was designated as a point of contact for any parental concerns; many of these calls went to the resource room teachers, but they generally felt that there was little they could do because they had no authority over their teammates; other calls went to the principal.

The team agreed to use a peer buddy system during sixth grade. In seventh grade, Nathan said he did not want to do this anymore and that he could do it himself. The middle school did have a number of group assignments during the year, which tended to have a fixed membership based on student self-selection. Reports were required to be submitted in the student's handwriting, although one each year was done as a slide presentation. The written reports were difficult for Nathan and he struggled to finish them, often with loud protestations at home. Parent requests for modifications were denied, with the rationale that Nathan needed to handle written assignments before starting high school.

The school psychologist continued some of the work that had been begun in elementary school on self-monitoring of mood, calming, and learning more about Nathan's triggers. The psychologist felt that Nathan had made such good progress that sessions could move on to an as-needed basis during seventh grade, with regular monitoring. Nathan had a number of incidents each year in which his behavior spiraled out of control, getting louder and more upset, until he ended up being sent to the office. He was known to the behavior support team, but he was not formally referred because instructors did not view his difficulties as severe enough to require an FBA or a new BIP.

Nathan enjoyed playing on school sports team and received recognition for this. The coaches had very different styles and requirements regarding academic achievement and homework; some wanted the students to come to practice as soon as classes were dismissed. At the beginning of his first season, Nathan demonstrated poor sportsmanship after an official's call—he swore, kicked the ground, and complained loudly about the call. The coach took him out of the game and did not speak to him. Nathan's parents supported the coach's actions. But, Nathan argued that he had been treated unfairly, first by the referee and then by the coach. He continued on the team, but he also remained resentful toward this coach. Nathan became known as something of a sore loser to his teammates.

The middle school behavior support team did not view Nathan as requiring specific transition supports to high school. They anticipated that he would take an academic course load that would provide the basic requirements for his high school diploma. They did recommend two periods a day of resource room services.

Nathan has made the transition to high school, where he seems to enjoy hanging out with his basketball teammates from middle school. He is planning to try out for the freshman basketball team. His resource room teacher is concerned that he is hanging out with the wrong crowd. He has already had a number of office referrals for being late to class and once for storming out of a class. Despite this, Nathan is doing well with three of his six teachers. The three who are displeased with him submitted referrals to the guidance department. One, when calling his parents, expressed that Nathan's behavior needed to be handled at home. Nathan goes to the resource room, but he has protested to the teacher that his friends make fun of him for being assigned there. His resource room teacher works with him on assignments from each of his classes. Because he was not highlighted as needing specific behavioral supports, there is no specific behavior plan in place, nor was anybody designated to serve as a parental contact.

What sense do we make of these two scenarios? Nathan is a classified student with a host of needs, although perhaps mild in comparison with students with significant disabilities. The first scenario presented an optimal situation in which the transitions went smoothly, supports were delivered, problems were anticipated, and planning focused on Nathan's most likely needs in the next setting. The second scenario is less rosy; even though people are caring and supports are being delivered, communications are not as regular, planning is driven by the immediate situation, and the prevailing philosophy is *if it ain't broke, don't fix it*. It seems less cohesive. It is not hard to see that there are two trajectories here—one that looks pretty good for Nathan, and one that promises a greater level of difficulty for him in the next few years. Let us examine these two scenarios from two perspectives—first, that of Nathan and the people surrounding him, and second, from the systems level in terms of the things teams need to do to keep things running smoothly.

SUCCESS BEGETS SUCCESS

Nathan's elementary school FBA and BIP led to changes that, in turn, created a host of positive outcomes. His problem behaviors became less frequent, going to zero in some cases. He began using replacement behaviors, even recruiting reinforcement from others without specific coaching. As Nathan enters middle school, his better outcome team supports these developments. Nathan continues to grow, even flourish.

What has changed for Nathan? He has learned that he can regulate his behavior. This has a distinct effect on others; he is no longer the one who is out of control. Peers respond to him differently, seeking him out at times. He broadens his social networks and participates in a wider range of activities. He relates differently to teammates. He goes to the movies. Even his parents do not seem so bad. Nathan begins to feel better about himself, more confident, less like an outsider.

Teachers also view Nathan differently. They no longer think of him as a student they have to look out for. Rather, they think of him as the student who is really working on pulling himself together. They understand that a few situations are still difficult, but that with a little bit of guidance, Nathan usually does the right thing. Teachers are gratified by working with him. He even extends thanks when offered support.

Nathan's parents have become empowered. They have worked with the school, and their child has improved. They have seen him make gains that are directly attributed to the hard work of the teaching staff, and they are appreciative. They know what works for Nathan and that when concerns came up during his middle school years, the staff collaborated with them to address his problems. At this point, they know that if Nathan begins to have difficulty, they will be able to advocate for a course of action in a way the special education team is going to hear.

It is what education is supposed to accomplish—students use the skills they learn to learn more, do more, explore the world, and become more competent. It is the reason that most of us chose the professions we did—we wanted to be agents of positive change. Nathan is better prepared for the world and is more likely to leave his accomplishments behind.

THE DOWNWARD SPIRAL

In the alternate scenario, Nathan approached middle school with a recent boost in some of his academic, social, and self-regulatory skills from his elementary school experience. His middle school team tended to view him as fairly competent and not at any particular risk, because his problem behaviors were not that frequent. And, because he was a classified student, Nathan was not likely to be suspended for the disruptions he might cause. They delivered the services identified in the IEP, made changes with the input of Nathan and his parents, and provided enough monitoring to ensure his safety and meet all regulatory requirements. Despite this, it is clear that Nathan is not moving in the direction that we would really like.

What has changed for Nathan? He has experienced some success in regulating his behavior, but others do not really notice. He knows he has a reputation for going off in a way that intimidates others, but he does not really get himself in trouble. In fact, when he talks back to a widely disliked teacher, other students seem to enjoy it. He enjoys the group of friends he has made through sports, and does not really like all the other students who seem to think they are better than him. Nathan is a teenager—his identity is with his small group of peers.

Teachers see Nathan as just another kid who is on the cusp between making it and getting into trouble. They know he has his ups and downs, and they generally like him because he seems to be trying. They believe that Nathan's behavior problems should be managed outside the classroom: at home, with the school psychologist, and in the guidance office. They will do the best they can in their classrooms, but if he misbehaves, he will be treated like any other student.

Nathan's father and mother are acutely aware that they are the parents of a teenager. Trying to put his difficulties into perspective, they recall that their friends also have had confrontations with their adolescent children. They understand that the school faces many challenges, but they have a lingering feeling that their son is not getting what he needs. They raise this point at every committee on special education meeting, but they do not get any real satisfaction. They wish they knew what to ask for, remembering that he seemed to do well for a time in elementary school.

Is not-so-good Nathan a system failure or the outcome of a child with a quirky temperament and learning disabilities? Obviously, we cannot tell for sure, and it may not be an either–or question but, instead, a bit of both. We want to suggest that the actions a team takes to sustain positive momentum can carry a student to a higher level. Table 24 highlights key factors contributing to the success of long-term supports. Some of these are, no doubt, familiar to readers; all are essential to achieving success in PBS at the level that affects quality of life.

SYSTEM-LEVEL SUPPORTS

Schools are the context for *Positive Strategies* efforts in the area of behavior change. As context, schools are small societies, with their own cultures, values, rules, expectations, jargon, and traditions. The school is also the context for the behavior support team, which operates in the environment of all of these factors. In the Nathan examples, we would argue that *his* day-to-day school activities have much in common with other schools—classes, hallways, lunch time, lockers, and sports. The day-to-day routines for the teachers in the two examples may also be similar, but the organizational cultures are likely to be distinctively different. How does the organization affect the *Positive Strategies* team?

Table 24. Factors contributing to the success of long-term supports

Organizational commitment to excellence
Administrative support for immediate and long-term efforts
Team leadership, role taking, responsibility, and accountability
Student and family involvement in assessment and planning
Revise the behavioral intervention plan: fade unnecessary elements and modify and add others as needed
Provision of booster sessions during difficult times
Continual assessment of barriers to inclusion and typical activities that the student does not access
Acknowledgment of accomplishments: social, academic, self-regulatory, communicative
Ongoing contact with family regarding progress and outcomes
Planned transitions between school years, teachers, and settings
Designated point person for communication
Emphasis on long-term accomplishments: peer acceptance, friendships, quality of life

Of course, the context for behavior (as discussed in Chapter 3) is key to both understanding and changing it. In the first scenario, Nathan benefited from a caring and dedicated team who worked in partnership and coordination with his family. Although administrative support might not have been visible to the family, it enabled Nathan's team to dedicate the necessary time and resources. Effective PBS requires an organizational commitment to excellence and administrative support for both immediate and long-term efforts. Our second scenario is not intended to portray school staff as uncaring or ineffective. It is entirely possible that each teacher who worked with Nathan sincerely wished to help him. Without a schoolwide PBS effort to sensitize them, or specific training in PBS to afford them the proper skills and knowledge to conduct an intervention, the staff could hardly be expected to take a different perspective. PBS requires an explicit shift in philosophy, attitude, and behavior, but these changes cannot be accomplished overnight. A better way is only possible for students when it can be envisioned by those who support them.

CLASSROOM AND TEAM EFFORTS

For students at risk for problem behavior, a classroom that is organized, structured, and supportive of self-regulation can make a measurable difference. For the portion of students who will inevitably have problems despite a well-run classroom, the effective, even prolonged efforts of a student support team are crucial. The bulk of this book has been devoted to supporting teams to initiate and sustain change, so we will not attempt to reiterate those strategies.

PREPARATION FOR TRANSITION

For students at risk, and for students with established problems, foreseeing challenges inherent in new contexts is crucial to maintaining change. As mentioned earlier, one important element of preparation for transition is forecasting the settings and situations that are likely to serve as future setting events and antecedents. When this is done, team members can help students rehearse upcoming situations. Should a student experience a lapse into problems that had previously remitted, experienced team members are in a position to provide booster sessions to the student (and the staff): rehearsing alternative behaviors, role playing, helping to select reinforcers, and so forth.

Preparation for transition might also entail having the current student support team meet with staff members who will work with the student in the next school year or setting; designating a leader or point person within the new team may ease communication and build confidence for the student and family. We have worked with elementary school teams who arranged orientations for middle school staff. These meetings included the middle school team, the student's family, the behavioral consultant, and two members of the student's presumed team for the next year. In one instance, the family brought a brief videotape of their child as an introduction; in most cases, a photo sufficed. These transition preparations were more than information sharing and planning. They were the beginnings of new partnerships.

ALWAYS STRIVE FOR MORE

The best long-term plans are dynamic ones, with details that evolve in response to ongoing assessments of progress. Once problem behavior is sufficiently reduced, or even ceases, the team's attention should turn to assessment of barriers to full inclusion and participation in typical activities. What is the student not doing that other students do? These issues cannot be considered without full partnership with family, especially because some of these goals need to be addressed in the community.

CONCLUSION

In conclusion, we offer our readers caution, suggestions, and thanks. We hope that this book helps you appreciate both the inherent promise of individualized supports and the diligence required to make an impact. So, we caution you to be patient with yourselves, your colleagues, your students, and their families. Done well, PBS rallies the best talents of all team members and brings results much greater than any one person can hope to accomplish. Gains can seem long in coming, and you may find yourself feeling that you would like more expertise in one aspect or other. This is good. It means that you are still learning and that you are reaching outside comfortable, if well-worn, strategies to bring novelty and creativity to the process.

As for suggestions, we have made many already, but we close with this: enjoy! Teamwork, family–professional partnerships, and student accomplishments are not always easily won, but they can be fun and are quite rewarding. Behavior interventions are sometimes derided as mechanistic; although we do not believe they are, we also know that your humanity and thoughtfulness dignify this work in ways that no book can instruct. *Positive Strategies* is about being able to look back and say, "We did the best we possibly could have." If you commit yourself to this process, we believe you will be able to say, "Together, we accomplished this." Because the best change occurs over the long run, you may not always bear witness to changes in the quality of your students' lives, but their origins can be traced back to your efforts.

Lastly, we offer gratitude. Thank you for your time, your endurance, and your willingness to work with your partners to implement the *Positive Strategies* process. More importantly, thank you for your commitment to bringing out the best in your students.

References

Anderson, D.H., Munk, J.H., Young, K.R., & Cummings, L.E. (2006). *Improving academic skills within a schoolwide system of positive behavior support.* Paper presented at the 3rd International Conference of the Association for Positive Behavior Support, Reno, NV.

Achenbach, T.M., & Rescorla, L.A. (2001). *Manual for the ASEBA school-age forms and profiles.* Burlington, VT: University of Vermont, Research Center for Children, Youth and Families.

Baer, D.M., Wolf, M.M., & Risley, T.R. (1968). Some current dimension of applied behavior analysis. *Journal of Applied Behavior Analysis, 1,* 91–97.

Bandura, A. (1977). *Social learning theory.* New York: General Learning Press.

Bandura, A., Ross, D., & Ross, S.A. (1961). Transmission of aggressions through imitation of aggressive models. *Journal of Abnormal and Social Psychology, 63,* 575–582.

Barnett, D.W., Bell, S.H., & Carey, K.T. (1999). *Designing preschool interventions: A practitioner's guide.* New York: The Guilford Press.

Bijou, S.W., Peterson, R.F., & Ault, M.H. (1968). A method to integrate descriptive and experimental field studies at the level of data and empirical concepts. *Journal of Applied Behavior Analysis, 1,* 175–191.

Blakeslee, M.A., Sugai, G., & Gruba, J. (1994). A review of functional assessment use in data-based intervention studies. *Journal of Behavioral Education, 4,* 397–413.

Bratton, S.E. (1998, December). How we're using value-added assessment: A Tennessee school district charts the effects of instructional staff on student outcomes. *The School Administrator.* Retrieved August 5, 2006, from http://www.aasa.org/publications/saissuedetail.cfm?ItemNumber=4266&snItemNumber=950&tnItemNumber=951

Bricker, D., Pretti-Frontczak, K., & McComas, N. (1998). *An activity-based approach to early intervention.* Baltimore: Paul H. Brookes Publishing Co.

Bronson, M.B. (2000). *Self regulation in early childhood.* New York: The Guilford Press.

Brophy, J.E. (1996). *Teaching problem students.* New York: The Guilford Press.

Buckley, J., Schneider, M., & Shang, Y. (2004). *The effects of school facility on teacher retention in urban school districts.* Washington, DC: National Clearinghouse for Educational Facilities. Retrieved July 19, 2006, from http://www.edfacilities.org/pubs/teacherretention3.html

Carr, E.G., & Durand, V.M. (1985). Reducing behavior problems through functional communication training. *Journal of Applied Behavior Analysis, 18,* 111–126.

Carr, E.G., Horner, R.H., Turnbull, A.P., Marquis, J.G., McLaughlin, D.M., McAtee, M.L., et al. (1999). *Positive behavior support for people with developmental disabilities: A research synthesis.* Washington, DC: American Association on Mental Retardation.

Cattell, R.B. (1965). *The scientific analysis of personality.* Harmondsworth, England: Penguin Books.

Chapman, D., & Hofweber, C. (2000). Effective behavior support in British Columbia. *Journal of Positive Behavior Interventions, 2,* 235–237.

Chiu, L.H., & Tulley, M. (1997). Student preferences of teacher discipline styles. *Journal of Instructional Psychology, 24*(3), 168–175.

Cole, C.L., & Levinson, T.R. (2002). Effects of within-activity choices on the challenging behavior of children with severe developmental disabilities. *Journal of Positive Behavior Interventions, 4,* 29–38.

Colvin, G., & Fernandez, E. (2000). Sustaining effective behavior support systems in elementary schools. *Journal of Positive Behavior Interventions, 2,* 251–253.

Conners, C.K. (1989). *Conners teacher rating scale.* Toronto, Ontario: Multi-Health Systems.

Cothran, D.J., Kulinna, P.H., & Garrahy, D.A. (2003). "This is kind of giving a secret away . . . ": Students' perspectives on effective class management. *Teaching and Teacher Education, 19,* 435–444.

Crimmins, D.B., & Farrell, A.F. (2006). Individualized behavioral supports at 15 years: It's still lonely at the top. *Research and Practice for Persons with Severe Disabilities, 31,* 31–45.

Crimmins, D.B., & Woolf, S.B. (1997). *Positive strategies: Training teams in positive behavior support.* Valhalla, NY: Westchester Institute for Human Development.

Cummins, R.A. (1997). Assessing quality of life. In R. Brown (Ed.). *Quality of life for people with disabilities: Models, research and practice* (2nd ed.). Cheltenham, England: Stanley Thornes.

Dawson, C.A. (2003). A study on the effectiveness of Life Space Crisis Intervention for students identified with emotional disturbances. *Reclaiming Children and Youth, 11*(4), 223–230.

DeMagistris, R.J., & Imber, S.C. (1980). The effects of life space interviewing on academic and social performance of behaviorally disordered children. *Behavioral Disorders, 6*(1), 12–25.

DeVries, R., & Zan, B. (2003). When children make rules. *Educational Leadership, 61*(1), 19–23.

Donovan, M.S., & Cross, C.C. (2002). *Minority students in special and gifted education.* Washington, DC: National Academies Press.

Downer, J.T., & Pianta, R.C. (2006). Academic and cognitive functioning in first grade: Associations with earlier home and child care predictors and with concurrent home and classroom experiences. *School Psychology Review, 35*(1), 11–30.

Duncan, G.J., & National Institute of Child Health and Human Development Early Child Care Research Network. (2003). Modeling the impacts of child care quality on children's preschool cognitive development. *Child Development, 74*(5), 1454–1475.

Durand, V.M. (1990). *Severe behavior problems: A functional communication training approach.* New York: The Guilford Press.

Durand, V.M., & Crimmins, D.B. (1992). *The motivation assessment scale administration guide.* Topeka, KS: Monaco & Associates.

Dwyer, K., Osher, D., & Warger, C. (1998). *Early warning, timely response: A guide to safe schools.* Washington, DC: U.S. Department of Education.

Ervin, R.A., Radford, P.M., Bertsch, K., Piper, A.L., Ehrhardt, K.E., & Poling, A. (2001). A descriptive analysis and critique of the empirical literature on school-based functional assessment. *School Psychology Review, 30,* 193–210.

Eshleman, J.W. (2000). *Commentary on the dead man's test.* Retrieved August 10, 2006, from http://members.aol.com/johneshleman/comment09.html

Evans, I.M., & Meyer, L.H. (1985). *An educative approach to behavior problems.* Baltimore: Paul H. Brookes Publishing Co.

Fan, X., & Chen, M. (2001). Parental involvement and students' academic achievement: A meta-analysis. *Educational Psychology Review, 13*(1), 1–22.

Farrell, A.F., Kimball, L. & Crimmins, D. (2005). Unpublished raw data.

Felce, D., & Perry, J. (1995). Quality of life: Its definition and measurement. *Research in Developmental Disabilities, 16,* 51–74.

Feldman, M.A. (1990). Balancing freedom from harm and right to treatment for persons with developmental disabilities. In A.C. Repp & N.N. Singh (Eds.), *Perspectives on the use of nonaversive and aversive interventions for persons with developmental disabilities.* Sycamore, IL: Sycamore.

Fink, A.H., & Janssen, K.N. (1993). Competencies for teaching students with emotional-behavioral disabilities. *Preventing School Failure, 37*(2), 11–16.

Finn, C., & Sladeczek, I. (2001). Assessing the social validity of behavioral interventions: A review of treatment acceptability measures. *School Psychology Quarterly, 16,* 2, 176–206.

Fox, J., & Davis, C. (2005). Functional behavior assessment in schools: Current research findings and future directions. *Journal of Behavioral Education, 14,* 1–4.

Frede, E.C. (1995). The role of program quality in producing early childhood program benefits. *The Future of Children, 5*(3), 115–132.

Freeman, R., Eber, L., Anderson, C., Ervin, L., Horner, R., Bounds, M., et al. (2006). Building inclusive school cultures using school-wide positive behavior support: Designing effective individual support systems for students with significant disabilities. *Research and Practice for Persons with Severe Disabilities, 31,* 4–17.

Galloway, S. (2006). Quality of life and well-being: Measuring the benefits of culture and sport: Literature review and think piece. *Scottish Executive Social Research, 12,* 4–97. Retrieved August 15, 2006, from: http://www.scotland.gov.uk/Resource/Doc/89281/0021350.pdf

Gardner, H. (1993). *Multiple intelligences: The theory in practice.* New York: Basic Books.

Gardner, W.I., Cole, C.L., Davidson, D.P., & Karan, O.C. (1986). Reducing aggression in individuals with developmental disabilities: An expanded stimulus control assessment and intervention model. *Education and Training of the Mentally Retarded, 21*, 3–12.

Goldstein, A. (1999). *The PREPARE curriculum: Teaching prosocial competencies* (Rev. ed.). Champaign, IL: Research Press.

Goldstein, A., & McGinnis, E.M. (1997). *Skillstreaming the adolescent: New strategies and perspectives for teaching prosocial skills.* Champaign, IL: Research Press.

Goode, D. (1994). *Quality of life: International perspectives and issues.* Cambridge, MA: Brookline Books.

Gray, C. (2000). *The new social story book: Illustrated edition.* Arlington, TX: Future Horizons.

Gresham, F.M. (2004). Current status and future directions of school-based behavioral interventions. *School Psychology Review, 33*(3), 326–343.

Grskovic, J.A., & Goetze, H. (2005). Evaluation of the effects of Life Space Crisis Intervention on the challenging behavior of individual students. *Reclaiming Children and Youth, 13*(4), 231–235.

Guin, K. (2004). Chronic teacher turnover in urban elementary schools. *Education Policy Analysis Archives, 12*(42), 1–30.

Hall, T. (2002). *Differentiated instruction: Effective classroom practices report.* Wakefield, MA: National Center on Accessing the General Curriculum.

Hanft, B.E., Rush, D.D., & Sheldon, M.L. (2004). *Coaching families and colleagues in early childhood.* Baltimore: Paul H. Brookes Publishing Co.

Helmstetter, E., & Durand, V.M. (1990). Nonaversive interventions for severe behavior problems. In L. Meyers, C.A. Peck, & L. Brown (Eds.), *Critical issues in the lives of people with severe disabilities.* Baltimore: Paul H. Brookes Publishing Co.

Holburn, S., & Vietze, P.M. (Eds.). (2002). *Person-centered planning: Research, practice, and future directions.* Baltimore: Paul H. Brookes Publishing Co.

Horner, R., & Sugai, G. (2000). School-wide behavior support: An emerging initiative. *Journal of Positive Behavior Interventions, 2*(3), 231–232.

Horner, R.H., Carr, E.G., Strain, P.S., Todd, A.W., & Reed, H.K. (2002). Problem behavior interventions for young children with autism: A research synthesis. *Journal of Autism and Developmental Disorders, 32*, 423–446.

Ingram, K., Lewis-Palmer, T., & Sugai, G. (2005). Function-based intervention planning: Comparing the effectiveness of FBA function-based and non-function based intervention plans. *Journal of Positive Behavior Intervention, 7*, 4, 224–236.

Jackson, L., & Panyan, M.V. (2001). *Positive behavioral support in the classroom: Principles and practices.* Baltimore: Paul H. Brookes Publishing Co.

Jones, V., & Jones, L. (2003). *Comprehensive classroom management: Creating communities of support and solving problems* (7th ed.). Boston: Pearson.

Kehle, T.J., Bray, M.A., Theodore, L.A., Jenson, W.R., & Clark, E. (2000). A multi-component intervention designed to reduce disruptive classroom behavior. *Psychology in the Schools, 37*(5), 475–481.

Kendall, P.C. (1992). *Stop and think workbook* (2nd ed.). Ardmore, PA: Workbook Publishing.

Kennedy, C.H., Horner, R.H., & Newton, J.S. (1989). The social networks and activity patterns of adults with severe disabilities: A correlational analysis. *Journal of The Association for Persons with Severe Handicaps, 15*, 86–90.

Kern, L., Hilt, A.M., & Gresham, F. (2004). An evaluation of the functional behavioral assessment process used with students with or at risk for emotional and behavioral disorders. *Education and Treatment of Children, 27*, 440–452.

Kincaid, D., Knoster, T., Harrower, J.K., Shannon, P., & Bustamante, S. (2002). Measuring the impact of positive behavior support. *Journal of Positive Behavior Interventions, 4*, 109–117.

Knoster, T.P. (2000). Understanding the difference and relationship between functional behavioral assessments and manifestation determinations. *Journal of Positive Behavior Interventions, 2*, 53–58.

Koegel, L.K., Koegel, R. L., Boettcher, M., & Brookman-Frazee, L. (2005). Extending behavior support in home and community settings. In L.M. Bambara & L. Kern (Eds.), *Individualized supports for students with problem behaviors.* New York: The Guilford Press.

Koegel, L.K., Koegel, R.L., & Dunlap, G. (Eds.). (1996). *Positive behavioral support: Including people with difficult behavior in the community.* Baltimore: Paul H. Brookes Publishing Co.

Koegel, L.K., Koegel, R.L., Harrower, J.K., & Carter, C.M. (1999). Pivotal response intervention I: Overview of approach. *The Journal of the Association for Persons with Severe Handicaps, 24*, 174–185.

Lehr, D., & Brown, F. (1996). *People with disabilities who challenge the system.* Baltimore: Paul H. Brookes Publishing Co.

Lindsley, O.R. (1991). From technical jargon to plain English for application. *Journal of Applied Behavior Analysis, 24*, 449–458.

Lohrmann-O'Rourke, S., Knoster, T., & Llewellyn, G. (1999). Screening for understanding of student problem behavior: An initial line of inquiry. *Journal of Positive Behavior Interventions, 1*, 35–42.

Lohrman-O'Rourke, S., Knoster, T., Sabatine, K., Smith, D., Horvath, B., & Llewellyn, G. (2000). School-wide application of PBS in the Bangor Area School District. *Journal of Positive Behavior Interventions, 2*, 238–240.

Losen, D.J., & Orfield, G. (Eds.). (2002). *Racial inequity in special education.* Cambridge, MA: Harvard Educational Publishing.

Lucyshyn, J.M., Dunlap, G., & Albin, R.W. (Eds.). (2002). *Families and positive behavior support: Addressing problem behaviors in family contexts.* Baltimore: Paul H. Brookes Publishing Co.

March, R.E., Horner, R.H., Lewis-Palmer, T., Brown, F., Crone, I., Todd, A.W., et al. (2000). *Functional assessment checklist for teachers and staff.* Retrieved May 11, 2004, from http://www.pbis.org/files/FACTS.doc

Marzano, R.J., Marzano, J.S., & Pickering, D.J. (2003). *Classroom management that works: Research-based strategies for every teacher.* Alexandria, VA: Association for Supervision and Curriculum Development.

Matheson, A.S., & Shriver, M.D. (2005). Training teachers to give effective commands: Effects on student compliance and academic behaviors. *School Psychology Review, 34*(2), 202–219.

McCombs, B.L., & Whisler, J.S. (1997). *The learner-centered classroom and school.* San Francisco: Jossey-Bass.

McFadden, A.C., & Marsh, G.E. (1992). A study of race and gender bias in the punishment of school children. *Education & Treatment of Children, 15*(2), 140–147.

Mendro, R.L. (1998). Student achievement and school and teacher accountability. *Journal of Personnel Evaluation in Education, 12,* 257–267.

Meyer, L.H., & Evans, I.M. (1989). *Nonaversive intervention for behavior problems.* Baltimore: Paul H. Brookes Publishing Co.

Nakasato, J. (2000). Data-based decision making in Hawaii's behavior support effort. *Journal of Positive Behavior Interventions, 2,* 247–250.

National Center for Education Statistics. (2001). Teacher preparation and professional development: 2000. Washington, DC: U.S. Department of Education. Retrieved September 28, 2005, from http://nces.ed.gov/surveys/frss/publications/2001088

National Council on the Accreditation of Teacher Education. (2006). *National Middle School Association middle level teacher preparation standards.* Retrieved August 2, 2006, from http://www.ncate.org/documents/ProgramStandards/nmsa.pdf

Nersesian, M., Todd, A.W., Lehmann, J., & Watson, J. (2000). School-wide behavior support through district-level system change. *Journal of Positive Behavior Interventions, 2,* 244–246.

New York State Office of Mental Retardation and Developmental Disabilities. (1998). *Strategies for Crisis Intervention and Prevention—Revised.* Albany, NY: Author.

Nichols, A.S., & Sosnowsky, F.L. (2002). Burnout among special education teachers in self-contained cross-categorical classrooms. *Teacher Education and Special Education, 25*(1), 71–86.

O'Neill, R.E., Horner, R.H., Albin, R.W., Sprague, J.R., Storey, K., & Newton, J.S. (1997). *Functional assessment and program development for problem behavior.* Pacific Grove, CA: Brooks/Cole.

Office of Special Education Programs. (2002). *Twenty-fourth annual report to Congress on the implementation of IDEA.* Retrieved September 28, 2005, from www.ed.gov/about/reports/annual/osep/2002/sectioniv-pdf

Patterson, G.R., DeBaryshe, B.D., & Ramsey, E. (1989). A developmental perspective on antisocial behavior. *American Psychologist, 44,* 329–335.

Porter, A.C., & Brophy, J. (1988). Synthesis of research on good teaching: Insights Institute for Research on Teaching. *Educational Leadership, 45*(8), 74–85.

Quinn, M.M., Gable, R.A., Fox, J., Rutherford, R.B., Van Acker, R., & Conroy, M. (2001). Putting quality functional assessment into practice in schools: A research agenda on behalf of E/BD students. *Education and Treatment of Children, 24,* 3, 261–275.

Repp, A.C., & Singh, N.N. (Eds.). (1990). *Perspectives on the use of nonaversive and aversive interventions for persons with developmental disabilities.* Sycamore, IL: Sycamore Publishing Company.

Rice, J.K. (2006). *Teacher quality: Understanding the effectiveness of teacher attributes.* Washington, DC: Economic Policy Institute.

Rosenberg, M.S., & Jackman, L.A. (2003). Development, implementation, and sustainability of comprehensive school-wide behavior management systems. *Intervention in School and Clinic, 39*(1), 10–21.

Rosenthal, R., & Jacobson, L. (1968). *Pygmalion in the classroom.* New York: Holt, Rinehart & Winston.

Rutherford, R.B., & Nelson, C.M. (1988) Generalization and maintenance of treatment effects. In J.C. Witt, S.N. Elliot, and F.W. Gresham (Eds.), *Behavior therapy in education.* New York: Plenum Press.

Sailor, W., Zuna, N., Choi, J., Thomas, J., McCart, A., & Blair, R. (2006). Anchoring schoolwide positive behavior support in structural school reform. *Research & Practice for Persons with Severe Disabilities, 31*(14), 18–30.

Sanders, W.L., & Rivers, J. (1996). *Cumulative and residual effects of teachers on future student academic achievement* (Research Progress Report). Knoxville, TN: University of Tennessee Value-Added Assessment Center. Retrieved August 1, 2006, from http://mdk12.org/practices/ensure/tva/ tva_2.html

Schalock, R.L. (1990). *Quality of life: Perspectives and issues.* Washington, DC: American Association on Mental Retardation.

Schalock, R.L. (2000). Three decades of quality of life. *Focus on Autism & Other Developmental Disabilities, 15,* 116–127.

Scott, T.M. (2001). A schoolwide example of positive behavior support. *Journal of Positive Behavior Interventions, 3,* 88–94.

Scott, T.M., & Nelson, C.M. (1999). Using functional behavioral assessments to develop effective intervention plans: Practical classroom applications. *Journal of Positive Behavior Interventions, 1,* 242–251.

Scott, T.M., McIntyre, J., Liaupsin, C., Nelson, C.M., Conroy, M., & Payne, L.D. (2005). An examination of the relation between functional behavior assessment and selected intervention strategies with school-based teams. *Journal of Positive Behavior Interventions, 7,* 4, 205–215.

Scott, T.M., Meers, D.T., & Nelson, C.M. (2000). Toward a consensus of functional behavioral assessment for students with mild disabilities in public school contexts: A national survey. *Education and Treatment of Children, 23,* 3, 265–285.

Skinner, B.F. (1953). *Science and human behavior.* New York: Free Press.

Skinner, B.F. (1948). *Walden Two.* New York: Macmillan.

Snell, M.E., Voorhees, M.D., & Chen, L. (2005). Team involvement in assessment-based interventions with problem behavior: 1997–2002. *Journal of Positive Behavior Interventions, 7*(3), 233–235.

Stokes, T.F., & Baer, D.M. (1977). An implicit technology of generalization. *Journal of Applied Behavioral Analysis, 19,* 349–367.

Stronge, J.H., & Hindman, J.L. (2003, May). Hiring the best teachers. *Educational Leadership,* 48–52.

Sugai, G., & Horner, R.H. (1999). Discipline and behavioral support: Practices, pitfalls & promises. *Effective School Practices, 17,* 10–22.

Sugai, G., & Horner, R.H. (2002). The evolution of discipline practices: School-wide positive behavior supports. *Child and Family Behavior Therapy, 24,* 23–50.

Sugai, G., Horner, R.H., Dunlap, G., Hieneman, M., Lewis, T.J., Nelson, C.M., et al. (2000). Applying positive behavior support and functional behavioral assessment in schools. *Journal of Positive Behavior Interventions, 2,* 131–143.

Sugai, G., Horner, R., Lewis-Palmer, T., & Todd, A. (2005). *School-wide positive behavior support team training manual.* Eugene, OR: OSEP Center for Positive Behavioral Interventions and Supports. Retrieved December 1, 2006, from http://pbismanual.uoecs.org

Taylor-Greene, S.J., & Kartub, D.T. (2000). Durable implementation of school-wide behavior support: The high five program. *Journal of Positive Behavior Interventions, 2,* 233–235.

Thomas, A., & Chess, S. (1977). *Temperament and development.* New York: Brunner/Mazel.

Touchette, P.E., MacDondald, R.F., & Langer, S.N. (1985). A scatter plot for identifying stimulus control of problem behavior. *Journal of Applied Behavior Analysis, 18,* 342–351.

Turnbull, H.R., Turnbull, A.P., Bronicki, G.J., Summers, J.A., & Roeder-Gordon, C. (1989). *Disability and the family: A guide to decisions for adulthood.* Baltimore: Paul H. Brookes Publishing Co.

Tyler-Wood, T., Cereijo, M.V.P., & Pemberton, J.B. (2004). Comparison of discipline referrals for students with emotional/behavioral disorders under differing instructional arrangements. *Preventing School Failure, 48*(4), 30–33.

Utley, C.A., Kozleski, E., Smith, A., & Draper, I.L. (2002). Positive behavior support: A proactive strategy for minimizing behavior problems in urban multicultural youth. *Journal of Positive Behavior Interventions, 4,* 196–207.

Van Acker, R., Boreson, L., Gable, R.A., & Potterton, T. (2005). Are we on the right course? Lessons learned about current FBA/BIP practices in schools. *Journal of Behavioral Education, 14,* 1, 35–56.

Vaughn, B.J., & Horner, R.H. (1997). Identifying instructional tasks that occasion problem behaviors and assessing the effects of student versus teacher choice among these tasks. *Journal of Applied Behavior Analysis, 30,* 299–312.

Walker, H.M., & Horner, R.H. (1996). Integrated approaches to preventing antisocial behavior patterns among school age children and youth. *Journal of Emotional and Behavioral Disorders, 44,* 194–209.

Warren, J.S., Edmonson, H.M., Griggs, P., Lassen, S.R., McCart, A., Turnbull, A., et al. (2003). Urban applications of schoolwide behavior support: Critical issues and lessons learned. *Journal of Positive Behavior Interventions, 5,* 80–91.

Wehmeyer, M.L., Baker, D.J., Blumberg, R., & Harrison, R. (2004). Self-determination and student involvement in functional assessment: Innovative practices. *Journal of Positive Behavior Interventions, 6,* 29–35.

Wenglinsky, H. (2003). Using large scale research to gauge the impact of instructional practices on student reading comprehension: An exploratory study. *Education Policy Analysis Archives, 11*(19). Retrieved August 7, 2006, from http://epaa.asu.edu/epaa/ v11n19

Whitebook, M. (2003). *Early education quality: High teacher qualifications for better learning environments—A review of the literature.* Berkeley, CA: Institute of Industrial Relations.

Winett, R.A., & Winkler, R.C. (1972). Current behavior modification in the classroom: Be still, be quiet, be docile. *Journal of Applied Behavior Analysis, 5,* 4, 499–504.

Wolf, M.M. (1978). Social validity: The case for subjective measurement or how applied behavior analysis is finding its heart. *Journal of Applied Behavior Analysis, 11,* 203–214.

Wright, W., Horn, S.P., & Sanders, W.L. (1997). Teacher and classroom context effects on student achievement: Implications for teacher evaluation. *Journal of Personnel Evaluation in Education, 11,* 57–67.

* Appendix

TABLE OF CONTENTS

Communication Style Assessment

Purpose: A questionnaire used to determine the student's functional communication skills, that is, by what means does the student make his or her wants and needs known. It is used as a component of the assessment of student–environment fit.

Completion time: Approximately 10 minutes, plus any additional time spent in team discussion.

Directions:

1. Complete the information requested at the top of the form.
2. The form should be completed by one or more individuals familiar with the student's communication, either individually or through a collaborative team process.
3. Respond to each question as specifically as possible. Include examples that illustrate typical communication skills.
4. Consider and list all modes of communication a student uses. When more than one system of communication is used (e.g., verbal language and picture system), indicate the circumstances under which the student employs each mode. For bilingual students, note languages, oral and written proficiency, and patterns of use (e.g., English at school, other language at home and in community).
5. If any of the questions are difficult to answer, defer to the observations of those who spend the most time with the student, but include differences observed across school, home, and community.

Analysis and interpretation: This questionnaire elicits information on functional communication skills. In contrast to formal assessment of speech and language skills, it focuses on self-expression in everyday life. Examining practical aspects of communication is essential because many problem behaviors serve communicative functions. Since intervention plans frequently involve teaching functional communication skills, it is helpful to know more about the student's current abilities.

Use of information: Understanding functional communication skills is essential to developing an effective behavior intervention plan. Specifically, the team may use this assessment to establish instructional objectives and whether a student needs communicative supports. Any recommended changes in this area should be coordinated with the Individualized Education Program.

Communication Style Assessment

Name: ______________________ Date: ______________

Completed by: ______________________________________

What methods of communication does this student regularly use to make himself or herself understood (e.g., speech, augmentative system, gesture, picture system, object cues, vocalizing)?

How does this student express likes and dislikes?

What methods of communication (e.g., speech, gesture, sign language, object/tangible cue) are generally used to communicate with this student?

What methods of communication does the student's family use with him or her?

Does the student's family use a language other than English at home? If yes, how proficient is this student in English? In the other language?

What types of information does the student communicate spontaneously (e.g., signal needs, direct others, request information, share information, express interest, disengage)?

How does the student gain your attention when you are not paying attention to him or her? Once you attend to him or her, how is the interaction maintained?

How does the student ask questions for directions, information, personal needs, or assistance? Under what conditions does he or she solicit such assistance?

How does the student communicate choices or preferences? What strategies are used to facilitate such communication?

Does this student have a daily schedule of activities? How do others explain transitions and schedule changes?

Learning Style Profile

Purpose: A checklist that assesses the student's response to different aspects of the instructional environment. It is used as a component of the assessment of student–environment fit.

Completion time: Approximately 10 minutes, plus additional time spent in team discussion.

Directions:

1. Complete the information requested at the top of the form.
2. The form should be completed by one or more individuals familiar with the student as a learner, either individually or through a collaborative team process. If respondents have difficulty reaching consensus during a group discussion, members should complete the *Learning Style Profile* individually and discuss results together.
3. The form denotes several dimensions—learning style, reinforcers, instructional design, and setting factors. Responses are based on direct observation of the student's response to different instructional variables.
4. If many items are rated as **?** (unsure), the team may need to conduct more thorough observation or assessment of the student's learning attributes.
5. Once all items are complete, teams review the form and identify the five items that are most critical to optimal instruction for this student.

Analysis and interpretation: Team members review responses to the *Learning Style Profile* section by section, noting areas of clear consensus and those for which context may be a factor (e.g., prefers one type of reinforcer or task type in math and another in language arts).

Use of information: The goal of this form is to identify areas of potential mismatch between the student's learning style and the characteristics of the instructional environment. Results guide instructional decisions, such as method of prompting, task duration, scheduling within a day and across a week, use of interpersonal strategies during instruction, environmental variables (e.g., temperature, lighting, noise level), and the availability of reinforcers that are appealing and motivating.

Learning Style Profile

Name: ______________________________ Date: ______________

Completed by: ____

Each section below presents dimensions that affect engagement and learning. For each item, circle one response that describes the conditions under which this individual learns best. Circle **?** if you are unsure and **NR** when the condition is not relevant. On completion, review all responses and mark the five items most critical to the design and delivery of instruction for this individual. If completed by a team, please keep in mind that learning style, instructional design, and reinforcement needs may vary by instructional content and setting.

INDIVIDUAL LEARNING STYLE	**Critical**
Preferred mode for processing information—visual / auditory / tactile / combined / ?	______
Preferred position—seated / standing / lying down / varies / ? / NR	______
Previous activity—preceded by physical activity / preceded by a quiet activity / ? / NR	______
Mealtimes—before meal or snack / after meal or snack / ? / NR	______
Time of day—morning / afternoon / evenings / varies / ? / NR	______
Time of the week—early in the week / midweek / late in the week / weekends / ? / NR	______
Most effective type of prompt—physical / visual / verbal / varies / ?	______
Tolerance for prompt fading—requires prolonged use of prompts / moves easily to less direct prompting / responds with time delay / varies / ?	______
Response to new situations—looks around / disengages / laughs, cries or vocalizes / manipulates materials / engages with people / other ________________ / ?	______
Response to inactivity—daydreams / vocalizes / becomes restless / manipulates materials / other ________________ / ?	______

REINFORCER ASSESSMENT	**Critical**
Preferred type—social / tangible / free time / self-reward / combined / varies / ?	______
Type of social—brief praise / prolonged social contact / physical contact / public posting / varies / ? / NR	______
Type of tangible—food / toys / preferred items / clothing / money / privileges / special activities / varies / ? / NR	______
Use of free time—break from task / relaxation time / time off / varies / ? / NR	______
Self-reward—pride in accomplishment / engaging in sensory-motivated activities / varies / ? / NR	______
Tolerance for reinforcer fading—requires prolonged, high level of reinforcement / moves to intermittent schedules easily / varies / ?	______

INSTRUCTIONAL DESIGN **Critical**

Group size—one-on-one / small group / large group / varies / ? ______

Style of interaction—friendly or familiar / stern or formal / varies / ? / NR ______

Task variety—single activity at a time / working on variety of tasks / varies / ? / NR ______

Task type—open-ended tasks / tasks with a clear starting and ending point / varies / ? / NR ______

Task familiarity—familiar / new / varies / ? / NR ______

Task difficulty—easy / moderate / difficult / varies / ? / NR ______

Transitions—signaled / occur on schedule without other notice / varies / ? / NR ______

Daily schedule—clearly explained and followed / tolerates changes without notice / varies / ? / NR ______

Activity level during task—stationary / some movement / physically active / ? / NR ______

Length of time on task—less than 5 minutes / 5–15 minutes / 15–30 minutes / greater than 30 minutes / varies / ? ______

INSTRUCTIONAL SETTING **Critical**

Noise/activity level—in quiet areas / in active areas / ? / NR ______

Lighting level—in soft, dimly lit areas / in bright, well-lit areas / ? / NR ______

Temperature—cool / warm / ? / NR ______

Location—indoors / outdoors / community locations / home / ? / NR ______

Appearance—clean, uncluttered area / "messy," stimulating areas / ? / NR ______

Preference and Interest Assessment

Purpose: A questionnaire that prompts identification of student interests, preferences, likes, and dislikes in support of more effective engagement. It is used as a component of the assessment of student–environment fit.

Completion time: Approximately 10 minutes, plus time spent in consultation and discussion.

Directions:

1. Complete the information requested at the top of the form.
2. Questions may be completed by individuals or through a collaborative team process.
3. Responses to the first three items should refer to the setting in which the respondent relates to the student (i.e., school for a teacher, home and community for the parent).
4. In considering activities the student engages in spontaneously, reflect upon recent requests for materials and activities (e.g., books, games, toys, crafts, music, sporting goods, play date, computer, car ride, television, and so forth).
5. Responses related to use of free time (item 4) refer to school, home, and community. When discussing support, indicate type and amount of assistance necessary to enable the student to engage in activities.

Analysis and interpretation: Analysis is qualitative. The team evaluates the above information to consider changes in instructional content and activities to improve engagement and social interaction. Discussion focuses on the potential common elements of preferred and non-preferred activities.

Use of information: Results assist teams to identify ways to increase access to preferred activities as a means of enriching the daily experience and diminish compulsory participation in non-preferred activities. The team may also examine whether instruction can be integrated into spontaneous activities to expand routines and interests.

Source: Turnbull, Turnbull, Bronicki, Summers, and Roeder-Gordon (1989).

Preference and Interest Assessment

Name: ______________________ Date: ______________

Completed by: ______________________________

What are three activities that this student most enjoys? Please note how often, where, and with whom the student engages in these activities.

Activity	How often?	Where?	With whom?
1.			
2.			
3.			

What are the three activities that the student likes least? Please note how often, where, and why the student is expected to perform these activities.

Activity	How often?	Where?	With whom?
1.			
2.			
3.			

Name three activities that the student engages in spontaneously. Please note how often, where, and with whom (if anyone) the student engages in these activities.

Activity	How often?	Where?	With whom?
1.			
2.			
3.			

Please note the types of activities that the student does in his or her free time. How much support is required to do these activities in each setting?

Setting	Activity	Level of support
At school		
At home		
In community setting		

What activities has the student indicated he or she would like to do that are not currently available? Where would these occur? How much support is likely to be required to do these activities?

Setting	Activity	Level of support

Social Network Assessment

Purpose: A questionnaire used to identify individuals who are significant in the student's life. It is used as a component of the assessment of student–environment fit.

Completion time: Approximately 10 minutes, plus additional time spent in team discussion.

Directions:

1. Complete the information requested at the top of the form.
2. Identify persons who are most significant to the student, even if their interactions are relatively infrequent. Indicate the types of activities the student engages in with these individuals and where this occurs. Consult the student, family, team members, and other school staff to obtain a clear picture of social contacts.
3. Indicate which individuals the student seeks out, note the style and quality of interaction, and consider the type and extent of influence this person has on the student.

Analysis and interpretation: Given the nature of these questions, analysis of the responses is largely descriptive. Teams may use the information to evaluate factors such as the

- Number of people the student has regular access to
- Type and number of opportunities the student has for meaningful social interaction
- Reception and social support the student enjoys from others
- Quality of social interaction skills the student employs
- Opportunities the student has to interact meaningfully with peers within and outside school.

Use of information: Social relationships are critical for students; the extent and quality of relationships is an indicator of interpersonal relatedness, social skills, and quality of life. This tool is designed to heighten awareness of significant social relationships. Students whose socialization experiences are predominated by family members, teachers, school personnel, and paid caregivers may demonstrate corresponding social isolation and skills deficits. For students who do not exhibit obvious disabilities, this area is often overlooked. This information informs the student profile developed as part of the functional behavior assessment and serves as a basis for formulating intervention goals.

Source: Kennedy, Horner, and Newton (1989).

Social Network Assessment

Name: ____________________ Date: ____________

Completed by: ____________________

Who are the important people in this student's life? What is a typical activity or interaction that the student might have with that person? Where is this most likely to occur—at school, at home, or in a community setting?

	Who	Activity	Where
Family			
Peers and fellow students			
Friends			
Neighbors			
Paid support providers			

Does the student seek out people to do things with? What types of activities does this include?

With whom does this student spend the most time?

With whom would this student like to spend more time?

Incident Log

Purpose: A form that provides a quick and efficient means of documenting behavioral incidents in school settings. The form is organized to allow for most entries to be checked off. It may be used as part of the functional behavior assessment process for a student or as a routine means of recording behavior incidents. The form may be adapted for use in different settings.

Completion time: One to two minutes per occurrence of the behavior.

Directions:

1. Complete the items at the top of the form.
2. Check off information within each category and provide written responses to open-ended questions.
   - Time
   - Location
   - Setting events
   - Antecedents
   - Behavior
   - Consequences
   - Function
3. Once this information is documented, users may note in the final section the degree to which this incident and the circumstances surrounding it are typical or unusual for the student.

Analysis and interpretation: After collecting 10 to 20 completed forms for a specific behavior, use a blank copy to tally responses in each category. The summary form can then be reviewed to identify recurring patterns of time, location, antecedents, or consequences for a particular behavior. If no clear pattern emerges, teams should log additional incidents and supplement with other assessment methods.

Use of information: The information collected using the *Incident Log* is helpful in determining recurring antecedents, consequences, or setting event variables that relate to behavior. The *Incident Log* offers two advantages as an observational approach. First, because there are check-offs for many categories, collecting data is relatively efficient. Second, the form prompts staff to consider a variety of possible factors they might not have otherwise contemplated.

Source: Goldstein (1999).

Incident Log

Name: ______________________________ Date: ______________

Completed by: ____

Use this log to document triggers, behaviors, and consequences. Select a typical episode to log and analyze; summarize several incidents by transferring data to single summary form.

Context/time: When did the incident occur?

Day of the week—Monday / Tuesday / Wednesday / Thursday / Friday

Time of day—before school / morning / lunchtime / afternoon / after school

*Period, class, subject, etc.*______________________________

*How long before normal activity resumed?*______________________________

Context/location: Where did the incident occur?

Classroom	Hallway	Community	Gym	Other:__________
Outdoors	Worksite	Bathroom	Cafeteria	Other:__________

Setting events: Note likely setting events below.

1. ______________________________
2. ______________________________
3. ______________________________
4. ______________________________
5. ______________________________

ANTECEDENT	✔		✔
Teased by a student		Frustrated on a task	
Physically provoked by a student		Expected to work independently	
Bored or understimulated		Pleasant activity interrupted	
Negative interaction with peer		Transition	
Negative interaction with adult		Routine was changed	
Redirected or reprimanded		Not given instruction	
Asked to do something difficult		Noisy or crowded place	
Denied a request		Required to wait	
Did poorly on an assignment		Not receiving attention	

TYPE OF PROBLEM BEHAVIOR	✔	Notes
Physically aggressive		
Verbally inappropriate		
Destroyed, mistreated property		
Noncompliance or defiance		
Removed self from setting		
Self-stimulation, injury		
Was disruptive		

CONSEQUENCES	✔	Notes
Sent to office		
Reprimanded		
Restitution		
Punitive consequence		
Obtained desired object		
Parent contacted		
Redirected		
Talked to staff		
Obtained activity		
Resumed activity		

FUNCTION	✔		✔
Escape/avoidance		**Tangible**	
Difficult task		Food	
Prolonged work		Object	
Social demands		Activity	
Attention		**Sensory**	
Peer		Stimulation	
Adult		Sensory input	
Group		Habit	

NOTES

Scatter Plots

Purposes: A grid for recording the occurrence of behavior across time of day and day of the week. This observation method may be used to quantify the baseline rate of a behavior, as well as to track response to intervention over time. The *Scatter Plots* are most useful with moderate-to high-frequency behaviors.

Completion time: A few seconds per occurrence of behavior; less than 2 minutes per day.

Directions:

1. Complete items at the top of the forms. Because the plots are used for an extended period of time, note dates on which the data were gathered.
2. Note the behavior(s) to be observed.
3. The *Scatter Plots* may be used several ways:
   - If a behavior occurs during the observation interval, the observer may: 1) shade the box in the grid completely (one behavior per interval); 2) place a slash mark or shade half the box for the first occurrence of a behavior; complete an X or darken the remaining half of the box for a second behavior (record two incidents per interval); and 3) use tally marks for each occurrence of behavior in the observation interval.
   - In all applications, if the target behavior does not occur, the box is left blank.
4. Conduct baseline observations for one to two weeks. For students who follow a multiday class cycle, record behavior for one to two repetitions of this cycle. For high-frequency behaviors, a shorter period may be sufficient to identify patterns.
5. Time sampling procedures may be considered for very high-frequency behaviors. For example, the team might record entries for three mornings and two afternoons weekly (or some comparable combination of time intervals) as a sample.
6. Collect data throughout the period of assessment and during intervention. The *Scatter Plots* can also be used to track the increased use of replacement skills.

Analysis and interpretation: Data are analyzed by visual inspection to identify patterns of occurrence and nonoccurrence. The team may identify specific intervals associated with the problem behavior. Follow-up interviews may then reveal locations, activities, or personnel associated with these intervals. If no discernible pattern emerges initially, teams may decrease the recording interval (e.g., from 30 to 15 minutes) and examine patterns within sessions.

Use of information: Understanding the pattern of a behavior helps teams generate hypotheses about function. Information may also be used to identify times of the day or days of the week that may require short-term prevention and long-term accommodation strategies.

***Scatter Plot* forms:** Attached are two Scatter Plot formats. The first allows teams to establish the length of the recording interval, and it can be used for three academic weeks. The second uses a 30-minute interval and can track two separate behaviors across four academic weeks.

Adapted from Touchette, P.E., MacDondald, R.F., & Langer, S.N. (1985). A scatter plot for identifying stimulus control of problem behavior. *Journal of Applied Behavior Analysis, 18,* 342–351. Adapted by permission.

General Scatter Plot

Name: ____________________ Date: ____________

Completed by: ______________________________

Time interval	Monday	Tuesday	Wednesday	Thursday	Friday	Monday	Tuesday	Wednesday	Thursday	Friday	Monday	Tuesday	Wednesday	Thursday	Friday

Behavior-Focused Scatter Plot

Name: ______________________________ Date: ______________

Completed by: ______________________________

BEHAVIOR #1

Time	M	T	W	R	F	S	S
8:30–9:00							
9:00–9:30							
9:30–10:00							
10:00–10:30							
10:30–11:00							
11:00–11:30							
11:30–12:00							
12:00–12:30							
12:30–1:00							
1:00–1:30							
1:30–2:00							
2:00–2:30							
2:30–3:00							

BEHAVIOR #2

Time	M	T	W	R	F	S	S
8:30–9:00							
9:00–9:30							
9:30–10:00							
10:00–10:30							
10:30–11:00							
11:00–11:30							
11:30–12:00							
12:00–12:30							
12:30–1:00							
1:00–1:30							
1:30–2:00							
2:00–2:30							
2:30–3:00							

Antecedent–Behavior–Consequence Chart

Purpose: A form for recording observed antecedents and consequences for specific behaviors. This is best used with relatively low-frequency behaviors. For high-frequency behaviors, establish a sampling method (e.g., first 10 minutes of each instructional period) or complete at times when behavior is likely to be problematic (e.g., waiting for the bus).

Completion time: One to five minutes to record each occurrence of behavior.

Directions:

1. Complete items at the top of the form.
2. Record the date, time, and observer for each occurrence.
3. As soon as possible after behavior occurs, record events that preceded (antecedents) and followed (consequences). Be concrete; note observations from the perspective of what the student is likely to have experienced. Consider context issues such as individuals, activities, demands, and level of stimulation present. Note antecedents and consequences even if there is no apparent link with behavior.
4. When time sampling, select observation periods of adequate duration that reflect typical activities and routines.
5. When it is difficult to record because of competing demands on time (e.g., instruction and class management), designate an alternative method for obtaining observations, such as teaching assistant or related service provider.
6. Vary recorders and compare their observations.
7. To ensure adequate sample, maintain data collection throughout baseline period (one to two weeks or longer); alternatively, observe until a minimum of 10 incidents are recorded.
8. During the intervention period, use the *Antecedent–Behavior–Consequence Chart* periodically as a means of ongoing assessment; select and sample representative intervals (e.g., one day every two weeks).
9. Recording high frequency behaviors may involve high time demands. To render the chart more useful, use time sampling or employ after first reducing incidents of behavior.

Analysis and interpretation: To analyze these data, review and categorize information from the *Antecedent–Behavior–Consequence Chart.* To simplify analysis, organize antecedent events around different stimulus classes (e.g., presence of certain caregivers or peers, activities, locations). Consequences may be organized to represent different functional classes (e.g., attention was provided, attention was withdrawn, task was withdrawn, tangible item was received). This chart, however, is subject to error from inadequate sampling (i.e., insufficient duration, missed incidents), erroneous recording, observer bias, and errors of interpretation. One cautionary note is that this chart can be somewhat time consuming to complete. Another potential concern is analysis of the findings may require a relatively high level of experience and can be time consuming.

Use of information: A thorough observational analysis using an *Antecedent–Behavior–Consequence Chart* can be an invaluable component of the functional behavior assessment. Similar to the *Incident Log* and the *Scatter Plot,* this chart helps identify functional relationships among behavior, its antecedents, and consequences. Antecedent information may provide insights into schedule, staffing, activity, or other factors that trigger the behavior. Consequence information helps identify maintaining variables and reinforcers for the behavior so that environmental alterations can be made.

Source: Bijou, Peterson, and Ault (1968).

Antecedent–Behavior–Consequence Chart

Name: ______________________________ Date: ______________

Completed by: ______________________________________

Date and time	Antecedent conditions (Include location, activity, persons, etc.)	Behavior (Describe what happened.)	Consequences (State what followed the behavior.)

Setting Events Checklist

Purpose: A checklist to identify potential influences of setting events on problem behaviors. The form provides specific examples of potential setting events across four categories: physical, learning and self-regulation, social-emotional, and environment and routines. The form can only be used with low frequency events, including behaviors that occur less than once per week or for outbursts in the frequency of a commonly encountered behavior (e.g., increase from a daily average of 2 behaviors to a day on which 10 incidents occur).

Completion time: Approximately 2 minutes to complete; additional time is required to consult parents or others to obtain information from other settings.

Directions:

1. Complete items at the top of the form.
2. After problem behavior occurs (or on the day of the outburst), indicate setting events that preceded it and check off the time frames within which they occurred.
3. When considering the longstanding category, attempt to ascertain whether a condition had an impact on the behavior in question. Some setting events are rather enduring; the checklist prompts the user to consider their influence on particular incidents of behavior. In other words, an attention deficit may be ever-present, but the *Setting Events Checklist* requires the respondent to consider whether it contributed to the incident being logged.
4. Family consultation by phone, e-mail, or in person may be needed to assess setting events in different environments.
5. Contact other school personnel who interacted with or observed the student on the day of or the day prior to the incident. Survey them regarding potential setting events. When numerous individuals routinely interact with the student, it may be helpful to gather people together for a brief meeting or circulate the form to ensure that the checklist contains all relevant information.

Analysis and interpretation: Analysis of the data requires that information from several *Setting Events Checklists* be synthesized and summarized. To do so, transfer findings reported on multiple forms to a single blank checklist. Once this has been done, teams look for patterns of co-occurrence among behavior incidents (or bursts) and related setting events (denoted singly or in combination). In making these determinations, it is important to look for two important patterns. First, setting events that consistently occur prior to problem behavior warrant consideration in the planning process. Second, some long-standing concerns may contribute to challenging behavior and, therefore, need to be addressed in the behavior intervention plan. Others may not contribute, but may nonetheless be reviewed as part of an assessment of the student–environment fit.

Use of information: There are two ways to use data from the *Setting Events Checklist*. First, the behavior intervention plan may include program modifications or supports that help the student manage the impact of setting events; these supports can be provided as long-term accommodations or on an as-needed basis for transitory influences. Second, the assessment can signal the need for intervention in different life domains. For example, if sleep disorder is a known setting event, the behavior intervention plan might specify an intervention for sleep difficulties and a contingency plan for days when the student is sleep-deprived.

Source: Gardner, Cole, Davidson, and Karan (1986).

Setting Events Checklist

Name: ______________________________ Date: ______________

Completed by: ______________________________________

Check the appropriate column for events according to their time frame. For long-standing influences, note only those that contribute to the current incident or behavior.

Setting events (by type)	Same day	Day before	Within week	Long-standing
Physical				
Mealtime changed or meal missed				
Sleep pattern (including duration) atypical or insufficient				
Medications changed or missed				
Medication side effects				
Appeared or complained of illness				
Appeared or complained of pain or discomfort				
Allergy symptoms				
Seizure				
Chronic health condition				
Other (specify):				
Learning and self-regulation				
Specific disability (specify):				
Learning difficulties (specify):				
Low frustration tolerance/impulsive				
Short attention span				
Poor organizational or planning skills				
Anger management problems				
Atypical sensory needs				
Other (specify):				
Social-emotional				
Anxious				
Irritable or agitated				
Depressed, sad, or blue				
Experienced disappointment (specify):				
Refused a desired object or activity				
Disciplined or reprimanded, especially if atypical				
Fought, argued, or had other negative interaction(s)				

Setting Events (by type)	Same day	Day before	Within week	Long-standing
Social-emotional*—continued*				
Difficulty with peer(s) (specify):				
Chronic/acute stress in home or community (specify):				
Other (specify):				
Environment and routines				
Routine was altered; change in activity, order, pacing				
Routine was disrupted				
Change in caregiver or teacher				
Absence of preferred caregiver or teacher				
Was "made" to do something				
Change in school placement (specify):				
Changes in living environment (specify):				
Other (specify):				

Functional Behavior Assessment Worksheets
Student Background

Name: ______________________ Date: ______________

	Completed by	Date
Individualized Education Program and recent progress		

(Note classification; summarize major goals and comment on their relevance to problem behavior.)

	Completed by	Date
Current placement		

(Note location, type, staff-to-student ratio, inclusion opportunities, related services, etc.)

	Completed by	Date
Medical and related conditions		

(Note conditions affecting mood and behavior. List medications, especially for behavior, and effects.)

	Completed by	Date
Family consultation		

(List family concerns.)

	Completed by	Date
Previous interventions		

(Summarize results of individualized, classroom, or schoolwide interventions.)

Student–environment fit		

(Overview of learning style, reinforcers, preferences, and needed accommodations that relate to behavior.)

Is a formal consideration of student–environment fit indicated? ☐ Yes ☐ No

Functional Behavior Assessment Worksheets
Defining and Prioritizing Behavior

Name: ______________________________ Date: ______________

BEHAVIOR

Using behavioral terms, describe the behaviors of concern. Provide actual or estimated frequency for a given unit of time (e.g., 15 times per day, 2–3 times per week).

Behavior		Frequency
1		
2		
3		
4		

IMPACT

For each of the behaviors (as numbered above), check off the statements that apply.

	Behavior			
	1	2	3	4
Poses a physical or health risk to the individual				
Places others at risk for injury				
Causes property damage				
Is a significant concern to student's parents				
Interferes with learning				
Interferes with participation in school				
Interferes with participation in community				
Disrupts classroom or other school routines				
Precludes participation in less restrictive environment				
Has recently escalated in frequency or intensity				
Is an antecedent to other behavior problems				
Other:				

CONCLUSIONS

Based on this review of frequency and impact for each behavior, indicate priority of target behaviors. As needed, provide a brief rationale.

First priority behavior: ______________________________

____

____

____

Second priority behavior: ______________________________

____

____

____

Functional Behavior Assessment Worksheets
Assessment Steps

Name: ______________________ Date: ______________

STEP 1. DEVELOP STUDENT PROFILE

	Completed by	Date(s)
Gather background information		
Consultation with family		
Complete Student Background		
Define and prioritize behavior		
Complete Defining and Prioritizing Behavior		
Assess student–environment fit		
Communication Style Assessment		
Learning Style Profile		
Preference and Interest Assessment		
Social Network Assessment		
Other:		

STEP 2. ASSESS BEHAVIOR

	Completed by	Date(s)
Interviews		
Student		
Parent or family		
Teacher (identify):		
Other (identify):		
Observations		
Incident Log		
Scatter Plot		
Antecedent–Behavior–Consequence Chart		
Other:		
Checklists and Questionnaires		
Motivation Assessment Scale (MAS)		
Functional Assessment Checklist for Teachers and Staff (FACTS)		
Setting Events Checklist		
Other:		

STEP 3. ANALYZE RESULTS

What *setting events* were identified?	Physical	Learning and self-regulation	Social-emotional	Environment and routines
What *antecedents* are consistently associated with the target behavior?	**Person(s)**	**Place(s)**	**Task or activity**	**Conditions**
What *consequences* maintain the behavior? What *function* does it serve?	**Escape/avoidance**	**Attention**	**Tangible**	**Sensory**
	☐ Difficult task ☐ Prolonged work ☐ Social demands	☐ Peer ☐ Adult ☐ Group	☐ Food ☐ Object ☐ Activity	☐ Stimulation ☐ Sensory input ☐ Habit

What *other* consistent consequences were found?

What setting events or antecedents identified are associated with *low* rates of this behavior?

STEP 4. DEVELOP HYPOTHESIS

_______________________________ engages in

[student's name]

_______________________________ when or after

[problem behavior]

_______________________________, because when student does

[antecedent]

_______________________________.

[typical consequence]

This is more likely to happen when _______________________________

[setting event]

and because _______________________________.

[setting event]

STEP 5. TEST THE HYPOTHESIS

Conduct an experimental manipulation of setting events (slow triggers), antecedents (fast triggers), and/or consequences. Note baseline conditions (no change), conditions that were altered (interventions or accommodations), and results. Although more detailed documentation may exist elsewhere, use this space to summarize the test findings and conclusions.

☐ **Check here if formal hypothesis testing was deferred.**

☐ Setting events	Results	Dates

☐ Antecedents	Results	Dates

☐ Consequences	Results	Dates

RECOMMENDATION

Based on the results, should the working hypothesis be altered in preparation for the behavior intervention plan?

____

____

____

What aspects of the hypothesis test should become part of the behavior intervention plan? What are the team's next steps?

____

____

____

Behavior Intervention Plan Worksheets

Name: ______________________________ Date: ______________

Behavior: | Functional behavior assessment dates:

Hypothesis (from functional behavior assessment):

STEP 1. BRAINSTORM POTENTIAL SOLUTIONS

A. Prevention: List setting event and/or antecedent modifications that might reduce target behavior. Check those validated by the functional behavior assessment.

- ☐
- ☐
- ☐
- ☐
- ☐
- ☐
- ☐
- ☐

B. Replacement behaviors: List replacement behaviors meeting the same function as problem behavior; consider coping skills that may reduce effect of setting events.

STEP 2. PREVENT OR MINIMIZE OCCURRENCES OF PROBLEM BEHAVIOR

A. Short-term prevention strategies

Setting event or antecedent targeted	Strategy	Implementation plan	Outcomes
Staff responsible:		Start date:	1st review date:

B. Long-term accommodations to improve student–environment fit and social/academic success

Setting event or antecedent targeted	Long-term accommodation	Implementation plan	Desired outcomes
Staff responsible:		Start date:	1st review date:

STEP 3. MANAGE CONTINUING INCIDENTS OF PROBLEM BEHAVIOR

Early signs of problem behavior:

Steps to take in response to early signs of behavior:

Response to incidents of behavior: Include plan to resume activity or return to context.

Steps to take following an incident: Describe procedures for incident review and strategies to minimize inadvertent reinforcement for problem behavior.

☐ **Preparation required:** Consider staff training, student supports, and other efforts needed.

☐ **Crisis intervention plan is needed.**

Staff responsible:	Start date:	1st review date:

STEP 4. REPLACE PROBLEM BEHAVIOR WITH ALTERNATIVE BEHAVIORS OR SKILLS

Alternative #1:

Skill area:	☐ Self-regulation ☐ Communication ☐ Social skills ☐ Academic ☐ Other
Current skill level:	☐ Uses skill inconsistently ☐ Has prerequisites or aspects of skill ☐ Lacks this skill
Support needed:	☐ Formal instruction ☐ Improved motivation system ☐ Assistive or adaptive technology
Long-term goal and benefits:	

Initial instructional plan: Include procedures, instructor(s), frequency, setting(s), materials, and reinforcement.

Ongoing instruction: Include plan to fade prompts and reinforcement as skill is generalized to other settings.

Staff responsible:	Start date:	1st review date:

Alternative #2:

Skill area:	☐ Self-regulation ☐ Communication ☐ Social skills ☐ Academic ☐ Other
Current skill level:	☐ Uses skill inconsistently ☐ Has prerequisites or aspects of skill ☐ Lacks this skill
Support needed:	☐ Formal instruction ☐ Improved motivation system ☐ Assistive or adaptive technology
Long-term goal and benefits:	

Initial instructional plan: Include procedures, instructor(s), frequency, setting(s), materials, and reinforcement.

Ongoing instruction: Include plan to fade prompts and reinforcement as skill is generalized to other settings.

Staff responsible:	Start date:	1st review date:

STEP 5. MONITOR AND EVALUATE CHANGES IN BEHAVIOR, USE OF REPLACEMENTS, AND OUTCOMES

A. Monitor rates of problem behavior and use of replacement behaviors or skills

Problem behaviors and tracking methods	Baseline (Number per unit of time or opportunity)	Goal achieved (Rate at which plan is considered successful)	Review required (Rate at which plan modification is needed)
Replacement behaviors and tracking methods			

B. Evaluate generalized outcomes and impact of changes on academic and social performance

Skill area	Setting	Expected outcomes and benefits	Evaluation method
☐ Self-regulation ☐ Communication ☐ Social skills ☐ Academic skills	☐ School ☐ Home ☐ Community		
☐ Self-regulation ☐ Communication ☐ Social skills ☐ Academic skills	☐ School ☐ Home ☐ Community		
☐ Self-regulation ☐ Communication ☐ Social skills ☐ Academic skills	☐ School ☐ Home ☐ Community		

Procedure for modifying behavior intervention plan: Indicate how changes will be made to plan.

Staff responsible: Start date:

STEP 6. MAINTAIN POSITIVE CHANGES OVER TIME AND ACROSS SETTINGS

Periodic review: Outline plan to maintain change into future and enhance quality of life.

High-risk circumstances: Develop support plan that anticipates predictable future challenges.

Plan for relapse: Assuming initial success, outline plan for managing recurrence of problem behavior.

Staff responsible:	1st review date:

Index

Page references followed by *t* or *f* indicate tables or figures, respectively.